The Farther Frontier

The Farther Frontier

Six Case Studies
of Americans and Africa,
1848–1936

Lysle E. Meyer

SUP

Selinsgrove: Susquehanna University Press
London and Toronto: Associated University Presses

© 1992 by Associated University Presses, Inc.

All rights reserved. Authorization to photocopy items for internal or personal use, or the internal or personal use of specific clients, is granted by the copyright owner, provided that a base fee of $10.00, plus eight cents per page, per copy is paid directly to the Copyright Clearance Center, 27 Congress Street, Salem, Massachusetts 01970. [0-945636-19-9/92 $10.00 + 8¢ pp, pc.]

Associated University Presses
440 Forsgate Drive
Cranbury, NJ 08512

Associated University Presses
25 Sicilian Avenue
London WC1A 2QH, England

Associated University Presses
P.O. Box 39, Clarkson Pstl. Stn.
Mississauga, Ontario,
L5J 3X9 Canada

The paper used in this publication meets the requirements
of the American National Standard for Permanence of Paper
for Printed Library Materials Z39.48-1984.

Library of Congress Cataloging-in-Publication Data

Meyer, Lysle E.
    The farther frontier: six case studies of Americans and Africa, 1848-1936/Lysle E. Meyer.
        p. cm.
    Includes bibliographical references and index.
    ISBN 0-945636-19-9 (alk. paper)
        1. Americans—Africa, Sub-Saharan—Biography. 2. Africa, Sub-Saharan—Discovery and exploration—American. 3. Africa, Sub-Saharan—History—1884-1960. 4. Africa, Sub-Saharan—History—To 1884. I. Title.
DT352.7.M49   1992   90-50770
967.03′1—dc20   CIP

PRINTED IN THE UNITED STATES OF AMERICA

Contents

Preface	7
Acknowledgments	11
1. Thomas Jefferson Bowen and Central Africa: A Nineteenth-Century Missionary Delusion	15
2. Jungle Adventure: Paul Du Chaillu and the American Image of Africa	33
3. In the Service of the Khedive: Charles Chaillé-Long and Egyptian Expansionism	63
4. Henry Shelton Sanford: A Yankee in the Colonial Opening of the Congo	102
5. John Hays Hammond and the Jameson Raid: Engineering a Capitalist Revolution in South Africa	128
6. Carl Akeley and the Preservation of African Mammals	160
Conclusion	199
Notes	202
Bibliography	241
Index	259

To Diane, Erik, and Tim

Preface

The history of Europe's contact with sub-Saharan Africa is an old one. Because of long, sustained relations between Europeans and black Africans, and due particularly to the heavy European involvement in the African continent during the colonial period, there is a large body of literature on the subject. America's relationship with black Africa, on the other hand, has not been so long nor so intense. Consequently its history is a comparatively modern one. It was only in the 1960s that serious attention was focused on this chapter of America's interest in the outer world. Historian Peter Duignan was the leader in this study and over more than twenty years he, in collaboration with several colleagues, continued to fill lacunae in the record while encouraging others to devote their energies to this area of research.[1] Duignan made especially important contributions through his bibliographical work.[2] Other historians followed this trail and produced general surveys[3] of the subject as well as specialized studies. We now have a good understanding of the scope and variety of America's connection with Africa. The general histories available are very useful but, of course, they do not provide extended treatment of the individual experiences that fill their pages.

This collection of essays examines selected individuals who were involved with Africa in various capacities in the second half of the nineteenth or early twentieth centuries. That period saw the trans-Mississippi frontier draw Americans from disparate walks of life who were seeking opportunities or adventure not readily available in the long-settled areas of their country. The virgin West did indeed absorb the energies of many such restless people for decades. For certain others, however, there was a more distant, more mysterious, and more exotic part of the world that attracted their attention—Africa. In a sense, Africa became their alternate frontier.

The six men discussed in these studies represented various occupational pursuits and were concerned with distinct parts of the continent at different times, which to some extent reflects the broad diversity of Africa's experience with the West in the age of imperialism. These Americans might be considered secondary historical figures, but their activities nevertheless are linked to significant phases of the Western world's contact with Africa for almost a century. Moreover, their interesting experiences contain drama and adventure equal to that of better-known, more celebrated outsiders who became identified with Africa.

The book's first focus is on the work of a dedicated missionary, Thomas Jefferson Bowen, who, during the 1850s, labored among the Yoruba people in the country now known as Nigeria, which was not yet much traveled by white men. In fact, he was the first Westerner to visit many parts of Yorubaland. Bowen's ideas about Africa—both while planning his mission and later when recounting his experiences—indicate much about the West's perception of Africa at that time. The next subject is Paul Du Chaillu, an explorer who made some sensational and controversial discoveries in Gabon, in west-central Africa in the 1860s. Through his popular writings he had a great impact on America's image of tropical Africa that has gone almost unnoted. Quite a different story is that of Charles Chaillé-Long, the subject of chapter 3. A soldier-explorer, he served the ruler of Egypt in the Sudan, Uganda, and in East Africa. Later, in a private capacity, he worked as an attorney in the mixed courts of Egypt. The period involved is that between 1869 and 1882. His career sheds light on the relatively little-known Egyptian territorial expansion of that period. Chapter 4 deals with a diplomat-entrepreneur, Henry Shelton Sanford. His association with the Belgian king, Leopold II, in the period 1876–90 put him in the midst of the European diplomacy that created the "scramble" for African territory, the classic case of European imperialism in that age. The area with which he was most concerned was the Congo Basin of Central Africa. John Hays Hammond, a mining engineer who worked in South Africa, is the focus of chapter 5. His was the briefest involvement in Africa, 1893–96, but politically the most significant since he was one of the ringleaders of an abortive revolution, the Jameson Raid, in the Boer territory known as the Transvaal. He thus was a key actor in a crucial event in the history of that region. Hammond also was important in the early development of deep-mining in the gold industry. Finally, there is the story of Carl Akeley's deep attachment to Africa from 1896 to 1926. Taxidermist, hunter, naturalist, and museum designer, Akeley roamed East Africa on five expeditions and collected animal specimens for his great exhibit hall in the American Museum of Natural History. His contribution toward America's appreciation of Africa's animal life was enormous.

Certainly African history has sufficient intrinsic importance and provides more than enough examples of indigenous achievement to interest us, but this writer has found that students and others sometimes are drawn more easily into the fascinating story of modern Africa by vicariously following the steps of their countrymen who went there during the period of awakening European interest prior to colonial partition or subsequently when it was under foreign rule. The ideas and deeds, both accomplishments and failures, of these intrepid men, mirror those of many other outsiders who went to Africa in those days and therefore stand as testimony to the foreign approach to this huge, often little-understood land mass once commonly called the Dark Continent.

Acknowledgments

The author acknowledges the assistance of numerous librarians in the course of his research: the American Museum of Natural History, New York; the Field Museum of Natural History, Chicago; the Johannesburg Public Library; the Library of Congress, Manuscript Division; the Ohio State University Library, Columbus; the Rhodes House Library, Oxford; the Sterling Memorial Library, Yale University, New Haven, Connecticut; the Library of the Southern Baptist Convention, Nashville, Tennessee; the University of Rochester Library; and the Interlibrary Loan Office of Moorhead State University, Moorhead, Minnesota. Special thanks are due to Moorhead State University for providing research grants in the early phases of the project. For constructive suggestions after they read all or parts of the manuscript I am indebted to John Trainor and William Kenz. When preparing maps I was fortunate to have expert help from the geographers Warren D. Kress and David L. Rosberg of North Dakota State University. I also want to express my gratitude to Connie Lillehoff and Eunice Nygard for their excellent typing as well as for other assistance in getting the manuscript ready for publication. Finally, I must thank Norman R. Bennett, editor of the *International Journal of African Historical Studies* (formerly *African Historical Studies*) for permission to republish material from the following articles:

"Henry S. Sanford and the Congo: A Reassessment." Vol. 4 (1971).

"Thomas J. Bowen and Central Africa: A Nineteenth Missionary Delusion." Vol. 15 (1982).

# The Farther Frontier

1
Thomas Jefferson Bowen and Central Africa: A Nineteenth-Century Missionary Delusion

The student of missionary history recognizes early the fact that many Christian missionaries overseas were astonishingly ill-prepared for their work. The record for nineteenth-century Africa furnishes numerous examples. This is not to say that these evangelists were lacking in zeal or determination or to ignore that some of them contributed in certain ways toward the benefit of Africa. But in general, those who accepted the call to the "Dark Continent" knew little about the societies they hoped to redeem from "barbarism." In those few cases where programs for missionary training existed before the turn of the century, they were grossly inadequate, suffering from both the racial prejudices and abysmal ignorance of Africa that prevailed at the time.

The very nature of the missionaries' objective, of course, determined that they often would become a disruptive factor in African life. Their meager understanding of the continent's geography and ethnic complexity only compounded the problem. This represented a major contribution to the intellectual climate in Europe that led to the conquest and partition of Africa. Badly informed missionaries went into the field and proceeded to misunderstand and misrepresent African culture in their writings, thus perpetuating distorted images. Although most missionaries involved in this process were Europeans, a number of Americans also contributed to the West's regrettable misunderstanding about Africa that in some quarters has lingered on to the present time. And one of them, Thomas Jefferson Bowen, perhaps more than any other American churchman who worked in nineteenth-century Africa, popularized the civilizing mission that became so much a part of the subsequent colonial era, even though his own country was little involved in African affairs.

Thomas Jefferson Bowen (*Courtesy of the Southern Baptist Historical Library and Archives, Nashville, Tennessee*).

The initial American effort in Africa that is clearly recognizable as a missionary endeavor was that of two Virginia ex-slaves, Lott Cary and Colin Teague. Cary, a Baptist, was instrumental in founding the Richmond-African Missionary Society in 1815. He and Teague began their labors in Liberia, on the continent's western coast, in 1827. An interdenominational body, the American Board of Foreign Missions, was established in 1828 and it recognized the importance of Africa. But its first agent was not sent there until 1833, his destination, Liberia. For some years this territory, which contained several struggling settlements of American ex-slaves, remained the principal target of missionary enterprise. The first to work elsewhere were representatives of the American Board who arrived in Gabon, equatorial West Africa, in June 1842. Some colleagues were at work on nearby Corisco Island by 1850.[1]

Bowen, the first American missionary to Yorubaland, was a Georgian with a military bent. In 1836 at the age of twenty-two he raised a company of soldiers to help suppress Creek Indian uprisings in his home state and in Florida. Having acquired a taste for martial action, he shortly afterward rode to Texas and offered his services to the newly established republic. He acquired a commission and during three years of fighting Indians and Mexicans who threatened widely scattered settlements, he earned command of a regiment. Apparently he was a good soldier and he admitted that he became much enamored of military life. Yet his developing religious convictions made it impossible for him to continue such a career. By November 1839 he had resigned his commission and returned to Georgia where, in late 1840, he experienced his religious "awakening." The conversion was complete; thereupon Bowen began to preach and in 1842 he was ordained in the ministry.[2] But evidently the domestic pulpit and the adventure of circuit riding did not bring him the satisfaction he sought. This new "soldier of the Lord" decided to win converts in the mission field. Bowen, who had little formal education, at an early age developed a great interest in books. His broad range of reading included works that introduced him to Africa, a land of pagan peoples.

Bowen was associated with the Southern Baptist Convention (SBC). As a result of differences over the slavery issue, this group divorced itself from the American Baptist Convention in 1845 and established its own mission authority. American Baptist missionaries had operated in Burma since 1813 and in several other Asian territories since 1836. Following the split within the Baptist community in the United States, two missionaries in China chose to become affiliated with the Southern Convention. China was thus the first SBC mission and it remained the largest overseas enterprise for a century. West Africa had attracted some interest and the SBC was considering that area as a possible field for its evangelizing labors. Thus the first annual report of the SBC's Foreign Mission Board optimistically stated: "China is open. Africa is accessible."[3] But the convention had some difficulty procuring financial support for its foreign missionaries. New projects received careful scrutiny before being funded. The scheme Bowen presented to the SBC Foreign Mission Board in 1848 was far more ambitious than any other projects reviewed by this body. In view of the unique character of Bowen's plan and what it demonstrates about the state of knowledge in midnineteenth century American mission quarters, the genesis of this project is worth noting.

It has been suggested that the work of the Englishman Thomas F. Buxton, the untiring enemy of slavery and proponent of commercial expansion as a prime civilizing agency, was a great influence behind the extension of missionary activity in West Africa.[4] While this is probably true as far as a general awakening of interest in the continent is concerned, especially in British evangelical and trading circles, there is no evidence that Buxton's writings were known to Bowen. In any case, the British missionaries responding to Buxton's appeals were primarily concerned with the more familiar coastal region where the slave trade had been concentrated. Bowen, on the other hand, was looking to the deep interior. By 1848 a number of European explorers had penetrated to the western Sudan, the most famous of them Mungo Park, René Caillié, Richard and John Lander, Dixon Denham, and Hugh Clapperton, all of whom had published accounts of their journeys. Bowen knew of their widely reported accomplishments but, with the exception of later references to the Landers' journal, he never indicated that he had read their books in researching his project.

The recorded sources of Bowen's information include such common reference sets of the time as the *Penny Cyclopedia* and *Chamber's Miscellany*.[5] Certainly such materials left much to be desired by modern standards, yet one scholar claims that the former work was as authoritative for its time, on many topics, at least, as the *Encyclopaedia Britannica*.[6] But the most important authority Bowen consulted was a fellow Georgian, W. B. Hodgson. A linguist and specialist on the Berber and Fulani peoples, a natural scientist who delivered papers on a variety of subjects before learned societies, Hodgson published two books on northwestern Africa that were pertinent to Bowen's interest. Indeed,

Hodgson probably provided the inspiration for Bowen's scheme. We know that the latter relied heavily on Hodgson's *Notes on Northern Africa*, in which can be found opinions about the geography and people of Africa that Bowen made his own.[7]

It was Bowen's belief that a great opportunity for the Christianization of the continent lay in the western Sudan, an area that he, following the practice of several writers, referred to as "Central Africa." The territory that had captured his imagination was concentrated "between Timbuctos [sic] and the mountains."[8] Such a vague identification was in keeping with the still obscure picture of the African interior common in Europe and the United States at the time. He meant the land around the great bend of the Niger River and Hausaland to the east. The dry climate of this region was said to be healthier for white men than the pestilential coastal belt, but the principal attraction for him was the character of the area's people.

Influenced by Hodgson, Bowen saw the Fulani, one of the major groups in the Sudan, as the key to the regeneration of Africa. They were, he wrote, "so different from other Mahometans [sic] that they might prove a people made ready for the lord."[9] This indicates that he was probably unaware of the several Fulani jihads, those militant Islamic reform movements of the eighteenth and nineteenth centuries that had produced significant theocratic state systems in the western Sudan, the most impressive in Hausaland. Bowen thus could naively suggest that these puritanical, crusading Muslims "might embrace the Gospel and go forth as missionaries into every part of Africa."[10] Regarding their religion, he felt that "the ideas of Mohametanism [sic], however inferior and pernicious in themselves, were yet an advance upon the original Negro beliefs."[11] In other words, by having embraced Islam the Fulani were to be considered halfway along a progressive path from heathenism to Christianity![12]

This notion was not then so ridiculous as it seems today, given the reports of explorers that had noted the civilized cultures and relative commercial prosperity of the Sudanic peoples who were, presumably, ready to expand their contacts with the outside world.[13] And it was popular through much of the nineteenth century to see trade and Christianity advancing together through the wilds of Africa. Bowen thought that trade would become one of the principal means by which Christianity would be introduced throughout the continent.[14] If the Fulani were important traders, in his opinion they were obviously more advanced than other groups and, accordingly, they should be more receptive to the

Christian message. And in order to make the region appear more acceptable as a mission field to white Baptists, Bowen repeatedly distinguished the Fulani racially from Negroes who, he estimated incorrectly, probably did not comprise half of Africa's inhabitants.[15]

With the Niger's course finally charted by the Landers in 1830, it was natural for outsiders to view the great river as a sure route to the vast, promising interior. Visionary hopes of swiftly opening the Niger country to European trade and evangelization were dashed, however, by the disastrous expeditions of Macgregor Laird in 1832 and the group sponsored by the British government in 1841.[16] Attention was diverted temporarily to the other areas almost exclusively along the coast or not far from it. British missionaries began working along the Nigerian littoral in the 1840s, some Anglicans venturing sixty miles inland to the town of Abeokuta. This was a center of the Egba people, a sub-group of the great Yoruba language family. After some early difficulties, a British mission station was established at Abeokuta in 1846. There were then no European missions—and none contemplated—in the distant region Bowen called "Central Africa."

When Bowen's plan for a mission was laid before his board, a committee was appointed to consider its feasibility; this body issued a favorable report in January 1849. After recruiting two associates, one of them a young black man who had just purchased his freedom, Bowen then received his formal appointment on February 22.[17] His instructions directed him to make his way to the Sudan or to "some adjacent country." It was decided that a suitable location for the first station was the town of Igboho, situated on the northern edge of Yorubaland and believed, correctly, to be close to Fulani country.[18] In fact, the Sokoto Caliphate and Empire, a great Fulani-dominated state created by the jihad launched in Hausaland by Usuman dan Fodio in 1804, had absorbed the Yoruba town of Ilorin, fifty-five miles east of Igboho, as an emirate in about 1824.[19] Although Ilorin remained ethnically mixed, with a large Yoruba population, it was indeed part of the Islamic sovereignty that Bowen regarded as the key to all of West Africa.[20].

Bowen's party set sail from Providence, Rhode Island, in mid-December 1849 and accomplished the Atlantic crossing in normal time but, due to their ship making numerous stops along the West African coast, they did not put ashore in Monrovia, Liberia, until seven weeks later. It was Bowen's intention to reach Badagry, on the so-called Slave Coast, from where they would proceed through

Yorubaland. But they did not want to arrive at that port in the rainy season, so Bowen and his associates decided to remain in Liberia until the next dry season. His white colleague, Harvey Goodale, convinced him that they should invest their time working among the Gula people of the interior, since one of their chiefs had requested missionary-teachers. Bowen, who preferred catching a ship to neighboring Sierra Leone in the hope of finding a Fulani who could teach him that important language of the Niger country, reluctantly agreed to accompany him to the Gulas. It took them almost four weeks to reach their destination, the village of Sama, where Goodale soon obtained a grant of land for their mission and a farm. Shortly after their arrival, however, Goodale was taken ill and within a month was dead of a tropical fever. After burying his companion, Bowen, also suffering from fever, returned to the coast.[21]

While in Monrovia for ten weeks where he recuperated, Bowen was confirmed in his belief that the Africans of the coast were inferior types who would prove difficult to convert. Although he recognized some exceptions, such as the Mandingoes, he considered the coastal peoples generally a wretched lot. Those Africans, particularly the inland groups, who displayed physical features resembling those of white men and whose clothing covered most of their bodies, were easily rated as superior.[22] Four months in Liberia, while perhaps instructive in some respects, were nevertheless a frustrating period for the man who felt compelled to reach the inner part of the continent. And he was now alone. When it was time to leave Liberia, Bowen found it necessary, because of personality conflicts, to leave his black coworker, Robert Hill, in Monrovia.

The voyage by schooner down the coast took another six weeks. Bowen finally landed at Badagry on August 5, 1850. He soon discovered that due to chronic civil war that raged through Yorubaland, he could not travel to Igboho. It was possible to go to Abeokuta, however; and so, greatly disappointed, Bowen made his way sixty miles northeastward to that town. It was there that he would spend most of his time until he returned to the United States in 1853. Thus he had reached the territory now known as Nigeria.[23] But the period in Abeokuta was a depressing one. Since the Anglicans, Henry Townshend and the distinguished Yoruba ex-slave, Samuel Crowther, already had established themselves as missionaries there, Bowen did not want to interfer in any way with their work.[24] Such professional delicacy, along with repeated attacks of malaria, limited his activities.

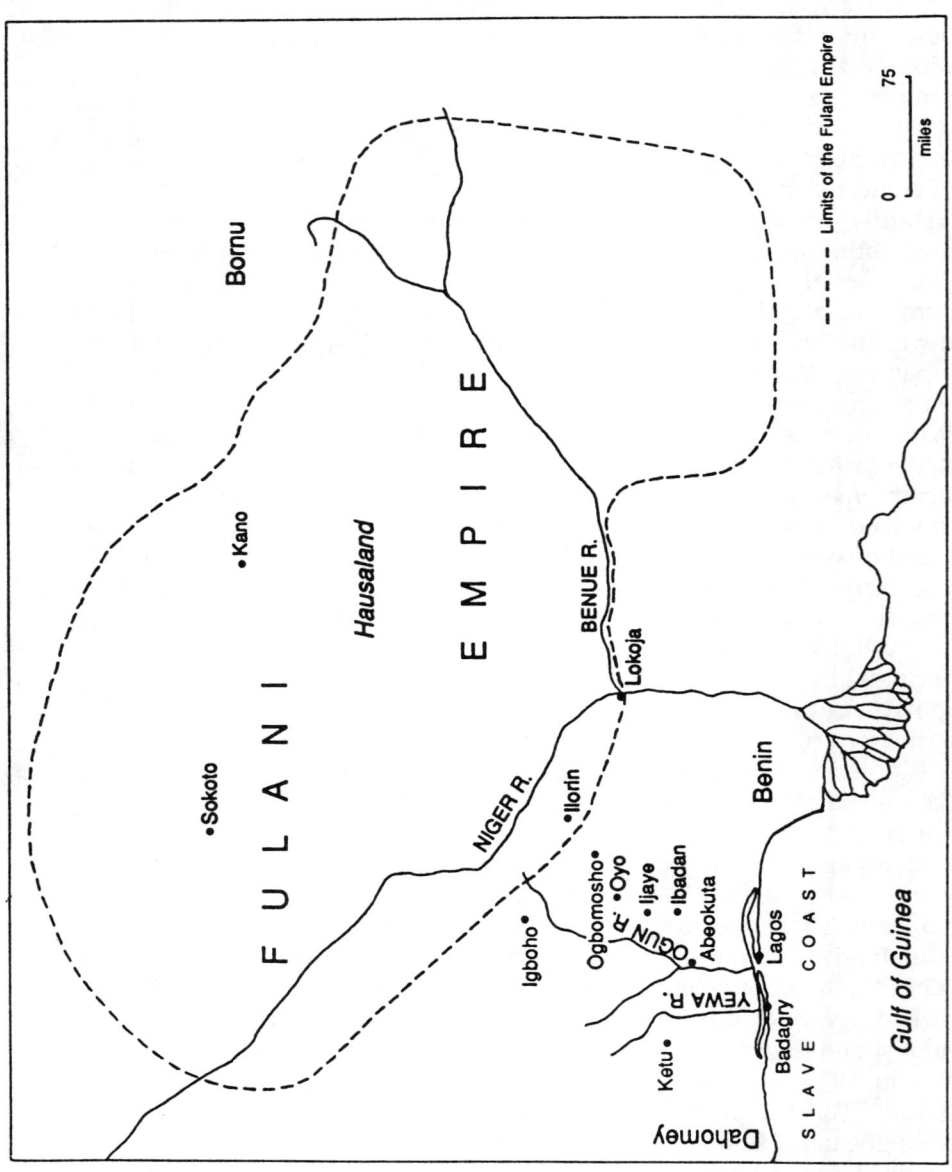

Yorubaland and Nigeria in the mid-19th century.

Abeokuta was one of several towns founded by refugees from the north who fled from the power struggles and slave raiding that engulfed Yorubaland following the collapse of the once great Oyo Empire in the early nineteenth century. Especially hard hit by the chaotic situation were the Egba Yoruba, many of whose original towns were destroyed. Seeking a haven, Egba refugees established themselves in Abeokuta in 1830, and in the following decades this center continued to attract Egbas fleeing from insecurity elsewhere.[25] In addition, a number of Egbas who had been enslaved, shipped from the coast, recaptured by the British navy's antislave trade patrol, and finally freed in Sierra Leone, began to return to Yorubaland after 1839. Many of these Sierra Leonians or "Saro" settled in Abeokuta.[26] This urban community developed as a loose confederation of townships established by various groups migrating from the north. Each of the townships or wards within the city was under the authority of the ward's branch of the secret society, the Ogboni, and the township's military leader, the Ologun. At the center there was the Alake, the elected chief of the senior township, who served as a head arbitrator but who wielded no authority over the whole urban population. Executive power, such as it was, was shared by an elderly triumvirate of chiefs who exerted their authority through the Ogboni Society.[27]

Missionaries considered this relatively new community as an excellent base from which to Christianize the whole Niger country.[28] And there were grounds for such optimism. The refugees settled there welcomed the missionaries because they sought the latter's help in defense against hostile neighboring states, while the Sierra Leonians, most of whom were Christians, wanted to maintain their connection with Western culture through the missionaries and rendered them valuable assistance.[29]

Besides studying the Yoruba language while delayed in Abeokuta, the restless American also drew from his military experience to assist the townsmen in repelling an attack by the powerful forces of Dahomey, a major kingdom to the west. Gezo, the ruler of Dahomey, had been hostile toward Abeokuta for some years. He saw the establishment and success of Abeokuta and other new Egba towns as an impediment to his own expansion aimed at the conquest of Yorubaland[30] and, more specifically, he bitterly resented the Egbas' capture of Dahomey's royal chair and its national emblem, an umbrella made of various animal skins, during an earlier military encounter in 1844. Gezo would have paid dearly to recover the umbrella, but the Abeokutans had burned it.[31] Now, in early March 1851, he sought revenge.

The Dahomean army made extensive preparations for its drive on Abeokuta, and these had been witnessed by British officers visiting Gezo's capital of Abomey. They had then warned the Egba chiefs of the impending attack, thus enabling them to ready Abeokuta as well as other towns along the invasion route.[32] Arriving before the strongly defended Egba center with erroneous advice from the chief of another Yoruba town, the Dahomean forces were about 16,000 strong, 6,000 of whom were females, the famed and widely dreaded Amazons. This was one of the largest armies ever assembled in that part of Africa and it was an uncommonly disciplined one. Unwisely, the attackers, with their Amazons in the van, charged their target at midday (rather that at night as originally planned) and against the strongest part of the wall. The defenders, about equal in total numbers and all armed with guns, put up a determined resistance. Bowen provided tactical advice and constant encouragement in helping them repulse ten assaults. It resulted in a rare defeat for Gezo's forces who then withdrew.[33]

Bowen was now a minor celebrity. The prevalent belief in the region had been that any town permitting residence to white men would be destroyed by its enemies. But when word spread that Bowen's assistance and that of the other missionaries had helped to save Abeokuta from a feared enemy, it enhanced the white man's image. He found that his reception in neighboring towns was better in some cases than before the battle. Contributing to the relatively greater freedom of movement for missionaries was the treaty Britain exacted in 1852 from a number of Yoruba chiefs, by which they agreed to protect the Christians and permit them to move about at will.[34] Yet travel could still be difficult. The civil strife, brigandage, and suspicion of outsiders were far from ended. When Bowen ventured to other settlements he was usually unable to accomplish more than visiting a few chiefs and, despite the British treaty, was sometimes insulted and rebuffed. Indeed, several towns would not even admit him.

Bowen had tried on several occasions, for example, to visit the western Yoruba state of Ketu but was denied permission by its king. When, after three months, the American finally was invited in, he found others in the area opposed to his presence and, as a result, the ruler's house was burned down and an attempt was made to poison the white stranger. Bowen attributed this hostility toward him to the widespread superstition that ill-fortune would befall any community that admitted white men. But among those in Ketu who opposed the king's invitation to the missionary were some supporters of the king of Dahomey and they may have sought vengeance against the American for his role in defending Abeokuta from Dahomey's recent attack.[35] Bowen nevertheless persisted in his effort to preach in Ketu until, advised by his host to leave, he returned to Abeokuta. Although in this period he failed to reach his objective, the town of Igboho, Bowen was able to proceed to Ijayi, an important town where he won permission to build a mission station. Here he spent a few months introducing those inhabitants who were curious, to some fundamentals of his faith.

Continually frustrated in his efforts to reach the land of the Fulani, Bowen did become more familiar with the Yorubas and he came to respect them as an impressive people even if they did not quite measure up to his Fulani standard. In fact, he realized that he might have to be satisfied by working with this group for the indefinite future.[36] In between increasingly severe bouts with malaria and other tropical maladies Bowen gained a good working knowledge of the Yoruba language and thus a better understanding of the culture. The Yoruba were an urban people settled in numerous towns, some of which contained many thousands of inhabitants, and in more peaceful times engaged in a varied trade with one another. Such Africans therefore exhibited some of the characteristics associated with the supposedly superior groups of the north. Even though most Yoruba were idolators in missionary eyes, they presented favorable prospects for instruction. The large population of Abeokuta, which included many refugees from other warring towns, Bowen overconfidently asserted to be "fast to receive the Gospel."[37] It happened, therefore, that Bowen's conception of "Central Africa" began to change. Whereas originally the area most identified by that designation was Hausaland, his new view expanded far to the south to include all of Yorubaland. Indeed, it now embraced all but the coastal forest. And this was the message he brought with him when, in need of recuperation after enduring Africa's fevers and having received his mission board's advice that he not try to work alone, he sailed for home in August 1852.

Almost a year in the United States enabled him to promote a Yoruba mission and to find others to help him in the field. By the time he embarked once again for Africa in July 1853, he had acquired a wife and two coworkers. The Reverends J. S. Dennard and John H. Lacy and their spouses were appointed to the Yoruba mission. Bowen's persistent appeals must have been quite persuasive with a foreign mission board hard-pressed for money and with good reason to question the wisdom of mission work in war-torn Yorubaland. But the rigors of life in West Africa had not abated. Within a year after their arrival in Yorubaland, one colleague and his wife were dead and the other couple was forced by illness to return home. Bowen and his bride were left to carry on themselves.

Pushing on to Ijaye, they set to work building a chapel and awaited reinforcements. Eventually two other missionaries arrived, and by 1855 additional Baptist stations had been established at Lagos on the coast and at Ogbomosho beyond Ijayi. Although sickness continued to prostrate Bowen and his wife for long periods, and in 1854 they lost their infant daughter to disease, the growth of the mission system revived his ambition of carrying operations into the Sokoto Caliphate as he originally had planned. When an associate was available to take over the Ijayi station, the Bowens moved fifty miles south of Ilorin and only twice that distance from the Niger. It presented an opportunity not to be missed. A fellow missionary, William Clark, who had joined them in December 1854, made a preliminary visit to Ilorin in July 1855 and returned believing that the way northward was open to them. Some weeks later, desiring to confirm this encouraging report and intending to establish his principal base there if permitted, Bowen also traveled to Ilorin.

During the previous years Bowen had met a number of Muslims. They were to be found in almost all Yoruba towns[38] and he occasionally sought them out, initially to test his theory that they would be relatively receptive to Christianity. It is interesting to note that he prepared himself for such contact by examining the Koran, but it took him some time to become sufficiently aware of the confident religious pride with which most Muslims held to their faith. This helps explain his surprise when Muslims who heard his preaching expressed no interest in Jesus.[39] In discussions Bowen made them uncomfortable by commonly referring to their "sin" of polygamy.[40] Even though he never completely lost hope that ultimately he could reach the Muslims' minds and hearts, and he continued to engage them in disputations, he concluded that the "Koran is like smoke in the eyes of all who believe it."[41] Now, at long last, he was in a Muslim center and better able to judge the prospects for evangelism among such a people.

In Ilorin he encountered a Fulani ruling class who provided him with further evidence in support of his racial ideas. A Fulani, he reported, "might be black, brown or almost white, but some were very handsome had might have passed for 'sharp-nosed' people of any [presumably European] country." He classified them as "by far the most interesting, intelligent and energetic people in Central Africa."[42] The Yoruba, about whom he had been so complimentary in his recent correspondence, now fell considerably lower on his scale. "Yoruba is called an uncivilized nation. I began to have the same feelings and I was sorry that I must go back to Ijaye even for a few months."[43] His first impressions of Ilorin, then, were extremely favorable and reminiscent of his early grandiose pronouncements in enlisting support for his original mission proposal.

> I never saw an honorable man nor a modest woman in Africa till I reached Ilorin. The number of people who can read and write surprises me. I now see more plainly than ever that Central Africa [specifically Hausaland or the Fulani Empire] should be our field of labor.[44]

It appeared to him that he had reached the threshold of the great central Sudan. He expressed his intention to advance as soon as possible to Nupe beyond the Niger, with the next destination being Sokoto, the Fulani capital.[45] It all depended, of course, on Ilorin's ruler granting him access to the route northward. After a promising initial meeting with the local emir, Bowen was denied permission to set up a mission station. Moreover, it soon became clear that he would not be allowed to travel beyond this southern gateway to the Fulani Empire. It would have been foolhardy for a Muslim leader to have acted otherwise, especially since the political situation in Ilorin was rather delicate at the time.

After all, the Fulani conquest of Ilorin was a relatively recent one. And the conquerors were still an ethnic minority in what was a Yoruba community. Naturally, some Yoruba in the area, particularly those who had not embraced Islam, had not accepted foreign rule gracefully. These and others who had fled in the wake of defeat to towns such as Ijayi were an opposition element that the Fulani could not ignore.[46] Having come from Ijayi and Ogbomosho, whose relations with Ilorin were often strained, Bowen might well have been seen as an agent of enemy Yoruba seeking to undermine the Muslim regime. More important, however, was the fact that a Fulani ruler's position depended not just on military force but, as far as his Muslim subjects were concerned, on his role as defender of the faith.[47] Not surprisingly, then, the Christian missionary was turned back. In reflecting on this development later, Bowen, who by that time had the wisdom of hindsight, unconvincingly sought to minimize his failure. "I was not much disappointed for I had always feared that the Mahometans [sic] would not receive us as missionaries."[48] Whatever his feelings, he had no choice but to retreat to Ogbomosho where he continued his work among the Yoruba until his final departure from Africa in 1856.

Bowen's dream of a Christian central Africa was never realized. His Baptist successors sensibly contented themselves with Yorubaland and with neighboring areas in the south. But others did not. To whatever extent missionaries tried to learn from the experiences of their peers, they would have been confused by Bowen's reports on the feasibility of a mission to the Muslim regions. In a letter published in late 1856, he stated that "most of them [the Muslim Fulani] desire missionaries, though they know our doctrine and designs,"[49] whereas in his book, which appeared in the following year, he described his failure to get beyond the first Islamic center he encountered where there was no interest among Muslims in his Christian message. In any event, the agents of the Church Missionary Society, British Anglicans who had been active early in the Nigerian field, picked up the banner abandoned by Bowen. They stubbornly and unsuccessfully pursued the objective of converting the Islamic Sudan until the end of the century.[50]

British colonial authorities for a time unwisely supported this futile endeavor and thereby helped to provoke great hostility in northern Nigeria. By the early twentieth century they realized their mistake and, in order to promote better relations with the northern districts, the British High Commissioner (1900–1906) and later Governor (1912–13) in the north, Frederick Lugard, prohibited missionaries from entering Muslim areas without the local emir's consent.[51]

Belatedly the Church Missionary Society grasped what Bowen reluctantly had to acknowledge: namely, that the practitioners of traditional African religions were far more appropriate subjects for proselytization than African Muslims. The considerable missionary success in Nigeria was to be recorded not in the north but in the southern regions. And the Baptist station system founded and nurtured through trying circumstances by Bowen played a part in that process.

Although he never became a spokesman for British imperialism—which had not yet loomed as a dominant factor in Nigeria during his time there—Bowen nevertheless espoused another form of large-scale foreign intrusion. Once retired from his African labors, he became interested in the colonization of American blacks in that part of Africa most important to him; indeed he stated that he would devote himself as much as possible to the cause of colonization.[52] Removal of black freemen from the United States, he argued, would not only solve the problem of their unassimilability, but it would give them the opportunity to control a vast commercial network in central Africa and lead to a black Christian empire embracing the Sudan.[53] By this time Bowen had developed an even stronger belief that trade would be the prime instrument in reforming African life. "I plead for commerce in [the] Sudan as one of the most powerful means for the creation of that wealth, science, and art, which are indispensable to civilization."[54] Thus, if regular missionaries could not achieve Bowen's original objective, black Americans were to accept the challenge in a somewhat different form.

While in Africa Bowen had been in communication with the American Colonization Society, his letters to its officers occasionally appearing in the society's journal, the *African Repository*. This organization, founded in 1817, was white-led and counted among its members and supporters many slave-owners whose main interest in colonization was as a means of ridding the country of "troublesome" free blacks. It, along with affiliated state colonization societies, had established settlements in West Africa that became known as Liberia. The latter, when Bowen visited it in 1850, was still a struggling community that he found badly situated in the fever-ridden coastal belt. Although he had some praise for the achievements of the black American settlers there, Bowen was convinced that the interior regions, particularly Yoruba country, offered far better prospects for such ventures.

Published in 1857, Bowen's book, *Central Africa: Adventures and Missionary Labors in several countries in the Interior of Africa from 1849–1856*, described his experiences in the mission field and presented his views on how the more highly developed Christian world should proceed in transforming the black lands south of the Sahara. It was an influential statement in those circles concerned with Africa. Reviews of the book appeared in various newspapers and missionary periodicals, and the American Colonization Society provided extended coverage of it in the *African Repository*.[55] Bowen's favorable account of Yorubaland, already partially circulated in his earlier correspondence, impressed the organization's directors who now saw that area as a possible site for future colonization. Liberia by that time had become an independent republic divorced from the Washington-based society's direction, although the latter continued to extend financial assistance and occasionally sent some new settlers there. While Bowen did not discourage the group's interest in Yoruba territory, he cautioned patience until influential black leaders could be won over. If the society identified itself prematurely with such a project, he advised, it could be the "kiss of death" because of black distrust of white-sponsored colonization.[56]

Although most blacks remained opposed to leaving the United States as a solution to their problems, a growing number of spokesmen found that option more attractive in the 1850s.[57] Generally these men looked upon the American Colonization Society as a tool of the Southern slavocracy, and therefore believed it necessary to establish their own movement. One such late convert to emigrationism was the Presbyterian minister and ardent abolitionist, Henry Highland Garnet. In 1858 he helped found the African Civilization Society, which had among its aims the establishment abroad of "a grand center of Negro nationality from which [would] flow streams of commercial, intellectual and political power which [would] make colored people respected everywhere." Garnet believed that cotton grown by American blacks in their own colonies somewhere in the tropical world would find a ready market in England, ultimately replacing slave-grown cotton and thereby contributing significantly toward the eradication of both slavery in America and the slave trade within Africa.[58]

Like certain other black leaders seeking a suitable location for foreign settlements, Garnet found Bowen's case for Yorubaland quite persuasive.[59] Working out of his church in New York, he began to promote removal of his people to that part of Africa at the same time that Bowen, responding to what he perceived as the "new emigration feeling among the blacks," was addressing large crowds of Garnet's followers in New York, outlining the opportunities awaiting them in the areas familiar to him.[60] Bowen thus was associated with the traditional colonization movement as well as the newer black emigration forces, apparently hoping that eventually the two could combine efforts for the realization of a project very important to him. And in fact, a tenuous bridge was formed when the New York State Colonization Society decided, in late 1858, to back colonization in Yorubaland.[61] It certainly must have appeared to him at that point that his proposals were well on the way toward implementation.

Garnet invited Bowen to return to Yorubaland to superintend the association's colonizing operation, the stated objective of which was the "evangelization and civilization of Africa."[62] Although for a time after his return to the United States in 1856 Bowen had hoped that he could work in Africa again in some capacity to further his dream, poor health and concern for his family prevented him from doing so. However, in 1858 a black-led exploring party, linked to the African Civilization Society,[63] reached Yorubaland and, following Bowen's path, generally confirmed his findings.[64] A treaty permitting settlement was negotiated with Egba leaders in Abeokuta. The Yoruba chiefs indicated a willingness to accept blacks from America but insisted that they be governed by local law and authority.[65] Bowen wanted each settlement, in the beginning at least, to be regarded as an American trading post and thus come under the protection of the American flag.[66] Before 1857 he had not expressed any interest in seeing his country's flag follow the faith into Africa and he made scant mention of it later. Yet it is clear that he, like certain other missionaries, was not averse to his government assisting in such an important "civilizing" enterprise. In fact, he took steps to bring this about.

Just before he lent himself to efforts to interest free blacks in a return to Yorubaland, Bowen had been in league with other lobbyists in advocating governmental funding for a fact-finding mission to the Niger region for the purpose of initiating trade with the Yoruba kingdoms and their neighbors. Various parties had, through the 1850s, been urging official U.S. exploration of West Africa. The American Colonization Society, for example, backed the move for a Niger exploratory mission because it hoped that resulting trade with that area would lead to regular American shipping service to West Africa which, in turn, would provide a boost to Liberia's chronically depressed economy. The early weeks of 1857 saw Bowen very active in Washington, speaking before sundry groups about the potentialities of American trade with the peoples in his sphere of experience. And his remarks were not ignored by the press. It was a well-organized campaign directed at the important sources of influence in the State Department and on Capitol Hill. In February 1857, the U.S. Senate voted twenty-five thousand dollars for a Niger exploration venture which, its sponsors assumed, would be directed by Bowen. Despite his testimony before its Commerce Committee, the appropriation was lost in the House of Representatives.[67]

Bowen's strategy for returning American blacks to Yorubaland and their eventual expansion into the Muslim Sudan, though it was espoused by others, including some influential black leaders, was of course never implemented. Not only was the Yoruba movement plagued by an insufficiency of funds, but the American Civil War understandably reduced blacks' interest in Africa.[68] But what he proposed was an invasion that probably would have disrupted Nigerian peoples no less than European imperialism was to do. The blacks who took up his idea planned on establishing their own nation-state that would, as Liberia supposedly was doing, provide indigenous Africans with the keys to their moral and cultural improvement while extending political control over them. In their own fashion the black emigrationists inspired by Bowen would have carried the "white man's burden" with them.[69]

And Bowen would have found great satisfaction in such a development. As was the case with his more famous contemporary, David Livingstone, Bowen had developed a respect for certain African peoples and some of their institutions, but in the end he, like Livingstone, came to believe that tribal society itself was the principal obstacle to Christianity and progress.[70] To facilitate the necessary transformation of the incomplete indigenous culture, Livingstone eventually advocated white colonization,[71] whereas Bowen, convinced by his observations of Sierra Leonians in Yorubaland that blacks could more readily instruct and inspire Africans than white men, saw the settlement of Christian ex-slaves as Africa's hope. In his vision it was to be a Westernizing trio of missions, colonization, and trade. As the history of its conquest and colonial rule was to demonstrate, this combination of forces, though not exactly in the form Bowen proposed, certainly was instrumental in reshaping Africa's development.

After completing a dictionary of the Yoruba language, which was a major contribution to linguistics,[72] Bowen went on to serve from 1859 to 1861 as a missionary in Brazil and subsequently as a Confederate military chaplain during the American Civil War. But shortly after his return from Africa he had begun to suffer from recurrent mental illness, which became increasingly severe in his later years. He died in a Georgia asylum in 1875.[73]

This American missionary-explorer undoubtedly served his cause faithfully and deserves the admiration of those who glory in the saga of an expanding Christian Church. At the same time, it should be clear that in resisting first Bowen's advances and then those of the black emigrationists influenced by him, some African leaders were seeking to prevent what ultimately became a wholesale assault on their way of life, of which the missionaries were only the precursors. Bowen's Central Africa scheme stands as a glaring example of not only the West's unfortunate ignorance of the wider world but, in particular, its arrogance when confronting African civilization.

2
Jungle Adventure: Paul Du Chaillu and the American Image of Africa

In 1889 Paul Belloni Du Chaillu published his second book on Scandinavia and was recognized as an authority on the history and culture of the Nordic peoples. When he died in St. Petersburg fourteen years later he was in the initial stage of research for a book on Russia. Yet these projects of his later years have relatively little to do with his place in history. Actually, Du Chaillu's considerable reputation during his lifetime was gained from his adventures in lands far removed from the cold climes of northern Europe. Indeed, he was one of the best-known explorers of Africa. Even though he receives little attention in modern surveys of foreign contact with Africa, his books on the Dark Continent were among the most widely read works of their genre.[1] He thus had a far greater influence on American ideas and impressions about Africa than is generally known.

There is considerable confusion about Du Chaillu's parentage and place of birth. Most biographical reference works and obituaries indicate that he was descended from French Huguenot stock and born in New Orleans,[2] while others list Paris as his birthplace.[3] Such disagreement suggests that Du Chaillu was not consistent in supplying information about himself, and the reason for this seems to be related to a certain insecurity he felt about his ancestry. An Englishman who became closely acquainted with Du Chaillu through mutual friends in British geographical circles stated with great certainty that his friend was born on the Indian Ocean island of Réunion (before the Revolution of 1848 known as Bourbon) of a French father and a mulatto mother.[4] If, as seems probable, Du Chaillu wished to conceal his mother's mixed parentage because of racism in the United States, he might well have been intentionally vague about his origins, especially to Americans.[5] But evidently he was more willing to confide to an English friend the then embarrassing fact that all his forebears

Paul Belloni Du Chaillu (*Courtesy of Harper and Row, Publishers*).

were not Caucasian. Another creditable acquaintance stated that his mother, who died while Paul was a small child, was Italian,[6] which would not preclude her having been a mulatto. Nowhere in his many writings, however, did Du Chaillu provide the slightest reference to his mother, which further suggests that he did not wish to bring attention to his maternal roots. The American scholar, Henry Bucher, Jr., who researched Du Chaillu's background more thoroughly than anyone else, suggests that since his father did not register the birth of a son, but did admit to siring two daughters, Paul probably was illegitimate.[7]

Even the date of Du Chaillu's birth is in dispute. The date, July 31, 1835, has been commonly accepted, but there is reason to question it. We know that he arrived in the United States in 1852 and obtained a teaching position in a girls' school the following year.[8] It is doubtful that a foreign youth of eighteen would have been given such a post. One of his students later recalled that when Du Chaillu commenced his duties as a French instructor, he claimed to be twenty-seven years old.[9] Even allowing that he might have assumed a more mature age in order to gain the position, he probably would not have exaggerated it by ten years. Michel Vaucaire, Du Chaillu's sole biographer, discovered his subject's only published reference to his age in a French edition of one of his books in which he allows the reader to calculate the year of his birth as 1831.[10] This is as authoritative an answer as we can expect.

Paul's father, Charles Alexis Du Chaillu, was a trader who first worked on Réunion and then became the agent of a La Havre firm on the Gabon River in equatorial west Africa until, in 1848, he was named supply-master for the French naval and colonial stations in the Gabon estuary.[12] During the 1830s he resided in France and it appears that Paul accompanied him and began his schooling there. The elder Du Chaillu was back in Gabon by the mid 1840s where Paul followed him between 1848 and 1850.[13] The young man evidently attended schools run by both the Protestant and Catholic missions near Libreville. And by age fifteen he was employed as a minor clerk by the local colonial administration.[14]

The territory of Gabon was a French sphere of interest. In 1473 the Portuguese navigator, Lopo Gonçalves, reached the mouth of the Gabon River, thus initiating European contact with that African region. His countrymen, though they developed a much stronger interest in the Congo region to the south, continued over the years an occasional trade along the Gabon coast, and eventually other Europeans competed with them. Slaves became the principal objective of the white traders although ivory, rubber, and various hardwoods were important. By the late eighteenth century the French were the most active in the Gabon business, some seventy companies having contacts there.[15] But trade would not remain the sole French interest.

In 1818, following the Napoleonic wars, France became the seventh European state to abolish the slave trade and subsequently contributed a few ships to the naval effort along the west African coast to suppress the traffic across the Atlantic. Although they had earlier identified the Gabon area as an appropriate site for a commercial and naval base, it was not until 1839 that the French, prompted by the initiative of a naval officer, Edouard Bouet-Willaumez, took possession of the Gabon estuary and, through a treaty with a local chief, a small strip of land on the southern bank. By 1842 France also had territory on the north bank where a fort (Fort d'Aumale) was constructed in the following year. The local Mpongwe were generally friendly and cooperative,[16] which not only encouraged traders and naval authorities but also missionary groups. Of the latter, Presbyterians representing the American Board of Foreign Missions, were the first to arrive in 1842, situating themselves a few miles from where the fort subsequently was erected. French Fathers of the Holy Spirit followed in 1844 to establish a rival Catholic mission adjacent to the military station.

The major French base in West Africa was in Senegal; Gabon was only a small outpost far to the south, on a very unhealthy coast and certainly not a choice assignment for naval officers stationed there. Emulating the British practice of settling at Sierra Leone "recaptives" intercepted by their antislave trade patrol, the French, in 1849, established such a settlement for their own liberated slaves near Fort d'Aumale and called it Libreville. It was impractical if not impossible to return recaptives to their places of origin. A common "dumping" center, therefore, was the preferred solution to the problem of what to do with such unfortunate victims of the slave trade. But the French were more calculating than humanitarian in the establishment of their asylum for recaptives. Gabon was reported to be an area with great agricultural potential; it was said that cotton, rice, ground nuts, coffee, sugar cane, and tobacco could be grown successfully there if the Africans could be induced to provide the labor. When the indigenous population did not readily volunteer to grow such export crops, French authorities proposed that a freed slave colony might fulfill the need for cultivators. Consequently, Libreville was intended basically as an agricultural experiment with "captured" if not slave labor.[17] The freed Africans, however, failed to cooperate in

French "development" plans, refusing to work on plantations. They preferred instead—as many of their ex-slave counterparts in Sierra Leone and American-sponsored Liberia did—to engage in trade, thereby interfering with established indigenous commercial networks. Relations between the few hundred ex-slaves and the coastal Africans, consequently, were not always cordial.[18] This, then, was the place where Paul Du Chaillu began his African adventures.

During his first few years there, Du Chaillu hunted, traded with the Africans, and acquired knowledge of local languages and cultures. In a land where there were few Europeans, missionary establishments commonly were popular meeting places for the white community. Although the Catholic and Protestant missionaries in Gabon were suspicious of one another, Du Chaillu became a regular visitor of both. He became close friends of the American Presbyterians John Leighton Wilson and his wife, in whose home he spent much time.[19] Curious about the little-known interior, Du Chaillu roamed inland on several occasions. He hunted in the vicinity of Cape St. Johns, some miles north of the Gabon River in what is now Equatorial Guinea. During one of his trading ventures up the Gabon his boat capsized, nearly drowning him. Deserted by his African guides and having lost all his food and supplies, he struggled for four days before reaching the American mission station where he was succored by the Wilsons. This life, though exciting at times, offered little promise at that point in Du Chaillu's life. Wilson helped convince him that he should seek his fortune elsewhere, that in fact Wilson's own American homeland presented attractive opportunities for him.[20]

Bringing with him a load of valuable ebony wood, Du Chaillu landed in the United States in 1852. Through the influence of Wilson he obtained a position as a French teacher at the Carmel School for girls in Carmel, New York. A former pupil there remembered him enduring ridicule from students and fellow teachers alike because of his small stature (he was five feet, four inches tall and weighed about one hundred pounds) and poor command of English.[21] While undergoing this introduction to American life, he initiated the process for becoming a naturalized citizen but, despite his ongoing appeal, citizenship was never granted.[22] If Du Chaillu therefore was officially not a citizen, he was nevertheless by his own estimation—and those of everyone else, until the historian Henry Bucher's modern sleuthing—an American. And I will consider him one here.

The new immigrant found that many people were interested in

Africa. He was encouraged to think that he might be able to capitalize on this curiosity by returning to the Gabon country for an extensive exploration, the published description of which might be a profitable enterprise. But such an undertaking would require funding, which a young man of such modest means could not himself provide. Word of his African experience apparently spread, and some influential people took an interest in him. They arranged for support of his projected African trip from scientific societies in Boston and Philadelphia to which the adventurer would ship examples of African wildlife.[23]

Du Chaillu's stated mission was to discover more about the peoples and natural history of the Gabon region and to collect samples of its animals. This was in accord with his fascination with various stories about the mysterious interior he had heard about earlier but had not been able to confirm. One of his primary goals was to find the gorilla. Another objective was to determine if missionary and trading posts could be established in the inner plateau. Though he did not emphasize it, another, more ambitious objective was to penetrate far enough into the mountainous interior to discover the sources of the Congo River.[24]

Taking passage on a three-masted schooner, Du Chaillu arrived in Gabon in December 1855. He spent some time in the coastal district, reacquainting himself with the Mpongwe people, who predominated along the lower Gabon river, and preparing for work in the interior. What manner of association existed between Paul and his father at this time is unknown. The latter died in 1856, presumably before March when his son left the Gabon estuary for exploration to the south. All Du Chaillu tells about his loss is that he "was soon alone among the Africans." For about four months he was a guest at the American mission post at Baraka, about eight miles up the Gabon River. His old friend Wilson had retired from his African labors but a replacement, William Walker, offered hospitality and in exchange was tutored in French by his guest.[25]

The Mpongwe were avid traders (as one observer put it, "The love of trade is their ruling passion"[26]) who controlled commerce with the interior and in their large dugouts carried on a lively coastal trade southward to Cape St. Catherine. Du Chaillu was intrigued with the credit or "trust" system by which European merchants advanced trade goods to the Mpongwe, expecting them to return from their interior contacts with profit enough to share. But he was also critical of this operation because it encouraged Africans to cheat their white partners who too often lost their investment.[27] Understandably, the Mpongwe were suspicious of

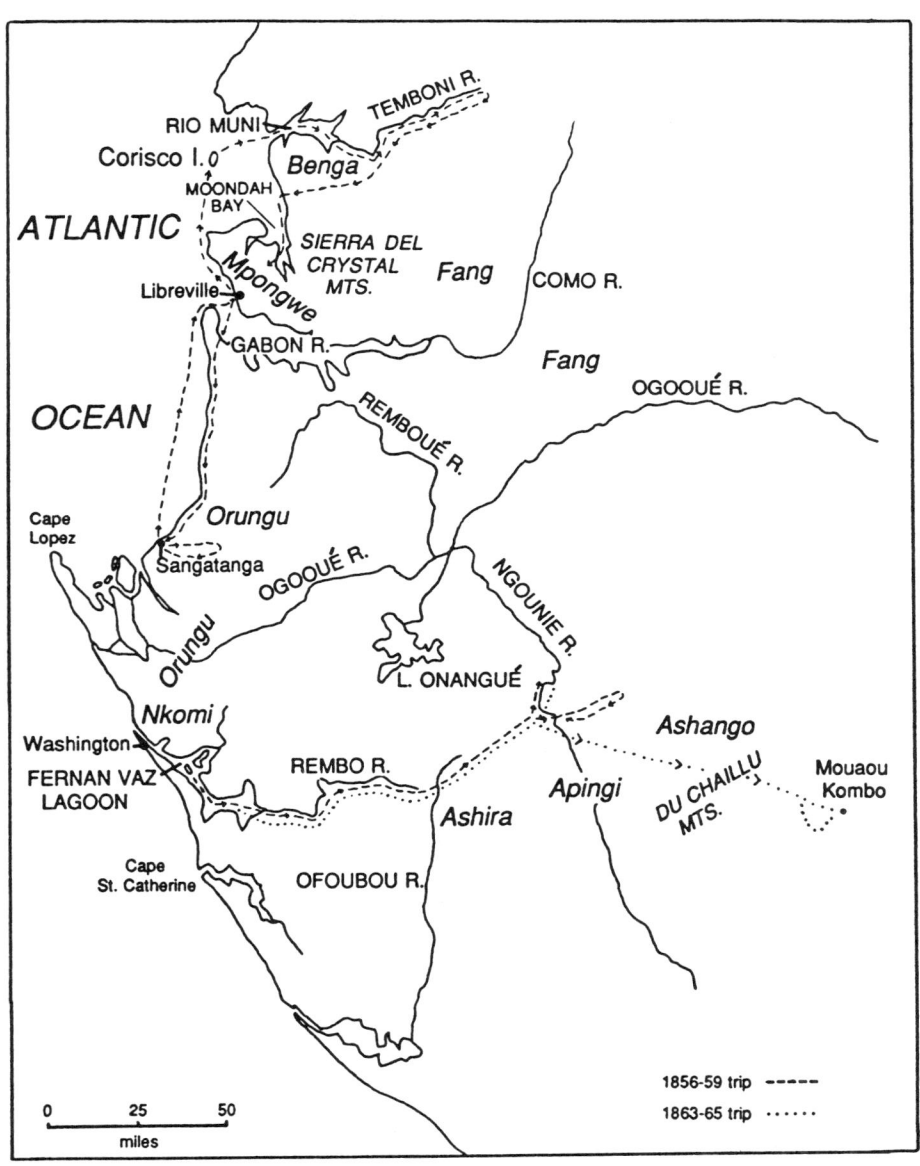

Paul Du Chaillu in Gabon, 1856–1865.

outsiders who might threaten their monopoly. Aware of Du Chaillu's earlier trading activities, they tried to discourage his intended journey inland by frequent tales of dangerous creatures that inhabited the forest. He managed to convince them that he was there only to explore and gain knowledge.[28] Eventually, Mpongwe, including several district chiefs, befriended the white man and accompanied him on major legs of his expedition.

His first trip took him south of the Gabon River where, principally in the vicinity of Sangatanga, he observed the slave trade. As he often would do when describing other African practices, Du Chaillu brought a relatively dispassionate, objective perspective to the subject. He found that there were different forms of involuntary servitude in that part of Africa and that domestic slavery, in contrast to the foreign slave trade, was a rather benign form in which the slaves were often treated humanely and their rights respected.[29] Most of the slaves he encountered were from the far interior, having been passed along from one group of traders to another until they reached the coast. Although the prominent coastal groups such as the Mpongwe usually no longer sold their own people, other communities, including the Orungu around Cape Lopez, and especially those south of Cape St. Catherine, often sold debtors, sorcerers, adulterers, and cheats to the Portuguese slavers who persisted in the Atlantic traffic.[30]

Du Chaillu considered himself as much a hunter as an explorer and while traveling in Orungu country he took the opportunity to shoot various animals and birds, which he prepared for museums and scientific societies. Altogether he would stuff some 2,000 birds (60 of which he claimed to be newly discovered species) and 200 quadrupeds on his first African expedition, most of which he brought back with him.[31] This was tedious work, consuming many hours of his time, but it certainly helped to make him a more serious naturalist.

His next journey took him north of the Gabon. After visiting American missionaries on Corisco Island about ten miles off the coast, he proceeded to the Muni River, which today separates Gabon from Equatorial Guinea. In the company of some Seke (Du Chaillu's "Shekiani"), a people located to the east of Mpongwe lands, and their chief, he ascended a tributary of the Muni, then trekked overland about one hundred miles through the forest to Fang country. He was then in the Sierra del Crystal mountains. During this march inland, he was deeply impressed by the immensity and, sometimes, the eerie silence of the forest. He very effectively evoked the sense of mystery and exotic beauty of these surroundings in his later account of the trip.

The Fang, an important interior people who today outnumber all other ethnic groups in Gabon, were reported to be cannibals and as such they intimidated their neighbors but excited the morbid curiosity of Europeans. Originally situated in eastern Cameroon, the Fang, responding to population pressures in the eighteenth century, migrated southward into the Gabon forests where there had been sparse previous settlement. By the midnineteenth century they had pushed close to the Ogooué River, thus cutting off the Mpongwe and related coastal groups from expansion eastward.[32] Du Chaillu commonly was thought to be the first white man to visit the Fang in their own territory (and he did nothing to dispel this assumption) but actually the Reverend Wilson made his way to one of their villages on the upper Gabon River in 1848.[33] However, Du Chaillu certainly capitalized on his more extended encounter with this people when he penetrated more deeply into Fang country. He found the men handsome: "the finest, bravest-looking Negroes I saw in the interior." In fact, he judged the Fang to be racially distinct from coastal groups.[34] Their women, on the other hand, he considered among the ugliest in Africa, presumably because of their filed teeth and red body paint. While repulsed by the Fangs' consumption of human flesh, especially their alleged willingness to eat the bodies of those who died of disease, he praised the design and orderliness of their villages. The arms of this warrior people, which included poisonous arrows and beautifully ornamented axes, received particular attention in his report of several-weeks' contact with them.

During this period Du Chaillu realized another ambition that, like his desire to meet the Fang cannibals, had been nurtured by the stories he had heard along the coast since he first set foot in Africa. He became the first non-African to see a live gorilla in its natural state. This animal fascinated him so much that he took every opportunity to hunt it and observe its behavior. His descriptions of the gorilla generated considerable controversy, aspects of which will be considered below.

Since his Seke escorts were unwilling to continue further into Fang territory and the latter also were unwilling to help him travel eastward in search of an idyllic plateau country, Du Chaillu was forced to turn back to the coast. The journey back was difficult, especially after his guides returned to their homes and left him on his own. Moreover, the rainy season had begun. Sometimes he was fortunate enough to find local villagers who were willing to assist him in traversing some dense mangrove swamps that fell in his path. One of the most dramatic episodes at this time was Du Chaillu's confrontation with the *bashikouay*, large army ants. The forest was infested with these voracious, irresistible insects, and many creatures were fleeing before them. Like the others, he was forced to run for his life.[35]

Once recovered from these exertions he resumed exploration in February 1857, south of the Gabon River. He initiated this venture by taking a small ship down the coast to the region of Fernan Vaz, now known as Omboué, located some sixty miles south of Cape Lopez. The people of this district were Nkomi, whom Du Chaillu called "Camma." Along with the Mpongwe and several other coastal or near-coastal societies they comprised the significant Myene-speaking group. Having decided this area would be the principal focus of his work, he obtained the local authority's permission to build a small base. In April, with Nkomi assistance, he constructed a settlement composed of several modest structures, which he called the City of Washington, probably to honor his newly adopted homeland's greatest hero. Except for a break of about two months at Baraka, Du Chaillu spent almost two years hunting and traveling out of Washington. During this time he pursued gorillas on several occasions and prepared numerous animal specimens for shipment across the Atlantic. He also explored several tributaries of the Ogooué River, penetrating about one hundred fifty miles inland.[36] Although he had every right to be proud of his accomplishment, Du Chaillu was less than honest in claiming to be the first white man to have seen these rivers, since American missionaries preceded him to the Ogooué in 1854, a trip about which the hunter-explorer must have known. Furthermore, there is some evidence that, contrary to his oft-stated boast, Du Chaillu was not always without white companions on his explorations.[37]

By June 1859, after some forty-two months in bush and forest, which included many harrowing experiences, such as his poisoning by a cook and bouts with fever that required a steady intake of quinine, Du Chaillu decided it was time to take his leave of Africa. Accompanied by many crates of his animal specimens, he arrived in the United States toward the end of the year. In his adopted country once again he found many new doors opened to him. There seemed to be an insatiable interest in his recent adventures; consequently, he was flooded with speaking and dinner invitations. It was not long before a major publishing house saw potential in an account of the trip. Harper and Brothers Company thus began a long and mutually rewarding relationship with the young explorer. Prof. S. Kneeland, a zoologist at the Massachusetts Institute of Technology, already had helped him to classify his animal collection, to prepare some lectures, and to compose an article published in 1860 by the Natural History Society of Boston. Now this authority agreed to assist Du Chaillu with writing the book.[38]

These were busy days, made somewhat unpleasant by a negative reaction to the aforementioned article. In a magazine critique a naturalist pointed out some discrepancies in Du Chaillu's identification and description of a certain otterlike animal, in effect calling into question the explorer's qualifications for scientific work.[39] But this episode was only a mild preliminary to even more difficult times ahead for the novice collector of exotic species.

The British were also interested in his discoveries. Du Chaillu gladly accepted an invitation from the prestigious Royal Geographical Society to present his specimens to and share his experiences with that organization. What he encountered in England was immensely satisfying and flattering to him until his first book, *Explorations and Adventures in Equatorial Africa*, was released while he was there.[40] He retained the full support of his hosts throughout his visit, but others were not reluctant to point out errors or oversights in his published work. The highly respected German explorer, Heinrich Barth, who had recently spent five years investigating the western and central Sudan under British governmental auspices, in effect declared Du Chaillu an amateurish charlatan whose claims were patently fraudulent. His main criticism concerned Du Chaillu's lack of scientific expertise and proper surveying instruments.[41] Although Barth's charges were restricted to a German scholarly journal, they became known in British scientific circles. The controversy hit London newspapers and periodicals and raged for several months.[42]

After purchasing Du Chaillu's collection of animal specimens, the British Museum put them on display. Subsequently John Edward Grey, a comparative anatomist and head zoologist at that institution, asserted in a letter to *The Times* that these exhibits neither provided new knowledge nor supported the explorer's various claims about African fauna. Furthermore, Grey charged that Du Chaillu borrowed illustrations from books without crediting them.[43] An English trader with extensive experience in Gabon, Robert R. N. Walker, published some stinging denials of the data and claims in Du Chaillu's book.[44] Such detractors also doubted the accuracy of his maps and, perhaps most insulting to a hunter, his shooting skills.[45] The beleaguered author felt obliged to respond, first by a letter to *The Times*[46] and then in a new preface to his book. Here he admitted his use and minor alteration of previously published plates without direct credit but lamely explained that he made "repeated" references to such works in his text.[47] It became increasingly difficult for the target of such skepticism to stoically bear his burden, even though he could claim some prestigious supporters.

At a meeting of the Ethnological Society on July 2, 1861, the explorer and controversial Orientalist, Richard Burton, delivered a paper on cannibalism, which was followed by Du Chaillu's comments. A member of the audience, T. A. Malone, then addressed some offensive questions to the latter, the point of which was to cast doubt about the veracity of his recent book. Following a verbal exchange, Du Chaillu rushed over to the man, spat upon him, and called him a coward when he sought protection from the meeting chairman. Although some of the audience had departed by that time, many persons were witness to the affair.[48] Malone later urged the society to bar his attacker from any of its subsequent meetings.[49] Burton and others, however, came to the American's defense, insisting that Malone had used insulting language, thus intentionally provoking him.[50] Nevertheless, by that time Du Chaillu already had apologized to the society—not to Malone—for his behavior.[51]

Clearly, he was finding that geographical and natural science could arouse great emotion and that London was the world's most important center for the examination and debate of such subjects. Other explorers would find themselves the centers of stormy controversies as African discovery continued through the century amid great scrutiny and popular interest.[52] It is now evident that Du Chaillu went too far in claiming to have discovered many new species of birds, and his critics in the scientific community noted that he borrowed excessively from earlier writers on the natural history of Gabon.[53] Ultimately, however, Du Chaillu would have the satisfaction of seeing himself vindicated on some questions. As more information came in from other travellers and explorers, his estimates of distance and geographical locations were shown to be relatively accurate. And, with some notable exceptions, his descriptions of various animals as well as data on African cultures were confirmed.[54]

The most important and long-lasting problem related to Du Chaillu's early work was his discussion of apes, especially the gorilla. The largest of the apes was then the least known of the primates. Skeletons and skins of the animal occasionally had been seen and examined by European missionaries and traders over the years and several captured gorillas had been examined, but the outside world had only the vaguest impressions of this great beast derived mainly from exaggerated folktales. The first scientific report on the gorilla, based on study of a skeleton provided by the Reverend Wilson from Gabon, was published in 1847.[55] The missionary also had collected many gorilla stories during his years of service in Gabon. In his own book on the region, published in 1856, Wilson characterized the beast as hideous, ferocious, and "one of the most frightful animals in the world."[56] He saw a man whose calf was nearly torn off by a gorilla and relayed the story that a gorilla would take a gun from a man's hand and crush the barrel between its jaws.[57] Du Chaillu demonstrably was influenced by both Wilson's views (he reported, for example, that one of his own men was killed and his gun barrel bent by a gorilla during the first expedition into the Fernan Vaz hinterland,[58]) and local African lore, but his own firsthand experience, which included several encounters with large male gorillas in the jungle, he claimed to be the main basis for his portrayal. He devoted many pages of his first book—and those that followed—to a depiction of the gorilla as an extremely aggressive brute, a true killer-ape that pounded its chest before attacking anything that stood in its way. Despite mounting skepticism and contradictory evidence through the years, Du Chaillu generally held to this view,[59] although in his second book he said that during later hunts, gorillas sometimes ran from him.

Among those who gave little credence to Du Chaillu's description of the great primate's habits was Winwood Reade. This minor English novelist, it seems, was disturbed by Du Chaillu's book and the attention it was receiving. What especially frustrated him about the controversy over the book was the inability of any scientific expert to establish authoritatively the author's alleged errors. He therefore took the amazing step of going to Africa himself to investigate (thereby setting an exceedingly demanding example for future book critics!). Reade disarmingly insisted that he went there "thoroughly unbiased," but it is difficult not to believe that his mission was motivated by a desire to disprove Du Chaillu's claims. His trip included five months in Gabon's gorilla country where he tracked the animal on several occasions but never saw a live gorilla in the forest. Consequently, all his findings were based on interviews with local inhabitants, particularly hunters, some of whom had worked for Du Chaillu. Reade's informants admitted that the diminutive American had indeed shot numerous animals but not gorillas. These elusive creatures, they said, were killed only by Africans; Du Chaillu, as did other white men, obtained their carcasses in exchange for cloth, powder, and tobacco and then skinned them. Reade accordingly declared that when it came to gorillas, Du Chaillu was merely a pretender who added nothing of value to earlier knowledge, inferring that all of the latter's information had come from others.[60]

In responding to Reade's charges, Du Chaillu maintained that two of those Africans who denied that he killed gorillas had not been present when he hunted the beasts and the other witness, who had accompanied him, could have lied for numerous reasons. Du Chaillu also pointed out that there was a ready market for gorilla skins and skeletons, since museums and scientific institutions wanted to add them to their collections, yet for some years he had been the only one to bring any specimens out of Africa. This, he suggested, should appear strange if, as Reade contended, skins could be so easily purchased from African hunters. Finally, the defiant hunter challenged his defamers (or their agent) to accompany him to Gabon where he would kill five or six of the apes in two years or forfeit £4,000 ($20,000).[61] Despite this interesting defense, Reade's case against Du Chaillu as a gorilla hunter, although not conclusive, appears to be a strong one. Nevertheless, it is still hard to believe that a hunter with Du Chaillu's considerable experience and his long-developing curiosity about gorillas, would have been put off by African guides—as Reade, the novice in Gabon, was—and satisfied to leave the jungle without shooting at least one of the twenty-one gorillas whose skins he brought out of the country.

As later research proves, Reade was correct in countering Du Chaillu's contention that gorillas attack men. That they are shy, retiring denizens of the rain forest we now know with certainty, although when cornered they are known to challenge their antagonists. Some modern writers have speculated that Du Chaillu portrayed the animals as vicious assailants out of a sense of guilt once he realized that what he had killed were evasive and harmless.[62] Perhaps more likely is that Du Chaillu misinterpreted some of the gorilla's actions. This would have been a natural reaction of one confronting such a formidable, frightening animal along an obscure jungle path. Du Chaillu probably saw raging bluff as aggression. He did, though, intentionally exaggerate its ferocity, perhaps, as commonly believed, in response to his American publisher's urging. In any case, his frequent references to the canine fangs of this normally peaceful herbivore are examples of misleading sensationalism. But other points once commonly labeled fabrications are not. Reade and others categorically denied Du Chaillu's report that the apes beat their chests,[63] a behavior witnessed by many people later and definitely established as characteristic of the male gorilla.[64] And there were those who disbelieved Du Chaillu's account of the gorilla that "made the woods ring with his roar."[65] This practice of the ape also has been confirmed by extended observation, one naturalist estimating that such roars "are among the most explosive sounds in nature . . . [which] under favorable conditions . . . carry far more than a mile."[66]

Some of his gorilla data, it must be noted, stood the test of time. Burton, already an experienced student of things African (albeit a negrophobe) and in 1861 posted to the equatorial island of Fernando Po as British consul, was so intrigued by Du Chaillu's discoveries that he had to investigate certain matters for himself. Carrying Du Chaillu's book with him and supposedly "checking every statement" in it, Burton generally had praise for the American's work. He confirmed most of Du Chaillu's findings, including those on the gorilla. [67] With due allowance for Du Chaillu's errors on its ferocity, one of the most respected modern gorilla specialists credits him as "basically a competent and reliable observer . . . whose [account] remained as one of the most accurate for a hundred years."[68]

While searching for gorillas, Du Chaillu saw some apes that seemed to warrant separate classification and in his first book he said they were neither gorillas nor chimpanzees. On the basis of casual sightings he suggested that these creatures, which he called *nshiego mbouve* and *kooloo kamba*, respectively, were distinct species, the head of the latter resembling that of man more closely that did those of other primates.[69] The nshiego mbouve was said to build roofed nests. Such startling information was often the target of his critics, and since he had brought back only one primate skeleton, that of a gorilla, he could do little to prove the existence of the others. Moreover, the illustration of the nshiego mbouve in his book looked much like that of a chimpanzee. After deliberating the matter and consulting with scientists, Du Chaillu eventually agreed that the unusual apes he detected in the trees were probably types of chimpanzees, for that is how he referred to them in subsequent writings. Despite his concession on the point, however, some experts thought his kooloo kamba might be a hybrid of a gorilla and a chimpanzee; consequently, it was not excluded from some zoology textbooks until well into the twentieth century.[70]

Du Chaillu's revelation about cannibals was either disturbing or too astonishing to many of his readers. He pictured repulsive scenes in one village where piles of human bones were found next to his hut while, nearby, strips of human flesh were being smoked. He said he passed a woman who was carrying a cut of human thigh," just as we should go to market and carry thence a roast or steak."[71] Again the skeptics wondered if his imagination had run wild. Both Burton and Reade made special efforts during their own trips to Gabon to see the Fang who were alleged to be man-eaters. The former, admittedly not the most impartial observer, spent one day among them and, while he could not accept certain features of Du Chaillu's description of their habits, he satisfied himself that there was anthropophagy among them.[72] Reade visited the Fang for a longer period and in his books provided an extended discussion of their strange dietary customs. After carefully interviewing some Fang, he was convinced that they ate human flesh and specifically corroborated Du Chaillu on this point.[73] Although he did not witness the grisly details related by the American, he claimed to have "thoroughly investigated" and believed the highly unlikely report that the Fang disinterred human corpses of neighboring peoples and ate them.[74] Even the missionary William Walker is said to have confirmed accounts of this ghoulish Fang practice.[75] Later in the century, that strangest of all Victorian travelers to equatorial Africa, Mary Kingsley, reached the Fang who, she admitted, were her favorite Africans. Despite her admiration for them, however, she could not deny their cannibalism.[76]

Most modern Africanists dismiss all charges of Fang cannibalism. They trace them to the coastal peoples, particularly the Mpongwe, who allegedly maligned their interior neighbors so as to discourage any other traders from trying to make direct contact with them. Credulous whites, according to this thesis, then passed on the tales, thus perpetuating a myth, sometimes in order to make their work in equatorial Africa seem more hazardous.[77] Apparently such fearful characterizations of the Fang did serve for a time to keep outsiders from threatening the Mpongwe trade monopoly, but logical and satisfying though this reasoning may be to those who refuse to concede anthropophagy, it does not put the matter to rest. Typically, social scientists discussing cannibalism insist that unless visitors personally witnessed the practice, their reports of its existence are without value.[78] Yet, if this criterion were applied consistently to all ethnographical research, much important, long-accepted intelligence obtained through interviewing would be rendered invalid. Cannibalism undoubtedly was a guarded activity, known to be abhorrent to other peoples, and probably was restricted to a small elite.[79] It evidently was not readily admitted by those who indulged in it and was hardly a ritual to which foreigners were invited. Firsthand observation of it by aliens necessarily would be rare or nonexistent. But it would be a mistake to reject all indirect evidence of the practice. Apart from the findings of

Burton, Kingsley, Reade, and numerous others, there is evidence from Fang oral tradition that some groups ate prisoners of war as the ultimate punishment of despised enemies and in order to terrify others.[80] Some African scholars, including the most widely respected Gabonese historian who assiduously investigated his peoples' oral records, now acknowledge Fang cannibalism.[81] The phenomenon did exist in the midnineteenth century.

Du Chaillu, therefore, was not contributing toward the continuation of a myth. But he definitely was guilty of gross sensationalism, as was the case when he described the gorilla. If there were signs of cannibalism in the villages he visited, he distorted the picture to an absurd degree and thereby seriously undermined his credibility. It was a major element in provoking the skepticism that confronted him in London.

Following such embarrassing contention in Britain, the idea of a return to Africa might have suggested a needed escape to the harassed author. In order to prove his earlier journey was all he said it was, and determined to bring back examples of his most controversial finds, especially live gorillas, Du Chaillu decided to return to Gabon. Impressive sales of his book provided the money to outfit his new expedition, but his American publisher also contributed extra funds for gifts to be distributed during the trip.[82] Preparations were indeed extensive. He hoped to cross the continent from the west coast to the headwaters of the Nile and then descend that river to the Mediterranean. A huge undertaking of that kind required great quantities of provisions and equipment. His list of supplies indicates that he planned on being in Africa for some time. Included were 72 pairs of lace boots and 24 pairs of shoes. The unpredictable nature of the territory and inhabitants ahead necessitated more extensive protective measures than he considered essential on earlier marches. There were 13 guns for his own use along with 250 flintlocks for his bodyguard.[83]

Even more important for this exploration was his scientific emphasis. Seeing that many questions about his first mission related to his failure to take precise geographic bearings, he went to great trouble to do it correctly this time. For example, he took instructions in the use of the most modern scientific instruments so that his computations of location, distance, and altitude would not be challenged.[84] Hence, his equipment included sextants, chronometers, barometers, and a prismatic compass. Of course, he also packed various materials for preserving larger animals, along with many bottles in which to collect insects. And for those things that could not be brought back, Du Chaillu acquired the latest in photographic gear, wisely believing that pictures could help prove his claims. Clearly, this was to be more than a casual stroll through the woods.

Ships sailing to Gabon were few; furthermore, Du Chaillu wanted to land at the mouth of the Fernan Vaz, not a normal stop for those vessels regularly operating in West African waters. He felt compelled, therefore, to charter a small steamer for his special use. To defray some of the enormous cost of such a plan, he arranged with the captain to carry trade goods on the return voyage.[85]

Leaving London in early August 1863, they sighted the Gabon coast on October 8. Landing was extraordinarily difficult because a point of land that had once offered a protective entry to the river had been washed away. The African canoes carrying the explorer's heavy baggage had to contend with very rough surf and one of them, carrying Du Chaillu and his precious instruments, capsized. Though he was saved, the instruments were either lost or ruined. Du Chaillu quickly wrote to the Royal Geographical Society, whose director, Sir Roderick Murchison, had become his strong supporter, explaining that he had exhausted his funds fitting out his expedition and could not afford the loss of his instruments. Fortunately, the society agreed to replace them.[86] But this occasioned a delay of several months. In the meantime Du Chaillu engaged in trade and sent two cargoes to England before resuming his exploration.[87] When his second expedition set forth into the interior, it included over seventy porters carrying his goods. It was now October 1864.

For over a year the large party pushed eastward, headed for the interior plateau. Du Chaillu had a group of ten Nkomi bodyguards who were entrusted with his most valuable equipment. Though they could sometimes be irksome, these men were indispensable associates without whom even such an intrepid, resilient explorer as Du Chaillu probably could not have survived. The regular carriers commonly were recruited along the way, as up-country villagers picked up the loads of those who fulfilled their contracts and returned home. Not all of them, however, carried out their obligations. Desertions were a constant problem; not only were bearers lost, but they took valuable goods with them.

When he reached Shira (Du Chaillu's "Ashira") country a smallpox epidemic temporarily halted progress. Many local villagers died, as did several of his Nkomi guards.[88] Village heads frequently associated the epidemic with the presence of the white man, making it difficult if not impossible for him to pass through some communities. The expedition was delayed in Mayolo, for example, for almost two months before permission was granted to proceed to the next village. The further the explorer penetrated into the interior, the more suspicious the local inhabitants were of his strange entourage. Mutiny among his carriers and greater demands for gifts by village chiefs continued to drain both the frustrated Du Chaillu's enthusiasm and the expedition's badly depleted resources.

The motley column reached mountain territory by June. They now were among the Massangou people whom Du Chaillu called Ashangos. Close by were some settlements of pygmies, and he definitely did not miss the opportunity to visit these shy, retiring forest-dwellers.[89] The existence of a pygmoid race in Africa was suspected since the time of brief, obscure references in ancient Egyptian literature. Several reports of such Africans had been published in the eighteenth and earlier nineteenth century but they were not based on direct contact. Du Chaillu had heard reports of such "dwarf-people" on his first expedition but dismissed them as "loose and exaggerated" tales.[90] Now he became the first white man to see such Africans. Describing these "Obongos'" color as "dirty yellow," he detailed their physical peculiarities and way of life, noting a symbiotic relationship with their taller neighbors who traded plantains and iron implements to the little hunters in exchange for meat.[91] Because of the pygmies' simple technology, he placed them lower on the scale of intelligence than other Africans. In fact, he later estimated that they were "little above the chimpanzee."[92] Exciting though such a discovery must have been to the young explorer, his main concern was further progress into the equatorial plateau. But, unfortunately, in the village of Mouaou Kombo his group was repulsed.

One of Du Chaillu's Nkomi retainers accidentally shot two Massangou villagers. Nothing he could do would satisfy the victims' relatives. The incident provoked the wrath of the local people not only against Du Chaillu and his Nkomi, but also against the Mobana porters who had carried the expedition's goods into Mouaou Kombo. There was no choice but to beat a hasty retreat. For some distance the party was under attack, trying to avoid being hit by poisoned arrows. In their fright, Du Chaillu's men dumped their loads and fled through the trees. In this way photographs, instruments, animal specimens, and notebooks were lost.[93] Happily, because the careful Du Chaillu had made three copies of his records, the one he carried himself survived. During the fray he and several of his men were hit, one of them dying of his wound.

Finally reaching friendly territory after their desperate struggle, Du Chaillu managed to fight off the poison from two arrows that nicked him.[94] Gradually his group, glad to be out of Massangouland, made its way back to the coast. After a brief rest and recuperation, Du Chaillu took leave of his faithful African friends and, luckily finding a ship available, embarked for England in late September 1865. It had been a grueling, discouraging experience and his last in Africa.

Back in Britain, he soon began writing a new book about it[95] and occasionally recounted his adventures from a speaker's rostrum. To his relief, his second journey, as well as the published record of it, did not provoke nearly as much controversy as their predecessors. Some of his earlier critics had tempered their judgments in light of subsequent knowledge and, in particular, in recognition of Du Chaillu's more scientific handling of his second mission.

At a meeting of the Royal Geographical Society on January 8, 1866, the now more seasoned explorer delivered a long presentation on his recent travels, which served as a preview of his upcoming book, and was applauded by Winwood Reade, among others.[96] Yet there were some doubters. In fact, the chairman of the meeting, J. Crawford, found Du Chaillu's report on the existence of a dwarf people incredible.[97] Since this negative reflection on his findings was reported in the press, the explorer found it necessary to respond in a letter to *The Times*, averring his personal contact with, and examination of, the diminutive people generally called pygmies.[98] Surprisingly, his old nemesis, Reade, who had visited Gabon in early 1862, offered his support for the presence of pygmies there on the basis of stories he had heard from a number of Africans.[99] It would not be long before other explorers, such as George Schweinfurth and the redoubtable Henry Morton Stanley, substantiated the existence of pygmies in equatorial Africa. Again Du Chaillu was vindicated.

His life after jungle exploration was comfortable and fulfilling. Now a respected Africa expert, he was often invited to address learned societies and other organizations. Such affairs sometimes took him abroad. In the 1870s he developed an interest in Scandinavia that prompted long trips to Norway and Sweden.[100] But most of his time was spent in the United States, his principal residence being New York, where, as a well-known *bon vivant* and man-about-town, he enjoyed the friendship of some rich and important persons.[101] In 1869 Du Chaillu first lectured to young people. There followed many such engagements, as large audiences attended his talks in Boston and New York.[102] He sincerely enjoyed these contacts with boys and girls and, though he did not necessarily plan it, his listeners became avid readers of his books. If youngsters so eagerly responded to his oral tales of Africa, he would satisfy a wider audience with his pen.

From 1868 to 1903 Du Chaillu had the satisfaction of knowing that his was a major name in the book trade. During that period he published nine titles that dealt with Africa. All were based on his first two books and became very popular with the reading public.

From the first, the winning combination of cannibals, gorillas, and pygmies was unmatched in the annals of exploration literature for its appeal to an audience of any age seeking vicarious thrills in the astonishing exploits of such an engaging pathfinder. Intended especially for young readers, most of these books went into numerous editions, one being reissued as late as 1936, sixty-eight years after its initial printing. His writings emphasized adventure, contained numerous illustrations, and were heavily sentimental. In his *Country of the Dwarfs*, for instance, Du Chaillu excludes discussion of serious exploration as well as political matters, concentrating instead on personal relationships along the line of march.[103] Using a conversational style that must have endeared him to many a teenager, he could engage his reader with such a beginning as this:

> Now, boys, fancy yourselves transported into the midst of a very dense and dark forest, where the trees never shed their leaves all at one time, where there is no food to be had except what you can get with your gun and where wild beasts prowl around you at night while you sleep.[104]

With colorful language he reworked old material throughout the series, some events reappearing in several books along with familiar opinions and descriptions. It was a successful formula that made the author a rich man.

Du Chaillu was, in fact, one of the most widely read authors of his time—and for many years afterward. It is important, therefore, to inquire about the image of Africa that he conveyed to the many people touched by his writing.

Though he considered himself a hunter, Du Chaillu was not a man of violence. He did not rush into the Dark Continent with a chip on his shoulder, in the mode of H. M. Stanley, determined to intimidate and impress its inhabitants with the power of the white world. Indeed, this was a friendly, patient little man who, unlike most other explorers, went into the bush with some understanding of local languages and cultures. Consequently, he was better prepared to interpret behavior that was often inexplicable and thus sometimes provocative to other outsiders who then acted in a hostile manner toward the indigenous population.

At the same time, he naturally resented those who took undue advantage of him. During his second expedition he was enraged by Africans' desertion and pilfering, yet when returning through their country he tempered his anger and eschewed revenge, recognizing that some of those who had ill-used him had been slaves all their lives and knew no better.[105] Certainly this was not a typical Western reaction. Blacks, he believed, should be judged as individuals. In his opinion, they showed a great range of intelligence and ability within their groups, some of them demonstrating imaginative minds and very effective speaking skills, whereas others were clever liars and cheats.[106]

The self-declared American viewed Africans as people with the same human emotions and needs as any others. When in the midst of a smallpox epidemic, he was sincerely moved by the devastating loss of life sustained by the villagers, some of them his close supporters.[107] Du Chaillu developed warm friendships with black men. Always willing to credit those who helped him, he generally found Africans ready to offer whatever food and shelter they had available. Even in times of scarcity, those he encountered in his travels presented the best provisions to their guest. Admittedly, some of his hosts were in awe of the strange white man about whom they had heard, but in other instances he came upon them with little notice, and still their welcome was genuinely friendly and supportive. This is a common scene in his books. His readers, therefore, might be encouraged to view Africans as simply fellow human beings of another skin color, people with the normal range of good and bad, bright and dull, industrious and lazy, who were warm and hospitable toward foreigners who were not perceived to be a threat to them. Unfortunately, though, there were other, invidious images in Du Chaillu's writing that presented Africans in a different light.

If Du Chaillu was relatively objective and less condemnatory than other whites when recounting his experiences with Africans, he was still a man of his time who harbored stereotypical views of the continent and its people that were current in the midnineteenth century. Confidently believing that Western civilization was superior to any other cultural system, he consequently found those African practices that resembled Western ones most worthy of praise. The Puno (Du Chaillu's "Apingi") people, for instance, were not as migratory as certain other interior groups in Gabon, and in their neat, permanent villages Du Chaillu discovered that the concept of private property was not unknown to them. At least certain types of trees planted by a man around his house were his exclusive property. These characteristics, along with the willingness of Puno men to do some of the agricultural labor, earned them high marks. Accordingly, he considered them more advanced than neighboring peoples.[108] As a rule, however, Du Chaillu judged the groups of inner Africa, those who had little or no "civilizing" contact with, specifically, the Arabs in the east, with Islam in the north or with the Boers in the south, as inferior.[109]

Yet skin color was not necessarily linked to his racial ranking. The very dark peoples of West Africa, particularly the Wolof and Fulani, clearly impressed him. As he explained, since their noses were not so flat nor their lips so thick as those of other Africans, they were thus more admirable. The "negroes of the Senegambia country," he estimated, "are far superior to those found in other parts of Africa, not only in looks, but in intelligence." In particular, they were "a far superior type than the Congo negro" who received most attention in his books.[110]

Du Chaillu subscribed to some pseudo-scientific notions that influenced theories of race in his day. Judging the Shogo (Du Chaillu's "Ishoga") as superior to the Shira, he noted that the former "generally had finer heads, broader in the part where phrenologists place the organs of ideality."[111] In this respect he joined a host of explorers who popularized the belief that certain African physical traits distinguishing them from Caucasoids denoted stupidity, brutishness, or degradation.[112] Africans, he acknowledged, showed that in certain ways they were the equal of Europeans. In bargaining, for instance, they were as shrewd as white men—that is, in anything "that did not require mental labor and forethought." They failed, in his view, when it came to memory and reflection, "perhaps through laziness."[113]

When discussing African culture, Du Chaillu was not always disparaging, but his distaste for certain practices received considerable attention. Sorcery and witchcraft were, in his Christian eyes, not only an abomination but a major cause of African backwardness. A seemingly all-pervasive superstition kept the African in an intellectual morass, preventing his progress toward rational thought and inquiry.[114] Nor could the alleged weakness of the African temperament be ignored, even by this traveler who had been aided and befriended by so many of them. Referring to an especially discouraging experience with his carriers during the second expedition, he resorted to a wholesale categorization by stating, "I well knew the hypocrisy of the African character."[115]

In the fashion of almost every nineteenth-century writer on Africa, Du Chaillu had much to say about the childlike nature of the people. There are numerous situations in his books where blacks stare in amazement at his shooting exhibitions or show their wonderment at his tools and instruments, the products of an advanced, industrial world which in his estimation, an African society could never imitate. In addition, the Africans he described were often witlessly credulous, ready to believe what to him were the most outlandish stories and explanations.

It should not be totally unexpected, therefore, that Du Chaillu, despite his acknowledgment of some commendable features of African humanity, would present a rather negative summary appraisal of the African's place in history. The sub-Saharan part of the continent, he asserted, had never in the past supported a high civilization and, unless uplifted by a higher race, it would not in the future do so. If left to themselves, Africans would soon fall back to—indeed many had never escaped from—barbarism.[116] Thus Du Chaillu joined the mounting chorus of those who insisted that in order for blacks to become more useful members of mankind they must be brought to higher standards by superior types, preferably Christian Europeans. One modern scholar, perplexed by such uncomplimentary views following the more commendatory opinions found elsewhere in the two exploration books, perceptively suggests that by the time he concluded the second manuscript, the tired and sick[117] explorer probably was still embittered by the disappointment of his unfulfilled mission.[118] In any case, such judgments, placed at the end of his book, *A Journey to Ashango-Land*, tended to erase whatever positive impressions were conveyed in preceding pages, leaving the reader with a largely unsympathetic image of Africa.

Du Chaillu's books were in much demand. No other author writing about Africa in the nineteenth and early twentieth centuries published as many separate titles in as many successive editions. Copies of these works must have been found in most American public libraries; thus they were among the most readily accessible sources of knowledge about Africa. It is not unreasonable to conclude, therefore, that Du Chaillu had more to do with American's conception of Africa for over a half century than any other author.[119] And certainly in this regard his books for young people played a major role. Not only did his youthful readers carry their early reading impressions with them into adulthood, but many adults also read these works. Furthermore, in an indirect manner Du Chaillu had even further influence on the formation of images of Africa.

One of the most successful publishing ventures in history is Edgar Rice Burroughs's Tarzan series. Introduced in a cheap pulp magazine in 1911, this fictional hero of the African jungle became the subject of twenty-six books, an immensely popular comic strip, and almost fifty films.[120] It is difficult to estimate the great number of people all over the world who have read such literature or have viewed the motion pictures based on them. But, regrettably, there is no doubt that many persons since 1911 have acquired their ideas about Africa largely through such sources.

The origins of the Tarzan character are not fully clear, although its creator admitted some debt to Rudyard Kipling's *Jungle Books* and the novels of H. Rider Haggard.[121] Burroughs also had a strong interest in classical mythology that apparently contributed to his development of the Tarzan stories.[122] The immediate inspiration for some aspects of the original tale was a magazine story telling of a shipwrecked sailor who survived in Africa after being assisted by a she-ape.[123] Once the character's outline was devised, however, and Burroughs decided on Africa for the setting, he had to learn something about that still shadowy land in order to work out many details of his protagonist's adventures. He explained that he carefully studied the accounts of Africa's explorers—though he did not identify them—in the Chicago Public Library, looking especially for "data concerning the flora and fauna... and the customs of native tribes."[124]

There is no definite proof that Burroughs consulted the works of Du Chaillu, but the internal evidence strongly suggests the latter was probably his major source of information. *Tarzan of the Apes*, first in the series, is set in the rain forest zone, specifically in the Congo region not far distant from Du Chaillu's Gabon territory. The latter was one of only a few explorers who had written extensively about that part of Africa and, as just noted, his books were indisputably the most readily available to the common reader. The descriptions of the jungle in the Tarzan books recall Du Chaillu's earlier writing about the dark equatorial forests. It is particularly easy to attribute Burroughs's frequent depiction of large animals to his probable familiarity with Du Chaillu's works in which are found numerous hunting scenes and extended sections on wildlife.

Tarzan is, after all, the adopted son of an ape mother who suckles and rears him with her own kind. The reader of the Tarzan novels meets apes on almost every other page, as Burroughs sets forth their ferocious appearance and regular habits in language obviously reminiscent of Du Chaillu's widely read work on the subject. Burroughs even had Tarzan beat his breast in the manner of gorillas when he defeated an adversary, while uttering a spine-chilling roar of victory much like that reported by Du Chaillu for an attacking gorilla. Another common practice of Tarzan is his roping of passing animals from the trees above which seems much like a story related (but not believed) by Du Chaillu that the gorilla concealed itself in trees and pulled up animals from below with its feet.

Also suggestive of Du Chaillu's influence here is his claim in *Explorations and Adventures in Equatorial Africa* that there were two species of great apes other than gorillas and chimpanzees, one of which seemed more humanlike than the others. It is often overlooked by Tarzan fans that his particular apes are not gorillas but another species, more intelligent than the latter, that often built their nests in trees much like the form described by Du Chaillu for his *nshiego mbouve*. Burroughs, borrowing the idea, simply made his new apes larger and more intelligent than all their anthropoid cousins. Certainly, no other author could have provided the creator of Tarzan with as much material on apes nor with the notion that another type of great primate might coexist in the equatorial woods with both of the others. No other explorer of Africa, moreover, hunted so extensively and provided such lengthy particulars on Africa's other animals in his books as did Du Chaillu by the time Burroughs conceived his jungle yarns.

To whatever extent Burroughs depended on Du Chaillu for information on African peoples and their ways of life, he tended, in his early books, at least, to seize upon the negative features found in the explorer's writing. As Tarzan first encounters blacks, for example, they appear less admirable than his ape friends. Savage though he is himself, he is repulsed by African villagers' torture of a captured animal before they kill and eat it in a scene quite similar to one in Du Chaillu's first book.[125] These tribesmen bear an unmistakable resemblance to the Fang. Du Chaillu had described the latter as having "their teeth filed, which gives the face a ghastly and ferocious look."[126] Burrough's first-mentioned Africans, also cannibals, were likewise repulsive but now in more exaggerated terms. "Their yellow teeth were filed to sharp points and their great protruding lips added still further to the low and bestial brutishness in their appearance."[127] As did the Fang, so these fictional Africans used arrows that were dipped in a thick, reddish-colored, poisonous vegetable sap.[128] Finally, even the ape-man, Tarzan, shared Du Chaillu's contempt for the African male's apparent disinclination to engage in agricultural labor that was commonly the responsibility of women.[129] The parallels here are too striking to be coincidental; they indicate, I believe, Burroughs's extensive borrowing from and, in some instances, imitation of Du Chaillu. Thus the Tarzan literature would carry some of the explorer's viewpoints to a much wider readership than he would have captured with is own publications.

In assessing Du Chaillu's importance in the history of America's contact with Africa, one must recognize the multifaceted nature of his work. In the field of exploration he cannot be credited with any major discoveries. Yet his data on the coastal region of Gabon and on various sections of the interior were very important for all parties concerned with the territory. Especially significant was his report on the Ogooué River delta proving that several streams were not separate rivers, but merely branches of that major river. Others, missionaries, official French agents, and travelers such as Reade and Burton added to the developing picture of this part of western equatorial Africa, but Du Chaillu accomplished more and probed deeper than the others.[130]

In the course of his journeys, and in preparing for them, Du Chaillu became a naturalist. He introduced the Western world to new species of tropical fauna even though he was guilty of overestimating his achievement here. In addition to data provided in his books, the specimens he shipped from Africa to museums and various zoological societies must have been, for their time, significant contributions to science. Some of this material could not have been superseded for at least a generation. Of particular value are his ethnographical disclosures. Lacking the scholarly background of a Burton but nevertheless possessing a keen eye for the major elements of African culture, Du Chaillu proved to be as perceptive a reporter as any other traveler of the period.

Since his adopted country was not then nor later inclined toward any official involvement in Africa, it cannot be said that Du Chaillu was a pathfinder for American imperialism. Whatever intelligence of his was used for such purposes would have assisted the French who, almost reluctantly, expanded their sphere in Gabon as the scramble for equatorial Africa accelerated in the 1880s. But Du Chaillu definitely did espouse Western enlightenment of the Dark Continent. Early in his travels he summarized the condition of Africa that called out for salvation.

> I thanked God that I was not a native African. These poor people lead dreadful and dreary lives. Not only have they to fear for their enemies

among neighboring tribes, as well as the various accidents to which a savage life is especially liable, such as starvation, the attacks of wild beasts, etc., but their whole lives are saddened and embittered by the fear of evil spirits, witchcraft and kindred superstitions under which they suffer.[131]

He could dream, however, "of forests giving way to plantations of coffee, cotton and spices; of peaceful Negroes going to their contented daily tasks; of farming and manufacturing, of churches and schools."[132] Here was food for thought for those idealistic Europeans who would go out in some numbers to "improve" their poor, benighted, black brethren. The message was akin to that of David Livingstone, only the most famous of those who urged the assumption of "the white man's burden."

Many white travelers in nineteenth-century Africa noted commercial possibility there. As a one-time trader himself, Du Chaillu naturally had a more-than-passing interest in the subject. While trading was not one of the professed objectives of his expeditions, he could not ignore all the opportunities that presented themselves. During his 1856–59 exploration he arranged for about one thousand five hundred pounds of ebony logs to be carried to the coast for shipment to the United States in order to help cover his expenses.[133] And he hoped, as a secondary fruit of that trip, to acquire ivory, wax, and rubber from the interior peoples.[134] In describing the customs and activities of the communities through whose lands he passed, the explorer often noted their interest in trade and the nature of goods they exchanged. Ivory, rubber, and hardwoods merited most attention as Du Chaillu thus informed his readers.

Like so many observers of the African scene in his day, he stressed the need to develop an expanded legitimate trade that could replace the traffic in human beings that was not just a part of the trans-Atlantic trade but a regrettably endemic African institution.[135] Many articles, such as firearms, powder, tobacco, brass, and iron had become very desirable among Gabonese groups but were never available in sufficient quantities and therefore very expensive.[136] Deep in Puno territory he found vast quantities of palm trees and estimated that "thousands of tons of oil might easily be made . . . and transported on rafts by water to the seaboard, if only the trade could be opened."[137] In fact, the agricultural potential for cash crops, he said with some exaggeration, was limitless.

> Any crop will grow in this virgin soil, and it needs only the cunning hand and brain of the white man to make this whole tract become a great producing country.[138]

There were special appeals to his adopted countrymen. They were told that American cotton goods were among the items in great demand among interior peoples.[139] As he traveled in Nkomi country he noted the wide expanses of land covered with rubber vines. This potential, he insisted, should be exploited by Yankees.

> It was enough to make a trader's mouth water to see it. . . . Here are chances for a commerce which I think our American merchants will not long leave unworked. And then we may hope to see a real and enduring civilization step in and help these poor natives upward a little.[140]

These encouragements to traders were typical of exploration literature throughout the century as the lure of profit-making was couched in humanitarian terms.[141] But not many Americans would respond to such enticements. One American trader, Richard Lawlin, who had preceded Du Chaillu to Gabon, operated a factory at Cape Lopez for over twenty years.[142] The other traders working in that part of Africa were mainly Europeans.[143] Yet the U.S. government did have enough interest in the region to appoint a consular agent there in 1856. Official dispatches from that post indicate that there was little American commercial activity, most of the trade being in English hands.[144] From 1860 to 1863, for instance, only three American vessels a year, all of them from Lancer, Bishop and Company of New York, stopped in the Gabon area.[145] With the opening of the American West, manufacturers and traders alike were so preoccupied with the domestic market represented by westward settlement and increasing immigration that foreign commerce gained comparatively little attention. Nevertheless, a popular American magazine, referring to Du Chaillu's revelations about trading opportunities in his first book, gave the false impression that he had "laid bare, for the operations of our enterprising commerce, a large region . . . which (would) take first rank in the world's commerce."[146] West central Africa was not to become an important target of American trading firms.

It is not as an explorer, hunter, naturalist, or promoter of Western penetration of Africa that Du Chaillu is most important, though he was all of them. It is, rather, as a writer, a popularizer of a certain view of Africa, that he made his great impact on the

American consciousness.[147] Not only in his own books which, it must be admitted, presented many objective judgments of the land and its people along with other, less flattering portrayals, but in the works of those he influenced, preeminently Burroughs, who fancied the negative characteristics Du Chaillu related, there was conveyed a simplistic, sometimes distorted picture of Africa that to this day has dominated the ordinary American's thinking. The continent came to be seen basically as a jungle infested with exotic creatures, many of them deadly and dreadful, a land inhabited by barbarous tribes of the strangest and least respectable kind. This image, unfortunately, is the principal legacy of Paul Du Chaillu. It is ironic, in a way, that this should be so when we recognize that he was one of the least ill-intentioned toward the continent or its peoples; in fact he had a liking and respect for them unsurpassed within the explorers' fraternity. But he chose to visit and write about one of the most exotic, most mysterious—thus most fascinating—parts of the Dark Continent and, because his numerous books provided an exciting literary experience, they were notably successful in their time, enjoying a long period in print. They did more than the works of anyone else—at least before Burroughs—to mold opinions about their subject.

3
In the Service of the Khedive: Charles Chaillé-Long and Egyptian Expansionism

While it cannot be said that American military personnel have established a venerable tradition of mercenary service in the armed forces of other nations, nevertheless there are some interesting examples of it. Perhaps the most famous case is that of John Paul Jones who, following celebrated exploits for his adopted country during the Revolutionary War, became an admiral in the navy of Catherine the Great. It was after the American Civil War, however, that the greatest number of American veterans considered military employment abroad an acceptable option. At the termination of that conflict numerous officers from both sides found themselves unemployed, some with no attractive prospects. Thus in 1869, when the government of Egypt announced that it was seeking ex-Union and ex-Confederate officers for service in its military forces, there were men ready and willing to accept the invitation.

Egypt was nominally a part of the Ottoman Turkish Empire, but ever since the early nineteenth century, when it had come under the direction of Muhammad Ali, an Albanian adventurer commanding a contingent in the Ottoman army, Egypt had become increasingly autonomous.[1] Muhammad Ali in fact had sent his armies into Syria in the 1830s, successfully challenging his titular superior, the Ottoman sultan, who ruled that territory. Syria became an Egyptian possession. Egypt's threat to Turkish power in the Levant was indeed formidable in that era but, due to the intervention of the European powers, especially Great Britain, which did not prefer to see Turkey crushed or even seriously weakened, the Egyptian pasha's ambition of replacing Turkey as the dominant force in the Middle East was thwarted. Consequently, he had to relinquish Syria in 1841.

Africa was another sphere of interest to which Egyptian leaders since the time of the pharaohs had given their attention without—at least until the last part of the nineteenth century—provoking much European concern. Muhammad Ali's troops conquered a major part of the vast Sudan in the 1820s. At the confluence of the White and Blue Niles the base of Khartoum was established as the administrative capital and a governor was appointed. Egypt then set about exploiting the Sudan up to the time of Ismail's assumption of leadership in Cairo in 1863. Little was done to develop the territory. The Egyptian administration there occasionally tried to introduce reforms, but generally was best known for neglect and inefficiency.

The Khedive Ismail's vision of Egypt's imperial role in Africa far exceeded that of his modern predecessors. It encompassed not only a new order for the Sudan, but expansion into neighboring territories as well. The creation of a revitalized and enlarged African empire was intended to enhance the power and glory of Egypt as it became more involved in international diplomacy with the great powers. Such ambitions could not, however, be reconciled with Egypt's position as a dependency of the Ottoman Empire. In the tradition of his precursors, therefore, one of Ismail's major objectives was to win complete independence from Turkey. And although he ultimately emphasized diplomacy and financial inducements in trying to achieve that end, in the 1860s he had not ruled out military means.[2] Thus he took steps to build a better, more modern military establishment.

Foreigners from various countries would find their way into Egyptian service under Ismail, some of them Americans. This was not the first time U.S. citizens had worked for Egypt. In fact, three Americans had accompanied Muhammad Ali's forces on their invasion of the Sudan in 1820–21. George Bethune English, a convert to Islam who was chief of artillery on that expedition, was the most prominent of them.[3] In the second half of the nineteenth century Egyptian leaders recognized that European nationals possessed expertise that could be useful to them. Although Europeans would be employed in some numbers, their Egyptian superiors were always somewhat uneasy about Europeans' ultimate loyalty to Egypt, about the conflict of interest that such men might face. This was especially true in the case of British and French employees whose countries were rivals in the eastern Mediterranean and whose interest in Egypt bore careful watching. The United States, on the other hand, had no political ambitions in northeastern Africa, and Americans in Egyptian pay might reasonably

Charles Chaillé-Long (*Courtesy of the Library of Congress*).

be expected to be more loyal and dedicated to furthering the cause of the Khedive's government than some of their European counterparts.

Ismail would hire fifty Americans, some of them ex-Union officers, others former Confederates, and a few civilians. There were usually not more than thirty in service at any one time.[4] Most of these men left Egypt in 1878 when the Khedive's financial troubles precluded their continued employment, but one held on until 1882 when the British occupation began.[5] The idea of recruiting American officers who supposedly were free of Europeans' designs on Egypt was advanced in 1868 by Blaque Bey, Turkey's first minister to the United States and thus an unlikely one to be helping Egypt strengthen its military posture that could be detrimental to the Ottoman sultan's imperial authority. In any case, this agent of the Porte was married to an American woman who was the sister of Thaddeus Mott, an ex-Union cavalry officer who had developed good connections at the court of Khedive Ismail. Between them, Mott and his Turkish brother-in-law convinced the Egyptian leader, who had followed the American Civil War with considerable interest, that able veterans of that conflict could be valuable to his regime.[6] Mott's brother, Henry, served as the Khedive's American agent and he solicited the recommendations of Gen. William T. Sherman, general-in-chief of the American army, for superior men who might be interested in foreign service.

But even before this effort began, one American had already applied for a position. Having heard in late 1869 that the French military mission to Egypt was being recalled, an ex-Union soldier, Charles Chaillé-Long, saw a chance to return to military life, this time in an exotic part of the world that had begun to interest him. His letter of inquiry had reached the Khedive of Egypt who decided to accept him as the first of his American officers. Chaillé-Long's commission was dated March 2, 1870. Soon thereafter others were recruited, including Charles Pomeroy Stone, who, despite General Sherman's strong recommendation, had a checkered war record and thus seized this opportunity to prove his detractors wrong.[7] He now helped select others for work in Egypt and soon won appointment as the Khedive's chief of staff. In April 1870, Chaillé-Long and the first few American officers arrived in Egypt, followed in August by a group of twenty more led by General Stone. Chaillé-Long's five-year contract designated him a lieutenant colonel in the Commissary Department, a position that hardly suggested what an adventurous, far-ranging experience he would have in the Nile Valley and beyond.[8]

Charles R. W. Long was born at Princess Anne, Maryland, July 2, 1842. His Huguenot paternal great-great grandfather, Pierre Chaillé, had settled in eastern Maryland in the late seventeenth century. The family took pride in the fact that several of its members served as officers of Washington's Continental Army. When the Civil War began, the young man was completing his studies at Washington Academy in Maryland.[9] Drawn to the conflict, he enlisted in the Maryland Infantry Volunteers, Eastern Shore Regiment, on October 2, 1862. In March 1865 he was promoted to captain, and on June 15 of that year was honorably discharged. The only special note in his military record refers to his brief appointment as aide-de-camp to Gen. A. P. Schoeff in 1865. There is no mention of combat experience although, never averse to padding his record, he later claimed to have seen action in several battles.[10] The postwar period saw Long drift to New York City where, from 1866 to 1869, he worked for a cotton commission firm and tried his hand at writing. He claimed to have written for the "commercial and literary press," but his work remains unidentified.[11] It was probably at this time that he began to identify himself by the addition of the patronymic prefix "Chaillé" to his name. But he did not legally change his name until 1870. Chaillé-Long's years in New York were dull and unpromising, so he decided to return if possible to military life.

Enamored of things French, he unsuccessfully sought a commission in the French army through a recommendation from a former Confederate, Maj. Gen. Dabney H. Maury.[12] However, after subsequently learning that Egypt was considering the enlistment of American officers, he aggressively pursued that opportunity. Fellow Marylander and American Secretary of War, Montgomery Blair, was induced to write in Chaillé-Long's behalf, and the U.S. consul in Cairo also made inquiries for him.[13] The latter informed him, however, that the Khedive was no longer adding to his forces.[14] Undaunted, the persistent applicant finally achieved his objective after addressing his entreaties to Thaddeus Mott.[15] So off he went, convinced that adventure and renown would be his destiny in the East.

The Egyptian leader extended quite liberal terms to his new American officers. Their salaries were equal to those of U.S. Army officers of equivalent rank. In addition, their transportation to and from Egypt was paid, and they received free housing and forage for two horses. Those assigned to distant parts of the empire were to receive supplementary pay and free rations. Life insurance and pensions for widows and children also were provided.[16]

Unfortunately, it was not long after their arrival in the ancient land of the Nile that the Americans learned that Britain and France had communicated to Ismail their opposition to his military expansion program, including the enlistment of American veterans and acquisition of American munitions, because it was intended for the Khedive's challenge to Ottoman suzerainty.[17] Ismail was in no position to ignore the message, and thus he had to find ways to use his American personnel that would not be construed as a threat to Turkey. Moreover, traditional cronyism and bureaucratic obstructionism in the Egyptian army prevented their placement in important staff posts or field commands, which were reserved for Egyptians.[18] The major exception, of course, was General Stone's commission as chief of staff of the Egyptian army. The other Americans could aspire to nothing more significant than advisory positions and leadership of exploring expeditions and scientific assignments such as cartography and geological work.[19]

Chaillé-Long, for example, initially had no important responsibilities and, like a minor foreign service officer, was relegated to guiding important visitors around Cairo and its environs. It was in this capacity that he traveled briefly in northern Egypt touring with Gen. William Sherman and Emperor Dom Pedro II of Brazil.[20] During one period he was given some lesser administrative tasks in Alexandria where he idled away much of his time.[21] For four years this was a rather casual, desultory existence for the most part, as Chaillé-Long amused himself with his horses, the French theater, and nights at the opera.[22] In a record of his career that he later submitted to the U.S. Congress in support of his request for a regular army pension, which was denied, Chaillé-Long indicated that he had been appointed as "Chief to Staff to the general in chief" in 1870 and that he also was a French professor at the Cairo military academy,[23] yet such posts are not mentioned in his autobiography. In any event, he was assigned direction of several sections of the general staff, headquartered in the historic Cairo Citadel, in 1873. Some writers suggest that his personality was such that he did not win many friends among Egyptian officers and was often shuttled from one minor job to another.[24] This seems to be accurate. Certainly there was no glory to be won in such desk work. But his fortunes changed when he was posted to the Sudan.

Since its conquest by Muhammad Ali's troops, the Sudan had endured decades of harsh exploitation by Egypt. In addition to lamentably high taxation, the area was identified with the slave trade. In fact, it was Egypt's imposition of central authority and pacification of large areas in the 1820s that permitted the long-established slave trade to expand to major proportions. The region most severely affected was the largely negroid southern Sudan.[25] Some of the slave traders, including a few Europeans, were organized into large commercial establishments that gained virtual control of the vast districts they worked, and they became a major force in Sudanese affairs. Moreover, with their wealth and connections in Cairo, these firms were an influential element in Egyptian politics.[26] Great Britain, having taken the lead in eradicating the Atlantic slave trade earlier in the century, gradually turned its attention to the traffic in slaves elsewhere in Africa, including that in the Sudan. The arrival of Christian missionaries in the 1840s, furthermore, resulted in increased attention being focused on this abominable condition in the Sudan. Consequently, pressure began to mount for a campaign to end the despicable business. Some effort in this direction was undertaken in the 1850s but little was accomplished.[27] It was only when Khedive Ismail gained power that Egypt made the slave trade a major state target.

Educated in Europe, sophisticated, familiar with European institutions and procedures, the Egyptian ruler was influenced by the same humanitarian spirit that inspired the abolition movement in Europe. He wanted to transform Egypt into a modern state along European lines. And, seeking respect and recognition from the Great Powers, he had to attack the slavers. In addition to domestic modernization, Ismail's plans for Egypt also included imperial expansion. Not only should the Sudan be brought more firmly under Egyptian control, especially the extreme south, but adjacent lands too should become Egyptian possessions. His ambition for an Egyptian empire was directed particularly to the Great Lakes region, the Upper Nile Basin.[28] By coincidence, in 1863, the same year that Ismail succeeded Muhammad Said as ruler, the British explorers John Hanning Speke and J. A. Grant appeared in Cairo after following the course of the Nile from near Lake Victoria. Their work was the culmination of a long search by a number of explorers for the source of the Nile. Speke and Grant reported on the lakes region, emphasizing the large, relatively advanced societies there that represented potentially important new markets for foreign goods. Consequently, the Royal Geographical Society, which had sponsored the exploration, urged the British government to encourage Egypt to extend its authority over the area.[29] Khedive Ismail, seeing both economic and political advantages, needed little coaxing.

The first phase of the Khedive's design for expansion required the conquest of the southern Sudan, mainly to suppress the slave trade there but also in order to establish a solid base for penetration into other territory.³⁰ Because Egyptians charged with carrying out his plans in the Sudan were undependable, largely due to corruption, Ismail chose several Europeans for the task. The first of these was the British explorer Samuel Baker who had gained fame for his travels in Ethiopia and for the discovery of one of the Nile sources, Lake Albert Nyanza, in 1864. Baker was a determined commander who carried the Egyptian flag to the border of Uganda, but his ruthlessness alienated many of the people he had ostensibly come to help. In any event, Baker eliminated many of the slavers along the Nile and established Egyptian authority, represented by a chain of river stations, where it had not existed before. Equatoria Province, as the southernmost part of the Sudan was now called, was secured. In the western regions of Bahr el Ghazal and Darfur, however, which had not come under Baker's purview, extensive slaving operations continued unabated, as the Khedive's agents there failed to carry out his orders. Moreover, the slave traders whom Baker had forced away from the Upper Nile had simply moved into the Bahr el Ghazal. When Baker finished his work in 1873, his employer was convinced that it was necessary to replace him with another European. The Khedive's choice was Charles George Gordon.

Gordon (1833–85) is one of most romantic and tragic figures in the history of European involvement in Africa. He first gained public attention when, on leave from the British army, he served the imperial government of China by leading an army of irregulars in the suppression of the Taiping Rebellion in the early 1860s. For that exploit he became commonly known as "Chinese" Gordon. In the course of a later assignment for Britain, he happened to be in Constantinople in 1873, where he made the acquaintance of Nubar Pasha, Khedive Ismail's prime minister, who explained his chief's goal of destroying slavery in the Sudan. Seeing this as a noble cause, Gordon later agreed to take up leadership in Baker's place, again having been granted leave by the British War Department. When offered the same £10,000 ($50,000) salary as his predecessor, he would accept only £2,000 ($10,000).³¹ A devout but eccentric Christian fundamentalist who had a deep sympathy for the downtrodden, he wanted to show the Khedive and his palace clique that "gold and silver idols are not worshipped by all the world," especially since he was convinced that all wealth in Egypt came from exploitation of the peasants.³²

Gordon's title was "Governor of the Equatorial Provinces." For combatting the slave trade he was instructed to establish a series of posts along the upper Nile that would facilitate pacification of the surrounding areas and the maintenance of communication all along the river to Khartoum. Gordon, furthermore, was advised to win the confidence of the local chiefs as far as Uganda and, if it was deemed necessary in order to stop intertribal warfare, to impose his indirect control over them.[33] Evidently Gordon accepted the Sudan mission in late 1873 only after the Khedive assured him that he had no desire to annex territory but, rather, only wanted to end the slave trade and encourage legitimate commerce.[34] If this was the English idealist's attitude at the start of his African work, his opposition to Egyptian imperialism would weaken later.

Northeastern Africa thus became the scene of Gordon's labors for about seven years. It would end in 1884 when, after interrupting his service in the Nile Valley for varied experiences in India and southern Africa, he returned to the Sudan where he was cut off by the Mahdi's forces and killed in Khartoum, thereby becoming one of the most popular heroes of his age. It was this unusual man with whom Chaillé-Long would now be associated.

Some writers have asserted that because he had learned Arabic (actually he knew little of the language at that time) and shared the Khedive's distrust of the British, Chaillé-Long was recommended to Ismail as a good colleague for Gordon.[35] Chaillé-Long himself claimed that he was sought out by Gordon and asked to join his staff; the specific invitation supposedly was as follows: "My dear Chaillé-Long, will you come with me to Central Africa?"[36] While it is possible that the young American was recommended by someone at court or perhaps by General Stone, it is doubtful that Gordon would have taken the initiative in recruiting him. In fact, Gordon, who was impatient to leave Cairo for the Sudan and indeed was in Egypt for only a very short time, reported that "an American named Long [the name by which Gordon always referred to him], a colonel in the Egyptian army has asked to come with me and if I can, I shall take him."[37] It is likely, therefore, that the bored, unabashed climber seeking a more exciting life contacted Gordon and personally requested to accompany the famous Englishman.[38] He won appointment as his chief of staff.

What is more controversial is the matter of Chaillé-Long's alleged meeting with Ismail. He affirmed that before leaving on assignment with Gordon on February 21, 1874, he was called to the royal palace on the twentieth and during an audience with Ismail, was issued secret orders to go with his commander to Gondokoro where he was not to tarry long before pushing on to Uganda. There he was to "obtain a treaty," presumably creating an Egyptian protectorate.[39] Writing many years after the alleged event, Chaillé-Long suggested that Ismail had heard of Henry Morton Stanley's intended expedition to East Africa and now ordered him to forestall Stanley or any other outsider who might be heading for Uganda.[40] Nowhere is there any confirmation of this. Instead, the evidence disputes it. In the first place, when his meeting with the Khedive is supposed to have occurred, Stanley had not yet announced his decision to return to Africa on the spectacular three-year journey that would take him to Uganda. It was made public only in August 1874. Even rumors about a possible Stanley expedition probably would not have been circulating as early as February. Therefore, there would have been no mention of Stanley who, in any event, as a putative American journalist would not have been perceived as a threat to Egypt's interest in the Great Lakes region.[41] It is possible that the Khedive was concerned about the mission of Verney Lovett Cameron, sponsored by the Royal Geographical Society, to assist the great missionary-explorer David Livingstone in his East African work. Cameron started out from the East African coast in early 1873 and by February 1874 was still deep in the interior. It was widely believed that Cameron had official British backing,[42] a rumor that could have reached the Khedive's ear in Cairo. But Chaillé-Long's interview with Ismail probably never took place.

It is odd that the American, always eager to boast about any recognition granted to him, did not mention secret Khedival orders in his first book, published in 1876, covering his adventures while in Egyptian service. In that volume he says that his decision to travel to Uganda was inspired only by his inclination to make a contribution to the still incomplete knowledge of the Nile sources.[43] Gordon, moreover, makes no reference to Chaillé-Long having separate orders, something he would have discovered at some point if they had in fact been issued. Finally, it is highly unlikely that the Egyptian ruler would have risked alienating his newly appointed governor by withholding from him notice of his aide's extraordinary assignment. In fact, in further contradiction of Chaillé-Long's story, Gordon received a dispatch from Ismail, including a letter from the Khedive for King Mutesa of Buganda (one of the major states in Uganda). Gordon was instructed to send the letter and some appropriate gifts to Mutesa in the Khedive's name.[44] Actually, Gordon already had sent Chaillé-Long on such a mission two weeks earlier.[45]

A reasonable explanation is that in an effort to inflate the significance of his mission and to avoid having to identify his

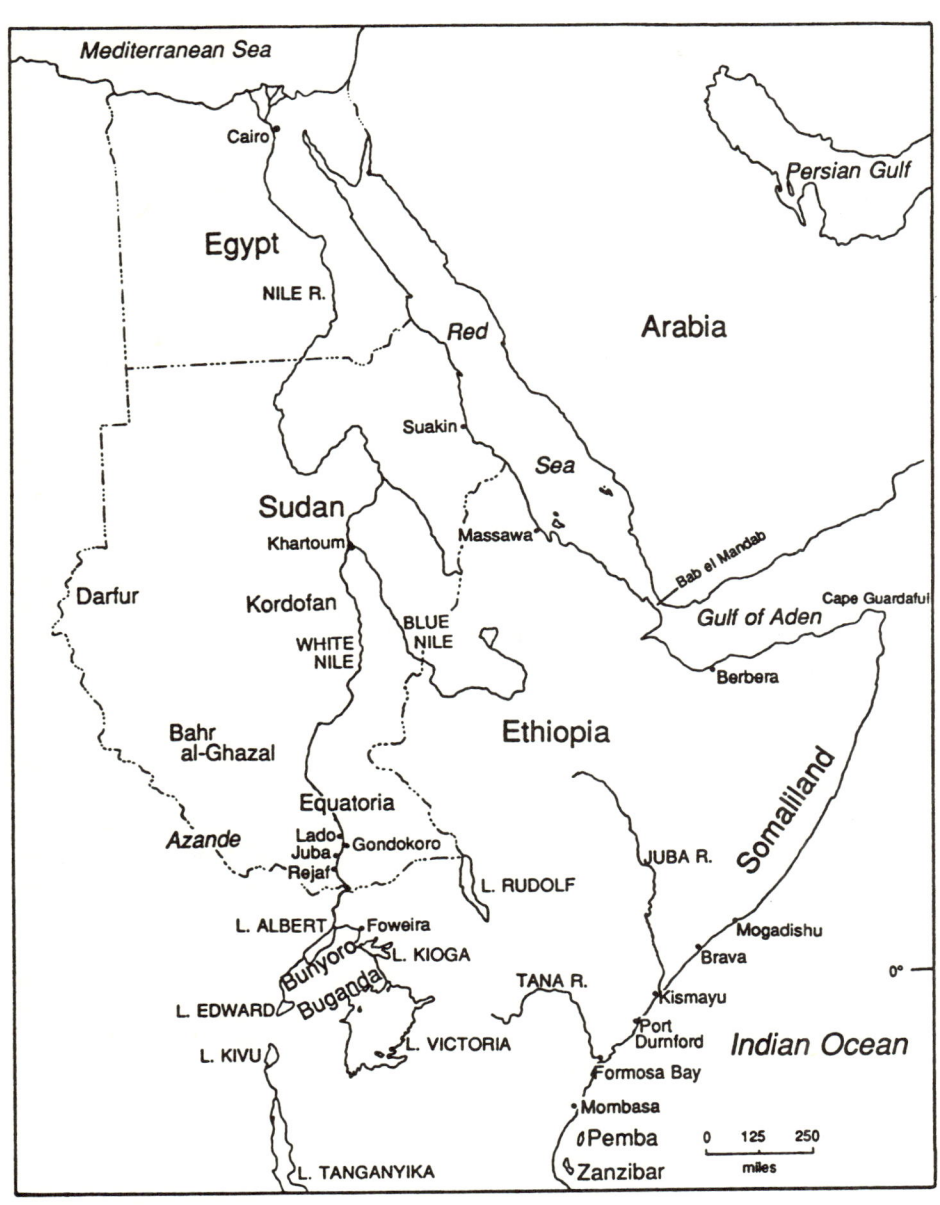

Chaillé-Long's Northeastern Africa.

accomplishment with Gordon's command, Chaillé-Long in his later books recorded it as an independent charge from the Khedive. Unlike Gordon, who was not interested in fame or public adulation, Chaillé-Long yearned for recognition and was not above deceit to gain it.[46]

Gordon quickly assembled his staff, an international group of two Americans, two Britons, a Frenchman, three Germans, and an Italian, and proceeded southward into the baking Sudan.[47] They arrived in Gondokoro, some one thousand seven hundred miles up the Nile, on April 16. This site, used previously by Baker, was designated as the new governor's headquarters for conducting his campaign against the slavers. However, since his baggage had been delayed, Gordon left Gondokoro after six days and headed back to Khartoum to get it. This trip kept him away four months, thus delaying major work. During his absence, however, Chaillé-Long set out for Buganda, apparently requested to do so by Gordon who thereby was complying with the Khedive's orders.[48]

The land associated with the Great Lakes of Africa was the scene of numerous human migrations over many centuries. As a result it contained a population of considerable ethnic and linguistic diversity. Bantu and Nilotic peoples had settled there, the latter in some prominent cases displacing the earlier Bantu inhabitants. By the midnineteenth century the most important tribal states in northern Uganda, the region that Chaillé-Long would traverse, were those of Bunyoro-Kitara, east of Lake Albert, and Buganda, west of Lake Victoria. But there were scores of smaller chiefdoms all along the Upper Nile and interlacustrine area, which were often the prey of their larger, expansive neighbors. By the 1860s wars here increasingly were encouraged by the involvement of slavers who came in from Equatoria. Bunyoro-Kitara had been the dominant kingdom for centuries but by the mid-1700s it had overextended itself and decline was well underway. Meanwhile Buganda, which originally was an offshoot of Bunyoro-Kitara, was clearly on the rise. Under strong monarchs, this state extended its control in several directions while developing a bureaucratic administrative system.[49]

By the time Ismail assumed authority in Egypt, Buganda had become the premier but not unchallenged power between Lakes Albert and Victoria. Its king, Mutesa, had established extensive trade contacts, one of them involving Arab and Swahili middlemen, linking his land to the eastern coast. Mutesa headed a relatively prosperous kingdom with an abundant agricultural and herding economy. The despotic sovereign could call upon a large army to impose his authority over the many clans and tribes within his sphere.[50] Aware of Cairo's desire to absorb the interlacustrine lands and the trouble Bunyoro-Kitaro had experienced when swashbuckling Samuel Baker tried to impose Egyptian rule over that territory in 1872, Mutesa realized that he should exercise a cautious diplomacy in dealing with such representatives of the outside world. The arrival of Zanzibari[51] traders provided him with a source of firearms. In addition he felt he could rely on these men from the east as allies if the need arose. Thus, when Mutesa heard that a new white man had been appointed to govern the southern Sudan, the wily king of the Baganda took steps to acquire information about this possible threat to his people.[52]

When Gordon first arrived at Gondokoro in April, he found Mutesa's emissary awaiting him. This was Ba Beker, a major official at the Bugandan court, who presented Gordon with some impressive ivory tusks and told him that his king wished to be visited by the new Egyptian authority. Mutesa specifically requested someone who could teach him the Koran, as well as others who could be useful in his court.[53] Subsequently Gordon dispatched Chaillé-Long with many gifts. Apparently Khedive Ismail had intended that two Muslim teachers would accompany this expedition, but for some unknown reason they did not make the journey.[54] Chaillé-Long was fortunate to have Ba Beker, who had just recently traversed the country leading to Buganda, join him on the trip. In addition to W. F. G. Kellerman, an Alsatian who had become Chaillé-Long's valet in Khartoum, only two Sudanese soldiers from the local Egyptian station and three other Africans formed the excited white officer's "staff" for the march south. That small band was not alone, of course; there were some three hundred porters to carry the baggage.

As far as Chaillé-Long was concerned, the purpose of the mission was twofold: he intended to help clear up the still not completely solved puzzle of the Nile sources, specifically to establish the actual relationship between Lakes Victoria and Albert and, officially, he was expected to initiate formal relations with Mutesa.[55] He confided later that he had been instructed to convince Mutesa that he should send his ivory north, rather than eastward to the coast with the Zanzibaris, and thus enable Egypt to gain a monopoly over this profitable trade.[56] For his part Gordon, who envisioned an eventual Egyptian sphere of interest in Uganda, probably saw Chaillé-Long's contact with Mutesa as a necessary preliminary step which, once the American's report was evaluated, would enable Gordon to proceed accordingly.[57]

Carrying cottons, silks, jewelry, and precious gems for gifts, the party set out on April 24. An armed escort joined them as far as Foweira, the last Egyptian outpost on the Sudanese Nile, beyond which they would be on their own. Chaillé-Long managed to obtain a horse, the only one in Gondokoro, for his use, although the country en route was often not good for riding. The white horse, nonetheless, proved quite helpful when they reached their destination. Unfortunately it was the rainy season, and the travelers had to endure almost two months of depressing equatorial precipitation. The conditions for travel became progressively worse as they advanced into territory whose inhabitants, long victimized by slavers and often engaged in internecine warfare, were known to be hostile toward strangers. Several of Chaillé-Long's black retainers were killed in the first confrontation with the Mogi, but the column was not held up for long. Fever was a far more worrisome threat on this trip, for almost everyone was prostrated by it at one time or another.

When they reached Bunyoro-Kitara, the weary party crossed territory controlled by Rionga, cousin and rival of Kaba Rega, the king of Bunyoro-Kitara who was unable to assert his authority over the entire country. When Samuel Baker had passed through this area in 1872, he had fallen into conflict with Kaba Rega and, seeking to eliminate him, had attempted to replace the king with Rionga. Baker had succeeded only in intensifying a civil war already underway. Kaba Rega managed to maintain his power in the southern half of Bunyoro-Kitara. Rionga now welcomed Chaillé-Long but endeavored to impress the visitor with his importance. After a brief stop with this chief, the expedition resumed its progress through more rain and marshy terrain until, on June 10, they reached territory under the control of Mutesa. Here there were maintained roads (when dry the red clay surfaces were actually swept), which made their transit easier. Messengers had been sent ahead announcing the coming of a "great prince" to confer with the king.[58] Mutesa sent out one of his chief ministers to greet the latest representative of Egypt in central Africa who was told he and his entourage must wait several days while the ruler prepared for their arrival. Ultimately, after marching two more days, they reached the Baganda capital on June 20. This was Rubaga, situated a few miles from the western shore of the great lake called Ukerewe by the Africans and recently named Victoria by the explorer Speke.

Riding into Rubaga in his ornate Egyptian staff uniform at the head of his large column, Chaillé-Long must have cut quite a figure in spite of the ill health that he and many of his followers suffered. His horse, particularly when spurred to a gallop, was indeed a strange, even terrifying sight to the throng that gathered around their king for this occasion. Though undoubtedly impressed, the latter concentrated more on demonstrating his own power. During their initial interview, Mutesa ordered thirty of his subjects beheaded in the American's presence. This repulsive demonstration only confirmed his visitor's opinion that Africans were by nature cruel and cowardly.[59] Yet, Chaillé-Long was in general favorably impressed with Buganda (if not with its sovereign); compared with other territories he had seen, this land and its people were quite commendable. The fact that the Baganda wore long robes, in contrast to the nakedness of most tribesmen encountered on the upper Nile, was in itself enough to win his high praise. This, and the fact that many Baganda displayed some Caucasoid physical features made him rate them higher than most other blacks. The "softening" of Negroid characteristics he attributed to contact with Arabs.[60] As he observed his surroundings, Chaillé-Long noted the comparatively productive land, the variety of crops, the superior cattle (he rated them equal to European breeds), the tanning industry, and the high quality of iron-working.[61]

During his month in Buganda, when he was not ill and wondering if he could survive fever and dysentery, Chaillé-Long did his best to gain Mutesa's agreement to export his ivory by way of the Nile when the American proved the feasibility of that route. But that exploration should be preceded, he insisted, by his examination of Lake Victoria. Speke and Grant had been the only previous Europeans to see Africa's largest lake but, Chaillé-Long thought, they had not ventured out on it. It took much coaxing before the reluctant Mutesa gave his American guest permission to do that.

For his maritime excursion he was escorted by one thousand two hundred men in a large fleet of boats. It was his hope to determine the exact size of the lake by crossing and exploring it carefully, but Mutesa would not allow him to accomplish such a feat. Like his people, the king harbored superstitions about the lake and the people on its eastern side, but Mutesa also feared that the white stranger might perish if he went too far from shore, for indeed the waters of this inland sea could become quite rough.[62] Although frustrated in this instance, Chaillé-Long consoled himself with the knowledge that at least he was the first European to sail on the great lake. Even that distinction, however, was denied him. He declared in *Central Africa: Naked Truths of Naked People* that he was the first white navigator on Victoria, but must have been shocked when another writer soon pointed out that both John H. Speke and J. A. Grant, each on different occasions, had accomplished the feat a decade earlier during their joint exploration to the sources of the Nile. Chaillé-Long, it appears, had seen Speke's account of his travels but neglected to read it carefully. Moreover, he probably ignored Grant's book.[63]

Despite Mutesa's objections, he was determined to make his return trip to Gondokoro on the Nile. This was necessary, in his view, because it was Egypt's plan eventually to put steam vessels in service from Lake Albert to Lake Victoria, but only if the Nile linking them permitted it. And if he could succeed in covering that portion of the river, he would be credited with a significant geographical discovery.[64]

In his 1876 account of the Buganda visit Chaillé-Long claimed that Mutesa agreed to close his ivory trade with the coast and to divert it to Egypt. He further states that the king was "made a willing subject [and] his country . . . created the southern limit of Egypt."[65] This, sadly, is a misrepresentation; the proud, wily African leader would never have agreed to such terms. It is notable that nothing was said in Chaillé-Long's first book about a formal written agreement with Mutesa. In subsequent accounts, on the other hand, the author asserted that with the assistance of an Arab interpreter he negotiated a treaty with the king on July 19, 1874, the effect of which was to make "the entire Nile Basin an Egyptian protectorate."[66] Furthermore, he maintained that this treaty "was officially proclaimed by the Egyptian Ministry to all the powers, England included."[67] Yet there is no evidence to support his case. Mutesa, of course, did not have the authority, even if for some reason he was willing, to confer such control upon Egypt. Gordon, Chaillé-Long's immediate superior, surely would have known about any treaty yet made no reference to it when acknowledging Chaillé-Long's work in Uganda. In fact, after the American's return, Gordon considered it important to establish a treaty relationship with Mutesa, something he himself planned in 1876 but was unable to carry out.[68]

In departing from Buganda Chaillé-Long sent his horse and five hundred-man escort provided by Mutesa along the land route to Mruli where they were to await him. He would explore the Nile between Lakes Victoria and Albert. Therefore he trekked to Urondogani, about sixty miles north of where the Nile flows out of Lake Victoria and the point at which Speke had been forced by threatening tribesmen to leave the river in 1863. There were eight in his party, including one of Mutesa's daughters who was presented with seven additional young women as gifts from the king. The other females Chaillé-Long gave to his aides and to chiefs who helped him along the way, something he was not comfortable doing but, given the circumstances, he rationalized, it was the best solution. Rather than insult the king with whom Egypt desired closer relations, however, the Baganda princess was kept with the expedition and eventually was placed in a Cairo school.

The descent of the river began on August 7 in four flat-bottomed boats. Through dense papyrus growth along the Nile and through the seemingly endless rain they slowly advanced. After four days of difficult paddling they entered a broad expanse of water that appeared to absorb the river. It was a lake dotted with countless islands of papyrus and water lilies, which made passage through them almost impossible for those unfamiliar with the many channels. For five more days the boats struggled along before regaining the main stream of the river.

The body of water Chaillé-Long had discovered is a shallow reservoir that in the Early Pleistocene Age was connected to Lake Victoria as one vast lake covering an immense territory. Following their separation, the larger lake's overflow continued through the centuries to maintain the other in existence but only as a very shallow basin. Its depth is only about seventeen feet.[69] Chaillé-Long named the lake "Hussein," after Egypt's minister of war, and saw this discovery, in connection with the section of the river he traced beyond it, as demonstrating indubitably that Lakes Albert and Victoria were indeed linked by the Nile, a point hotly debated until then.[70] Not content with that claim to fame, he went on to theorize that the thick vegetation on his lake, when it dried out, could no longer hold back the Nile whose heavy wind and rain then pushed the water forward, thereby causing the river's annual flooding.[71] This erroneous notion was never taken seriously and serves only to demonstrate that its originator was merely trying to emulate the many other explorers who in their books provided explanations—not always well-informed—of the phenomena they observed. The finding of the lake, however, would be credited to him (but not, as explained below, without some dispute) as a component in the solution to the Nile riddle.

On the approach to Mruli, which was in sight by August 17, the little flotilla was attacked by forty boats of Kaba Rega's men. By sustained and accurate gunfire at close range, the American officer and his men inflicted heavy losses on the enemy who lacked firearms, just keeping them at bay. After a desperate conflict, during which Chaillé-Long was slightly injured, his boats passed

Mruli, which obviously was not a safe haven and where there was no sign of his land expedition that was expected to meet him. Down river on the nineteenth they were delighted to meet some boats from the Egyptian post at Foweira. Having exhausted their scanty food supply, the ragged, hungry group was now treated to fish and potatoes along with friendly conversation. Soon they were in Foweira, nothing more than a tiny, desolate station but nevertheless able to provide a much-needed respite.

Recuperation was slow and only partial at this place where Chaillé-Long stayed for about three weeks. The remaining journey to Gondokoro by land and water took over a month and, considering the extremely debilitated condition of the travelers, was a punishing ordeal. Once there, Chaillé-Long received Gordon's sincere congratulation. The latter sent a report of the Uganda mission to the Khedive, accompanied by a recommendation for his aide's promotion to colonel, which was later conferred. The governor-general then encouraged him to take leave in Khartoum in order to recover his health. Two months of relaxation, good food, and medical attention brought much improvement, although recurrent fever would plague him for the rest of his life, one of the costs paid by most white men who worked in Africa for extended periods. His next assignment would require some of the same strength of body and will he had exhibited earlier.

While in Khartoum, Chaillé-Long, following instructions, had arranged for additional troops to be sent to Gordon for garrison duty in Equatoria. By this time Gordon had learned that Sudanese were preferable to Arabs as soldiers for work on the upper Nile. The former could more successfully tolerate the climate and fevers that took a far higher toll among the men of the north. Either Chaillé-Long was not so acutely aware of this or, as was probably the case, he was unable to procure enough Sudanese.[72] In any case, when Gordon was informed that four hundred Arabs were en route, he was furious. In order to save as many of these men as possible, he wanted them moved to a less pestilential area than Gondokoro. Always a demanding task-master impatient with those around him who were guided by less rigorous standards, Gordon had formed a low opinion of Chaillé-Long that was only aggravated by the latter's poor selection of reinforcements. The Uganda mission had won Gordon's praise and he was pleased that the greater maturity his chief of staff had acquired through that experience would make him more useful in Gordon's plans.[73] But it did not take long for Gordon to change his opinion. First he complained of Chaillé-Long's procrastination and forgetfulness and ultimately could not tolerate him.[74] Gordon was a difficult man for subordinates to be around in the best of times. Now, given the difficulties of the equatorial environment and the backward, frustrating Egyptian system with which he had to contend, he was often guilty of offensive treatment of his staff. He let Chaillé-Long know that it would be better if they did not have to be near one another.[75] In his judgment, consequently, it must have seemed a fitting assignment for Chaillé-Long to take many of the newly arrived troops to the west.

Ostensibly the purpose of this project was to open a route through Nyangbara country, a people whose hostility toward outsiders had blocked trade with the Makaraka area, which was rich in ivory. The Makaraka were a branch of the Azande, a large ethnic group who were prominent over a broad territory astride the Nile-Congo watershed. Azandeland and some of its eastern approaches were considered good locations for Egyptian bases, both because there were supposed to be relatively large populations there, and because the area was reputed to be comparatively healthy. True to form, however, Chaillé-Long had more than official goals. He also wanted to reach the unknown land of pygmies, some examples of whom he had seen and, since his vision apparently was not obscured by the realities of African geography, he hoped to make his way to the Atlantic.[76] Such grandiose but impractical ambitions might have seemed heroic to his readers in 1876, but certainly were extraneous to his official responsibilities.

Setting out from Lado[77] in early 1875, the caravan comprised 20 Sudanese troops, a detachment of more than six hundred Arab soldiers, 150 carriers and, as Chaillé-Long's personal guest, M. Marno, a representative of the Geographical Society of Vienna. For his staff he had the services of two dependable men who had been with him on the Uganda trip. A seven-days' march through mostly open grassland brought the expedition to Nyangbara territory where its commander prepared for defense against these warlike Africans who were notorious for their use of poisoned arrows. But only one small skirmish ensued, resulting in only a single fatality among the intruding force.

Subsequently arriving at the camp of a friendly chief, probably among the Fajulu people, Chaillé-Long found a group of several hundred young women who had been given to the local leader as presents by other chiefs in the district. He won his host's permission to distribute the women, who were not considered slaves, to his officers and men. The latter, previously not enthusiastic about being stationed for two-year assignments in the posts Chaillé-Long was setting up in this remote country, now found their positions more attractive. Sensitive to how this might appear in the record, especially in view of Egypt's announced determination to "civilize" the Sudan and terminate involuntary servitude, Chaillé-Long in his account of this episode, insisted that this peculiar arrangement was perfectly acceptable to all involved.[78] Moreover, in a later article he tried to make it seem more respectable by adding that all the couples were married by a Muslim "clerk."[79]

The country through which he was passing had, for some years, been the scene of slave-raiding and associated warfare, which understandably made the inhabitants fearful of strangers, though not always hostile toward them. The Azande, whom Chaillé-Long next encountered and whom he and others at that time called Niam-Niam, were feared warriors. In most cases they had been able to protect themselves from the worst depredations of the slavers. Organized under paramount chiefs and subchiefs, the Azande had acquired some firearms during the 1860s.[80] These agriculturalists were interested in trade, however, and possessed a large quantity of ivory. Some Azande were widely believed to be cannibals, a practice Chaillé-Long intelligently attributed to extreme privation in earlier times but which, he then assumed, had become a habit. He was told that the consumption of human flesh generally was found only among the most remote groups.[81] But Chaillé-Long was not a keen, sophisticated, or learned observer of African civilization and his characterizations are sometimes suspect.

Having established a few stations along his line of march at which were posted contingents of soldiers, Chaillé-Long decided, after several weeks among the Azande, to retrace his steps and return to Lado with the large load of ivory he had obtained. His journey had taken him about 150 miles into territory considered wild and dangerous, although topographically most of it was savanna woodland, unlike the more difficult terrain, including swamps and heavy forest, found near the Great Lakes. Contrary to some estimates,[82] he was not the first white man to penetrate the area. In addition to Egyptian Arabs, a few European missionaries and traders had been there in the 1850s and 1860s. Most prominent, perhaps, among the latter was Andrea de Bono, a Maltese who had organized a network of stations for moving ivory and gold to the Nile.[83] If Chaillé-Long could not claim to have made any original discoveries during this journey, he could nonetheless report to the Khedive that his government's authority was made more apparent than before.[84]

On the return trip he allowed 600 Azande to join his expedition. They had begged for an opportunity to exact revenge against their old enemies, the Nyangbara. Together with many others who joined the American's party, they made the column 1,375 strong. Included were pygmy and Azande individuals whom the commander intended to bring with him to Cairo as examples of the exotic peoples found in western Equatoria whose study might be useful in explaining human evolution![85]

As expected, the return trip was perilous because the Nyangbara were waiting for them in large numbers. This time there was more combat, but Chaillé-Long's people inflicted all the casualties. He paid special tribute to the fighting prowess of the Azande among his force. The decisive defeat of the Nyangbara was sufficient, in the American's opinion, for him to declare the road to Makaraka open.[86] He was back in Lado on March 20, 1875, and from there he made his way to Cairo where he was duly received by Khedive Ismail and feted by the small American community. This was probably the high point of his career in terms of public acknowledgment. Khedival plaudits and recognition from the local geographical society provided some of the glory he had long sought. And he hoped the same would be forthcoming in Europe.

A well-deserved leave of absence being granted, the Khedive's American officer traveled to Paris. Chaillé-Long was a Francophile who, fluent in the language, felt quite at home in the land of his forefathers. In tribute to his accomplishments, the Paris Geographical Society invited him to address its members.[87] His remarks were published shortly thereafter in the society's *Bulletin*. Here was the style of life that suited him even if he did not have the means to support it very long. But before he could obtain an extension of his leave in order further to explore the delights of the French capital, General Stone recalled him to Cairo. Yet another adventure awaited Chaillé-Long in a different part of Africa. This was to be his last assignment from the Khedive's government.

Early in his reign Ismail recognized the importance of East Africa in his plans for Egyptian expansion. The construction of the Suez Canal, underway since 1859, would enhance the Red Sea route's significance to major trading companies, and the European powers, especially Britain, could be expected to show greater interest in northeastern Africa and in the Red Sea region. Apart from its concern about any potential European designs on the area, the Egyptian regime was naturally drawn to its eastern frontier zones and neighboring territories.

One of Khedive Ismail's first moves in the east was to eliminate confusion regarding sovereignty over the Red Sea coast. In 1865 and 1866, the Ottoman sultan was persuaded to cede the disputed ports of Massawa and Suakin, including their associated districts, to Ismail. The territories stretched from Cape Elba in the north (close to the border between Egypt and the Sudan) to the straits of Bab al Mandab, that is, essentially the entire Sudanese Red Sea littoral.[88] Then, in 1867, Egypt claimed the African coast from Suez to Cape Guardafui, thus including a portion of the Somali coast.[89] Governors were appointed and certain sites, such as the port of Berbera, were occupied by Egyptian forces. Only the port of Zeila, in the extreme north of what is today the Somali Republic, was still officially under Turkish suzerainty, but even that area was ceded to Ismail in 1875.[90] In response to British inquiries, the Khedive insisted that the principal purpose of these moves was the suppression of the slave trade and the promotion of respectable commerce.[91] Following long deliberations on the matter, Great Britain agreed to recognize Egyptian rights to the newly acquired territories.[92] It was obvious, therefore, that Egyptian imperialistic ambitions were growing in the direction of East Africa, and such expansion was being carefully monitored by the British.

During Samuel Baker's governorship in Equatoria, as Cairo's efforts to assert control over the upper Nile proceeded, the obstacles faced by Egyptian forces operating at such vast distances and in such hostile surroundings prompted the Khedive's planners to consider the East African coast in their calculations for taming the area where Baker was struggling. In 1871 General Stone conceived a strategy to help Baker by sending reinforcements to Mombasa on the east coast from where they would march 400 miles inland to Lake Victoria and then on through the interlacustrine region to Gondokoro.[93] Since the distance overland was relatively short, this route was thought to be a practical alternative to the more than 2,500-mile river and land connection between Cairo and Uganda. An expedition under the leadership of the American lieutenant Erastus Purdy was readied for this purpose. Chaillé-Long and another American officer were designated to participate in this work, their first task being the assemblage of gifts to be presented to such inland chiefs as Mutesa.[94] In addition to assisting Baker, Purdy's expedition was designed to achieve a political goal. He was expected to erect a military station in the vicinity of Mount Kilimanjaro which, if it had materialized, would have initiated Egypt's claim to the East African interior. And, while inland, Purdy was directed to carry out extensive exploration of the Great Lakes region.[95] This so-called Baker Relief Expedition waited four months for the signal to embark but it never came. When Cairo was informed that Baker had extracted himself from his predicament, Ismail abandoned the Stone scheme. Evidently the Khedive thought the idea a good one; however, he simply had lost the excuse he needed to mask what would have been a far-reaching thrust of Egyptian empire-building. The plan was filed but not forgotten.

By late 1874 Gordon was feeling the extent of his isolation and was embittered by the long delay in communication with the outside world. In his opinion, Khartoum, the only major center in the Sudan, was controlled by a corrupt, incompetent administration that obstructed his progress. The city, furthermore, was too far from his operations. His only link with it was an undependable steamer. Finally, the opening of a steamer service to Uganda, which was one of his major objectives and a key factor in the Khedive's whole design for Egyptian hegemony in the interlacustrine region, was proving to be a formidable task, the success of which he was beginning to doubt. No wonder, then, that the governor of Equatoria decided that a shorter, more efficient connection might be developed. Now he, like General Stone before him, focused on the East African coast as a possible solution to the problem. Gordon gave much attention to this project. A road, he believed, could be constructed from the lakes to the Indian Ocean.[96] Although Gordon himself explained his concept and proposed the coastal plan in a letter to one of the Khedive's aides on January 21, 1875,[97] he also refined the proposal after discussing it with Chaillé-Long just before the latter left for Makaraka country, and had him communicate it to General Stone four days later in what was a long, detailed report. In it was the argument that all the territory between the coast and Buganda must be acquired in order to insure success. And, according to Chaillé-Long, Gordon recommended that the American lead the expedition from the coast.[98] If Ismail was agreeable to his proposal, Gordon was in favor of eventually moving his own headquarters to Mombasa on the coast.[99]

It was months before the mail from Equatoria was received in Cairo, but once the Khedive was apprised of Gordon's strategy, he was intrigued by it. It might allow Ismail to resurrect the earlier project, which had appealed to him. Of course, he wanted to be cautious this time. He discussed the project with the Prince of Wales and Sir Bartle Frere, London's influential special commissioner in the effort to end the Indian Ocean slave trade, who had interviewed the Khedive in 1872. Both of these contacts found the idea a good one.[100] While Cairo deliberated, Gordon kept sending further suggestions and modifications of the original proposal. He had a poor understanding of East Africa's geography and political realities. His French map of East Africa distorted distances significantly and in general gave its reader an erroneous picture of the region.[101] He knew that the sultan of Zanzibar had claims to part of the East African littoral but was unsure about their extent. When Gordon became aware that Mombasa was under Zanzibari control he consequently decided that port should no longer figure in Egyptian plans. He advised the Khedive that the best means of gaining access to the interior would be via one of the rivers that flowed into the Indian Ocean. The Juba, whose mouth was at the Equator, was a likely choice, but the Tana, further south (in what is now Kenya) was believed to be navigable for a greater distance and preferable because it would provide a shorter route.[102] Ultimately Ismail and his counselors were won over to Gordon's altered plan.

The Khedive appreciated the Englishman's concern about Zanzibar's pretensions along the coast and Britain's possible support of the sultan's claims, but he intended to move anyway.[103] Sultan Barghash of Zanzibar visited Europe during the summer of 1875, appearing in England in June. While there he addressed the Royal Geographical Society, declaring that East Africa, including the territory around the Great Lakes, was "reckoned under our rule."[104] The London *Times*, in an editorial comment on the speech, pointed out that both Egypt and Zanzibar apparently were laying claim to the same lands and suggested that diplomatic negotiation on the question was in order.[105] An opportunity for this did present itself. While returning home, the sultan found it appropriate to stop in Egypt where he was Ismail's guest for two weeks. Barghash informed his host that Zanzibar indeed claimed the whole east coast up to Ras Hafun (about one hundred miles south of Cape Guardafui). Allowing that his small country was not on a par with the great states he had seen in Europe, he confided to the American consul in Cairo that he intended to do more to earn respect in the international community.[106] Thus Barghash indicated to the Khedive that as soon as he arrived home he would raise Zanzibar's flag over the Juba mouth and other coastal points.[107] It seems that an exchange of views by the two leaders took place in Ismail's palace, but nothing that might be characterized as negotiations leading to some understanding or mutual recognition of exactly what territories each could rightfully consider his, was accomplished.

Undeterred—in fact now spurred to action—Ismail refused to accept Zanzibar's exaggerated claims, although as a gracious host he did not communicate this to the sultan while he was in Cairo. "The mouth of the Juba," he asserted in a dispatch to Gordon, "belongs to us."[108] All territory south of it might be recognized as the sultan's, but that from the Juba north, some of it already occupied by Egyptian forces, must come under the Khedive's authority.[109] If diplomacy would not suffice to bring the sultan to heel, then force would be used. As far as the European powers were concerned, England being the primary actor, Ismail was convinced that his costly campaign against the Sudanese slave trade and his declared intention to fight it in the east would win London over to his position. The Khedive emphasized that his state could do far more toward establishing security and protecting legitimate commerce in the areas under consideration than the sultan of Zanzibar, and he took it for granted that this must be recognized by all interested parties.[110] From the perspective of Cairo such a posture might have seemed utterly reasonable, whereas from other quarters the factors in the equation were read differently and led to different conclusions.

By an odd turn of events, Gordon was now urging his employer to delay the operation until Gordon was in a better position to involve himself with it, but Ismail was determined to move. An expedition was hastily organized. Appointed commander was H. F. McKillop, a former captain in the Royal Navy and, since 1869, Egypt's director of ports and lights. Chaillé-Long, who had been led by Gordon to believe that he would lead such a mission, later claiming that Gordon suggested the American would become a "viceroy in the east,"[111] was second in command and would be responsible for the land phase of the venture. Urged to maintain secrecy, Chaillé-Long left Cairo on September 16 for Suez, where three companies of troops awaited him. His sealed orders directed him to sail five miles south before opening a second set of instructions. Having done that, he found himself instructed to continue his voyage through the Bab al Mandab to Berbera on the northern Somali coast where he would meet McKillop and two more companies of Egyptian soldiers.[112] This destination reached, the American delivered sealed orders to McKillop. In them the latter was told to speedily make his way to "our possessions south of Cape Guardafui," to the mouth of the Juba and to occupy the place by establishing a base that could support itself.[113] The ultimate objective was the opening of a road to the Lakes, the western end of which was Gordon's responsibility. Indeed, Gordon was to be the overall leader of the operation. McKillop was expected to await his arrival and place himself under Gordon's command.[114]

McKillop's ships stopped at several places along the east coast of Africa as they sailed toward their principal objective. Egyptian flags were raised at these points and local authorities pressed to accept the Khedive's authority. At the port of Brava, for example, Chaillé-Long led a show of force that resulted in Somali soldiers in Zanzibar's service fleeing the area. Egyptians were then stationed there to hold it.[115] The expedition arrived at the Juba on October 16 but, finding it impossible to land safely there, McKillop sailed a short distance southward to the established harbor at Kismayu. Overlooking the port they found a Zanzibari fort whose commandant ordered them to leave. When McKillop's request to land for water was refused, he held some local officials as hostages until he won the right to bring some of his men ashore. The following day, while the main force occupied a position along the beach, Chaillé-Long led a company to the rear of the town, which was undefended, and succeeded in taking both the town and the fort.[116] Hundreds of slaves, whom Chaillé-Long freed, were found there, thus confirming what Ismail and others had believed—that Zanzibar was abetting, not abolishing the slave trade.[117]

With the town secure, McKillop saw to the establishment of a base that would allow him to comply with the Khedive's other instructions. Chaillé-Long, for his part, led a small detachment of troops inland until he reached the lower Juba and there, on a high point commanding a good view of the river, set up a camp. In November Egyptian reinforcements arrived at Kismayu, bringing with them a steam launch, which Chaillé-Long used to further reconnoiter the Juba while another officer began a survey of the coastal vicinity. Ascending the river, Chaillé-Long found that it curved so far to the north that it could not have served as a feasible artery for reaching the Great Lakes.[118]

The military force at Kismayu was now one thousand three hundred men strong, including an artillery company and a cavalry contingent from Ismail's Palace Guard. There was even a camel corps for transport work.[119] It was quite an impressive little army for that part of the world and, as its commander, Chaillé-Long was eager to put his men to some important use. All were awaiting Gordon who had been directed to make his way from the Lakes to the coast. When he did so, this force might accomplish great things. But it was not to be. Surprising new orders had come. Dated October 29, 1875, but received in November, McKillop's instructions now called for him to leave the Juba vicinity, which was judged unfit for commercial traffic, and advance southward to Formosa Bay, which contained the mouth of the Tana River. If conditions there were found unsuitable, then the operation should be moved to Port Durnford (between Kismayu and Formosa Bay).[120]

Egypt's decision to transfer its forces closer to Zanzibar was an odd one. The full extent of Kismayu's deficiencies as a port and Chaillé-Long's discouraging intelligence about the course of the Juba could not, given the difficulty of communication, have been reported in Cairo before Ismail changed his mind. So the conditions at the coast seem not to have been the determining factor. Despite the Khedive's defiant tone in his correspondence regarding Zanzibar's extensive claims to coastal sovereignty, Ismail was aware that the sultan enjoyed British backing.[121] The Egyptian ruler, as noted above, had declared that his own territorial rights were more legitimate, or more likely to win international recognition, north of the Juba mouth. Nevertheless he now risked greater resistance to his project by moving south of that point into an area where Zanzibar's jurisdiction was more respected. And resistance was quickly forthcoming.

The British consul general in Cairo, informed of the McKillop expedition, told the Khedive in mid-November that Egypt was going too far in pursuit of imperial domain. Such a policy, he suggested, would create adverse public opinion in England, which could be detrimental to Egypt's credit rating.[122] But this was only the prelude. The official British "request" that Egypt withdraw its forces from the East African coast was received on December 3.[123] Ismail immediately complied, realizing that he was in no position to persist in the face of European opposition. At the same time, though, he protested to the British consul general in Cairo that Egypt's very costly expansion into Equatoria had been encouraged by London, which was now obstructing the Khedive's vital effort to develop a needed line of communication from the Upper Nile to the east coast.[124]

McKillop, who had taken his ships and men to Formosa Bay, finding that place an unsatisfactory anchorage, went slightly north to the old, important island port of Lamu whose harbor suited him. The town was defended, however, by a Zanzibari garrison and, rather than initiate further hostilities, Ismail's peripatetic admiral sailed farther north to Port Durnford. It was there that he received the order to return his forces to Egypt.[125]

This ended an affair characterized by one writer as "the craziest of all African adventures,"[126] which, in view of the numerous ill-conceived actions of the European imperialists, seems an extravagant assessment. Admittedly, though, it was an embarrassing fiasco that produced confusion and controversy in its wake. Egypt was obliged to retreat to the northern Somali coast, its jurisdiction over which now became the focus of extended negotiations with London. Only in 1877 was an agreement reached that recognized the Khedive's authority over the coast no farther south than Ras Hafun.[127] And even this was not secure; before another decade had passed, Italy would take control of this area as the European scramble for African territory reached a frantic pace and Egypt itself would be occupied by British forces. If anything was accomplished by the presence of Egyptians and their foreign officers in East Africa it was not what Ismail had in mind. By provoking the sultan of Zanzibar to assert his authority on the littoral more strongly and upgrade his military presence there, Ismail also made Barghash further acknowledge his ultimate dependence on Great Britain to underwrite his claims to territory. This, in turn, forced Zanzibar to move more diligently against the slave trade in order to please its patron.[128]

And where, it might be asked, was Gordon, the instigator of the project? Thwarted in his campaign to open communication and transportation along the whole Upper Nile, he remained deep in central Africa. His dejection over his situation was worsened by the poor quality of the troops at his disposal and his disappointment over the Khedive's choice of the Juba, rather than some point farther south, as a base for the East African operation.[129] He therefore totally rejected the plan and gave up the idea of trying to reach the coast, by which time, but unknown to him, the expedition had been recalled. Gordon's decision was not, as Chaillé-Long and others have suggested, a result of British pressure or his calculated disloyalty to Egypt.[130] And in any case, had he managed to push forward and link up with McKillop and Chaillé-Long, it would not have mattered because the fate of the project was settled elsewhere.

Various forces were aligned against Egypt's intrusion into East Africa, including English liberals who were unsure of the Khedive's good faith in eradicating the slave trade, as well as British officials and local traders in Aden who saw Egypt's arrival on the Somali coast as detrimental to existing commercial relationships.[131] Not the least of Ismail's opponents was the influential British consul in Zanzibar, John Kirk, who forcefully took up the cause of Sultan Barghash. His convincing opposition to the McKillop expedition did not, however, have a significant impact on London before the authorities there had issued their request that Ismail drop his project.[132]

The Egyptian forces actually did not complete their evacuation from East Africa until early 1876 since both McKillop and Chaillé-Long were down with malaria. Once in Egypt again, the latter recovered and then, in June 1876, began a six-month leave in Europe and in the United States. Resuming his duties in late 1876, he found little to do. There were no more exciting assignments for Ismail's Americans, a situation related to the depressed state of Egyptian finances. The Khedive's extravagant operations in the Sudan, Ethiopia,[133] and East Africa entailed enormous expense. His government had become deeply indebted to European bondholders, thus creating a crisis that would lead to Ismail's removal in 1879. Egypt's financial problems, therefore, necessitated a drastic reduction in programs. The Americans were not the only government personnel affected. But Chaillé-Long and others attributed their idleness to General Stone. Apparently referring to Stone's alleged excessive loyalty to Ismail, he regretted that the general "had forgotten what it was to be an American."[134] What certainly heightened their vexation was the absence of paychecks for several months. Fed up with the whole Egyptian scene, Chaillé-Long resigned from the Khedive's army and returned to the United States. When back in New York in August 1877, he had little but contempt for the Egyptian administration. Stone, he charged, was an incompetent imbecile and Ismail, "like all Orientals, too susceptible to flattery."[135]

Settling in New York again, this soldier-explorer must have viewed Western urban life as both stimulating and disappointing. He found work as chief clerk of police courts in the metropolis, a dull occupation for the intrepid traveler of untamed Africa. This was still a disciplined, ambitious man, though; his spare time he devoted to the study of law. By the time his four-year appointment in the courts expired in 1881, he had finished Columbia University Law School. Probably unable to find an attractive position in New York, he chose to use his legal training abroad. Despite his recent displeasure with the situation in Cairo, Chaillé-Long allowed Egypt to beckon him once more. He went back to the scene of his long service in uniform and there practiced law in the Mixed Courts of Cairo and Alexandria. Conceived in 1867 by Nubar Pasha, Ismail's able foreign minister, these were tribunals employing both European and Egyptian judges in cases involving foreigners, and were an attempt to placate Western interests while maintaining some check on Europeans' exploitation of capitulatory treaty rights and certain Egyptian customs that had reached a scandalous level.[136] They were opened in 1876.

Ismail, having offended the European powers by his reckless spending and failure to check a growing opposition movement in the army, had been removed from the throne through European influence in June 1879. His son Tewfik, considered easily manipulable, had been elevated to Khedive by British and French intrigue. Egypt's humiliation by Europeans, its economic woes and austerity measures forced on Tewfik's government had aroused Egyptian nationalists led by Colonel Ahmed Arabi. This officer, organizing certain army elements, instigated a movement in 1879 that aimed at reversing the alarming European encroachment on Egyptian sovereignty. Growing pressures from various disgruntled groups in the country and the Khedive's inability to keep foreign interests at bay, led to the Arabi revolt in 1881–82. As the rebel demands grew, along with their popularity, the European powers, fearing that the foreign debt might be repudiated, were aghast.

Colonel Arabi and his nationalist colleagues took control of the government in Cairo in late 1881, the Khedive unable to resist them. Radical elements among the Egyptian populace, troubled as always by poverty and hopelessness, were encouraged by the nationalist agitation and, in some parts of lower Egypt, turned to violence against foreigners. Chaillé-Long found himself in the thick of it. Earlier, Tewfik, fearing for his position in the midst of nationalist intimidation, had General Stone ask the veteran of earlier campaigns if he would recruit and take command of a palace guard that would serve the Khedive in emergencies. Chaillé-Long agreed to try to find experienced, loyal Egyptian and European veterans for this duty but, due to the confused state of Egyptian affairs, this proved difficult. He was engaged in such a task when Arabi's revolt reached its climax.[137]

When massacres of Europeans began in Alexandria in June 1882, all American consular officials there fled to Europe. The State Department, having received appeals from Americans in Egypt, instructed the American consul in Cairo to appoint Chaillé-Long acting consul in Alexandria.[138] From June 15 to July 11, Chaillé-Long opened the doors of the consulate building to provide a refuge for Americans as well as for other desperate foreigners in the city. Many Europeans had fled from violence elsewhere in Egypt, hoping to find safety in the port of Alexandria where foreign warships were in the harbor. It was estimated that fourteen thousand Christians had left the country and thousands of others were waiting to go.[139]

When the British government was informed that the Egyptians were installing shore batteries in Alexandria that were intended for use against the British fleet, it tried unsuccessfully to stop the project. The European powers could not agree on a multinational invasion of the country at that point, so the British decided on a naval bombardment of the threatening artillery installations. The Royal Navy's flotilla was augmented by the arrival of iron-clads on May 20, 1882 which, of course, were an additional provocation to Arabi's movement. In addition, there were American, French, and Greek warships—a total of forty at anchor in Alexandria.[140]

The British commander notified Chaillé-Long on July 10 that his shelling would soon begin and that the U.S. official should see that all persons under his protection go aboard the American ships in the harbor.[141] Chaillé-Long managed to get several hundred people to the ships even though many of them were not strictly entitled to American protection.[142] All other foreign consular offices were closed and their personnel accompanied the refugees to the ships. Chaillé-Long, however, kept his consulate open for stragglers despite the rumored threat of an attack on the foreign quarter by Arabi's forces.[143] Finally he left for safety aboard an American vessel.

Early on July 11, the bombardment commenced. This proved to be only the prelude to the British military intervention and takeover of Egypt in August. When the heavy gunnery ceased, there were fires in various parts of the city, due not, in most cases, to naval shelling, which had been restricted to the shore installations, but to the actions of mobs intent upon wreaking vengeance on European property. Chaillé-Long was anxious to reenter the city and do whatever possible to protect the consulate. Since the British commander was not authorized to land any of his men, the American acting consul prevailed upon the American naval commander to assign him a military contingent. Leading one hundred sixty sailors and marines, therefore, he returned to the European quarter on the other side of the harbor and there they tried to put out fires, working through the night of July 13 and into the following day. He discovered that rebel forces were nowhere in sight and encouraged the British and American naval authorities to dispatch more men to the Place du Consuls and to take over their property. Apparently the Americans' brave action served as an example, for British marines also landed a day later, although they did not leave the harbor vicinity.[144]

For a while much of Alexandria was in the hands of rioters and local marauders, including some desert Bedouin who had been attracted to the city by the disturbances. Even the royal palace was sacked.[145] Often blamed later for the lawlessness and destruction of property that occurred, Arabi, who was minister of war and headquartered in Cairo, did not know of the riot until late on July 11. When informed, he took immediate steps to restore order, which was accomplished quickly. Arabi actually did his best to save European lives.[146] The Egyptian army garrisons in Alexandria, however, failed to respond earlier because their commanders were not accustomed to initiating action without orders. And some of the local police were implicated in the mob violence.[147] The American forces certainly helped deter some destruction in the vicinity of their consulate, but Chaillé-Long, often tempted to stretch the truth in his favor, later claimed that his hasty intervention saved Alexandria from ruin.[148] Perhaps he can be forgiven for such exaggeration late in life, for he did demonstrate courage and initiative in the face of serious danger to himself and others for whom he was responsible. He clearly deserved the commendation he received from the American naval commander in Alexandria.[149]

After finishing his emergency duties and notifying the "fugitive" American consuls in Europe that they could now safely return to their Egyptian offices, he gave up his temporary position in August. Chaillé-Long hoped, however, that his exploits in July might get him recommended for a permanent consular appointment in Egypt. When this failed to materialize, he attributed it to the State Department's interest in covering up the poor performance of its agents in Egypt during the troubles; that is, if the consuls were not replaced, he contended, nobody would be encouraged to investigate their records.[150] Nor did he let the matter rest. In a letter to a French contact in 1883, which was quoted at length in the *New York Times*, Chaillé-Long complained that the same U.S. consular officials, neither of them American citizens, were deserting their posts once again in the midst of a cholera epidemic. Certainly, he argued, native-born Americans would make better representatives of their country overseas.[151]

During the remainder of 1882 and part of the next year, Chaillé-Long practiced law in Paris. Beginning in April 1883, he represented clients before the Indemnity Commission in Egypt. This body had been established to determine reimbursement for those who had lost property during the unrest of 1882. Able to draw from his own experience, he must have been an especially effective spokesman for European claimants. This would be his last work in Egypt. Because of the serious cholera problem he was unable to leave the country until September. Back in Paris he was party to an unsuccessful effort to obtain a concession for constructing a subway and elevated railway in the French capital. Finding too few professional opportunities in Europe, he returned to the United States in May 1884. But evidently he was still unable to erase Egypt from his vision, for he tried again to obtain the post of U.S. diplomatic agent to that country. He failed in this, he insisted, because his enemies prevented it. After working for several months on the editorial staff of the *New York Star*, however, the aspiring diplomat was successful in securing a position as consul general and secretary of legation in Korea. He held this appointment from President Grover Cleveland from 1887 to 1889. This Asian experience was the basis for his book on Korea, *La corée ou chösen, la terre du calme* (Paris: Matinal, 1894). From December 1890 to May 1892 the well-traveled American could be found yet once more in Egypt, but this time only as a distinguished visitor accompanied by his wife.

The remainder of his life was devoted largely to literary pursuits, including occasional articles for the Washington *Sunday Star* for a few years, but he continued to see himself as an experienced leader who could still be of use. His animosity toward Britain and its African expansion led him to proffer advice to France in the hope that it would more aggressively resist more British acquisitions. Knowing that the French were envious of the British position on the upper Nile, he approached French officials in early 1894 with the offer to lead two hundred thousand Ethiopians against the Mahdist forces then in control of the Sudan, declaring that such a force, recruited with the Ethiopian king's cooperation, could crush the Sudanese or, if they interfered, the British. This action supposedly would result in the Sudan becoming a French protectorate.[152] When the unrealistic proposal was rejected at the Quai d'Orsay, he continued in vain to push it before a French colonial group. Still not content to abandon his desire to taste military action again, he offered his services to the American army when the war with Spain began in 1898, but to no avail.

Of his personal life we know almost nothing. In 1890 he married Marie Hammond of Crown Point, New York, daughter of a congressman from that state, but the union was childless. Chaillé-Long's eventful life came to an end on March 24, 1917 in Virginia Beach, Virginia.

The experiences in Africa while in Egyptian service represented the highlights of his interesting career. And in the years after those adventures, Chaillé-Long assiduously guarded his record, responding to the least slight as well as major detractions. He produced numerous articles in scientific and popular journals, in both English and French, and was the author of seven books, five of which dealt with Africa. In most of these publications, besides the expected emphasis on his own accomplishments, the reader will find some repetitive themes. No one was to forget, for instance, that this venturesome American had discovered one of the lakes connected with the Nile sources. Shortly after reporting his Uganda mission he was unfairly accused of "manufacturing . . . secrets . . . to make his adventures the more marvelous."[153] Some writers credited others with finding the lake.[154] These early attacks on his credibility seem to have put him permanently on the defensive. He imagined sinister plots by his rivals to deny the truth of his findings.

Sir Richard Burton, himself one of the principals in a long controversy over the true main source of the Nile, encouraged the American to believe that Speke's erstwhile colleague, J. A. Grant, had encouraged others to ignore Chaillé-Long's work.[155] Undoubtedly more important, however, was Henry Morton Stanley's failure to recognize his contribution to discovery. Stanley knew of Chaillé-Long's visit to Uganda in 1874 but nowhere in his published work or in public statements did the acclaimed explorer acknowledge the other's trip through the portion of the Nile not previously seen by outsiders or his discovery of the shallow lake north of Lake Victoria. Given Stanley's fame and the great popularity of his books, this must have troubled Chaillé-Long acutely. Harry Johnston, at the time an officer of the Royal Geographical Society, confided to Chaillé-Long that Stanley was a leader in casting doubt on his discovery and creating ill-feeling toward him among the society's members.[156] It should not be surprising, therefore, that Chaillé-Long's subsequent references to Stanley were not complimentary.[157]

What was especially irritating was the geographical world's treatment of "his" lake. Although Chaillé-Long named his discovery "Lake Hussein," the Khedive preferred to call it "Ibrahim" and the loyal American officer accepted that name. That the lake today is called "Kioga" is probably explained by Gordon's influence. The latter, for a time unaware of Chaillé-Long's strong feelings on the subject, thought that geographical place names should be indigenous ones, those used by the local people. Thus he called it "Cojoa" or "Coja" and many Europeans used that name. Over the years it was gradually refined to "Kioga." Once thus established, the lake was so identified by major cartographers. Although Gordon later apologized to Chaillé-Long for contributing to the confusion,[158] the latter deemed it necessary to submit a series of appeals to geographic associations for corrections. The American Geographical Society, always warmly supportive of his work, complied with his wishes and awarded him a special medal in 1904, the public announcement of which gave him full credit for Lake Ibrahim.[159]

For years he tried to win equal treatment from the Royal Geographical Society, which he considered a more important and influential body, especially with map publishers. He even appealed to King Edward VII, a patron of the society, to intercede for him. Although the prestigious organization could not, it said apologetically, change the lake's name on its maps, seeing that "Kioga" had been in use for so long, it did agree to put the name "Ibrahim" in brackets. Then in 1907, George Goldie, president of the society, informed Chaillé-Long that his cause was a worthy one and that all maps produced by the society henceforth would designate the lake in question as "Ibrahim."[160] That action did not settle the dispute, however; the commonly accepted name of the lake throughout the world is "Kioga." And even though Chaillé-Long could go to his grave feeling somewhat vindicated on this issue, his name tended to become obscured in later commentary about the Nile sources. In one modern account of the exploration era, all those who traveled and mapped the route between Lakes Albert and Victoria are mentioned except Chaillé-Long.[161]

Another ever-present theme in Chaillé-Long's writing is the nefarious influence of Great Britain. Certainly the British swaggered through the period of Africa's partition carrying a heavy stick, but the readers of his books and articles get the impression that "Perfidious Albion" lurked behind every bush he passed. His conspiracy theory was first inspired by the belief that the British opposed his appointment as Gordon's chief of staff.[162] Then he became convinced that Stanley's expedition of 1874–77 that took him to Uganda was the brainchild of the British Foreign Office, which could never forgive Egypt's earlier advantage there and "coveted the treaty by which Mutesa recognized Uganda and the Nile Basin as Egyptian territory."[163] The ill-fated expedition of McKillop and himself to East Africa was turned back, he believed unreservedly, by the influence of the British agent John Kirk at Zanzibar and London's pressure on Gordon not to obey the Khedive's orders to link up with the coastal base. And his own failure to obtain a permanent American diplomatic post he attributed in part to British opposition to such an appointment.[164] Finally, he suggested to another writer that even the naming of his lake was due to the British desire, once they had assumed control of Egypt, not to be reminded of Egyptian precedence on the Upper Nile. Only in the case of Lake Ibrahim, he pointed out, was the name of the lake associated with the Nile sources changed from that established or endorsed by its discoverer.[165] Britain, in its plan for a Cape-to-Cairo African empire, was ready to run over individuals and nations, either African or European, to attain its goal. Chaillé-Long saw himself as merely one of many who had been unfairly discredited and denied for getting in the way of the British steamroller.

Probably the meanest of Chaillé-Long's literary attacks was that on Gordon. The lionized Englishman never publicly criticized his American chief of staff, but in private correspondence published after his death, Gordon censured him.[166] Chaillé-Long never forgave his former superior and those responsible for making such opinion public. He sought to discredit Gordon at every opportunity. As far as he could, the petty, embittered Chaillé-Long dragged the "martyr of Khartoum" off his pedestal, charging him with inadequate leadership, poor judgment, and excessive ambition. The widely admired hero was said to be unsuccessful in human relations with both Africans and Europeans.[167] Gordon was quoted as saying, "I cannot live peacefully with anyone I cannot kick."[168] The former governor-general of the Sudan's policies, judged Chaillé-Long, were ill-advised and not only exacerbated existing problems, but were instrumental in bringing about the rise of the Mahdi, a phenomenon that caused Gordon's death.[169] This was strong condemnation, the like of which was heard from no other quarter. Of all the disparaging things he said, none was more provocative than his report that Gordon regularly consumed brandy. Clearly, Chaillé-Long knew what he was doing; it was a carefully calculated attempt to mar the image of a man whose honored reputation he had come to resent bitterly. Gordon's defenders questioned his detractor's veracity and in general overreacted to what was only a description of a man oppressed by his surroundings using alcohol for medicinal purposes, not a charge of drunkenness. Gordon's reputation suffered little in any case, whereas the affair provided damning testimony to his former associate's vindictiveness.

Having spent more than a few years in several parts of Africa, Chaillé-Long had ample opportunity to observe and assess the continent's peoples and their cultures. His opinions reflect the man and his time, views not much different from those of most white men in Africa during the nineteenth century. But they were extremely narrow views. He saw most blacks as miserable savages, made so to some extent by their wretched environment. Echoing the judgment of Samuel Baker, he found that the African "does right only when he has not the power to do wrong."[170] Those "weak and inoffensive" travelers who trusted the blacks to do otherwise were, he complained, almost criminally wrong because that approach would only encourage the worst behavior.[171] Duplicity and treachery were said to be the natural tendency of Africa's people. Whole populations, he added, were averse to sustained labor and thus were held back economically.[172]

Chaillé-Long observed nothing indicating that the black African had any idea of a supreme being, perhaps because to him Africa was a place "accursed of God."[173] Unable or unwilling to look beyond the surface of cultures he could not easily understand after a casual glance, he declared with a pathetic certainty that Africans "had no tradition, no past."[174] Later anthropologists and other scholars would find among people he contacted rich cultures that contradicted practically everything Chaillé-Long reported about them. But, then, this can be said about the majority of European commentators of the nineteenth century. His tendency to dwell on what he interpreted as negative features of African life earned him some praise among those reviewers who were unreceptive to commentary from explorers and others who found redeeming qualities where, in these critics' opinions, they did not exist.[175]

Was there any hope, as Chaillé-Long saw it, for the future of African people? He prided himself in his rigid conviction on this matter, asserting that "I am one of those who believe in that limited point to which the Negro only [sic] can go."[176] Doubtless his position was molded, at least in part, by his Maryland experience. His family had owned slaves and he doubted that the latter could have been happier with emancipation.[177] If he could hold such thoughts about American ex-slaves, it should not be unexpected that he would be pessimistic about Africans' potential.

As was the case with so many other whites who visited Africa of his day, Chaillé-Long did differentiate to some extent when rating Africans. The Egyptians, of course, were not considered African; they were, despite the lethargy of the peasants, superior to blacks. In his estimation Egyptians were not only capable but the most appropriate ones for exploring and developing the lands of the blacks.[178] Among the blacks themselves, the Nubians, that is, northern Sudanese who had long been in contact with "superior" Egyptian Caucasians, if carefully selected and disciplined, could become an important civilizing element in the south. And some of the peoples he met near the Great Lakes showed special qualities that suggested they were definitely more advanced than most other blacks. They, he conceded, might be capable of higher development. Apparently, then, Chaillé-Long thought there was some possibility of uplifting blacks to a limited extent. Islam had proven the best religion for them and could be extended further among black populations, preferably by converted people such as the Nubians. Chaillé-Long's portrayal of the people he encountered and their prospects was, therefore, definitely not a flattering one. It would, along with so many others of a similar ilk, play a part in the miseducation of a reading public that would take generations to overcome.

As an author he did not receive any serious critical acclaim or much popular attention. His first book, however, provides the reader with as much vicarious excitement as most other works of the genre. *Central Africa* contains passages that betray the author's intention to magnify the import of his deeds, yet this was not unusual among his peers who produced such a stream of exploration and what might be called "soldiering for some prince" literature. *The Three Prophets* (1884) was primarily a vehicle for him to show Gordon in a bad light by emphasizing the latter's preoccupation with religion rather than with transforming Equatoria. The book drew little attention although it was an important influence on a few others who denigrated Gordon.[179] His memoir, *My Life on Four Continents*, is interesting, albeit excessively long. Although, as already noted, replete with inaccuracies, it still serves as the most comprehensive record of his career if read with caution.

Chaillé-Long is seldom remembered, and when his name does come into consideration it is most commonly in connection with his slander of Gordon. This is unfortunate, for his career, though admittedly not of major importance, is quite worthy of attention. He served Egypt in some significant capacities, and, at least until his final year as a soldier of the Khedive, was a loyal supporter of the Cairo government. To him, Egypt under Ismail was a force for advancing civilization, progress, and development. Both in Uganda and in western Equatoria he performed well, relaying to his employer important intelligence. The embassy to Mutesa, in particular, was a grueling challenge which, if not so long and hazardous as some better-known African explorations, nevertheless required in addition to physical stamina, great courage, and resourcefulness. The discovery of Lake Kioga helped to solve the question of the source of the Nile. Its significance does not match that of Baker's or Speke's contributions, but it is certainly noteworthy. Chaillé-Long was an instrument of Egyptian expansionism on the eve of the European colonial partition and his activities comprise a fascinating story.

4
Henry Shelton Sanford: A Yankee in the Colonial Opening of the Congo

In the diplomatic history of the partition of Africa one of the least understood participants is Henry Shelton Sanford. This American was deeply involved in the empire-building machinations of Leopold II, King of the Belgians, from 1877 until he became disenchanted with that monarch in the late 1880s. In this period he performed valuable services which helped to bring into existence that anomaly of colonialism in Africa, the Congo Independent State. Yet his various Africa-related activities and the motives that inspired them went beyond mere usefulness to a European ruler. Since his papers were cataloged in 1960, new interest has been directed to Sanford, and these, along with other materials, make possible a clarification and reassessment of his role.[1]

Born in Derby, Connecticut, in 1823, Sanford descended from a long line of New England forbears. His father, Nehemiah Curtis Sanford, was a prominent industrialist and land speculator who also served in the Connecticut legislature.[2] Following graduation from a private academy in 1839, Henry attended Washington (now Trinity) College in Hartford. Before finishing his second year there, he had to withdraw due to eye problems.[3] After his father's death about the same time, Sanford began to speculate in Western lands and invested in several Western railroads.[4] These ventures continued for many years. It seems that early in life he was strongly attracted to the investment opportunities in underdeveloped territories, the western and later the southern United States first capturing his imagination. But such business did not keep him in the country. In 1841 he made the first of many trips to Europe. These visits soon became a regular part of his life; indeed, he was to spend much of his time on the Continent.

While still relatively young, Sanford gained valuable diplomatic experience. Through the influence of a family friend who was the newly appointed U.S. minister to Russia, he was to serve as an

Henry Shelton Sanford (*Courtesy of the Henry Shelton Sanford Memorial Library and Museum, Sanford, Florida*).

attaché in the St. Petersburg legation in 1847. After six months there, Sanford used another connection to obtain the position of acting secretary of legation in Frankfurt, Germany. During his stay in Germany he studied law at the University of Heidelberg, receiving his doctor of laws degree in 1849. Now definitely drawn to a diplomatic career, Sanford enlisted the backing of his relatives and friends for a concerted effort to obtain a significant post. He was subsequently appointed secretary to the Paris legation in August 1849, where he could do more meaningful work. Upon the election of Zachary Taylor to the presidency in 1853, the American minister to France resigned. Until his successor arrived, Sanford advanced to the temporary rank of *Chargé d'affaires* and headed the legation. During that eight months of heightened status and responsibility, Sanford negotiated the first Franco-American postal convention. Then, in April 1854, he submitted his own resignation and made his way back to the United States.[5]

His inherited fortune enabled Sanford to mingle with European aristocrats, and their way of life apparently undermined his democratic Yankee ideals. His mother, disgusted with his ostentatious life abroad, upbraided him for hypocritically denouncing the idea of aristocracy while simultaneously aping that class.[6] Sanford's "un-American" demeanor provoked one of his countrymen visiting Paris to report his unfavorable image to President Pierce.[7] That Sanford had indeed developed a great admiration for Europe's royalty and upper class was to become more obvious in his later relationship with the Belgian king. In fact, this enamoration would help explain his naive credulity while working with that monarch.

During the 1850s Sanford became involved in Latin American affairs, representing his uncle in a contest with the Venezuelan government over offshore guano deposits and serving as agent for U.S. citizens in railroad negotiations with Columbian and Honduran authorities.[8] Besides adding to his income, these experiences fostered definite views about American foreign policy. He saw a need for greater U.S. commercial activity if it were not to be completely outstripped by European interests. Following this reasoning Sanford advised Washington to consider annexation of Latin American territory to insure access to commercial opportunities.[9] Here he was manifesting attitudes that strongly influenced his later philosophy concerning American enterprise in the Congo.

Time spent abroad did not prevent Sanford from cultivating important friendships at home. These contacts, including such key Republican leaders as Thurlow Weed and William H. Seward, were instrumental in winning him a diplomatic appointment from the newly elected President Lincoln in 1860. As minister to Belgium Sanford was an able officer, but he became a controversial figure mainly because of his special responsibilities as supervisor of Federal Secret Service in Europe and fiscal agent in charge of large sums. Despite some indiscreet actions in his zealous effort to serve the Union's cause while obstructing the Confederacy's, Sanford's multifaceted work made him Washington's most useful representative in Europe during the Civil War.[10] The Brussels post was his until 1869.[11] During this period he became acquainted with the Belgian king, Leopold, II, who was to become an important figure in Sanford's subsequent career.

Returning to the United States in 1870, but also maintaining a residence in Belgium, he continued with various business speculations. He acquired land in Florida and established the first sizable commercial orange groves in the state. The town of Sanford emerged in 1872. This land and its development became the owner's paramount interest during the 1870s. It led to his involvement in state politics where he failed in his attempts to become a Republican party leader so that he could represent Florida in the U.S. Senate. Sanford saw the Negro problem as the principal dilemma in Southern politics and unsuccessfully tried to divorce Republicanism from its black identification. It was in this context that he began to accept Negro emigration as a panacea.[12]

Generally, Sanford proved less than successful with business and investments. In the earlier years, when he based his financial position upon solid investments inherited from his father and followed the practical advice of shrewd relatives and friends, he remained wealthy and secure. But when projects promising quick returns increasingly enticed him, reverses followed. Sanford's fortune in the 1870s, based upon stock and bond holdings and salaries from offices in several companies, stood at $922,500.[13] This was seriously altered by the depression of 1873, as his securities plummeted and as investment income declined. Desperation bred at this time impelled Sanford to seek other schemes which would restore his financial footing. When mining, railroad, sugar, and marketing promotions failed in turn, he was compelled to liquidate his better holdings and stood in rather desperate straits by the late 1870s.[14] This being the situation, it is not unreasonable to suggest that when his friend Leopold described a grandiose African project, Sanford sensed possible opportunities for himself, not least of which was the chance, perhaps, to make a lucrative investment underwritten by a royal fortune. But such things obviously could materialize only after much exploration and development. In Africa Sanford eventually would seek a means to regain his lost affluence yet, clearly, he was not one to be driven primarily by the prospect of financial gain. He needed an inspirational cause, such as he had served in the Union during the American Civil War, to absorb his idealism, restless energy and driving ambition. This, too, he found in Africa.

After considering such areas as China, Formosa, Indo-China, the Philippines, and Argentina, the King of the Belgians finally decided on Africa as the most promising field for his imperialistic designs.[15] His first overt move was the summoning of a "geographical" conference in September 1876. This gathering in Brussels attracted twenty-eight delegates, including explorers, geographers, and others representing seven countries. Although no Americans were present,[16] invitations had been extended to Judge Charles P. Daly, president of the American Geographical Society (AGS) and John H. B. Latrobe, president of the American Colonization Society (ACS).[17] Ostensibly the king's objective in calling together these experts was to discuss means of civilizing Africa. This could be viewed as a genuine response to the growing humanitarian interest in the continent arising from the work and writings of an increasing number of explorers and missionaries. By calculated moves, however, Leopold also made the conference serve his private ambitions, the aims of which were not pre-dominately humanitarian.

In addition to discussing ways of establishing bases of operations for the proposed philanthropic work, the delegates founded an international committee and provided for national organizations to collaborate with it. Thus there appeared the Association internationale pour l'exploration et civilization d'Afrique central, usually known as the Association internationale Africaine (AIA). This was headed by an International Commission, which in turn deferred to an Executive Committee. Leopold accepted the presidency of the latter.[18]

Sanford probably became interested in this African project soon after it was announced, but his public involvement was somewhat delayed.[19] There was support in the United States for the declared objectives of the AIA and, shortly after the Brussel's conference, steps were taken to establish an American committee to support the association. Leopold had been disappointed by the absence of American representatives at the 1876 conference and was determined to involve influential parties in the United States thereafter. Particularly important to him was anticipated financial backing for his project from American philanthropists. The Belgian minister to

Washington was kept busy advancing Leopold's ideas to Daly and Latrobe. Both of them were won over by the humanitarian aspects stressed in the Belgian monarch's effective appeals and they in turn recruited other supporters.[20] A group of interested persons, including some missionaries, philanthropists, and two explorers with African experience, one of whom was Paul Du Chaillu, met at the AGS's New York office on May 8, 1877, where they established the American Committee of the International Commission of Brussels.[21] This decision was formalized and other matters concerning the emergent organization were attended to later in the month at the residence of William Tracy, an AGS officer who was closely associated with the new project.[22] The responsibility for selecting persons to represent the American committee at the pending AIA meeting in Brussels fell to Judge Daly, and he chose for that mission Henry M. Schieffelin and Sanford. The latter's appointment as a delegate suggests that he and Leopold were already working together on the king's carefully conceived plans. Sanford had no experience even remotely connected with Africa, nor did he hold any position in an appropriate organization that would justify his appointment. He once confessed that he knew almost nothing about Africa at the time. Indeed, it was due to Sanford's ignorance of Africa that Schieffelin, whose Africa-related experience included service as Liberia's *chargé d'affaires* in Washington, was named as a fellow delegate to assist him.[23] Some influence, it would seem, was exerted in his behalf so that he could return to Brussels as the official representative of the American committee.

The International Commission of the Association held its first and only meeting on June 21–22, 1877. Its main function was to implement the program formulated the previous year. Accordingly, it authorized expeditions that were to set out from the east coast into the interior for the establishment of "hospitable and scientific posts," and made a change in its Executive Committee.[24] Since Sir Bartle Frere, representing the English-speaking community in that body, resigned early in 1877 to accept the governorship of the Cape Colony, the conference unanimously selected Sanford to succeed him. No British delegates had come to Brussels, leaving Sanford as the sole Anglo-Saxon there.[25] "Regretting that some more competent and experienced American was not there to bear the honor, he nevertheless felt he should not decline.[26] One of the topics debated at the conference was the need of the AIA to have a flag. When the idea was accepted, various flags were considered, including the Belgian national standard. But Leopold immediately saw the impropriety of using his country's flag for his African operations. The design eventually adopted was that of a single gold star set in a blue field. This, it has been suggested, was proposed by Sanford.[27]

The king was quite pleased with the American's contribution to his second international meeting. Sanford already was close to Leopold but did not realize at this stage that the primary impulsion behind the African scheme was the king's desire for private gain and the possible opportunity to give his reluctant countrymen a colonial foothold. The American was not privy to all plans, and, like so many others at the time, he thought Leopold was foremost a philanthropist. While Sanford himself was not oblivious of the commercial potential of Africa, the evidence indicates that he was then more concerned with the humanitarian character of the operation.

While the king was considering how he might best turn his African operations in a potentially commercial direction, he made the acquaintance of another person who would become a key figure in his enterprise. This was the Welsh-American explorer, Henry Morton Stanley,[28] whose long expedition of 1874–77 had culminated in his tracing the Congo River to its mouth. His achievement had excited all those interested in the Dark Continent—and none more than Leopold, whose attention already had been drawn to Central Africa by the travels of Verney Lovett Cameron in 1873–75.[29] The royal promoter determined to concentrate his efforts to secure an African territory in the Congo region, and who more appropriate to undertake Leopold's business there than Stanley? Sanford was now put to work as the king's principal recruiter. Preliminary steps included Sanford's contacts with Stanley's employer, James Gordon Bennett, publisher of the *New York Herald*, from whom he elicited information on the explorer's economy, prudence, and reliability.[30] Accompanied by Baron Jules Greindl, Leopold's private secretary, he met Stanley upon the latter's return to Europe and endeavored to enlist him in the AIA's work.[31] Not initially successful in that, he remained in touch with Stanley, occasionally visiting him in England, until the two became friendly. Thus Sanford could keep before him the advantages of working for Leopold's organization. After failing to interest British officials in his Congo intelligence and realizing that London was not ready to follow his advice and intervene directly in Central Africa, Stanley finally succumbed to Sanford's persistence and agreed to join the king's service.

When Stanley first visited the Belgian royal palace in June 1878, he made a very favorable impression on his host. And he brought with him certain ideas about the commercial development of the Congo that inspired the king to organize a new venture.[32] By 1878 the AIA had ceased to exist as an entity apart from Leopold himself—he, in fact, was the association. The national committees associated with it had for the most part disappeared or failed to maintain their links with Brussels. Yet Leopold kept alive the fiction of a working international organization representing various interests and supported by national committees. It proved to be useful front for his own plans.[33] It was now time, the king decided, to strike out on a somewhat different path. By the end of the year, he founded the Comité d'études du Haut-Congo, which was intended to prepare the way for a major undertaking later by attracting capital. In addition to the king, it included an international group of bankers and merchant-investors committed to extending commerce and industry on the Congo by means of study and exploration.[34]

Sanford argued that Leopold should eschew the comité's commercial orientation until some of the laudable humanitarian objectives of the original association were achieved. While there was nothing wrong with the business aspect, he thought, it could follow later, after more fundamental work, and it need not be so identified with the royal name.[35] When the Dutch firm (Afrikaansche Handelsvereeniging) participating heavily in the comité fell into financial difficulties,[36] which in turn threatened the solvency of the latter, Sanford urged Leopold to capitalize on the situation by buying out all the subscribers. This, he argued, would prevent the king from being exploited by them and would also enable Leopold to restore to the Congo enterprise the purely philanthropic character it initially had.[37]

His statements at this time strongly suggest that Sanford was not yet fully apprised of the king's real intentions and that he believed Leopold, actually the promoter, to have been pushed into the comité by unscrupulous investors.[38] Undoubtedly, Sanford was keenly aware of the danger to the king's international image from his identification with self-centered business interests. He appreciated, furthermore, the political implication of the Congo expeditions amid the growing tangle of European states' territorial claims in Central Africa and foresaw that bold steps eventually might be necessary, at which time operations should be unencumbered by commercial considerations. When Leopold finally dissolved the comité in November 1879, it was not exactly for the reasons suggested by Sanford, but in order that the king would be free to impose a political character upon the Congo project.[39]

In August 1879 Stanley was back in the Congo, ostensibly serving the then nearly defunct comité but actually in Leopold's personal employ, where he established stations, built a system of communications, and negotiated treaties with African chiefs along the southern bank of the great river that gave the Belgian monarch monopoly rights of various kinds. These activities, as will be shown below, did much to focus attention on the region and to provoke the suspicion and envy of several European states. However, while Stanley was in Europe, Leopold's preoccupation during 1878 with the comité's problems delayed the explorer's departure for some months. When Stanley became restless, it was Sanford who maintained close ties with him,[40] all the while obtaining from him valuable information for Leopold's planning.[41] Their relationship was important not only because it contributed toward the king's success, but also for how it affected Sanford's attitudes. The latter came to depend upon Stanley for knowledge of Congo conditions. More important, he became infected with Stanley's optimistic appraisals of the area's potential. The explorer's influence on him is obvious in various positions Sanford took when advising Leopold and also in his later propagandizing in the United States.

Sanford wanted the United States to support the AIA's work. It was not only a question of his belief that the organization's humanitarian aims deserved the sympathy and cooperation of all the powers, but also his vision of ultimately great commercial opportunities for Americans in the Congo. Moreover, international complications were developing that required the AIA to seek aid and comfort from every quarter. As early as 1879 Sanford began his campaign to interest Washington in the Congo, requesting the secretary of state to instruct U.S. warships to insure that Portuguese claims to the Congo did not interfere with American rights there.[42] Consequently, the Navy Department ordered the cruiser *USS Ticonderoga* to visit the Congo and report on conditions there.[43] In the next presidential administration, that of James R. Garfield, Sanford successfully cultivated the friendship of Secretary of State James G. Blaine, whom he likewise requested to declare American opposition to threatened European military occupation of the Congo. Evidently Blaine was unwilling to take such moves at that time, but Sanford kept the issue before him so long as the former remained at the State Department.[44] Since he considered pressure from the American business world to be a decisive factor in influencing official policies, Sanford began to exploit his contacts to marshal support from that corner for Leopold's association. By 1878 he was concentrating on New York interests, particularly the city's Chamber of Commerce, which he addressed the following year.[45] All of these moves were only preliminaries, however; the major effort was forthcoming.

In 1883 it was decided in Brussels to seek U.S. recognition of the AIA's flag. Sanford already had mentioned such action to President Arthur in the previous year, and it is probable that he was most responsible for selling the plan to Leopold's cabal.[46] Fears of possible French or Portuguese maneuvers against the AIA encouraged these efforts to secure official American support.[47] Actually it was to be part of a two-pronged attack, as it was believed that France also might be induced to grant early recognition. Negotiations with Paris began about the same time as Sanford's mission.

Arriving in the United States on November 27, with full authority to negotiate in the king's name, Sanford's plan was to influence President Arthur, the press, the New York Chamber of Commerce, and the AGS—all having been contacted by him previously.[48] Success soon was realized, as Arthur mentioned support of Congo neutrality in his annual message to Congress only a few weeks after Sanford's return.[49] The generally cautious and conservative Secretary of State Frederick T. Frelinghuysen, was particularly interested in Africa and therefore he too gradually allowed himself to become more cooperative with Sanford than his predecessors had been. The secretary, in fact, was completely won over to Leopold's cause by Sanford's apparently authoritative and persuasive presentations.[50] As far as the press was concerned, Sanford could count on the *New York Herald*, Stanley's earlier employer, which came out for "friendly recognition of the Association's flag in late 1883,"[51] and the *New York Times*, also supporting that policy early the next year.[52] Sanford then managed to have the New York Chamber of Commerce, two influential members of which, Abiel A. and Seth Low, were longtime friends, pass a resolution endorsing recognition that was sent to President Arthur.[53]

As important as these steps were, Sanford's most decisive collaboration was that with Sen. John T. Morgan of Alabama, an avowed imperialist and chairman of the Senate's prominent Foreign Relations Committee. The two shared a belief in America's need for commercial expansion and, related to this, they agreed that Africa could hold the key to the country's color problem. Both men held strong hopes, definitely reminiscent of those identified with the earlier American colonization movement's attitude toward Liberia, that the Congo would attract unassimilable blacks who would in turn be instrumental in expanding trade between their "motherland" and the United States. In addition, they were endeavoring to eliminate race from Southern politics.[54] They were not alone, of course, in hoping that the Congo would draw off black Americans. Senator R. L. Gibson of Louisiana, among others, supported recognition of the Congo flag in the belief that, if handled correctly, the blacks voluntarily would return en masse to Africa since, as he later put it, "being around whites reminded them of their former slavery."[55] Morgan's involvement resulted in his committee obtaining a Senate resolution endorsing U.S. recognition of the AIA's flag.[56] This action, more than anything else, cleared the way for Frelinghugsen to implement that policy on April 22, 1884, when he and Sanford signed the formal declaration of recognition.

The diplomatic blitz employed by Sanford was not conducted solely in commercial centers or in the noisy halls of Capitol Hill. He had a reputation on both sides of the Atlantic as one who hosted the finest dinner parties. This "gastronomic diplomacy," as it was called,[57] upon which Sanford set great store, was put to good use in winning over important congressmen.[58] Mrs. Sanford joined her husband in Washington in early 1884, adding her charm as hostess during the long party season. Their home, the Everett mansion on G. Street, was the scene of many festive gatherings at which various dignitaries found the conversation turning about the Congo and the question of American recognition of the AIC. John Latrobe, who later recalled such pleasant evenings, was a frequent guest of the Sanfords, his experience with Liberia being used to impress government figures.[59]

While engaged in convincing American officials of the AIA's merits and justifying its recognition, Sanford admittedly disseminated Leopold's propaganda, including such claims that association forces were creating a network of native states that eventually would become self-governing on the order of Liberia. For this he has been labeled unscrupulous,[60] but an examination of his papers indicates that he actually believed most of the king's claims and was not acting with duplicity. Leopold was able to delude his associates by not clearly outlining his actual intentions.[61] While Sanford must have had doubts about specific details and the implementation of certain announced royal policies, he had no reason to believe that a system of native protectorates could not be established, which at some future point, after Western civilization prevailed, would give way to self-governing states. After all, Liberia needed considerable "supervision" before it achieved independence. Indeed, its unimpressive record since independence would have suggested longer tutelage for any other prospective native "free states." If during the period of white overrule the Congo was opened to trade and commercial profits followed, this was, according to the ethics of the period, perfectly consistent with the march of progress and the betterment of backward peoples. As for the apparent contradiction between Leopold's promises of free trade and the exclusive treaties his agents negotiated with Congolese chiefs, Sanford understood such tactics to be necessary in order to forestall protectionist powers such as Portugal or France from gaining the upper hand and preempting the philanthropic association. Sanford accepted the king's assurances and convinced others that neither taxes nor customs duties would be introduced.[62]

It has passed with little notice that the recognition declaration, probably composed in part if not entirely by Sanford, contained the following paragraphs:

> That the said Association and the said States [native states under association auspices] have resolved to levy no customhouse duties upon goods or articles of merchandise imported into their territories or brought by the route which has been constructed around the Congo cataracts; this they have done with a view of enabling commerce to penetrate in Equatorial Africa.
>
> That they guarantee to foreigners settling in their territories the right to purchase, sell or lease, lands and buildings situated therein, to establish commercial houses and to there carry on trade upon the sole condition that they shall obey the laws. They pledge themselves, moreover, never to grant to the citizens of one nation any advantages without immediately extending the same to the citizens of all other nations.[63]

Sanford did not take its contents lightly. It was his desire to see American merchants take advantage of the rights and privileges thus afforded them. Undoubtedly his personal ambition was to ultimately exploit these widened commercial opportunities in some fashion, but he was most concerned with what he saw as a matter of national interest.

With Leopold's main objective in Washington now realized, Sanford did not rest. Along with the like-minded Morgan he strove further to influence official policy so that the United States' entente with the association would be meaningful. In addition to a consular appointment, they urged that an investigatory commission be ordered to the Congo and, eventually, were to see both in service.[64] Sanford continued campaigning in commercial circles. Utilizing the press, especially the ever-cooperative *New York Herald*,[65] he did his utmost to awaken businessmen to the Congo's potential. New England's largest textile mills were induced to assay the market by sending out cotton and woolen samples.[66] Undaunted by his failure to elicit a greater, continuing response, he kept prodding, always convinced it was only a matter of time before Americans took their place next to Europeans in the Congo trade.[67] These were not the actions of one solely devoted to furthering a European monarch's ambitions.

Sanford's achievement in Washington did much to improve the diplomatic posture of Leopold's association.[68] The king was so pleased with his American associate's diplomacy that he urged him to seek an appointment from Washington as a special envoy to convince the European powers to follow the United States lead in recognizing the association as a state.[69] Such a mission, however, was not considered appropriate by Secretary Frelinghuysen and others.[70] U.S. recognition was followed a day later by a significant treaty that Leopold's agents signed with France. This agreement provided that in case Leopold's association (now known as the Association International du Congo [AIC]) could not continue its work in the Congo—and it was widely assumed that it would soon become insolvent—France would inherit all its territories and treaty rights.[71] This understanding with France was one of Leopold's most brilliant maneuvers; it brought him support in difficult days ahead from those who did not prefer to see a French takeover of the Congo if Leopold's operation were allowed to die.[72] The American treaty obtained by Sanford along with the king's bold stroke in winning the French accord hastened discussions in several capitals, which brought about the Berlin Conference in 1884. This important international assemblage occurred because of the heightening rivalry that developed among the European states as they became more interested in territorial acquisitions in Africa, particularly the Congo area.[73]

Since 1839 France had established claims to territory in Gabon, north of the Congo. In 1878 the French naval officer Savorgnan DeBrazza discovered that the Ogooué River in Gabon could serve as a route to the vast upper Congo system, thus bypassing the series of rapids that obstructed transportation on the lower Congo. Some interested parties in France now saw more potential in Gabon and its hinterland. Suspicious of the Belgian king's inten-

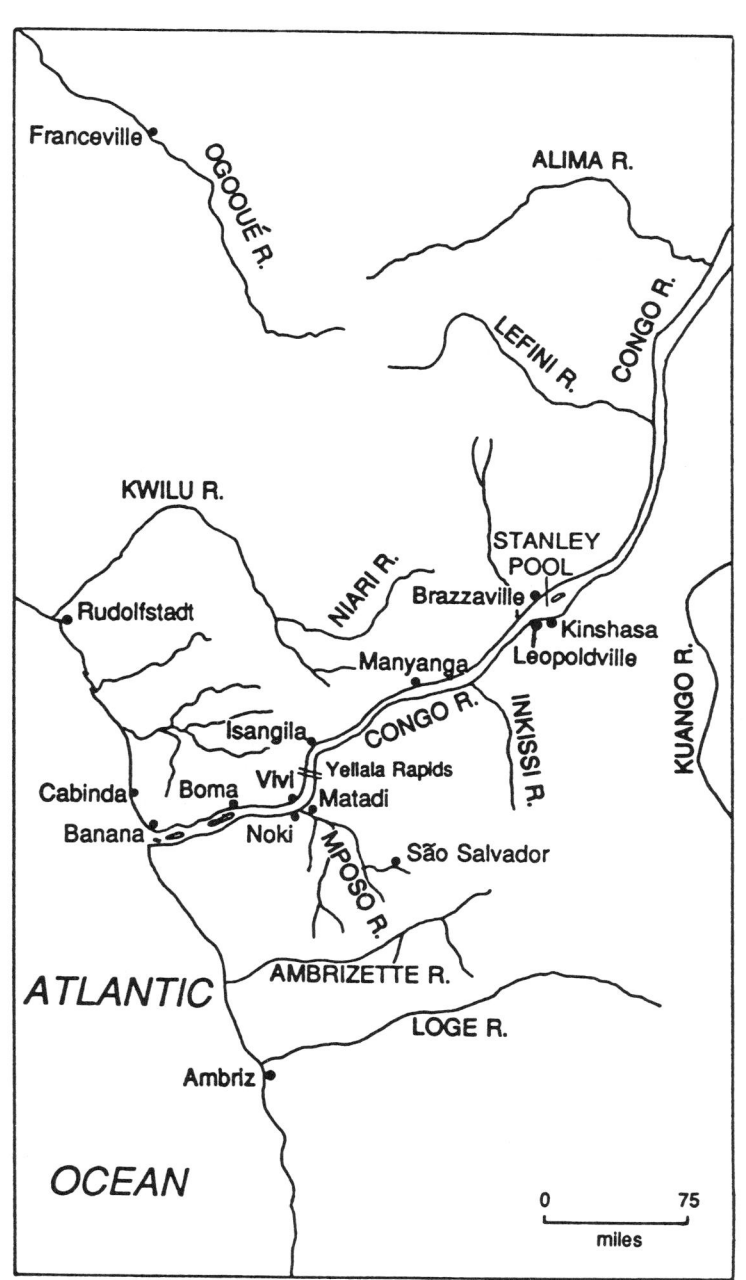

The Lower Congo, 1885.

tions in the Congo, especially after Stanley went to work for him, DeBrazza won official support for another mission up the Ogooué to forestall Leopold's forces from gaining control of the route to the rich upper Congo. By October 1879 he succeeded in reaching the broad, lakelike expanse on the Congo, ultimately known as Stanley-Pool, beyond which the river is navigable for about fifteen hundred miles. There he concluded one of several treaties with chiefs in that vicinity, which provided for French control over territory on the right bank of the greatest waterway in central Africa. Amid much popular enthusiasm these treaties were ratified by the French parliament in 1882. Obviously France was now in the thick of the competition for this important region.

Meanwhile, Portugal was beginning to reassert its long dormant claims to the Congo country that originated in the fifteenth century when Portuguese mariners had pioneered in Europe's contact with the whole of the west coast of Africa. And Lisbon was successful in enlisting British support for her position because London, promised favored treatment by the otherwise protectionist Portuguese, wished to prevent France from acquiring a dominant position that would be disadvantageous to increasing British trade with the Congo. An Anglo-Portuguese Treaty recognizing Portugal's claim to the Congo mouth and calling for Anglo-Portuguese regulation of Congo navigation was signed (but not ratified in Britain) in February 1884.

Finally, Germany became involved. Its imperial chancellor, Otto von Bismarck, sought to improve relations between his country and its recent enemy, France, and at the same time to thwart the policies of Britain which at first did not show proper respect for German's new territorial ambitions in Africa. Both Germany and France wanted to teach Britain a lesson and they took the initiative in calling for a conference to deal with the Congo question. When it met in the German capital from November 1884 to February 1885, the participants, representing the greater and lesser powers of Europe as well as the United States, considered various topics related to European imperialism in Africa, but the Congo was the area receiving most attention. Officially the conference was not to deal with territorial disputes and awards, but since it brought the principal disputants together it provided an excellent opportunity to work out solutions to rival claims even while the formal sessions were devoted to the discussion of other matters.

Sanford was a member of the American delegation to the conference. The principal representative was John A. Kasson,[74] U.S. minister to Germany and friend of Sanford, who had requested that the latter be appointed his associate, explaining to the secretary of state that a man of Sanford's experience would be especially helpful in "those outside preliminary conversations which often shape the actions of the conference in advance."[75] Kasson was another expansionist who favored a more determined American effort to exploit Africa's commercial potential and who was both favorably impressed with the Belgian king and sympathetic with the AIC's aims.[76] Still in league with Leopold, Sanford saw his role in Berlin in terms of doing everything possible to strengthen the association's position. As the latter was not entitled to official representation, Sanford and the Belgian delegation were expected to guard its interests. He clearly used his appointment toward that end and, while doing so, usually could count on the cooperation of his friend, Kasson. This was not considered prejudicial to American interests, for Sanford believed that his countrymen had most to gain by supporting Leopold's announced policies.

Besides advising Kasson on many matters, Sanford's principal work at the conference was his introduction of the so-called Sanford Railway Proposal. This provided that whichever power held the most territory on the lower Congo between Vivi and Stanley Pool when the conference adjourned, should win preferential right to construct and operate a railway around the troublesome cataracts on the lower course of the river.[77] In the Brussels palace it was considered extremely important that no other power should acquire railroad rights.[78] French and Portuguese opposition, however, determined that Sanford's endeavors in this instance would be unfruitful.

Actually it was outside the conference itself that Sanford carried out some of his most significant assignments from Leopold during this period. Early in December 1884, the French suggested to Sanford that the association should seek a private accord with them, and that Paris would be a more appropriate site for discussions.[79] Hard bargaining was anticipated when Leopold dispatched a special mission to the French capital to resolve the thorny territorial dispute, which then blocked agreements at Berlin. In addition to five Belgians,[80] Sanford represented the king in these negotiations. It was the stated opinion of the French ambassador to Brussels that Leopold's lack of confidence in his other emissaries accounted for Sanford's presence, and he advised Paris that the latter was a very important addition to the mission.[81] Leopold considered Sanford a valuable agent for the French discussions because of the latter's French contacts and because he represented the politically neutral and territorially disinterested United States.[82]

The principal territory disputed in Paris was the Niari-Kwilu region north of the Congo, which Stanley's officers had claimed for the association in 1883, before the French explorer DeBrazza could raise the tricolor there. It included three hundred miles of coastline and a river system extending back to the Congo. Leopold would not abandon it to the covetous French without a large indemnity for his outlay.[83] In fact, he let it be known that he was ready to leave the Congo if Paris did not accept his terms. While these negotiations continued, Sanford returned to Berlin where he knew the diplomatic environment to be more favorable for the association's position and he strove to enlist German support in Leopold's favor.[84] When Bismarck declined to oppose France on the issue and it became clear that the French were adamantly opposed to meeting Leopold's demands, Sanford advocated sacrifices by the king in order to secure greater political gains.[85] Once Leopold saw the need to adopt this conciliatory policy, in particular his relinquishment of the Niari-Kwilu territory, combined with French willingness to permit the association to raise a lottery in France in lieu of an indemnity, settlement was possible.[86] This was a giant step and, although territorial arrangements with Portugal remained to be settled,[87] by the end of February 1885, the association had won recognition treaties from all the important powers and thus emerged as the Congo Independent State.[88] This new and most unusual sovereign territory comprised some nine hundred thousand square miles and stretched from the Atlantic to Lake Tanganyika.

The conference culminated with the signing of the Berlin Act which, among other things, provided for a free trade zone in the vast Congo Basin and required the signatory states to work for the advancement of the African people by various means. Clearly, the Berlin assembly did not initiate the colonial partition of Africa but in producing the Congo Independent State and agreeing on a code of rules to prevent conflict among the powers claiming African territory, it certainly gave sanction to the so-called scramble for Africa that had already begun and would continue for some time.[89]

Sanford's role during the Berlin conference was a very significant one. It is reasonable to suggest that without his various contributions Leopold might well have had considerably more difficulty in creating his Congo State. The explorer Stanley later estimated that Sanford's work in Berlin was his most important service to the king.[90] American participation in the conference and his own activities there were, in his eyes, perfectly consistent with U.S. needs and were logical outgrowths of the Garfield and Arthur administrations' relatively outward-looking policies.[91] He saw his actions as in the best interests of all trading nations, including his own. Not only was he proud of his work at the conference and always ready to defend it, but he felt that it merited him more recognition.

There was, however, considerable domestic opposition to American participation at Berlin and specifically Sanford's role in it. Several leading papers kept the issue before the public in early 1885. Moreover, following the lead of prominent Democrats in the House of Representatives who were critical of the Republican administration for sending a delegation to Berlin, Grover Cleveland wasted little time after moving into the White House in 1885 in repudiating such action. Consequently, the Berlin Act never won Senate ratification.[92]

Having done as much to secure the association's place in the Congo, Sanford was not averse to seeking investment opportunities there. It was not simply a question of personal profit that motivated him, but also the belief that he could pave the way for American enterprise; and he was willing to demonstrate for his countrymen the value of the upper Congo for American trade.[93] Leopold was willing to accede to Sanford's modest request for the right to launch a small company to undertake commercial operations on the upper Congo. The Sanford Exploring Expedition, financed by American and Belgian capital, appeared in June 1886.[94] Its objective was the preliminary exploitation of the ivory and rubber trade of the hitherto untapped upper-river regions.[95] The company's work was to be completed by January 1888, at which time, Sanford hoped, it would give way to a more ambitious venture. To its founder the king promised use of his steamers for transport, various Congo State stations and other facilities, and all possible cooperation from state officials.[96] The enterprise suffered from assorted misfortunes, but not the least of its troubles was the blatant obstructionism of state officers. Only with great difficulty did Sanford come to realize that the state which he had helped bring into being was not friendly to his interests.[97] Promises made to him in Brussels went unfulfilled in the field, as his men found Leopold's Congo agents thwarting them in various ways.[98] Stanley, who had foreseen this development, considered Sanford a fool for his unbounded faith in Leopold's word.[99]

The Exploring Expedition's failure to return a substantial profit was a bitter defeat for Sanford, as was his inability to enlist American investors in the successor company. Striving to attract more Anglo-Saxon, but particularly American, capital, he appealed to leading businessmen such as John D. Rockefeller,[100] contacted large rubber companies[101] and broadcast his glowing predictions for the Congo's future[102]—all to no avail. He had to watch Belgians predominate in the new operation that evolved, the Société du Haut-Congo pour le commerce et l'industrie. Financially he was experiencing hard times. Failures in his Florida citrus enterprises made him put all his hopes in the Congo. To reach some degree of equilibrium, he managed to obtain an unattractive loan on his shares in the new company.[103] Apart from the monetary loss, perhaps the greatest blow to Sanford was his final realization that, despite his years' of faithful service and extremely significant contributions to King Leopold, he was not to receive special favors. Continued reports from the Congo had proved that state employees were not directed to assist Sanford's company. It seemed that, having no further need of him, the king had completely forgotten Sanford after 1886.

The Congo also proved to be a heavy drain on Leopold's resources. In attempting to demonstrate effective occupation of the vast territory and at the same time trying to pry it open to tap its wealth, he had depleted his private fortune.[104] A number of projects to raise additional sums were less than satisfactory.[105] The profits popularly associated with his Congo regime later were not destined to be realized for several years. Leopold thus decided that other avenues of income must be opened. According to the Berlin Act of 1885, which made no mention of exports, the Congo State was not to establish import duties for twenty years. Since exports as yet were few, the problem was one of revising the free trade provision agreed upon at Berlin.

At this time growing antislavery sentiment in Western Europe, effectively stimulated by the influential French cardinal, Charles M. A. Lavigerie, was pushing for a crusade against the so-called Arab (but mostly east coast Swahili) slavers in East and Central Africa.[106] The British, in particular, were alarmed at expanding Arab power there. Missionaries and their supporters called for official action. In London, Prime Minister Salisbury's government, viewing the Arabs in East Africa in terms of British interests on the Nile,[107] and also desirous of mounting more effective resistance to the maritime slave trade, believed an international discussion would be advantageous.[108] In order to avoid publicly taking the initiative, however, Salisbury suggested to the Belgian monarch that he convene a conference to study the whole question. One can imagine how delighted Leopold must have been. Having found such international gatherings immensely satisfactory in the past, he decided to use this meeting to obtain approval for his own political and economic objectives.[109]

The Brussels Anti-Slavery Conference opened in November 1889. In attendance were representatives of the powers that participated at Berlin in 1884–85, plus the Congo Independent State. Serving as U.S. delegates were Edwin H. Terrell, minister to Belgium, and Sanford. The State Department, again under James G. Blaine's direction, wanted to avoid the controversy surrounding American participation at the Berlin Conference and, accordingly, instructed Terrel that he was to serve as delegate "ad referendum" rather than as plenipotentiary.[110] Sanford had the same rank. It prevented the delegates from signing protocols but, after exerting considerable pressure on Blaine, they received the authority of plenipotentiaries.[111] Since Sanford's involvement at Berlin had been regarded as one of the principal blocks to U.S. ratification of the Berlin Act,[112] it is surprising that he was selected to serve in Brussels. There is reason to believe that even Blaine himself did not favor the appointment.[113] However, Sanford had influential friends, such as John Latrobe, who contacted Blaine in his behalf,[114] and, in terms of diplomatic experience combined with knowledge of the subject before the conference, Sanford had few peers. Terrel, a Texas lawyer ignorant of French and at his Belgian post only a short time, definitely needed an experienced hand to guide him.

Regarding the main consideration before the conference, the slave trade, Sanford recognized its evil effects and strongly desired to see its extinction. Yet he was no rabid Arab-hater, as were some of the crusaders. He went on record before the conference opened as opposing outright suppression as advocated by overzealous Christian philanthropists, and championed a gradual replacement of the slave trade by legitimate commerce.[115] At a time when few voices of moderation were heard, Sanford emphasized the commercial role the Arabs could play in Africa once they gave up slaving. Allowing for the obvious horrors of slave raiding, he felt that the Congolese had made net gains from their contact with the Arabs who had introduced rice cultivation and cheap American cotton by way of the Swahili coast. Nevertheless, he advocated a firm policy to deter continued slave trading; in fact those slavers who would not take up legitimate commerce should understand that they risked extermination.[116]

Just as he had done at the Berlin Conference, Sanford took much interest in the limitation of the liquor trade and exerted himself at the Brussels meeting to restrict the importation of cheap, often noxious alcoholic spirits.[117] He provoked the ire of many delegates when, just as it appeared that the liquor question was settled by nothing more than the imposition of a small tax on spirits, he proposed that the conference act to control the importation of "harmful" drink throughout Africa. Correspondence with his employees in the Congo and information provided by such experienced men as Stanley, had convinced him that Africa was indeed suffering from the growing consumption of imported liquor. He therefore suggested that each case sent to Africa bear the stamp of a certified chemist indicating its degree of purity.[118] If he was unrealistic in this, he was also demonstrating a sincere concern for Africa's welfare. And he had the full support of his government, despite the fact that American firms supplied a significant quantity of liquor to western Africa.[119] The Dutch, however, who were the foremost traders in intoxicating beverages, used their influence to squelch the American initiative.

The gun trade also won Sanford's attention. Although still devoted to the stimulation of American trade in Central Africa, he realized that on the arms issue commerce must not be the primary consideration, especially since Stanley definitely linked the gun traffic to the slave trade.[120] American arms manufacturers probably were enjoying a greater market in Africa than those of any nation. The favorite guns of the Arab slave raiders in that era, it was reported, were Remingtons. Winchesters were also popular among the East African Arabs.[121] Yet Sanford expressed his country's desire to limit the sale of such arms in any way that would best protect Africans from the slave traders and their allies.[122] Ultimately the conference decided to prohibit the importation of firearms and ammunition into the zone defined for liquor regulations. Outside that zone various restrictions were imposed.[123] Sanford's primary involvement at Brussels, however, concerned the question of import duties.

On May 10, after ten months of deliberations, the conference heard King Leopold's appeal for new sources of revenue. The Congo State's financial position was pictured as precarious, owing to great expenses in the early period and new burdens attending the antislave trade campaign. Having allowed the powers to indicate their intent to root out the evil, Leopold now offered them a logical means of accomplishing it. The Congo State was said to be the appropriate agency to carry out the task, provided its finances were strengthened. Accordingly, it was held essential that the "states of the conventional basin of the Congo" (as defined by the Berlin Conference) be accorded the right to levy a 10 percent *ad valorem* import duty upon all merchandise.[124] Preliminary soundings already had indicated that most of the powers were sympathetic with Leopold's position and would accept the proposal. Indeed, prominent members of the conference reminded the American minister that Leopold's bankruptcy was imminent and his Congo State's demise would find France, on the basis of its 1884 preemption treaty with the old association,[125] taking over the entire Congo basin.[126]

Sanford was aware of the fact that Leopold planned to move for import duties and made his opposition clear to Washington. Secretary Blaine was warned to resist any attempt by the Congo to alter the conditions agreed upon in the April 1884 exchange of declarations when Sanford had represented the AIC.[127] The principal argument Sanford used throughout this dispute was his firm conviction that American commerce would, in time, be extensive in the Congo if no artificial barriers were imposed. He wrote to President Harrison's office, "We are destined to be large traders there, and to be one, if not the greatest source of supply of manufactured goods in that region if we have access."[128] Later he predicted to Blaine that Central Africa would be "the greatest market for our domestic cotton goods outside of our own domains."[129]

Authorized to state their government's objection to any conference action, particularly one on import duties, which would represent an expansion of the Berlin Act, the Americans found to their chagrin that mention of said act invariably provoked reminders that Washington had not seen fit to ratify it.[130] Sanford, consequently, urged ratification, as he had in previous years. He was concerned that the administration and Senate should understand that, while the United States might hold the Congo State to the free entry provisions of the bilateral 1884 treaty, those provisions applied only to the actual territory of Leopold's state. The Berlin Act, on the other hand, prohibited import duties in a vast free trade zone throughout Central Africa from sea to sea. Therefore, if that act were modified by the erection of protective or revenue tariffs by the colonial powers, such action would affect areas other than the Congo where American trade was significant, such as East Africa. With Senate ratification, Sanford argued, Washington could hold out for free entry in the entire zone and the other signatory powers would be reluctant to annul that part of the Berlin Act while the Americans continued to enjoy its provisions.[131]

Sanford's stand against duties was one of personal commitment strengthened by disappointment in his own Congo ventures. Free entry for American products was not simply a selling point; to him it was a practical necessity, a valuable concession extended to the United States in exchange for recognition of the Congo flag in 1884. When Leopold now sought to cancel the concession, Sanford feared he would be identified with having involved his country in a diplomatic farce. Up to this time, it should be stressed, he believed his 1884 action to have been a real benefit to the United States. It thus became a matter of pride to demonstrate that he had not carried out his Washington mission solely to aid Leopold. He refused to accept the Congo State's pose of impending financial collapse. Not only did it offer no proof of insolvency, he contended, but with the proper economic reforms and special loans he long had advised, the problem would be quite manageable.[132] Leopold's agents could not deal with Sanford and failed to divide him and Terrell on the question.[133]

Sanford's determined resistance to Leopold was heightened by accumulating intelligence testifying to scandalous practices of Congo officials. As late as February 1889, he could publicly praise the king for his "civilizing influence" on the Congo, which would lead to the extinction of the slave trade.[134] But the conference opened his eyes. The British missionary, George Grenfell, was furnishing Sanford with confidential reports from the Congo on state personnel purchasing Africans and permitting Arab slave caravans to pass through their stations unchallenged. Leopold's employees, Sanford found, were actively bartering in human beings, frequently exchanging prisoners taken in skirmishes over ivory, or trading old women prisoners for younger attractive ones.[135] It was becoming clear to Sanford that the king, who had constantly posed as a foremost humanitarian, was actually involved in a great hoax. Leopold was carving out a personal empire in Africa with little concern for the cost of the undertaking to the area's people. He was using international concern about the slave trade to further his own ends. Everybody who had been involved in promoting his schemes, therefore, was in some degree guilty by association.

When Sanford, overcoming his earlier naïveté, began to see the picture in focus, the shock was overwhelming. He had believed in Leopold's grand gestures. In correspondence with the king and his ministers, with Stanley and various Americans, Sanford proudly remarked about his involvement in such noble, philanthropic work. While understanding that he and others might expect personal gain from the opening of Central Africa, Sanford was dedicated to the concept of the "white man's burden" and believed that the whole project must benefit Africa first. Obviously, the

Belgian monarch did not share these beliefs. If the Congo State now was successful in imposing tariffs, Sanford would not even be able to console himself with the thought that he at least had secured free trade privileges for American commerce.

Contributing further to Sanford's bitterness toward Leopold was the latter's unwillingness to allow black Americans to settle in the Congo, even on a trial basis. Sanford had long cherished the hope that such immigration would serve the needs of both the United States and Africa, but the king thought that ex-slaves would only prove troublesome and corrupt the Congolese.[136]

The United States faced great pressures in its opposition to import duties. It was averred that by defying the will of the overwhelming majority of the powers, America would be responsible for sounding the Congo State's death knell and thereby preventing a determined drive against the slave trade.[137] Leopold was quite willing to blackmail the powers with the threat of withdrawing from the Congo if import duties were not approved, and thus the onus of forcing this step was falling on the United States. Holland was the only other nation left opposing the duties, patently because of extensive Dutch commercial interests in the area. The Dutch were firmly in support of the American position.

Sanford used every tactic to prevent Washington's acquiescence, but to no avail. To the end he was unwilling to give up his country's right of free entry. At most he reluctantly agreed to a free list for certain American products or, failing that, arrangement for duties for only a limited time, but such concessions were unobtainable. He could not carry his point with the secretary of state. Blaine finally authorized Terrell to sign the act of the conference and the separate special declaration allowing a 10 percent *ad valorem* duty.[138] The Brussels Act itself, primarily dealing with the slave trade and the gun and liquor traffic, was acceptable to Sanford who saw it as "solely a philanthropic document for the protection of African races," yet he continued to oppose its ratification so long as the provision on duties was associated with it.[139] The U.S. Senate, nevertheless, after long deliberation, ratified the act in February 1892. By that time Sanford was dead. Having returned to the United States, he passed away on May 21, 1891. Five days earlier he had written to the Belgian ambassador in Washington. This letter summed up his feelings on the whole Congo question and pointed out Sanford's conviction that Leopold's recent policies were a denial of all that he, Sanford, had worked for. In his view the opportunity for a great Western civilizing mission, the opening for U.S. commerce, and the return of black Americans to the

Congo, the latter representing a possible solution to his nation's racial problem, were now ruined.[140] Although he died seeing none of these hopes in any stage of fulfillment, Sanford at least was spared witnessing the later horrors of Leopold's Congo, which would have further dashed his expectations.

Sanford was an appropriate colleague for Leopold II in the creation of the Congo Independent State. His diplomatic experiences in Europe and legal work in Latin America, his political concerns in the United States, and the attitudes he developed regarding America in the wider world, insured that he would make a valuable ally in the king's work. However, he has been viewed incorrectly as simply endeavoring to further that monarch's selfish ends. Impelled by the desire to participate in a great humanitarian project, Sanford also sought to obtain opportunities for American commercial expansion, in which he hoped to be involved. He further saw the Congo as an outlet for unassimilable American ex-slaves whom he regarded as a major political and social liability.

His services to Leopold were many, ranging from assistance in planning expeditions for the AIA, the recruitment of Henry Morton Stanley, the brilliant diplomatic feat winning U.S. recognition of the association's flag, to various important missions during the Berlin Conference of 1884–85. Throughout, he sincerely believed such efforts to be in the interests of Africa as well as beneficial to trading nationals, particularly his own. Completely taken in by Leopold's pose as primarily a philanthropist, the naïve American, who long had been enamored of European aristocracy, eventually realized his error. His own disappointing commercial venture in the Congo in the late 1880s helped reveal the king's intentions, which Sanford now interpreted as mainly self-seeking. Serving as an American delegate to the Brussels Anti-Slavery Conference of 1889–90, Sanford openly broke with his former idol and led an unpopular and unsuccessful fight against Leopold's move to reverse the commercial provisions of the Berlin Act. This represented his attempt to salvage for the United States the free trade advantages won through his own agency in 1884. To the end, he believed American traders and emigrant blacks, if unobstructed by such things as import duties, would capitalize on the Congo's potential, which he so persistently proclaimed.

Sanford was one of a group of expansionists, frustrated commercial empire-builders, that was unable to move significantly an inward-looking America toward the outer world. One historian has called these years the "period of preparation" for the "new empire" that the United States established in the late 1890s.[141]

Yet, even when American overseas commercial contacts multiplied significantly in that decade in response to the pressures of a more rapidly expanding industrial economy, it was Asia and, to a lesser extent, Latin America, but not Africa, with which the imperialists were concerned. Sanford's success in Washington in 1884 and the U.S. involvement in the Berlin Conference, which was the logical sequel to recognition of the AIC, were possible partly because of pressure and influence generated by him in the business community. This would support the contention of the economic determinists who see such influence as largely responsible for American expansion. Indeed, the fact that the Congo preliminaries were never extensively pursued was due to the belief of most American business leaders that, compared to other areas, Africa was simply too barbarous and unpromising. It was left to the Europeans, who of course had the political advantage there, to exploit.

5
John Hays Hammond and the Jameson Raid: Engineering a Capitalist Revolution in South Africa

The affair known as the Jameson Raid, which was a seminal prelude to the Anglo-Boer War, has received considerable scholarly attention. Thanks especially to the important study by Jean Van der Poel[1] and the more recent work of Denys Rhoodie,[2] most facets of this odd enterprise have been satisfactorily examined. A major participant in the plot behind Jameson's ill-fated filibustering expedition and the associated activities in Johannesburg was the American, John Hays Hammond. Although all studies of the raid acknowledge his presence during these events, and Hammond himself gives a lengthy account of his South African activities in his autobiography,[3] his importance has not been fully appreciated. The effects of his special influence on Cecil Rhodes's policies and his role in the conspiracy were far-reaching and deserve independent treatment.

At the time of the 1895 crisis in the South African Republic (or Transvaal) leading to the raid, Hammond was one of the world's leading mining engineers. Born in 1855 to a prominent San Francisco family, he was educated at Yale and at the renowned Royal School of Mines at Freiburg, Germany. Then he acquired his early practical experience, beginning in 1879, in the gold mines of California, Arizona, and Idaho and during brief employment with the United States Geological Survey. Subsequently he managed mining properties in Mexico, then explored for gold in Central and South America. Such positions demanded, in addition to scientific and technical knowledge, considerable resourcefulness since he had to command men in adverse circumstances. On more than one occasion Hammond found himself relying on raw nerve and strength of will during long periods in primitive surroundings. While in Mexico, for instance, he withstood repeated attempts to

John Hays Hammond (*Courtesy of Yale University Archives, Manuscripts and Archives, Yale University*).

assassinate him and his wife and successfully directed the defense of his mining community during a bandit siege.[4]

Work in late nineteenth-century mining camps was a rough, demanding existence that bred attitudes that Hammond carried through his career. The affluent young engineer earned the right to consider himself—and, indeed, was considered by his peers—a man of action and leader of men.

Hammond's reputation grew with his successful efforts in these several challenging areas as the mining world, not easily impressed, came to regard him as skillful and scrupulous. Having become a highly recommended expert, in 1884 he was named mining consultant for the premier West Coast iron works. In this capacity he served in various supervisory roles, assisted in labor disputes, and even was instrumental in winning for his firm the construction contract for the battleship USS *Oregon*.[5] Thus, when Hammond allowed himself to be lured to South Africa, he went as an acknowledged authority on all phases of mineral extraction and mine management.

Following the fabulous diamond strikes around Kimberley in the late 1860s, South Africa experienced one of the world's great gold rushes twenty years later. Capital derived from the diamond industry was thus readily available for rapid exploitation of the new El Dorado. The area in question was the Witwatersrand, commonly called the Rand, located in the South African Republic, an independent state dominated by Dutch-speaking whites, known as Boers, who were primarily rural pastoralists resistant to forces that would change their traditional way of life. The Rand attracted a flood of miners and adventurers from many nations whose crude camps soon gave rise to the city of Johannesburg. Not surprisingly, mining engineers found their services in great demand as the diamond magnates offered extremely attractive salaries to those experts who might help them plunge into the yellow reefs of the southern Transvaal. Figuring prominently in these developments were a number of Americans.[6]

The man who convinced Hammond to seek his fortune in the Rand was Barney Barnato, one of the most famous of the diamond kings, who had amalgamated his holdings with those of Cecil Rhodes to form the powerful De Beers Consolidated Mines, Ltd., of Kimberley. Now he was prominent in gold mining. From him the confident American won a beginning annual salary of $50,000 and arrived in South Africa with his family in the summer of 1893. In six months, however, because of Barnato's failure to act on Hammond's recommendations, the latter left his service. Refusing other offers, he soon became chief consulting engineer of Consolidated Gold Fields of South Africa (CGFSA), the Rhodes syndicate on the Rand, and also served in the same capacity with the British South Africa Company (BSAC), another Rhodes enterprise that controlled mining rights in the territories to the north eventually known as Rhodesia. Hammond's new contract called for $75,000 a year, profit-sharing, and the right to undertake other consulting work if it did not conflict with Rhodes's interests. Significantly, Hammond demanded, in the terms of his employment, that he "be responsible to Cecil Rhodes and subject to no interference from anyone else."[7] That Rhodes consented indicates his respect for his new engineer's reputation.

There is no question about Hammond's admiration for Rhodes. In his later days he stated that "Rhodes was the greatest personality I have ever met."[8] Attributing few faults to his employer, he saw in this so-called colossus of South Africa the personification of those ideals so important to himself. Rhodes he described as "remarkably upright in business, broad-minded, liberal and very farseeing . . . undoubtedly the greatest Englishman of the age . . . and he suits me to a T."[9]

The man who so impressed Hammond was driven by an *idée fixe*, namely, the extension of British interests through as much of southern Africa as possible, preferably behind the leadership of the Cape Colony. This would entail the federation or at least close cooperation of the two British self-governing territories, the Cape and Natal, with the two independent Boer states, the Transvaal and the Orange Free State. This objective was central to his grand design of creating a British sphere from the Cape all the way to Egypt. Enjoying the power derived from the fortune he won in the diamond fields and his position as prime minister of the Cape Colony since 1890, Rhodes could also exert his influence within governmental and financial circles in London. To further his expansionist schemes he created the British South Africa Company, which was endowed by royal charter in 1889 with quasi-governmental powers for exploiting newly won territory. With such advantages, Rhodes seemed destined to realize his dream. Yet by 1894 he was seriously challenged by the Boers in the Transvaal.

The northern Boer state had a redoubtable leader in Paul Kruger and was capitalizing on its position atop the rich gold reserves of the Rand. As revenues were wrung from the expanding mining operations, Kruger's government was enabled to spurn Rhodes's promotion of both a South African political federation or even a customs union; and more critical, the old Boer patriarch could now finance the construction of a rail outlet to Delagoa Bay on the Indian Ocean. This line, completed in 1894 and promising the Transvaal commercial independence, threatened to free the Boers from British influence and, combined with its gold income, allow their state to replace the Cape as the dominant factor in South African affairs. Exacerbating matters further, Kruger was establishing closer relations with Germany, already ominously based in Southwest Africa, thus presenting another challenge to British interests. Rhodes found this situation highly provocative.[10]

Among the trump cards in Rhodes's hand was the northern frontier. Across the Limpopo River, the Boers' northern border, was a vast territory ruled by the Ndebele chieftain, Lobengula. In addition to his own people, Lobengula held sway over the more numerous Shona. The always land-hungry Boers understandably were attracted to these African lands, but were edged out by the BSAC. Resorting to brazen deceit followed by naked force in dealing with the African ruler, Rhodes's agents had gained both Matabeleland and Mashonaland for the chartered company by 1890. They were then opened for white exploitation. Numerous ancient mine workings were known to exist there, which in earlier centuries had sustained gold-exporting black states such as the kingdom of Monomotapa. Folklore and cursory examinations had bred the popular notion that these regions were as rich in precious metal as the Rand. Rhodes wanted to believe this and he fervently hoped to see the development of a new bonanza land, perhaps even outstripping the Transvaal, which would help him finance his wider imperial goals and the intensifying competition with Kruger.[11]

With so much dependent on this great inland plateau now under his company, Rhodes invited Hammond to join a small exploratory party and undertake a thorough study of its mineral potential. And thus in August 1894, there set out from Bulawayo, Matabeleland, an expedition that would prove to be portentous for South African history. In a very real sense, this long trek gave birth to the plot involving the Jameson Raid. For two months, as they camped out in the wild veld, Hammond came to know intimately Rhodes and Dr. Leander Starr Jameson, the latter's personal physician and trusted associate, who a year before had led the BSAC's successful military effort against the Ndebele.[12] It was also an excellent opportunity for the others to appreciate fully that the American mining specialist was no flabby, effete functionary, but a man of action whose adventurous background could impress even such intrepid empire-builders as them. In light of subsequent developments it seems certain that they then marked Hammond as a strong, aggressive personality of their own breed, one upon whom they could depend in critical times.

The purpose of the trip was to "boom" the country. Anxious to broadcast glowing prospects based on scientific evidence, Rhodes originally planned for his group eventually to proceed to England in late October with promotional material in order to attract investment in the chartered company.[13] Despite an earlier negative appraisal of the territory by some specialists, Rhodes and Hammond had other expert opinion that led them to believe that a more comprehensive examination would foretell a great future in mineral extraction.[14] The American had no illusions about what was at stake. Not only was Rhodes eagerly awaiting a highly positive report, but others with BSAC stocks were encouraging Hammond to insure inflation of "chartered" shares by sensationalizing his findings. One of his associates pleaded with him, "For God's sake, old man, shake your pen up and sling a little more ink than usual and we will all sail on to glory."[15] In the end, however, Hammond issued a guarded, conservative report that naturally disappointed his employer immensely. Rhodes undoubtedly could have found another specialist to deliver the kind of judgment he desired, for the findings were by no means totally discouraging, but Hammond, who professionally was without guile, could not be party to such deception. Rhodes never considered hiring a less scrupulous expert nor did he attempt to induce Hammond to falsify his statement.[16] He went to London, without Hammond, to make the best of the situation with the company's board of directors. However, when facing the shareholders he described the prospects for the company's future in more favorable terms than the known facts warranted.[17]

It was clear, then, that while some gold would be extracted from Matabeleland and Mashonaland, there probably would never be another Rand. In addition to this shock, other, assorted public and private troubles at this time, not the least of which was his recurrent heart disease, intensified Rhodes's impatience and reckless proclivities.[18] Despite being somewhat slower than others in entering the race for claims on the Rand,[19] Rhodes and his partners did become substantially involved in gold mining, albeit not so enthusiastically as they had in the Kimberley diamond fields. Consolidated Gold Fields won control of some outcrop mines, although these were not the largest and most productive ones. Ironically, the company's spectacular profits in the period before the Jameson Raid resulted principally from the sale of most of its

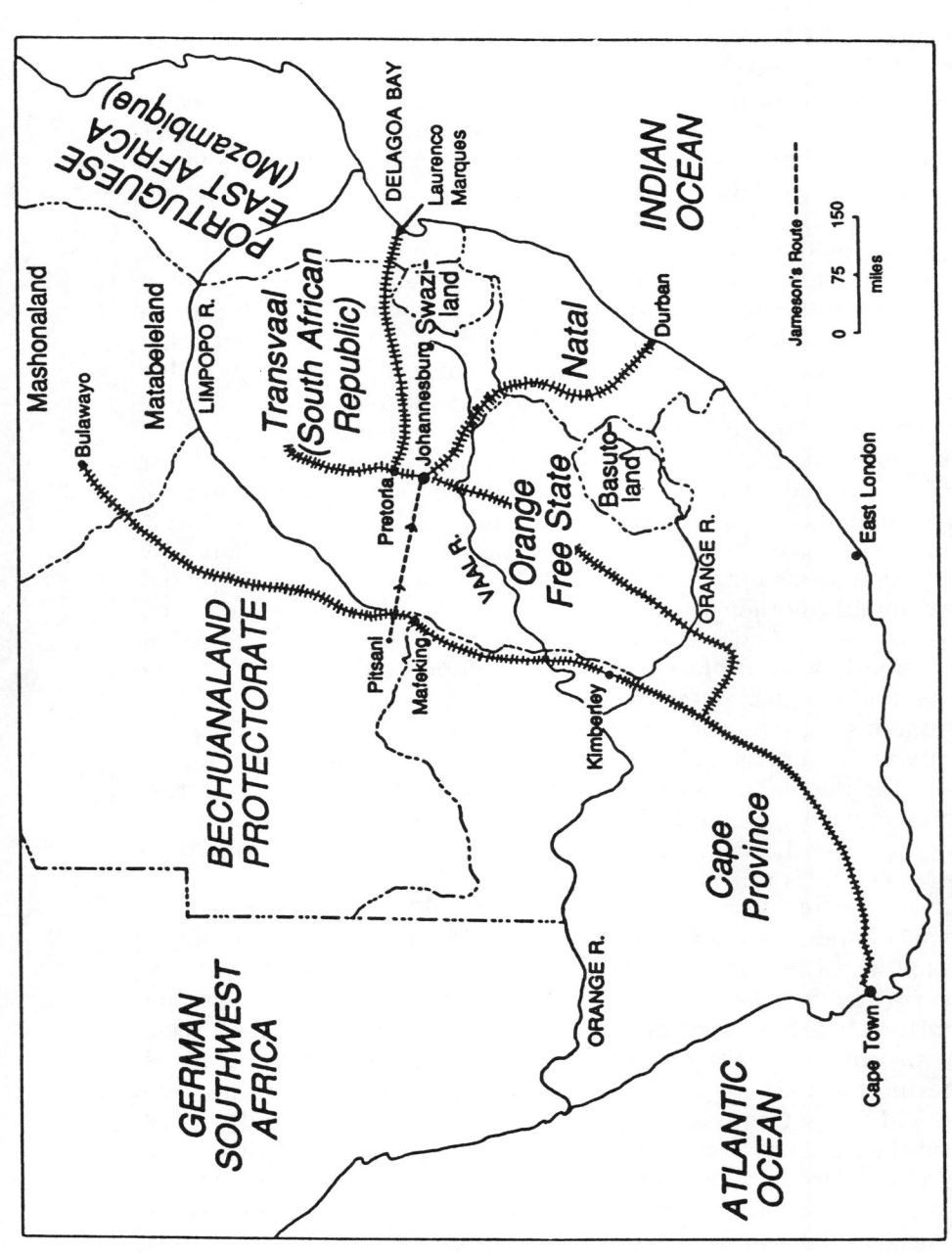

South Africa, 1895.

outcrop holdings and shrewd manipulation of the stock market.[20] Much of the capital so earned was invested in deep-level properties. While near-surface (outcrop) mining would continue for some years to yield gold in significant quantities, the future lay in exploiting deeper deposits, the importance of which was not appreciated until 1890. By that time some experts understood that the reefs or veins showing gold at the surface did not extend vertically into the bowels of the earth but instead dipped at varying angles and depths, generally flattening out, thus making their mining a feasible though costly undertaking.[21]

When Hammond joined Rhodes's Rand operations in early 1894, he quickly recognized the significance of deep mining and was instrumental in Gold Fields' acquisition of more deep-level areas, some of which became the best properties in the field.[22] This was still considered somewhat risky, since widespread skepticism persisted regarding mining far beyond the outcrops, but Hammond obtained outside professional confirmation of his optimistic projections for deep-levels[23] and committed his firm to rapid development of its new holdings. To Hammond and the team of engineers he led, must go much of the credit for solving the critical technological problems associated with mining at great depths. Because of his success, the rate of shaft-sinking swiftly increased, thus making the deep-levels extremely profitable.[24] Of course mining operations did not take place in a vacuum; the politics of the South African Republic bore heavily on the Rand enterprises.

While roughing it in the north with Rhodes and Jameson, Hammond contributed in another way to his employer's decision to deal forcefully with Kruger. The three discussed the Transvaal political scene at length and Hammond furnished the others with an enlightening report on developments in Johannesburg. He spoke of "impossible economic conditions" on the Rand and, drawing from his knowledge of mining camps elsewhere, he predicted a rising there if reforms were not forthcoming.[25] Rhodes could hardly have been ignorant of the general conditions on the Rand but he had been immersed in Cape affairs and in the opening of the northern territories; this intelligence coming from his circumspect head engineer must have had a special impact. It prompted Rhodes and Jameson to visit Pretoria and Johannesburg in October as they accompanied Hammond home from Matabeleland.[26]

Dissatisfaction with president Kruger's government was longstanding in the gold mining center and was based on real grievances. The mining community was fast approaching the Boer population in size—it outnumbered the Boers fourfold on the

Rand—and provided most of the state's revenue. Yet the Uitlanders, as the Boers called these foreigners, were almost completely denied meaningful participation in political life at the national level. Kruger believed that to give the vote to these outsiders with objectionable habits and beliefs would be tantamount to giving them control of his country. Since 1890 eligibility for the franchise required fourteen years' residence. It is clear that only a minority of the Uitlander population was interested in permanent settlement in South Africa and thus it has been suggested that the vast majority of them had little concern for the vote.[27] On the other hand, about 13 percent of the immigrants had brought their families along; they and even many of the unaccompanied males might well have contemplated sinking their roots in the country if conditions had been right. Such people must have been outraged by the law that withheld all state financial support from schools that permitted instruction in any but the Dutch language. They began to realize that they could not ignore politics if they wanted to protect their interests.[28]

The Uitlanders were particularly enraged by the Transvaal's conscription of them for military service against rebellious African groups for which they were to provide their own mounts and weapons. Even though only a few men were compelled to join the Boers in such combat, this issue was reported to be "the one occasion when the feelings of the Johannesburg community was most genuinely stirred."[29]

As far as the mining establishment was concerned, the scene was more disquieting from a business standpoint. Monopoly concessions, such as the one for the manufacture and supply of dynamite, were granted by President Kruger to certain favorites who proceeded to exploit the mining companies. Not only were the explosives supplied by these concessionaires expensive,[30] but they were of inferior quality, needlessly causing many fatal accidents.[31] Problems with African labor were an additional concern. Mine owners had little success when seeking government assistance in enforcing workers' contracts, ensuring their safe travel home, and controlling their consumption of alcohol.[32]

A railroad monopoly added to the burden, for resultant high freight rates were actually a considerable indirect tax that affected all consumers on the Rand. An American mining authority who investigated the South African gold fields claimed that it should have been possible to mine for half the cost that such conditions created.[33] It has been demonstrated that the weight of these economic woes and the state's peculiar mining regulations fell heaviest on the deep mines whose development was just beginning.[34] Since Consolidated Gold Fields was by 1895 counting heavily on deep-level operations, especially due to the advice and initiative of its chief engineer, to produce large profits, both Rhodes and Hammond were keenly sensitive to these developments.

The policies of the Kruger regime prompted the mining community to organize for redress of grievances. As early as 1888 a "political association" was formed in Barberton and in other eastern Transvaal mining camps, and it was hoped that the Rand would follow suit.[35] By 1890 an obscure Political Reform Association emerged in Johannesburg that plotted the overthrow of Kruger's government along lines quite similar to those followed later by others.[36] Evidently it did not survive beyond 1890. More significant was the Transvaal National Union, which appeared in 1892. This organization, representing primarily the professional and commercial groups, was a moderate vehicle for communication of grievances, which at its first public meeting was said to have attracted "all that is enlightened, influential and respectable in the town."[37] Conspicuous by their nonparticipation in the Union's work in its earliest years, for which they were berated,[38] were the major mine owners and capitalists of the Rand. The latter, fearing to become publicly political, resorted to discreet lobbying in Pretoria and bribery of officials whenever appropriate. Their organization was the Chamber of Mines, formally established in 1889 to speak for the industry and to create the optimum economic climate for it. Hammond headed the body in early 1894.[39] When dealing with the Boer government, however, neither the National Union nor the Chamber could boast of much success. After several years of frustration some important Uitlanders began to conclude that change would never be won through peaceful, constitutional means.

By the middle of 1894 industry leaders were becoming more politically involved. Lionel Phillips, Johannesburg manager of the important mining firm, Ekstein and Company, and now also president of the Chamber of Mines, surreptitiously made a substantial monetary contribution to the National Union. This was the first time any of the "Randlords" had encouraged the Union in such a way.[40] Moreover, some Johannesburgers formed a rifle association, presumably to prepare for possible military action should a confrontation occur with Kruger's forces, and this group too was the recipient of secret capitalist funding.[41] Hammond, about this time, took his first step in active opposition to the government by encouraging Americans, many of whom were employed by

CGFSA, to resist conscription.[42] Yet, despite their trials, the Uitlanders, particularly the capitalists and mine managers, hesitated to go much further than directing mild threats toward their tormentor.

This attitude was encouraged by the financial boom that began in 1894. South African gold shares became very popular in the London and Paris stock exchanges, bringing an injection of capital and a heady economic climate in Johannesburg as property values soared and prices for gold claims climbed as much as fiftyfold.[43] This so-called Kaffirboom had some trickle-down effect on the Rand population generally, and the relative prosperity, including good wages for white workers, diverted attention from politics. Reform leaders, however, foresaw that the financial bubble would burst eventually and that the old problems would remain. They tried to continue agitation through the boom and reminded Uitlanders that things could be better. The editor of the antigovernment Johannesburg *Star*, for example, was directed to keep political issues before the public.[44] Thus, the more determined leaders saw the need to exert pressure on Kruger's government by sustaining a potential for trouble among the aggrieved Uitlanders. Gradually this strategy came to include the possibility of revolutionary action.[45]

Meanwhile, Cecil Rhodes had concluded that he might utilize the mounting discontent on the Rand to unseat Kruger. What he envisioned was a plan whose general outline had been conceived in 1893 by Sir Henry Loch, the British high commissioner in South Africa. This involved the stationing of an armed force on the Transvaal's western border for the purpose of assisting an Uitlander rising, all of which would then be followed by the intervention of Her Majesty's high commissioner.[46] With Rhodes it was not simply a matter of helping the Johannesburgers to achieve their own ends but, if possible, bringing them under his influence, for the determined imperialist did not favor the idea of a revolt in the gold capital that resulted in an Uitlander republic controlled by other mining magnates, some of whom where his bitter rivals.[47] On a visit to London in late 1894, Rhodes made inquiries that encouraged him to think that he could obtain support from certain British officials for the way he was planning to establish a new order in the Transvaal.[48] By March 1895, he had managed to have Loch replaced as high commissioner by Sir Hercules Robinson, who previously had held the post and who was willing to work closely with Rhodes. Now the latter was ready to bring the Uitlanders into his scheme.

Important in this effort was Alfred Beit, an associate of Rhodes from the early Kimberly days. Now a wealthy partner in the prestigious Wernher Beit Company, which was heavily involved in the gold fields, particularly deep-mining, the London-based Beit returned to South Africa in mid-1895 and met in the Cape with Rhodes who enlisted him in the conspiracy. The two agreed to fund an Uitlander rebellion while Rhodes would furnish the BSAC military force under Jameson that would be readied in British Bechuanaland for a dash to Johannesburg's aid.[49] Rhodes was the architect of the plot, but Beit became a major participant from this point on; moreover, the latter's firm ultimately put up more money to finance the revolution than did Rhodes himself.[50] If Rhodes's goals in the enterprise were both economic and political, Beit's were primarily those of a financier. He did favor a South African federation but he did not share his friend's broader imperialistic designs. Beit acted primarily out of concern for the deep-level mines and for the adverse effects of Kruger's policies on them.[51]

Since Lionel Phillips, a major reform leader in Johannesburg, worked for Beit,[52] Rhodes hoped to use the latter to keep the shrewd Phillips from acting too independently. Phillips did not trust Rhodes completely but deferred to Beit's judgment on most matters related to the dynamic Cape premier.[53] It was decided, therefore, that Beit should proceed to Johannesburg where he invited Phillips and Charles Leonard, chairman of the National Union, to throw in with Rhodes, that is, agree to coordinate their respective preparations in order to enhance their chances for success.[54] Although the two Uitlanders were not fully in agreement with what they knew of the Rhodes plan at that juncture, the link between Cape Town and Johannesburg was established.

Hammond entered into these discussions since he was Rhodes's principal agent on the Rand, enjoyed his confidence, and was strongly in agreement with those who promoted reform. In addition, Hammond was considered a major representative of the non-English inhabitants of Johannesburg and those who "only wanted fair play and fair government."[55] The American engineer, already practically an Anglophile, sympathized with Rhodes's vision of an Africa enlightened by Anglo-Saxon civilization and developed by British enterprise, yet his main objective in the business-at-hand was more restricted. He had staked his reputation on the success of the deep mines that he was directing for CGFSA and he found intolerable the backward Pretoria regime's frustration of sound industrial management. A more friendly or more tractable government was for him a necessity.[56] Upon those among his reform-minded colleagues who might resist cooperation with Rhodes, Hammond could urge his belief that Rhodes's participation was indeed necessary for, apart from his welcome financial support, as prime minister of the Cape, Rhodes could bring that government's influence to bear on the situation.[57] In any case, he who had always been on the side of constituted government now joined the unusual conspiratorial clique whose radical activities would help to alter the historical course of South Africa.

By autumn, economic conditions were unsettling to those responsible for Rand industry, especially deep-mining. Even though the Rhodes and Beit firms astutely managed to weather the great depression in the stock market that lasted through the last quarter of 1895, this was not accomplished easily. Until all the complicated transactions were completed and the Wernher Beit and CGFSA portfolios were secure, the uncertain financial climate must have added to the burdens of the mining magnates and their managers.[58] Hammond and Phillips, as well as others working for the major companies, were deeply committed to the industry, not just as highly paid employees but also as investors themselves.[59] While the market was plummeting, a railway war between the Transvaal and the Cape saw the Cape line unload goods at the Transvaal border and move them to the Rand by ox-cart rather than pay increased rail tariffs imposed by the Kruger government. To prevent this evasion, the Transvaal president ordered the drifts (fords) across the Vaal River closed to wagon traffic after October 1, thus precipitating a crisis that focused attention on what Uitlanders perceived as Kruger's high-handed actions that forced up the cost of imported goods.[60] Delays and inefficiency on the Transvaal rail system already had brought complaints; now mines and engineering firms were worried about being deprived of essential machinery and losing valuable time—a particularly alarming prospect for the deep-level operations just getting under way.[61] The labor problem, furthermore, was becoming more acute. There was a serious shortage of African hands that prevented the mines from operating at full capacity. This, too, was blamed partially on Kruger's policies.[62] In other words, men who had careers and significant investments at risk and who wished to see the mines advance smoothly and rapidly to their maximum potential, were aroused. Kruger, they would charge, was out to ruin their industry.[63]

And preparations for overthrowing the Boer leader were continuing. Rhodes stepped up his negotiations with British officials for their assistance and backing. Jameson was in Johannesburg in September to discuss with the conspirators there the problems of supplying them with arms and of moving his troops to the city.[64] Then, in October, Hammond, Phillips, and Leonard journeyed to Cape Town for an important meeting with Rhodes. It is worth noting that Hammond made the trip separately in the company of Maj. Robert White, an officer in Jameson's BSAC police. Ostensibly the two were inspecting the latter's mining properties, but the fact that White had been sent to the Transvaal for the purpose of compiling a report on the state of Boer military preparedness in Pretoria and Johannesburg, strongly suggests that their ride west to the railhead at Mafeking was taken in order further to survey the area for Jameson's prospective march.[65] This would have been in keeping with Hammond's role as director of intelligence for the Rand conspirators.[66]

Arriving in Cape Town before Phillips and Leonard, Hammond consulted with Rhodes on the effects of the drifts crisis and then explained the position of the mine operators to Cape political leaders. The latter pledged their support if Britain should interpret Kruger's closing of the drifts as a breach of treaty obligations.[67] When the other Johannesburg reformers joined Hammond at Rhodes's Groote Schuur estate in late October, they worked out final arrangements for the revolt with their host. They found the latter's professed aims, namely, the protection of his heavy financial investments in the gold fields and the creation of a South African customs union, easily compatible with their own. The course of action decided upon required the Rand group to organize a revolt, seize the Pretoria arsenal, and retire to Johannesburg where, if necessary, they would be assisted by Jameson's force moving in from Pitsani in Bechuanaland. For his part, Rhodes would see that arms were supplied and insure that the high commissioner would swiftly step in and mediate.[68] It was also agreed that Rhodes's brother Frank, a former colonel in the British army, would superintend the military aspects of the Rand uprising; to screen his real task, he was appointed managing director of the CGFSA Johannesburg office. It was unanimously resolved, furthermore, that nothing would be done to disturb the integrity of the South African Republic. Of course, everyone understood that if the plot succeeded in bringing an extension of the franchise to the Uitlanders, they would control the state.[69]

The Cape negotiations led the small band of Rand reformers to constitute themselves as a secret "Reform Committee."[70] The committee would gradually expand its membership, but most of these were inactive.[71] In November, Jameson stopped again in the mining city to confirm certain details of the plot and probably to test the committee's resolve to carry out the revolt. The reformers decided that the rising should take place on December 26, but later it was acknowledged that this was too early, that December 28 would be more appropriate.[72] This was only the first of several schedule changes.

In order to have a pretext for entering the Transvaal with an armed force, Jameson requested that the reform executive provide him with a letter of invitation, which he could then date at the appropriate time. The letter, dictated by Jameson and stressing that Johannesburg was in danger of being overwhelmed by Kruger's army, was intended to justify his unusual action to the BSAC, the British government, and the wider public. It also would enable Jameson to inspire his men with a determination to rush to the beleaguered city whose women and children supposedly would be in jeopardy. Significantly, however, Jameson was not given carte blanche; the letter was to be used only upon the correct signal from the reform leaders.[73] Not only was Jameson required to await notification from the committee, but he must have received a personal communication from Hammond before crossing the border.[74] Most of the reformers expressed reservations about this document—indeed, Percy Fitzpatrick, a partner in Wernher, Beit and Company and secretary of the Reform Committee, refused to sign it, and others delayed affixing their names to it—but once he obtained Jameson's pledge not to move until the reform executive directed, Hammond readily signed, and thus reinforced Jameson's impression of him as determined and reliable, one who could stiffen the nerve of the weaker ones.[75] In fact, in a number of respects, Hammond was now the most significant conspirator in the reform group. Not only was he responsible for intelligence and the smuggling of arms into the city, but he was also the major representative and principal contact of Rhodes and Jameson on the Rand.[76]

Later in November Hammond journeyed to Kimberly to discuss final preparations with Rhodes, especially the shipment of guns from the diamond capital to Johannesburg. Rhodes had arranged for arms, ostensibly purchased for the BSAC, to be stored at his DeBeers facilities and then, under the supervision of Gardner Williams, the American who managed De Beers for Rhodes, transferred to the Rand where Hammond would oversee their concealment and eventual distribution.[77] On his return to Johannesburg, Hammond hired a carriage in Mafeking and carefully laid out a route for Jameson, which the latter found acceptable.[78] Another of Hammond's important tasks was the provision of supplies and remounts for Jameson's troop. Having scouted the proposed line of march, Hammond employed the American physician, Henry A. Wolff, to establish stations along the route where the riders could rest, eat and, at one location, find fresh horses.[79] To cover these and other expenses, Rhodes transferred BSAC funds to several bank accounts, the largest of which was the "development syndicate" account in Johannesburg's branch of the Standard Bank of South Africa. Hammond, one of four reformers authorized to make withdrawals, furnished Wolff with sizable sums for his provisioning work.[80]

There was more to this engineer-turned-conspirator's preparations for armed rebellion. One of the Uitlanders' principal military responsibilities was to attack the Boer arsenal in Pretoria. This objective, which contained thousands of weapons, comprised several buildings enclosed by a brick wall, a section of which was being repaired. The reformers were led to believe that the guard unit was not alert at night and therefore a surprise raid undoubtedly would succeed. To serve as a launching base, Hammond rented some land just outside Pretoria and hired men to pose as prospectors. These were fifty tough Americans, most of whom had been fired for various offenses from mines under his direction. Against the advise of others, Hammond judged them tractable and appropriate enough for the daring escapade he was planning. This strike force was to break into the arsenal, fill its wagons with as many guns as possible, ruin the rest, and quickly return to Johannesburg, thereby supposedly rendering the Boers defenseless.[81] The whole scheme had a rather naive, unprofessional character, and one suspects that Kruger's agents were not deceived by such moves, but it demonstrates Hammond's initiative and determination. No other reform leader was as deeply involved in so many aspects of the conspiracy as this American.

The first weeks of December were anxious ones for the plotters in Johannesburg. The reform leaders hired a man to create a special police force that would keep order once the rising occurred,[82] and they busied themselves recruiting prominent persons into the movement. This was frustrating work where the merchants were concerned, for they tended to oppose adamantly all talk of war or revolt.[83] Others held back for financial reasons, fearing for their investments. In at least one case where a man hesitated to join a cause that might further depress the stock market, Phillips offered to cover any such losses if he signed on.[84] The problem of engaging the general public was a sensitive one, as the reformers were always conscious of themselves as restrained, selective rebels rather than typical revolutionaries—long after the

Raid, Hammond, by then accustomed to using twentieth-century references, preferred to characterize the conspirators as Fascists rather than Bolsheviks.[85] The *Star*, whose editor, Frederick Hamilton, was both a friend of Rhodes and an important member of the secret Reform Committee, continued as the voice of reform, reiterating the sins of the Pretoria government and Uitlander pleas for more enlightened leadership. But public meetings for stirring up the masses were delayed until the most opportune moment.[86] To do otherwise, it was feared, would arouse the Boer authorities and, since the increasing number of miners entering the country from Australia and central Europe were thought to have been "reared on socialist agitation," possibly lead to trouble with the man in the street.[87] Clearly, though, some steps had to be taken to prepare the white laboring class for what was coming. On the twenty-third, George Farrar, manager of a major mining firm and known to be popular with the miners, addressed the work force at his East Rand Proprietary Mine, explaining how their welfare was dependent upon the prosperity of the mining industry as a whole, which was threatened by Kruger's ill-advised policies.[88] Similar gatherings took place at other mines during this period. Indeed, it was charged by their enemies that the reformers had to lecture the masses "night and day [to bring them] up to the pitch of protest."[89]

At the same time the progovernment *Standard and Digger News* attempted to counteract the *Star* by proclaiming the Pretoria regime as the workingmen's friend, and Kruger's agents endeavored to turn the Rand proletariat against their employers. This Transvaal "secret service," which had £50,000 ($250,000) for such purposes, evidently convinced some labor leaders that their people, most of whom earned relatively good wages, had nothing to gain by joining with the mine owners in the developing agitation.[90] The incongruous behavior of both sides, which perhaps startles the historian, must also have caused some soul-searching among the participants in these bizarre affairs.

Because of chronic delays on the railways and the great need for subterfuge, arms shipments from Kimberley were extremely slow. Apparently this and other considerations eroded the reformers' determination as the intended date approached. Early in December, in fact, Frank Rhodes suggested to Jameson that the revolt could not be effected until the following month.[91] Jameson, now just across the border with his 494 men (the original plan had called for 1,500 riders) in the dusty little camp at Pitsani, thought it would be sufficient to advise that Hammond should simply explain to the others the perils of delaying.[92] But Hammond was unsuccessful in this effort. Enthusiasm had waned. George Farrar confided to another member of the reform executive that he was almost ready to "chuck the whole business."[93] More important, Lionel Phillips was beginning to drag his feet, and this prompted the resolute Hammond to telegraph Rhodes on December 18 that Alfred Beit, having just arrived in Cape Town from England the previous day, must come to the Rand to reinvigorate his business associates.[94] Ironically, Rhodes prevented such a trip, however, because he feared Phillips might in fact convince Beit to pull out.[95] The predicament in the reform ranks was not, as one scholar argues, one in which there was no strong leader to keep the others in line, but rather a case of too many strong, assertive leaders who were preoccupied with business matters and probably suspicious of one another.[96] Admittedly neither Phillips nor Leonard were men of action but Hammond, even though he had never before organized a revolt, had shown himself to be a forceful, persuasive figure in earlier difficulties. In this instance, though, his associates were all intelligent, ambitious, and generally very careful Englishmen who undoubtedly distrusted Hammond to a certain extent because he was an American and a Rhodes man.[97] The fundamental problem, however, was the confusion and uncertainty about how the actual rebellion would take place and what the nature and outcome of the external intervention should be.[98] The doubts and indecision already taking their toll on the reformers were to be multiplied by the flag issue.

Two men who had sailed from England with Beit and who had then met with Rhodes reached Johannesburg on December 19 with the news that Jameson intended to march under the Union Jack and when in Johannesburg would raise it over the city.[99] Consternation followed this revelation. Of course, there were those among the reformers and in the general Uitlander population who, in Phillips words, "would have hailed the hoisting of the British flag,"[100] while others, in particular the Americans, were decidedly against it. For many of the latter this ordinarily would have been the case, but recent events had aroused among them even stronger feelings against John Bull. A boundary dispute between Britain and Venezuela led the United States to evoke the Monroe Doctrine and, in a bellicose statement on December 17, President Cleveland had identified his country's honor with stopping alleged British expansionism.[101] Covered in the Rand papers two days later, Cleveland's message further divided the reformers.[102] The flag question was not, as some writers contend, only a pretext for delay.[103] It was important not only to Americans but to many others who were sincerely interested in working only for internal reform of the Transvaal and not for a change of sovereignty. Hammond is said to have now become the champion of the Vierkleur, the Transvaal Flag.[104] When the revolutionary junta met to deal with the problem, Frank Rhodes had to assure the others that there was no private arrangement between himself, his brother, and Jameson to make the Transvaal British.[105] While perhaps somewhat reassuring, this was not considered adequate. Only Cecil Rhodes could calm such troubled waters and possibly get the revolutionary movement back in order.

Colonel Francis Younghusband, a correspondent for the *Times* of London recently dispatched to the Rand to report on the impending clash, was, strangely, sent by the reformers to contact Rhodes in Cape Town and to obtain clarification on the flag. The restless imperialist, who was by then being pressured from London to get the operation underway soon, made conflicting statements to Younghusband.[106] The latter's report to the reformers on December 25 emphasized Rhodes's preference for the British flag and threatened to destroy the movement in Johannesburg. Charles Leonard was told by Capt. Thomas Mein, an American who managed one of the largest mines, that "if this is a case of England gobbling up this country, I am not in it; otherwise I am up to my neck in it."[107] Rather than cancel everything, however, the reformers sent another representation to the Cape to secure a pledge from Rhodes that the Vierkleur would be retained. Charles Leonard and Frederick Hamilton were chosen for this important mission and until they succeeded, much was in doubt. Leonard, who had drawn up a manifesto outlining the Uitlander position, which he had intended to present to a mass meeting of the National Union on December 27, postponed that gathering, but just before leaving for Cape Town arranged for the manifesto to be published. This supposedly would give the populace time to consider all the issues before assembling together later.[108]

To make matters worse, other defects in the strategy became apparent. Surprisingly, for instance, when deciding on a date for the revolt, the planners had not anticipated that the Christmas holiday would bring throngs of Boer celebrants into Pretoria, thus hampering the seizure of the arsenal there.[109] As just noted above, Hammond had enlisted fifty Americans for this assault, keeping them on the outskirts of Kruger's capital until the right moment.[110] Now the scheme was seen as clearly impracticable. This was confirmed by one of Jameson's men who had been sent to the Rand to assist with military preparations.[111] Obviously the original timetable had gone awry, and nothing could be done until the first week of the new year.

Leonard and Hamilton conveyed to Rhodes a convincing description of the confusion and unreadiness on the Rand, and the latter satisfied these emissaries on the flag issue, thus enabling them on December 28 to telegraph reassurances to the reform executive that encouraged the group to "go on quietly" with arrangements and to work for an uprising in early January. Reflecting the reformers' recent decision to proceed without Jameson,[112] furthermore, Leonard insisted that Rhodes notify his impetuous doctor not to move from Pitsani.[113] Rhodes acquiesced, but did not follow through. As late as December 24, Jameson had been assured from Cape Town that the revolt would occur on the twenty-eighth.[114] Now he was told to start out a day later.[115] Finally, on the twenty-ninth he was sent a somewhat ambiguous message from Rhodes, instructing him to remain in camp a little longer, but he never received it.[116]

Jameson's restless troops were losing their spirit out on the hot, empty veld and their commander, fearful that the Boers would discover his intended purpose, concluded that the hesitant Johannesburg party needed a push from him. On the twenty-seventh he again requested that Hammond telegraph him that the affair would begin as planned.[117] At that point, of course, the American was just as determined as the other reformers to postpone it, but he also could appreciate Jameson's position. Hammond proposed to his collaborators that Jameson should move his men to Kimberley where Hammond would meet him and try to find a way to get them into Johannesburg. But this idea won no support; the others evidently no longer wanted anything to do with the external dimension.[118] Hammond therefore had to wire Jameson warning him not to attempt to precipitate events, that to do so would jeopardize the whole cause and bring him no assistance from the mining city. Additionally, two messengers were sent with the same warning, one on horseback and the other by train to Mafeking, it being assumed that at least one would get through to him by the twenty-ninth.[119] Ignoring these attempts to dissuade him, Jameson was apparently still confident his resourceful friend could rouse the laggards in Johannesburg. He telegraphed on the twenty-ninth: "Have great faith in J. H. Hammond, A. L. Lawly and miners with Lee Metford rifles."[120] Then, before striking camp and leading his men into Kruger's country, he stirred their sense of mission by reading aloud the letter obtained earlier from the reformers but now said to have been just received from the threatened city. The Jameson Raid was underway.

It would be twenty-four hours before the fretful conspirators on the Rand heard of the invasion. But there was growing concern among the population there, as rumors abounded and as fear of the unknown spread. Retail business already had declined drastically as stocks were not replenished due to the prevailing uncertainty. At the same time there was a great run on small arms.[121] Since the signs were foreboding to businessmen, the Mercantile Association considered the establishment of a town bodyguard for "preserving public order and protecting lives and property" in any possible emergency.[122]

Revealing Pretoria's suspicion that trouble might occur in the Uitlander center, seventy additional state police took up assignment in Johannesburg.[123] It appears that publication of Leonard's "manifesto," albeit provoking more discussion of the major issues than ever before, contributed to the heightened tension. Those who did not wish to become politically involved or who simply chose to avoid trouble left the Rand in considerable numbers; indeed, the trains could not accommodate the rush by Saturday the twenty-eighth.[124] As worried husbands sent their wives and children to Cape Town or Durban, some of those most concerned with the "sport of kings" shipped their race horses out of the crisis zone.[125] African laborers, too, were aware that something unusual was afoot. Twelve thousand Zulus reportedly sought required passes permitting them to leave while others were quietly slipping away.[126]

Various national or ethnic groups came together to decide on appropriate action. A number of Australians, desiring to make themselves useful in case of hostilities, assembled to form a special Red Cross brigade.[127] Irish and Scottish infantry brigades followed. On the twenty-eighth a deputation of about 60 Americans who had hitherto ignored the reform movement called on President Kruger in Pretoria, refusing to believe that a peaceful solution could not still be found to Uitlander problems. Hammond, who considered this party "undisciplined," heard them explain on the thirtieth how obstinate they had found the old Boer leader. They had in fact been vexed into telling him that in case of trouble they would be against his government. The American community decided to try once more, however, and another, three-member committee was sent to Kruger the following day to urge changes.[128] There were 500 Americans gathered to hear their report on the evening of the thirty-first.

By this time news of Jameson's move had been received and understandably there was great excitement. Since the Pretoria government had not been very accommodating on the list of grievances presented to it—indeed, the deputation to Pretoria stated that "it was hopeless to expect a single concession"—the reaction of those present was a pugnacious one, as almost all now joined the reform movement.[129] Foreseeing British intervention now that the crisis had escalated, some of the Americans expressed a willingness to accept the Union Jack, but Hammond asserted himself vigorously against those who would abandon the reformers' earlier decision to stick with the Transvaal flag. Exhorting the crowd to stand together with "ninety-nine percent of the population of the Rand" in support of "true republican principles,"[130] he earned a rousing show of support when he threatened to shoot the first man who tried to raise the English colors. All but a handful then shouted that they would fight against Kruger. Accordingly, after the meeting was adjourned, a "George Washington Corps" of 150 men was formed.[131]

Hammond was strongly identified with flag work that day. Earlier he had acquired a Vierkleur from a linen draper and brought it to his offices at the CGFSA building, which had become the headquarters of the newly proclaimed Reform Committee. This body was the old secret reform executive now enlarged.[132] It would be in constant emergency session for several days. The engineer-cum-revolutionary entered the room where his colleagues were in deliberation and proceeded to raise the Boer standard. The committee members to a man were persuaded by Hammond to stand and swear allegiance to the South African Republic.[133] Subsequently the flag was hoisted on the roof of the building where it remained for the duration of the crisis despite objections from CGFSA officials in Cape Town.[134]

Large crowds milled about the committee's office, seeking information and direction. Addressed by attorney J. W. Leonard, they were told that the reform leaders had all matters in hand, that their committee was in effect a provisional government for the Rand, which would provide for law, order, and defense.[135] Interestingly, proclamations eventually were printed that announced the provisional government with Phillips as acting president of an executive council consisting of Farrar, Fitzpatrick, and Hammond. These were to be distributed and displayed through the city if

Jameson arrived.[136] Seeing that an efficient leadership was at the helm and a professional military force was en route to help them, many people who had seen no possibility of effecting change, now ended their neutrality. More men volunteered for military service than could be armed or readily used.[137]

An attack on Johannesburg by Kruger's troops was considered a distinct possibility, especially if Jameson's column succeeded in reaching it. Indeed, the Reform Committee wired the British high commissioner in Cape Town that it had good reason to believe the Boers were ready to attack the city at any time and asked him to intervene.[138] Johannesburgers were warned not to do anything that might be interpreted as hostile action against the state, but at the same time various military companies that had sprung up were receiving arms and drilling.[139] Since the regular Transvaal state police were withdrawn on the thirtieth (although some officers continued to circulate in the city out of uniform in order to stay abreast of developments for their government), the Reform Committee had to replace them, but clearly a military force was being prepared that far exceeded normal police requirements. When word of Jameson's incursion came, there were 1,000–1,500 rifles, most still packed in oil drums or other disguised containers in which they had been shipped into the Rand, hidden in various mines.[140] About 1,500 more were still in transit hidden under bags of coke, and men had to be sent down the rail line to get them, along with the bulk of the ammunition and three Maxim guns.[141] In order to deter attack, various stratagems were employed to make Pretoria think that the Uitlanders were heavily armed. Appropriate rumors were encouraged and a theatrical touch was added when mining pumps covered in canvas were paraded through the streets, giving the impression that heavy artillery had somehow been procured.[142] Hammond contributed to this deception by cleverly misleading a Kruger spy about the true state of the reformers' armament.[143] A highly exaggerated report in the *Star* estimated that the number of men "who could be put under arms, and who are mostly at present under arms publicly and privately, is 25,000."[144]

For their safety, women and children living in the suburbs or near the mines were brought into the city where they could be looked after. And a relief fund was established for assisting the needy. As the new year began over £63,000 ($315,000) had been collected from a dozen individuals and firms.[145] The Reform Committee drew from this to feed and house dependent persons in buildings made available in the town center for this emergency.[146]

Besides these services, the committee's "Detective Department" saw to police duties, and its chief, A. Trimble, also administered an informal summary court.[147] Fears of disturbances by the more than 42,000 African workers on the Rand led to the closing of the canteens, the placing of guards around stored liquor, and the prohibition of black miners in the city streets; but apart from minor looting of abandoned homes, these blacks caused no real trouble. Mounted units patroled the streets where nervous merchants had boarded up their storefronts. For the special task of watching over the committee's headquarters, a carefully picked squad of men was sent in from Kimberley, and they enforced a tight security requiring passwords and careful identification of all visitors.[148]

Considering the general confusion and the fact that the mines were closed, a remarkable discipline was maintained throughout the crisis of the first week of January for which the reform leadership deserves much credit. On the other hand, as the added responsibilities and marathon committee sessions frayed their nerves, the amateur revolutionaries were not always above abusing their new power. Whereas the *Star*, which was practically the reformers' in-house organ, had continually directed strong criticism toward Kruger's regime, the provisional government of Johannesburg found it difficult to tolerate disparagement from the rival *Standard and Digger News*. Hammond personally confronted that paper's director and "advised" him to discharge a writer whom the reformers found particularly offensive.[149]

On New Year's Eve, Kruger's representatives brought proposals on the basic Uitlander grievances, including some concessions, to the Reform Committee. Since these were partly acceptable, Lionel Phillips led a small respondent delegation to Pretoria the following day. Upon their return, Phillips informed a large gathering that Kruger's government, through its negotiating commission, agreed to "earnestly consider" the Uitlander grievances and not to undertake hostilities against Johannesburg, provided that nobody there took hostile action against the government.[150] Even though the Uitlander deputation did not at the time formally agree to this stipulation, Phillips later insisting that the reformers were still free to begin military action,[151] there now existed what was virtually an armistice. The Johannesburg representatives did assume responsibility for Jameson's peaceful departure if he reached the city. Finally, Phillips pleased his audience by saying that the Reform Committee would stand behind Jameson, even though he had not been invited to come.[152] The inconsistencies of all this could only have further clouded the picture for people already quite befuddled by events. What Phillips failed to tell the throng in the streets was that he had complied with Kruger's request for the names of the Reform Committee leaders. The crafty old Transvaal President must have marveled at the naïveté of these supposedly sophisticated capitalists.

Closely related to this development was the action of the British high commissioner. Sir Hercules Robinson, who had been privy to much of Rhodes's scheming but who now wished to be seen as an honest broker, won Kruger's acceptance of his offer to mediate the Transvaal confrontation. Robinson had denounced Jameson's invasion immediately upon hearing of it, had ordered him to turn back, and had discouraged any cooperation with him. But the old and feeble British official did not begin his peacemaking work in Pretoria until January 6. In the original plan worked out between the reformers and Rhodes, it had been expected that the high commissioner would be able to move more quickly to mediate.[153] In the meantime much depended on Jameson's fortunes. That daring but foolhardy commander had led some five hundred men into the Transvaal, expecting to slice through any Boer opposition in the same fashion as he had overcome the Ndebele in 1893. After a demanding three-day ride to Krugersdorp, about thirty miles from Johannesburg, they encountered Transvaal troopers who had been following the column's progress. On January 2, following some confusion about the best way to get to Johannesburg, the invaders were lured into a Boer trap and, after suffering fifty-eight casualties, their commander surrendered. On the battlefield the victors found the letter of invitation to Jameson signed by Hammond and other reform leaders.

Subsequently a controversy arose, which to this day has not been fully resolved, over whether Jameson was to get aid from the Reform Committee. Some of his men insisted that the Johannesburg leaders informed Jameson before the battle that their city "had risen to man" and reinforcements would meet him at Krugersdorp.[154] It appears that Frank Rhodes had notified Jameson on January that he would send an "officers' patrol" to meet him just outside Johannesburg, but this was to be only a ceremonial escort, not military assistance.[155] On the fateful morning of the battle, however, Colonel Rhodes had received Jameson's request for an armed unit to join him. Colonel R. A. Bettington, commander of a mounted Uitlander detachment known as Bettington's Horse, asked to be sent out, but Rhodes reluctantly refused and instead sent his cavalry on various errands, all in the opposite direction. When an explosion occurred at a mine on the road to Krugersdorp, Bettington had an excuse to move in that direction, fully intending to reach Jameson.[156] Meanwhile Phillips and Hammond, worried about the unit's rather long absence, sent riders out. Gordon Sandilands, a member of the Reform Committee, caught Bettington's contingent about ten miles from the city and brought them back.[157]

The people of Johannesburg, heretofore rather well-behaved, turned unruly when Jameson's capture was announced. To the ordinary person, uninformed as he was of the Raid's background, Jameson was a gallant hero acting in the Uitlanders' interest. Throngs outside the committee's office wanted to know why a rescue mission had not been sent. Rumors of treachery and cowardice swept through the town and for a time the committee's safety was in doubt.[158] Phillips later concluded that the only reason their headquarters was not overrun was the mob's exaggerated impression of the reformers' strength.[159] Eventually calm was restored, but some Uitlanders were now more determined than ever to beat the Boers and wanted action.[160]

The fact of the matter was, however, that the provisional government was doing its best to prevent conflict. Its military units were kept occupied in drilling, digging trenches, and guarding a herd of cattle that would become essential in case of a long siege.[161] One force of a thousand men with two Maxim guns was situated in and around a children's home on a prominent hill about two hours' march from the town center; another group with the third Maxim was dug in on a commanding height called Hohenheim; while a third contingent was sent out to a place known as Aukland Park.[162] Nor was the other side idle. Boer soldiers had been occupying certain points around the city since December 30. Their strongest position was at the jail on Hospital Ridge, which now served them as a fort from where they had at least two artillery pieces trained on the Uitlander encampments.[163]

When it was prematurely reported on January 2 that Jameson was soon to reach Johannesburg, the Reform Committee, fearing his arrival would cause the Boers to bombard their positions, decided to seize the fortified jail. Hammond, evidently intent upon taking an even more active part in this fluctuating revolution, assumed command of an assault team to carry out this mission, but word of Jameson's surrender cut short the project.[164] Nevertheless, the situation remained ripe for a clash. There were several reports of Uitlanders being fired upon;[165] still the committee urged its people not to shoot back. When a Boer party raided their cattle herd and took some three hundred head, the guard did not retaliate.[166] Although some hotheads regretted this policy, it undoubtedly hastened a settlement.

The high commissioner's discussions with Kruger led to the former's apology for the invasion and agreement that Johannesburg should disarm unconditionally. Joseph Chamberlain, the British colonial secretary who had given his secret support to the Rhodes-Jameson plot to end Kruger's resistance to a South African federation, cabled his acceptance of these terms. And thus the Reform Committee received Kruger's ultimatum on January 6 that it must surrender all its arms or risk not only the lives of Jameson and his fellow captives, but also forfeit any support from the British government.[167] Sir Sidney Shippard, governor of British Bechuanaland, was sent into the Rand to encourage capitulation. His speech to the Johannesburg populace on January 7, in which he emphasized that compliance would ensure the safety of both Jameson and the reform leaders, was quite effective.[168] The revolt, such as it was, now was definitely over. The provisional government soon dissolved. Guns were turned in the following day.

The city gradually returned to normalcy as the Transvaal police resumed their regular responsibilities and the mines reopened. Boer authorities, however, were slow to be convinced that all the arms were being surrendered. After all, much had been done to make them think many more guns had arrived in the reformers' hands. On the night of January 9, Hammond and the other committee members, mistakenly believing that Great Britain would never permit them to be arrested, were taken into custody and all their assets frozen. Jameson and his men, most of whom were British subjects, were turned over to the queen's authorities for trial in England, but the Reform Committee, with primary focus on the ringleaders, was to be brought before a Transvaal court.

For his part, Cecil Rhodes was forced to resign the Cape premiership, and his cabinet fell. It was political ruin for him. He, along with Chamberlain and certain other British officials privy to Rhodes's plans, would have to endure the embarrassing trial of Jameson and a long parliamentary inquiry. Had he not threatened to expose Chamberlain's complicity in the planning of the raid, Rhodes probably would have lost his chartered company. The Jameson fiasco did indeed shake the high and the mighty.

Hammond and his sixty-four colleagues were not brought to trial until April. And the intervening several months were hard ones. Hammond fell seriously ill in his Pretoria prison and only partially recovered while released on bail. During that period his plight called forth a considerable show of support from his influential relatives, friends, and former associates in the United States. His wife worked tirelessly in his behalf, visiting Kruger and urging Hammond's American contacts to stress that he had not been a tool of Rhodes but, rather, had fought for republican principles and against injustice.[169] George Becker, an American geologist-engineer and Hammond's former superior on the United States Geological Survey, was in South Africa to conduct a mining survey and he approached Kruger before Hammond had been granted bail. He relayed Hammond's message that while he expected a heavy punishment, he hoped to be let out of prison because his physician predicted that, given his illness, he would not survive for long.[170]

The American consular agent in Johannesburg initiated, somewhat reticently, the official American involvement in Hammond's case by admonishing Kruger against "any illegal retention of the citizens of my country."[171] In time, considerable pressure was brought to bear on Washington as leading newspapers publicized Hammond's predicament and members of his engineering fraternity joined the campaign to help him.[172] Various members of Congress used their influence with the State Department, prompting Secretary of State Richard Olney to take a serious interest in Kruger's American prisoners, especially Hammond. Olney obtained British cooperation in this effort to afford Hammond all possible protection.[173] All those concerned for his welfare, however, realized that the Transvaal was definitely within its rights to try those implicated in the abortive insurrection and, despite their protestations to Pretoria, they knew the best they could hope for was a fair trial and leniency.

In late January all the Reform Committee prisoners except the five principal leaders, Hammond, Farrar, Fitzpatrick, Phillips, and F. Rhodes (Charles Leonard, also identified as a ringleader, had slipped out of the country and thus avoided arrest), were released on £10,000 ($50,000) bail. Later, because of his deteriorating health, Hammond was permitted, after furnishing £20,000 ($100,000) bail, to return to his Johannesburg home where he remained under close guard. Since his condition still failed to improve, he won permission to seek recuperation in Cape Town. It was apparent that the Transvaal's case against the major reformers would be a strong one and that an acquittal was unlikely. In fact, Hammond's attorney warned that a Boer jury "is bound to convict."[174] Some of Hammond's friends, therefore, advised him to escape while in the Cape.[175] This he refused to do and, when notified to appear for trial in late April, he returned to Pretoria. Their attorneys had advised the reform leaders to plead guilty to a "minor form" of treason, believing that the punishment would be no more than banishment from the country. Against his better judgment, Hammond joined the others in agreeing to such a plea. However, the legal system of the Transvaal was based not on the British but on the Roman-Dutch legal tradition, which evidently was not familiar to the defendants' counsel. The trial judge interpreted their acknowledgment of guilt and other particulars of the case through Roman-Dutch principles and rendered an unexpected decision.[176]

It took the Transvaal High Court only a few days to convict the chief Johannesburg conspirators of the charge of high treason and inciting a rebellion. On April 28, the four were sentenced to death. Shortly afterward Kruger received a petition for Hammond's pardon containing the signatures of 250 members of the U.S. Senate and House of Representatives, as well as that of Vice President Adlai Stevenson.[177] His conviction only spurred Hammond's supporters to continue lobbying for him. An attempt was made to have President Cleveland appeal personally to Kruger for clemency, but Secretary Olney argued that this would not be appropriate.[178] In any case, the Boer leader was deluged by petitions and appeals to spare the reformers. And these were not by any means all from abroad. There was much local sentiment in their favor. On one occasion 150 mayors representing urban and rural districts in different parts of South Africa visited Pretoria for this purpose.[179]

Ultimately, on June 11, after exploiting the situation for his own ends and letting the detested Uitlanders stew in their own fears, Kruger pardoned them. To gain their freedom, each of the four was required to pay a ($125,000) fine and, if he wanted to avoid total banishment from the territory, to swear to abstain from any political activity in the Transvaal for three years.[180] At least Hammond's ordeal was over. Two weeks later he and his family were at sea, bound for England. His departure marked the end of the most intensive involvement of any American in South African political life.

The actions of Hammond and his fellow Americans on the Reform Committee deservedly incurred the wrath of Kruger's government. But their complicity in the abortive Johannesburg revolt should not obscure their other important work. American mining engineers and other specialists made a gigantic contribution to the progress of South Africa's mineral industries. Indeed, without their extensive participation, especially in the gold fields, this phase of the country's economic life would not have advanced so impressively. American engineers came to dominate the field during a key developmental stage when about fifty of them were at work in South Africa in 1896.[181] Hammond, it should be noted, not only brought several other Yankee engineers with him to South Africa, but he and other industry leaders continued to hire the best graduates of American training programs and those who had made their mark in U.S. mining. This is the other, and hardly less spectacular, side of American involvement in South Africa during the late nineteenth century.

Headquartered in London from 1899 to 1902, Hammond maintained his lucrative association with Consolidated Gold Fields. During this period in Britain he observed the trial and conviction of Jameson for violating the Foreign Enlistment Act. The notorious doctor spent only four months in prison before resuming an active life which, remarkably, saw him become prime minister of the Cape. Hammond also was on hand when Rhodes was censured by a parliamentary committee. For his own part, Hammond honored his commitment to refrain from any political activity related to the Transvaal, which he interpreted to include written statements that might embarrass its government. Yet in 1897 his wife published her diary of the period from late December 1895 to June 1896. Although she disclaimed any political intent in this disarming little book, Natalie Hammond certainly reflected her husband's views about the intolerable stubbornness and obstructionism of Kruger's government that had provoked the reformers' attempt to displace him.

Right up to the eve of the Anglo-Boer War Hammond's work occasionally brought him back to the Rand on inspection trips. While there in 1899 he saw that the heightening crisis was bringing Boer and Briton to the brink of conflict and he consented to convey the Uitlanders' case to Kruger. Here was the ex-rebel facing the man whose policies had provoked him into a revolutionary conspiracy and who then spared his life. Since the Raid, the Transvaal had extended certain modest reforms to the mining community affecting education, the franchise, and local administration, but these could hardly satisfy a population so long denied and now led by a renewed reform movement calling loudly for British intervention.[182] And London was now much more concerned with the matter than in 1895–96. Consequently, Hammond met Kruger in an attempt to explain the need for major concessions in light of growing official British impatience and sympathy for the Uitlanders. For Hammond the whole scene must have created a sense of déjà vu. The Boer president refused to be alerted to the dangers facing his state; he preferred to think Britain would not go to war and assumed he could negotiate successfully with the queen's representatives. When he finally saw the need to compromise more seriously, it was too late.

Insistent British imperialism was not to be denied. The war between the two white forces in South Africa, which many said was inevitable, began in December 1899 and, after almost three years of bitter struggle, ended in a British victory. The union of South Africa's territories was finally achieved by a force of arms.

Hammond gave up his London office and returned to the United States in 1902, thereafter continuing to add to his prestige as one of the top men in his field. And he remained a consulting engineer for Consolidated Gold Fields until 1908, a responsibility that annually necessitated trips to South Africa. These visits enabled him to continue providing sound advice to the company. Even after his resignation in 1908, Hammond's services continued as he became the firm's major promoter in the United States. It was Hammond who encouraged investment in American enterprises such as light and power companies, oil, a dredging company and, yes, alluvial gold properties. In 1909, at Hammond's urging the Gold Fields American Development Company was launched.[183]

Already financially secure before taking up the challenge of the Rand, Hammond became very wealthy as a result of his South African work. Besides amassing a fortune from various mining, petroleum, and electric power ventures, he became a staunch Republican and a friend and advisor of several presidents. He even made a halfhearted bid for his party's vice presidential nomination in 1908. His South African experience, even though it was but a short interlude in his long and eventful life, nevertheless exerted a great impact on him. Over the years he regularly returned to that subject in his writings. He published various commentaries and reminiscences culminating in his two-volume autobiography of 1935, about a third of which is devoted to his days in South Africa.

Hammond consistently argued that the revolutionary conspiracy of 1895–96, had it succeeded, would have brought redress of grievances for the Uitlanders, which ultimately would have facilitated a rapprochement among all South African territories, thus preventing the Anglo-Boer War at that time. But, he believed, Germany would have been able to bring a still independent Transvaal to its side in 1914, enabling the Second Reich to conquer all of South Africa. Such a success in turn would have provided wealth and strategic advantages to the Germans sufficient enough to give them a world victory. Therefore, the Anglo-Boer war coming when it did, admittedly precipitated by the Jameson Raid, brought a needed British hegemony to South Africa that prevented a much more unfavorable sequence of events in 1914–18.[184] In such inflated terms did the prominent capitalist of later years try to justify his participation in earlier activities that might not be considered seemly for a man of his station and conservative philosophy.

6
Carl Akeley and the Preservation of African Mammals

Often considered nothing more than a skilled trade, taxidermy is not an occupation that normally would lead its practitioner to international prominence in several fields. But in the case of Carl Akeley it did. Because of his extraordinarily successful effort to raise his chosen vocation to the level of both an art and a science, he became an honored figure among naturalists. The foremost memorials to his achievement are the imposing exhibit halls named after him that are part of the great natural history museums in Chicago and New York City. And there is another, less conspicuous tribute to his work in wildlife conservation that is indicative of his multifaceted career. This is an animal reserve that he was most instrumental in creating in central equatorial Africa. Akeley's experiences in Africa were a major influence in his life. The fact that, according to his wish, Akeley was buried in that remote national park in Zaïre testifies to his compelling tie to the continent.

Akeley was a man of many talents who gradually turned them toward one major objective, the preservation of Africa's animals. This was to be accomplished by presenting vividly realistic displays of mounted specimens in major museums and by inspiring a concern for conservation in Africa. Through his own writings and those of other authors about him, as well as by presentations on the lecture circuit, he emphasized the rapid depletion of Africa's major mammals and the need to halt it. His work bore fruit when, in 1925, King Albert of Belguim decreed the establishment of Africa's first wildlife preserve. Unfortunately, the pleasure hunters' and poachers' assault on Africa's animals has continued since Akeley's time, despite some valiant attempts to stop it; this remains a critical problem in some countries. But without Akeley's pioneering steps, species such as the gorilla and elephant undoubtedly would be in even greater danger of extinction.

Carl Ethan Akeley *(Courtesy of the Field Museum of Natural History, Chicago, Neg. No. 5974).*

Akeley's interest in animals, particularly the thrill of hunting them and the fascination with mounting their skins, was acquired early in life. He was the second of four sons of a farmer who had moved to western New York from Vermont. Born in 1864, Carl (he preferred this to his given name of Clarence) grew up on a small, marginal farmstead. His family was frequently in economic straits and all had to work hard to survive. Yet there was some time for hunting and exploring adjacent woodlands. The Akeley property was located two miles from the village of Clarendon and about eighteen miles from Rochester, in a rocky lowland area containing both forests and swamps. With his gun and dog young Akeley frequently roamed over the country, becoming familiar with its varied fauna.[1]

His formal education was minimal: eight years of instruction at a nearby one-room school was all the solitary, nature-loving prospective farmer at first wanted. At age sixteen, however, the youth managed to complete six months of classes at Brockport Normal School. When he was about thirteen, Akeley borrowed a book on taxidermy from a friend and began to mount birds. This, rather than regular schooling appealed most to him. It did not take long before he realized that simple bird mountings were not satisfying his holistic sense of nature, that detached from their environment they could not be much appreciated. Consequently he decided to display his preserved birds against painted backgrounds. Toward this end the youngster took some painting lessons from a local art teacher in nearby Holly. Later, in Brockport he met an English painter-decorator who was also a taxidermist. This was David Bruce, who had been judged capable enough to prepare several animal mountings for a museum in Rochester. When, in 1882, Carl inquired about studying the trade under him, Bruce agreed to accept him as an apprentice but recommended instead that he go to a major taxidermy center in Rochester, Ward's Natural Science Establishment.

Henry Augustus Ward was a student and strong admirer of Louis Agassiz, Swiss-born-and-educated Professor of Zoology at Harvard University. A widely influential teacher and scholar, Agassiz emphasized the role of the research museum in science. Ward studied under Agassiz in the 1850s and subsequently taught geology and other sciences at the University of Rochester. Also a dedicated proponent of museums as centers for furthering natural history, Ward began to assemble and prepare specimens for museum collections, ultimately forsaking his faculty position in

1869 for full concentration on his zoological supply business.[2] The Ward Establishment, across the street from the University of Rochester, attracted a number of young men interested in science and natural history who later became important educators and leading museum officials.[3] It was a rather unique place, one that gave the novice zoologist, botanist, geologist, and taxidermist very beneficial experience.

Akeley was nineteen when, announcing to his parents that taxidermy was his choice for a career, he left home. He certainly had become unhappy there. His puritanical mother, supported by her relatives and others in the local farming community, had incessantly criticized his long hours of hunting and, especially, his preoccupation with taxidermy, both of which to her seemed totally unrespectable and unproductive.[4] Thus he sought and obtained a job at Ward's. Akeley naturally saw the move to Rochester as an exciting new challenge, although he soon found that employment at Ward's was neither easy nor highly remunerative. The proprietor was a hard taskmaster, one who simply wanted to fill his orders as efficiently as possible. Akeley quickly mastered the basics of taxidermy as then practiced, but the process was extremely primitive and gave him little satisfaction. Animal skins were crudely stuffed with straw or excelsior and stitched together so that the finished mounting conveyed some semblance of the live animal. Evidently Ward's clients, who wanted specimens for scientific reference, generally were satisfied with such work, the prices for which could be kept low. Better preparation techniques were known, but Ward, except in special cases, eschewed them, insisting that his customers would not pay for more meticulous work. Akeley quickly became disillusioned with mass-production taxidermy because he knew superior methods could produce more realistic specimens.

He and his coworkers suffered a hectic work schedule yet they developed a comradship that helped to sustain them. Akeley built a particularly strong friendship with William Morton Wheeler, who would become one of America's foremost biologists. Moreover, while at Ward's he made the acquaintance of a professor of biology at Rochester University, Harrison Webster, who was impressed with Akeley's scientific potential and encouraged the young taxidermist to continue his education.[5] Akeley thus decided to ready himself for the entrance examination to the Sheffield Scientific School of Yale University by studying geometry and Latin. Not being a natural scholar, however, and tied to a demanding work routine, he was unable to prepare adequately for the test. An illness, moreover, prevented him from taking the examination.[6] Yale would never count him on its rolls.

Because of his more innovative approach to his craft, Akeley experimented, often on his own time, with new techniques that did not please his employer. More disturbing to Ward, however, was the report that Akeley sometimes slipped away from his work place and napped in the shop's attic. Consequently, Ward fired him sometime in 1883.[7] The latter found employment in a small but busy taxidermy shop in New York. This was six months of dismal labor that held no promise for the future. When Ward agreed to take him back, therefore, Akeley returned to Rochester and remained with the firm for another three years. As he learned more about his field, constantly drawing upon his considerable mechanical aptitude and artistic sensibilities, Akeley continued to develop his skill. When he tried to apply his new methods on a broader basis to the work being done at Ward's, he was usually frustrated. Ward's was simply not the place for this imaginative and gifted taxidermist. In search of more fulfilling work, Akeley applied for a position in the taxidermy department of the American Museum of Natural History in New York, stating that "I believe that I can give you satisfaction in all classes of taxidermy and also on mounting small skeletons."[8] Although his bid was rejected at that time, Akeley some years later would earn himself an honored position with that major institution.

Before he left Ward's, however, Akeley was given the chance to demonstrate his ability as a taxidermist in a way that made him a minor celebrity. In 1885 Ward received word that an elephant owned by the great circus impresario, P. T. Barnum, had been killed and that Ward's should preserve the remains. This was no ordinary pachyderm. It was none other than the famous Jumbo, an African elephant that was featured in Barnum's circus parades and was beloved by North American audiences. While being led to its own railway car in St. Thomas, Ontario, the beast encountered an oncoming locomotive that could not be stopped before ramming Jumbo head-to-head. The elephant died shortly thereafter. Barnum could not give it up; he wanted the animal mounted so that Jumbo could continue to lead his troupe of performers into towns of circus-loving America. And thus Ward hurried off with Akeley and another employee to the accident scene. By the time they arrived, the animal's huge, now odoriferous carcass had been exposed to the hot summer sun for a day and a half. Needless to say, the task before Akeley was not a pleasant one. He was nauseated through most of the ordeal of removing the skin and bones. The hide, weighing 1,538 pounds, was detached in three pieces and shipped back to Rochester where Akeley, officially under the direction of J. W. Critchley, gradually became the principal designer of the project. Jumbo, Barnum insisted, must be available for the next spring's circus opening. Moreover, he urged Ward to "stuff" the skin as large as possible, even, he hoped, larger than life. The shattered skull had to be repaired and a way found to support the heavy skin that would endure the demands of circus use. It was the type of challenge to which Akeley would rise constantly during his career.[9]

Here was the beginning, albeit a crude one, of Akeley's development of modern large mammal taxidermy. Over a basic frame constructed of wooden planks strengthened by steel plates were nailed steamed basswood slats, curved to simulate the animal's shape. To this the hide was attached by many countersunk nails, which would prevent major shrinkage or stretching due to temperature changes.[10] Akeley did not consider this a permanent preservation, but it certainly served the client well for several years. Jumbo, its imposing mounted figure now carried on a low-wheeled platform, continued to be a headliner with Barnum's company until it was retired in 1888 for display at Tufts College.[11] Akeley became known as the man who stuffed Jumbo, one of the first elephants ever mounted by taxidermists in the United States. A close friend during that period was convinced that the Jumbo assignment and the peculiar problems it presented to him gave Akeley the inspiration for his later emphasis on the display of African mammals.[12]

Akeley left Ward's for good in 1886. His friend, William Wheeler, had returned the previous year to his home town of Milwaukee where he became a science teacher. Aware of Akeley's not yet abandoned interest in preparing for university entrance, he offered to tutor him if Akeley would come to Milwaukee. And he would help his friend get taxidermy assignments from the city's Public Museum. Wheeler's mother, furthermore, agreed to let Akeley use her barn for his work. It was an opportunity not to be missed. So Akeley went to the Midwest and there began an important phase of his professional life. The sign that soon hung outside one end of the Wheeler barn read C. E. Akeley's Studio of Scientific and Decorative Taxidermy. College and Museum Work a Specialty.[13] Much of the mounting he did at the time was through commissions from the museum.[14] As he had done when they worked at Ward's, the intellectual, broadly educated Wheeler spent some of his evenings reading to Akeley while the latter labored in his shop. On other occasions the pair could be seen at lectures and cultural events.[15] This association with Wheeler undoubtedly was a stimulating and rewarding one for the relatively uneducated Akeley; it exposed him to a world of ideas that in a degree compensated for his short time in the classroom.[16]

In 1887 Wheeler left the small German-English academy where he was teaching to take the post of director of the Milwaukee Public Museum. Established in 1883, this institution was destined to become a major progressive museum of its kind. Ward had visited the city in that year and had exhibited a natural science collection at the industrial exhibition that Milwaukee's business leaders had arranged. Later he convinced the museum officials that they should buy his specimen collection to be put in a permanent exhibit.[17] These items and a small library comprised the museum and were housed in the exhibition building. When he assumed the directorship, Wheeler wasted no time in making his museum a meaningful part of the community's educational life. He inaugurated a lecture series for schoolchildren and emphasized the importance of accurate, realistic displays of animals.[18] There was, of course, a place for Carl Akeley in this scheme.

Akeley had been a half-time employee of the museum since 1887 (at fifty cents an hour), which enabled him barely to cover his expenses. In 1889 he was promoted to full-time taxidermist, one of the few such positions in the country at that time.[19] This work, along with that he did in his own shop, occupied him so fully that he now recognized the impossibility of furthering his formal education. He and Wheeler were agreed that wildlife exhibits must be done in a more sophisticated manner if they were to be educational, but insufficient funding was a major problem. Akeley's earlier suggestions for fully authentic animal groupings were voted down by the museum board because its members did not believe they could raise the necessary money. When Wheeler took over, he supported his friend as much as possible, but limited resources dictated that ambitious new projects be put on hold. Nevertheless, Akeley continued to demonstrate his leadership in taxidermy. The construction of habitat groupings was his principal objective and he prepared some excellent ones in Milwaukee.

The presentation of preserved creatures amid plants and natural or artificial accessories, especially against a painted background—the common definition of a habitat group—can be traced to private museum exhibitions in New York and Baltimore about 1815. But these would not have been scientifically accurate and they had no influence on taxidermy.[20] Shortly after mid-century some bird taxidermists were using painted backgrounds to enhance their group presentations, although these did not reach museums at that time.[21] Similar work with mammals was slower to evolve. By 1880, however, an impressive orangutan group (without painted background) by W. T. Hornaday was on view in the American Museum of Natural History. About the same time, young Akeley in Clarendon, in addition to his amateurish but promising bird groups, did a boxed mounting of at least one mammal, a fox poised over a downed partridge against a painted background, that places him among the pioneering habitat taxidermists. His most notable construction for the Milwaukee Museum was the muskrat group done in 1890, a far more complete, complex combination of animals and plants than anything attempted theretofore, definitely a trend setting work in the field of museology. It still fascinated visitors there a century later. Wheeler helped him collect the animals in a local swamp along with birds native to the Milwaukee vicinity. Accented by artificial plants and convincingly centered by simulated water, this presentation, which included a painted background, set the standard for all institutions that wanted to replicate nature for the education of their viewers about animal behavior.[22]

By 1890 Akeley's impressive creations earned him the financial backing of several people that enabled him to purchase a small house for his taxidermy enterprise. After his regular hours at the museum he fulfilled work orders from different institutions and from private customers. In April 1892 he resigned from the museum to devote full time to his own practice.[23] Unfortunately, however, due to his insistence on complicated and thus expensive procedures, Akeley's shop was not a business success.[24] Professional recognition, on the other hand, continued to come in. The United States National Museum in Washington, D. C., commissioned him to prepare a horse for its collection. In 1891 his deer head won an award at the Sportsman's Show in Madison Square Garden, and officials of the spectacular 1893 Columbian Exposition in Chicago invited him to submit an example of his handiwork for its zoological exhibition.[25]

Meanwhile, William Wheeler had left the Milwaukee Museum in 1890 to undertake graduate studies at newly established Clark University in Massachusetts. While in the late stages of his doctoral program in biology, he accepted a teaching position at the University of Chicago. Soon granted a research leave in Europe, Wheeler studied with leading scientists in Germany and Italy. As he made his way back to the United States in 1894 he stopped in

London and there visited the British Museum, which owned an impressive display of mounted animals. Wheeler told Sir William Fowler of that institution about the brilliant taxidermy of Carl Akeley. Shortly thereafter, the latter was invited to London with the prospect of working for the prestigious British Museum.[26] Intending in 1895 to go to London for an interview, Akeley could not pass through Chicago without stopping at the recently opened Field Columbian Museum (later named the Field Museum of Natural History).

This was yet another museum touched by William Augustus Ward. For the World's Columbian Exhibition, that zoological supplier had assembled a large display of specimens valued at $100,000. Marshall Field, the department store tycoon, donated the funds needed to buy the collection for a new museum. Indeed, he gave the founding committee $1,000,000 and later earmarked $8,430,000 in his will for the institution that would bear his name. Thus, a foremost American museum began with ample money to gain international recognition.[27] The recently appointed curator of zoology there was Dr. Daniel G. Elliot, a highly respected scientist who gave Akeley a tour of the facilities, which were housed in one of the exposition buildings. Aware of his visitor's fast-growing reputation in taxidermy and eager to hire him, Elliot favorably impressed Akeley with his vision of what the emergent museum should be. Elliot was determined to establish spectacular exhibits that would merit international acclaim. They had a meeting of minds, and consequently Akeley gave up his London trip. Moving his business to Chicago, he began preparing exhibits proposed by Elliott.[28] The young preparator would spend the next fourteen years in the Windy City and while associated with the museum there he developed his long enchantment with Africa.

Appointed chief taxidermist at the museum in 1896, Akeley found most conditions in his new post to his liking. Especially pleasing was Elliot's invitation to join him for a collecting expedition to British Somaliland, the first such venture by an American museum in Africa. This experience was invaluable because it afforded him an opportunity to hunt and observe some of the African species he already had begun to prepare for the museum. Knowledge of the animals he was mounting was always a high priority in Akeley's taxidermy, but in the 1890s there was little published data or filmed materials available on Africa's wildlife. In any case, there was no substitute for fieldwork; now he would have five months of it.[29] Their party arrived in the Horn of Africa in

April 1896. Somaliland, inhabited by nomadic pastoral peoples, was a hot, arid country but one that contained a rich variety of animals. By September they had brought down 200 mammals, numerous reptiles, and 300 birds. In addition to their skins, skeletons and casts of heads and body parts of larger animals were shipped back. And Elliot was proud to report that many weapons, utensils, ornaments, and garments had been procured from local tribesmen. He felt justified in claiming that his institution now had the greatest collection of large African quadrupeds in the United States.[30]

The first hunt was undertaken in the hinterland of the port city of Berber while the expedition was waiting for sufficient camels, then in short supply, to carry their supplies south to the Ogaden region where the major collection would take place. In the Golis hills about thirty miles from the coast, Akeley and Edward Dodson, a young taxidermist from the British Museum whom Elliot recruited after learning that he had participated recently in another expedition in this territory, tracked the wild ass, an extremely shy creature that was considered a most difficult quarry. After a long pursuit, they bagged enough for a group mounting, but in the process they ran out of water in the parching desert area. Their guides were unsuccessful in efforts to find a water hole. To make matters worse, the party had to wait out a long sandstorm. Beginning to worry about survival in such grueling conditions, Akeley saw a small caravan approaching. Some Somali camel-riders passed by his position carrying goatskins full of milk but refused to part with any of it. As they departed, Akeley, deciding that his group's plight was sufficiently precarious, raised his rifle and threatened to shoot one of the riders if they did not spare some of their milk. This move succeeded and his party's thirst was soon quenched. Even though the liquid was sour and quite warm, Akeley later claimed he had never had a finer drink.[31]

On another occasion during this first venture in Africa, he had a terrifying encounter with a wounded eighty pound female leopard. According to Akeley, who was never known to exaggerate or falsify his own accomplishments, as the crazed cat chewed on his arm he somehow avoided the rear claws and fell on the animal's chest, his knees in its ribs. With his other hand he clasped the leopard's throat. Though his own strength was ebbing fast, Akeley managed to crush the animal's ribs as he choked it, and the leopard eventually ceased its struggle.[32] A few weeks later, while hunting oryx, he had a frightening brush with two lions about which he admitted "death was but an instant away."[33] These were indeed painful, life-threatening experiences that taught him important lessons for the future. For he was hardly through with Africa.

Akeley, who in 1902 married Wisconsin native Delia Denning, was back in the "Dark Continent" in October 1905. Accompanied by his wife, museum naturalist Edmund Heller, and experienced big-game hunter Vernon Shaw-Kennedy, he now headed a Field Museum expedition to the British East African Protectorate, later called Kenya. This part of East Africa was still rather unexploited as far as colonial real estate was concerned. After obtaining Uganda through an agreement with Germany in 1890, Britain allowed the chartered Imperial East Africa Company to establish a meager presence there and in the East African Protectorate. When the company collapsed in 1894, the British government assumed all responsibility for "developing" the territories, but it was slow going. A major step forward was the Uganda Railway, completed in 1901, which linked the Indian Ocean port of Mombasa with Lake Victoria. This provided a means of transporting interior products and materials to the coast, a facility that helped to draw white settlers to the attractive highland plateau area of the protectorate in the early years of the twentieth century. It was a wild colonial territory containing vast savannas teeming with game herds, a veritable hunter's paradise.

After more than twelve months' work, Akeley's team could show considerably greater results than what was obtained on the earlier venture. Seventeen tons of skins, skeletons, plaster casts, photographs, leaves, and other mounting accessories, along with anthropological materials, were added to the Field Museum's growing collection of things African.[34] The principal objective of the expedition was the elephant, which took the Akeleys into the Abedare Mountains about fifty miles north of Nairobi. A leading local elephant hunter, Richard Cunningham, was hired to facilitate the mission and to teach Akeley as much as possible about the huge, intelligent animal. During their several months in that region Akeley shot a bull and his wife brought down an even larger male at the base of Mt. Kenya further to the east. Although Akeley was disappointed because they failed to obtain enough of the best specimens for a group display, his long search for the pachyderms enabled him to observe their movements and behavior which served him well both for subsequent hunts as well as for the construction of accurately detailed mountings.[35]

When he resumed his regular duties in Chicago in early 1907, there were many projects awaiting his attention. The pair of elephant skins was the major one. Throwing himself into the work, Akeley strove to make these mountings the best ever done. And he had every right to be proud of the impressive results. His elephants were ready for public view in 1909 and placed in the central rotunda of the Field Museum. In 1920 these magnificent specimens were moved to Stanley Field Hall of the new museum where they still dominate the huge room. The beasts in fighting attitude became the most widely used symbol of the institution, appearing on stationary, checks, postcards, and souvenirs.[36] As Akeley and his carefully chosen staff brought their skills to bear on the task of giving lifelike expression to the preserved remains of African mammals, the "Akeley method" of taxidermy came into prominence. Until his time most taxidermy was so primitive it disgusted anyone familiar with the animals represented, and he determined not to be identified with it. The typical animal exhibits found in American museums or academic science departments were merely skins stuffed with straw or cotton, much like cheap upholstered furniture, and crudely set on a base. As the stuffing shrank or deteriorated, and as the poorly prepared hide aged, the figure gradually became unrecognizable.

Some of the more accomplished taxidermists, it must be admitted, were practicing a technique known as the Hornaday process, after William T. Hornaday, a former Ward employee who became director of the New York Zoological Park. This involved the construction of a straw form which was covered with wood lath and bound together. Clay was then applied, and over this rough animal shape the skin was stretched and glued. Invariably the clay cracked into pieces, leaving obvious depressions in the hide. Heavier plaster forms came into use, but fluctuating temperatures and atmospheric conditions caused the covering skins to shrink.[37]

In Akeley's new system nothing was spared to achieve a truly lifelike appearance. Manikins, which he considered the essential nuclei, were meticulously modeled in clay so that when the skins were applied they covered a form almost exactly like that of the actual animal. Naturally, this required precise measurements and, often, the construction of body casts immediately after the animals were killed. Some parts of a subject's skeleton, such as the skull and leg bones, were used in building the manikin. The mounting of the hide on the finished clay model, though sometimes done, was not practical since the latter was too heavy and cracked easily. Akeley, therefore, decided that it was necessary to make a plaster mold of the clay model and into the former, after first attaching a muslin liner, he worked layers of papier-mâché, strengthened with wire cloth. Shellac covered each layer of the papier-mâché. The end product was a light, strong, and moisture-proof manikin that revolutionized the field of animal mounting.[38]

Another requisite was a carefully tanned skin. Akeley devised a unique tanning process that produced a soft hide that would not shrink. Unlike the older method, which used a wet skin, Akeley stretched the dry skin over the manikin and attached it with a glue that contained no water, thus preventing shrinkage when the materials dried.[39] All of these tasks, of course, were more difficult when the taxidermist worked with the enormous integument of an elephant. Field preparations were particularly taxing. After a kill the hide, commonly weighing a ton, was quickly removed in three or more sections. Sometimes over two inches thick, it was then shaved to a quarter of an inch, a laborious procedure that took a gang of Africans days to complete. The skin was then salted and dried out in the sun before being wrapped in waterproof cloth and ultimately packed in zinc-lined boxes. Later, when the manikin was ready to receive the skin, the latter could be made flexible by soaking it in water.[40]

Akeley's Chicago period saw him broaden his activities. As he became better known, the lecture circuit beckoned. After all, his African experiences were exciting for audiences, especially since he typically illustrated his talks with the pictures he had brought back with him. Such public presentations, beyond giving him additional income, provided him with an excellent means of communicating his views on wildlife, something he was always pleased to do.[41] As a pioneer in modern taxidermy, Akeley was forced to improvise as he continually sought new means of accomplishing the things he wanted to do, constantly devising brilliant mechanical improvements for taxidermy, which in a few cases had broader application.

His invention of the cement gun is the prime example. To apply heavy coloring to habitat forms, such as artificial rocks, Akeley made a compressed air machine that sprayed thin, tinted plaster of paris. When Field Museum officials, knowing of the machine, became concerned about the deterioration of the stucco exterior of their building, they encouraged Akeley to apply his keen mechanical ability to find a way to repair it. Working with a young engineer who had helped him with elephant mounting, Akeley adapted the sprayer for concrete work. The apparatus served nicely as he supervised the restuccoing of the museum.[42] The potential uses of the device were many, and a number of backers came forth to finance its refinement and production on a commercial basis. A company was formed, which proved a success although it occupied almost all of Akeley's spare time between 1907 and 1909. Over a thousand of the machines were distributed before 1920. During the First World War the inventor was pleased to see his brainchild used for making concrete ships.[43]

Akeley's shop in the Field Museum became the place where many progressive professional taxidermists wanted to learn the new methods. So, the father of modern taxidermy, as he is often called, became a teacher. When he first came to Chicago, however, there was some secrecy about his work. In part this was his own doing since he did not want incompetent persons to try his methods, fail to produce satisfactory mountings, and then charge that the process was to blame.[44] But his superior, Daniel Elliot, also contributed to the mystery surrounding Akeley, fearing that other museums might copy Akeley's advanced system. For a few years Elliot kept his chief taxidermist and his shop from the public eye. Akeley's old friend, William Wheeler, claimed that Elliot kept visitors away and was especially suspicious of anyone, such as Wheeler for a short time, who was connected with the University of Chicago.[45] Gradually, though, the secrecy ended, and Akeley began to share ideas and procedures with other professionals. Since he wanted animal displays, whatever they were, to be accurate, convincing ones, he generously made available his expertise without compensation. He did this by demonstration on the job, as well as through lectures and publication, although in the latter case most writing was done after he left Chicago.

The Columbian Exposition building was always considered merely temporary quarters for the Field Museum. A new building was planned and in it, Akeley expected, there would be special rooms for his exhibits. For some time he had been envisioning, among other ambitious projects, a special hall of African mammals incorporating new display concepts that anticipated his later African Hall scheme in New York. The death in 1906 of the institution's greatest benefactor, Marshall Field, however, forced the planners to exclude some features of the proposed structure, including Akeley's exhibit halls. This was a severe disappointment. Added to his dejection over administrative reorganization and a growing incompatability with Elliot's successor as curator of mammals, it caused him to loosen his ties with the museum.[46] For some time he had operated his own taxidermy studio where he fulfilled a variety of contracts in the little spare time available to him. Now, on July 1, 1908, he gave up his staff position in favor of complete dedication to his own business. The museum agreed to furnish him with assignments worth at least $12,500 a year for five years, allowing him an extra three years in case of extended absence.[47] And it was not long before an extended absence occurred.

Akeley could not get Africa and its wildlife out of his mind. In 1908 he contacted the American Museum of Natural History (AMNH) and proposed an expedition to collect African mammals for that prestigious institution. Akeley certainly was no stranger to museum people in New York. He had earned national renown in his profession by that time and also had mounted a deer for the AMNH. The museum's director, Herman C. Bumpus, now saw his opportunity and agreed to have the museum underwrite Akeley's trip.[48] It began in the summer of 1909 and would keep Akeley in the field until late 1911. Once more British East Africa was the scene of Akeley's hunt. And, as in 1905–6, his wife joined him, along with an experienced hunter-sportsman, Fred Stephenson, and a somewhat unlikely participant, the famous and widely travelled *Chicago Tribune* cartoonist, John T. McCutcheon. The museum also assigned James Clark, an able taxidermist already working in East Africa, to be Akeley's assistant. The expedition was notable in several respects. Various mammals were on his collection list, but again he gave particular attention to elephants. Specifically, Akeley was commissioned to furnish the museum with a group of four or five elephants—bulls, cows, and calves—which would be mounted in the midst of a natural environment, a carefully designed woodland scene with distant perspective provided by a painted background. Bumpus intended that the display would be the dominant one in the museum.[49] After plodding through East Africa and the Upper Nile region of Uganda—in fact he visited Uganda twice—Akeley finally took a prize specimen that eventually became the center piece of his spectacular museum group exhibit. He had observed over ten thousand animals before he identified the right one. It was the increasing depredations of ivory hunters, said Akeley, that made it so difficult for him to find large male elephants with impressive tusks.[50]

The elephant hunt also produced many photographs. Akeley had become an excellent still photographer; as this expedition clearly proved, he had an artist's eye for details that made his work valuable for science and fascinating for the average viewer. *National Geographic Magazine* published a spectacular portfolio of his work that included a remarkable picture of an elephant embryo through about one-third of the gestation period.[51] In fact, this article was only a small sample of the vast store of information on the elephant, covering birth, resting habits, aggressiveness, and

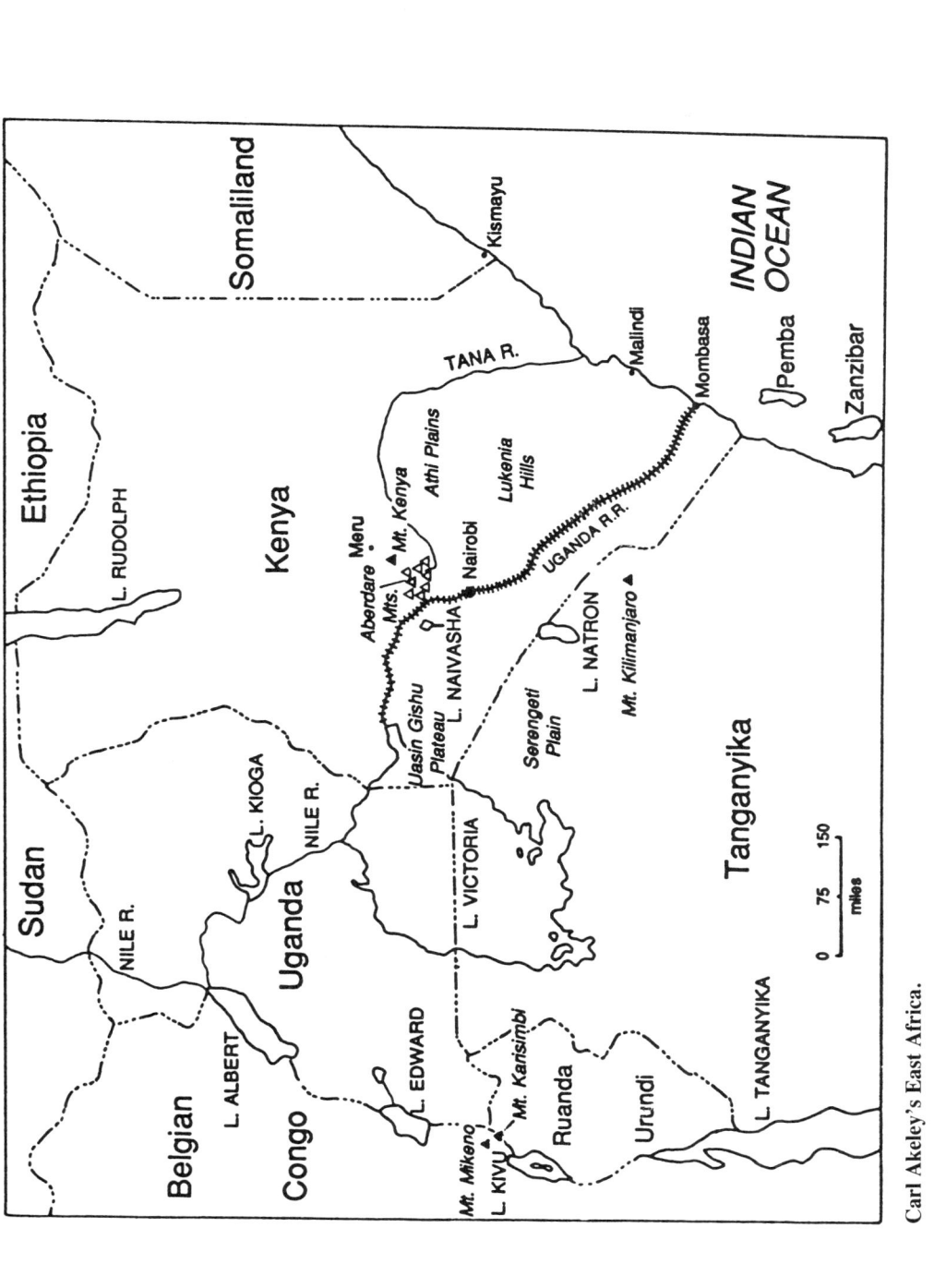

Carl Akeley's East Africa.

parenting, which Akeley now made known to science. Despite a severe illness contracted in the pestilential lowlands of Uganda, he continued to hunt there for almost a year. Recurring attacks of fever and dysentery forced him frequently to visit a missionary's home for recuperation.[52] Seeking more healthy country, he returned to the East African Protectorate. Akeley's blackwater fever worsened, putting him out of action for a few weeks as he was hospitalized in Nairobi and even thought by old African hands to be a terminal case.[53] Yet, again, his remarkably strong constitution pulled him through.

Once recovered, he resumed work on the Uasin Gishu Plateau in the western part of the territory. This area was famous for its lions. It was also the land of the Nandi, a pastoral people only recently pacified by British colonial authority. The Nandi warriors with their long spears were fearless hunters of lions, and Akeley planned to get motion pictures of their encounters. The objective was to obtain a sensational film that would prove valuable as an ethnological record as well as earn him enough money to further his African work.[54] One hundred African spear-men were paid to surround lions so that Akeley could then film the gruesome kill. It was a frustrating experience; numerous times as he was attempting to position his unwieldly camera, especially made for him by a leading London firm, the encircled lion charged and was quickly dispatched by the screaming Nandi before he was ready. Akeley realized that with the existing motion picture cameras such action probably never would be recorded. Therefore he made up his mind to devise a machine that would do the job and promised his disappointed wife that on their next expedition they would have the right camera.[55] In the course of his many unsuccessful attempts to get his pictures, however, Akeley's men killed ten lions. The animals were continually encircled and killed solely for his film project, which belied Akeley's professed concern with wanton waste of the continent's wildlife. It was his most flagrant violation of the conservation principles he would profess so widely.

Another memorable aspect of the 1909 hunting was Akeley's meeting with Theodore Roosevelt. The flamboyant ex-president was perhaps his country's most famous sportsman and conservationist. In his spacious home at Sagamore Hill on Staten Island, New York, the many trophy heads on the walls testified to his hunting experience. In 1895 he judged a taxidermy competition at the Sportsmen's Show in New York where Akeley's deer head won first prize.[56] Later he visited the Field Museum and asked to see the taxidermist-hunter whose work he admired, but Akeley was away at the time.⁵⁷ The two men finally met in 1906 immediately upon Akeley's return from East Africa when then-President Roosevelt invited him to dine at the White House. There was genuine mutual respect between them and they became friends. After swapping hunting stories, the diners discussed Roosevelt's upcoming hunt in Alaska when his term in office expired. Before the evening closed, Akeley had convinced the president that he should forego northern hunting and, instead, sample the big game of Africa. Indeed Akeley helped plan Roosevelt's trip.⁵⁸ The latter intended to send back some specimens to the Smithsonian Institution in Washington and Akeley convinced him to provide some elephants for the display Akeley was contemplating for the American Museum of Natural History.⁵⁹

Both men headed separate expeditions to the East African Protectorate in 1909 although they hoped it would be possible to meet somewhere in the field. Roosevelt's party, including his son Kermit, had been on the game trails for five months before Akeley arrived in the territory in September. The latter did not know the whereabouts of the other, yet by chance ended up in the same vicinity on the Uasin Gishu Plateau. They hunted together for a short time and each of the Roosevelts shot elephants that Akeley could use.⁶⁰ Around the evening campfire Akeley shared some intimate hours with this great personality who was at once scholar, outdoorsman, and world figure. And he developed a strong respect for the ex-president, admitting that "I learned to love him. It was then that I realized that I could follow him anywhere ... because I knew his sincerity, his integrity and the bigness of the man."⁶¹ Shortly after their collaborative hunt, Roosevelt's group left for Uganda and then followed the Nile to Egypt, his whole African adventure described in his popular book, *African Game Trails*.⁶² It had been a gigantic hunting extravaganza whose every phase received attention from the press. Akeley already had begun to speak out against indiscriminate slaughter of Africa's animals by visiting hunters but evidently could not bring himself to criticize his prominent friend for the 296 big-game kills of which the president's party boasted. Admittedly, many specimens were sent to the Smithsonian, thus significantly augmenting its collection, and other animals were shot to feed the Roosevelts' large expedition, but this does not account for numerous other slayings.

When informed of Roosevelt's unexpected death in early 1919, Akeley was deeply saddened. For several days he was unable to work. As he pondered his and the nation's loss he conceived a memorial to the ex-president. The original design was a small clay sculpture of the world with a lion sprawled over the top. A memorial committee was formed on which Akeley joined such notable close associates of Roosevelt as Henry Cabot Lodge and Gifford Pinchot. This body considered various proposals, including several lion designs by Akeley. He also sent models to the Roosevelt family, convinced that he had the most appropriate concept for honoring the great American leader he so admired. The family strongly favored the concept, devised by Akeley and the architect James Brite, of a giant granite lion in repose as the centerpiece of a large amphitheater at the top of a hill near Washington. Akeley saw it as "the shrine of the lion—a dream in granite."[63] But even the family endorsement was not enough. The selection process became very complicated as both the federal Committee on Monumental Memorials and the Arts Commission of Washington had to judge the architectural and artistic merits of the proposals. Long delays and criticism of his proposal discouraged him and, in 1925, he withdrew his design from the competition. Ultimately the idea of an official national memorial was dropped, and Akeley determined to honor the man in his own way as will be seen later.

During the 1909–11 safari, Akeley had another narrow escape from death while tracking animals. Rare were those hunters who survived close encounters with raging elephants, but Akeley was one of them. This episode occurred in the foothills of Mount Kenya in late June 1910 . Uncharacteristically surprised by the sudden appearance behind him of the great bull he had been stalking, Akeley could not get off a shot before two deadly tusks were almost in his face. As he grabbed one with each hand he was pushed to the ground, the tusks plunging into the earth while the rolled-up trunk crushed against his chest. The elephant kept raising its head and stabbing into the ground in an effort to finish him, moving away only after Akeley, knocked unconscious, lay limp before him. The only reason, it seems, that Akeley was not fatally smashed, was because the soft soil was not very thick and the underlying rock prevented the tusks from penetrating deeply enough. Fortunately, the beast charged off in pursuit of the African gun bearers and did not, as elephants were known to do, return and further mangle the body of its victim, Even so, Akeley suffered broken ribs and nose and his face was gashed open, exposing his teeth. Intermittently unconscious for about five hours, he was presumed dead by his men. After a tortuous ordeal he awoke to find his wife tending him. Runners had carried word of the mishap to her twenty miles back in the main camp. She had great difficulty finding Akeley after her guides lost their way trying to get back to him in the dark. Luckily, a Scottish missionary-doctor had been alerted and he managed to reach the Akeleys, but it took another three days to get the battered hunter to the nearest medical facility.[64]

Akeley's recovery required weeks of bed rest; it was three months before he could resume fieldwork. He must have realized that if he, like the proverbial cat, had nine lives he had used up most of them. The facial scar he carried the rest of his life reminded him of the costs of challenging the world's largest land mammal, yet he never lost his great respect for elephants and urged that they be protected from excessive human depredation. After such an ordeal, it is not surprising that Akeley had some doubt about his ability to face large game again. Even before he was fully recovered, therefore, he determined to test himself. Accompanying his wife on the perilous elephant paths once more, he demonstrated that he still possessed the strength of nerve that made him an accomplished hunter.[65] When he was firmly on his feet again, Akeley insisted on finishing the tasks of the expedition. Originally he had planned on visiting gorilla country, for the large primates had begun to interest him but, given the serious injuries he had sustained and the great distance he would have had to travel to reach gorillas in the Belgian Congo, this project was abandoned.[66] But he and his wife did travel again to Uganda for more months of elephant hunting. Finally, when they returned to the East African Protectorate, the resilient hunter had to be satisfied with completing his collection of buffalo and fulfilling an agreement to supply the Milwaukee Public Museum with hippopotamus and rhinoceros specimens.[67]

Leaving the Dark Continent behind him for a third time, Akeley returned to New York in November, 1911 and began his prominent employment at the American Museum of Natural History. Founded in 1869, that institution acquired its first permanent building in 1877 and by Akeley's time had become, in the words of a modern writer, "the grandest and most spectacularly laid out such repository in the Western Hemisphere."[68] Some of the most prominent New York plutocrats were proud to support it through the years. It was America's premier zoological museum, one that gave Akeley the fullest arena for his spectacular taxidermy while enhancing its own fame in the process. Months before, as he lay in bed recuperating in Africa, Akeley envisaged a splendid exhibit hall for Africa's mammals, a place where the public could see a re-creation of African wildlife the like of which would be available nowhere else. The concept he continued to develop in New York until in 1912 Akeley discussed it with Henry Fairfield Osborn, president of the museum, who encouraged him to take his proposal to the board of trustees. This he did in 1914, laying out his elaborate scheme for a huge room containing, in the center, elephants, rhinos, and some of his own bronze sculptures of African hunters, surrounded by forty habitat groups on two levels. The estimated cost at that time was one million dollars and time of completion ten years.[69] Part of the cost, Akeley hoped, would be covered by a motion picture series on the various stages of the project and other nature studies in Africa that would be distributed worldwide.[70] Favorably impressed, the board authorized work to begin, the first step being the construction of a detailed model, which Akeley soon completed. The major implementation of the plan would follow as funds were available. There was the rub. With the outbreak of the First World War, the trustees deemed it inadvisable to proceed with such a major undertaking. Thus began the long delay for African Hall, which plagued Akeley for the rest of his life.

Besides the backlog of taxidermy work that he tackled, Akeley continued as inventor. There was an obvious need among naturalists and others for a new type of field camera, one that Akeley was determined to build. After finding investors, he set to work fashioning one prototype after another that failed to satisfy him. When the original underwriters became discouraged and pulled out, he found a wealthy Clevelander who formed a syndicate to see the project through. The machine that was finally ready in 1914 was said by some who used it to be "the greatest motion picture camera ever invented."[71] Compact, versatile, convenient to use, it permitted its operator to make adjustments quickly, a feature Akeley probably stressed more than any other. Built to sell originally at $590 for the basic camera and $1,700 with all available accessories, including a special tripod, the device was quite expensive, but for many scientists, explorers, and others who demanded rugged, dependable photographic equipment, it was considered essential. For many years it remained in production, well-known among specialists all over the world, not the least of them Hollywood film makers.[72] Ten years after it was awarded its first patent in 1916, the Akeley Camera was still lauded as "one of the greatest instruments of its kind in existence."[73] Unfortunately, its inventor, who had sunk most of his savings in the initial stage of the camera's development, never earned much profit from it.[74]

World War I saw Akeley put his mechanical skills at the disposal of the U.S. Army. When his country entered the conflict, the

Army Signal Corps contracted to buy the entire output of his camera company. Since the manufacturing facilities were not yet ready for quantity production, however, the cameras had to be assembled by hand.[75] Arranging for the contract brought him to Washington where he was talked into working for the Division of Research of the Engineer Corps as a consulting engineer for ten dollars a day. The offer of a major's commission did not appeal to him; Akeley preferred to do what he could without going into uniform and binding himself more rigidly to a military routine. Most of his work for the Army he did in his New York camera shop and studio. Among his contributions were the invention of a papier-mâché searchlight mirror that could reflect even when hit by bullets, and valuable advice on the construction of concrete ships. He also helped to improve the armored tank.[76] The government took out several patents in his name on the devices he designed during the war.

In the postwar period Akeley continued to refine his process of animal mounting and in 1921 finished his four-elephant group, which had been underway since 1911. This was judged a "masterpiece" in the trustee's report of that year.[77] He also found time to publish an occasional article about his work and, more frequently, to accept lecture invitations. Of course he never ceased prompting the museum to bring his African Hall to fruition but, owing to inadequate funding, not much was accomplished. Until the new galleries were created, there could be no place to display most of the African animal skins in the museum's collection that awaited mounting.[78]

It was 1921 before Akeley could get back to Africa, when he made his first trek to gorillaland. While his museum provided some support for this effort, Akeley was forced to cover half of the cost himself. He exhausted his savings and borrowed an additional ten thousand dollars.[79] Moreover, given the need for additional financial backing, he agreed, no doubt reluctantly, to invite some wealthy nonprofessional hunters to join him. Appealing to outsiders for support of a collecting expedition had been a sore point with him. He had not wanted his expeditions to be seen as anything but scientific endeavors and, consequently, in 1912 had declined the museum's invitation to conduct an elephant-collecting trip to be financed by a subscription because he feared it would commercialize his work.[80] He told Osborn, furthermore, that his trips to Africa should not become a subject of newspaper publicity.[81]

Those who accompanied him in 1921 were close friends, Mr. and Mrs. Herbert Bradley of Chicago (Bradley, a wealthy attorney, had been one of the early investors in his camera company), their five-year-old daughter, Alice, her nanny, Priscilla Hall, as well as Martha Miller, Akeley's secretary at the museum. That a nononsense hunter like Akeley would accept a party with such a young child seems almost inexplicable but, he insisted, he welcomed the little girl in his party because her participation in the safari could help dispel the common perception, fostered by exaggerated tales from hunters and explorers, that Africa was an exceedingly dangerous place.[82] Apparently the Bradleys were so excited about joining an Akeley African journey that they ignored his admonition not to court publicity. Reproaching them, Akeley assured the Bradleys that he had placed discreet articles in the press that gave them "proper advertising without sacrificing the museum's dignity."[83] With such awkward preliminaries weathered, the so-called gorilla expedition left the United States in July.

Previously Akeley had seen only British territories in East Africa while on missions that were strictly professional. The rest of the exotic continent was *terra incognita* to him. On this trip, though, he travelled through much new territory for about two months, much like the average hunter-sightseer, before the real work began. Landing in Cape Town at the southern tip of the continent, they went by train through what were then the Union of South Africa, Bechuanaland, Southern and Northern Rhodesia, and the western edge of Tanganyika, followed by a river journey by steamer, then a shorter train ride in the eastern Belgian Congo and, finally, another boat cruise on Lake Tanganyika. The rest of the trip was overland to Lake Kivu, also in Belgian territory. Africans living near the line of march in this remote area must have been amazed by the scale of this intrusion by the outside world. It required six hundred porters to carry the expedition's supplies and equipment. At the northern end of the lake they were near gorilla country. There were still relatively few white men who had seen enough of the gorilla to provide definite information about it. Akeley had read everything available on the animal and disbelieved most of it. The writing of Paul Du Chaillu, which had been quite influential on the subject, he found particularly unacceptable. Long before he ever set eyes on the gorilla, Akeley intuitively felt, on the basis of his great knowledge of other wild creatures, that it was not the ferocious beast most people believed it to be.[84] To prove this was one of the principal purposes of his mission.

Deciding that he should track gorillas alone for a short time before the others joined him, an excited Akeley left his friends behind at Kissenyi, a small Belgian station on Lake Kivu, and pushed on to a Catholic mission post near the base of Mount Mikeno in the Virunga Range. Not far from there he was shown fresh signs of gorilla. In the rainy, slippery conditions on the mountain's slopes, Akeley sighted one of the elusive animals and, seizing what seemed a good opportunity, he shot his first male gorilla. It happened over a thousand feet up, and the big primate, fatally hit, tumbled down and barely missed falling into a deep chasm where it would have been lost. Since his tools were back at the base camp, and not wanting to waste time, Akeley set to work with only his pocket knife and his gun bearer's crude iron knife, skinning and roughly skeletonizing the body. This was accomplished in the very cramped, precarious spot where the ape came to rest. There followed the difficult task of getting the gorilla's remains out of there.

The next day saw Akeley photographing, cleaning, measuring, and preserving the skin and skeleton. And he made plaster casts of the face, feet, and hands. When added to the strenuous hunt itself, this labor proved taxing indeed for a man suffering from blood poisoning contracted several weeks earlier. Yet he continued at such a pace, frustrated by the shortage of trained guides and gunbearers that usually faced hunters that deep in the interior but determined to hold to a tight schedule. Not only did he bring down three more gorillas after enduring extremely trying circumstances, but somehow he found it possible to get the first motion pictures ever taken of wild gorillas. Eventually it became too much for him. When the Bradleys, notified that Akeley was sick, rushed to his aid, they found him in a very weakened condition.[85]

Debilitated or not, as host of the expedition Akeley had to see that his friends did some hunting. So they kept on the mountainous trail until Herbert Bradley brought down a fifth gorilla, an excellent huge, male specimen for Akeley's proposed museum grouping. All of this required practically constant movement, often in very damp, cold conditions against which the African workers had scanty protection. The regimen Akeley imposed on them made the majority of his men desert. Embarrassed by their action, the local chief later made them return, yet thereafter the porters frequently threatened to leave. This made it almost impossible for the vexed Akeley to provide his companions, while in gorilla country, with the most favorable experiences though, as Mary Bradley attested, he tried his best.[86]

During his three weeks around Mounts Mikeno and Karasimbi, Akeley observed from twenty-five to thirty gorillas and obtained about three hundred feet of film on one group. This acquaintance with the giant simian allowed him to present a description of its behavior that was at odds with prevailing notions. Lacking formal zoological training as a naturalist, Akeley nevertheless had become a sensitive, knowledgeable animal specialist whose study was careful and rather scientific for its time. The gorilla, he insisted, was generally nonaggressive. For this he offered considerable data, also pointing out that Africans in adjacent districts did not fear the animal. None of the beasts he tracked, furthermore, had attacked him. Nor did the gorilla live in trees, as several early writers had suggested. Akeley convincingly explained that they most often moved on all four feet, drawing upon his familiarity with the animal's anatomy to discount reports that it readily walked like a man. His reports provided measurements and weights that went beyond the previously accepted guesswork about the gorilla's size.[87]

Yet, as authoritative as his information was, there were doubters. The *New York Times*, for example, said his evidence on the gorilla's nonferocity was insufficient, concluding that the primate "certainly looks as if he could fight and as if he would if cornered,"[88] which Akeley would not have denied. Another gorilla trait emphasized by earlier commentators was chest-beating. Akeley was quite interested in proving that this was not indicative of aggression. After witnessing several examples of this behavior, Akeley could state that chest-beating was merely "a nervous expression of curiosity" for which there were equivalents among smaller apes.[89] In fact, however, Akeley did not completely prove Du Chaillu and others wrong on this point. It was only many years later, after more sophisticated, extensive research by other specialists that this rather intriguing practice of chest-beating was satisfactorily explained.[90] What Akeley made available to science was certainly a welcome addition to the world's understanding of the gorilla. Ironically, the facts about this animal that Akeley made available to the public made it seem less fearsome, and thus more easily shot, information that encouraged more whites to hunt them where they were not protected.

The adventure in these volcanic heights of equatorial Africa, in spite of the miserable cold that was encountered there, cast a spell on Akeley. As he took in a panoramic view of Mount Mikeno and its surroundings, he estimated it as the most beautiful landscape he had ever seen, a "veritable fairyland."[91] Later he wrote that "the morning on the slopes of Mount Karasimbi was the high spot of my African experiences."[92] This was the perfect country, he decided, to be captured in the background painting that one day would set off his mounted gorilla group. Akeley not only wanted the scene for his museum diorama, he also determined that this idyllic place was where he wanted to be buried.

It was after he returned from the gorilla expedition that Akeley gained most recognition in another field—sculpture. The taxidermy method he had introduced required modeling animal bodies in clay, first small-scale examples, then full size, something that he practiced to a fine art. The sculptures intended only as forms for manikins that would be covered with the animal's skin were actually works of art in their own right. Sculpture was a field that Akeley in his twenties considered as a possible career when he roamed through the extensive displays of masterworks in the Metropolitan Museum of Art. Although he eschewed it as a profession, he couldn't resist the impulse to prove that a taxidermist could be an artist and thus gain stature for his chosen field.[93] In 1915 he exhibited some of his work in various art shows, including one at the Pennsylvania Academy of Fine Arts. Later, when he began to build his models for African Hall, his friends, much impressed with the quality of these pieces, encouraged him to cast some of them in bronze. One of the most impressive results was "Wounded Comrade," depicting two elephants attempting to help a third stay upright and escape from its hunter. The most ambitious venture of Akeley the sculptor was the life-size bronzes of Nandi lion-spearing. The unforgettable scenes he witnessed in 1905 almost came to life in his 1925 groupings, each with three human figures. One set dramatically shows the poised hunters about to meet their prey; the other, entitled "Requiem," presents the triumphant Nandi with raised shields standing over a kill. In between was a third casting of two lions crouched for a charge.[94] These perfectly detailed works were intended as an important part of the African Hall exhibit (although they eventually were placed in an adjoining room) and can still be appreciated for the fine, realistic art they represent.[95] Other animal studies followed, which won Akeley accolades as a major figure in the sculptor's fraternity.

The only departure from the strictly natural studies was his provocative "Chrysalis," produced in 1924. In this bronze sculpture Akeley demonstrated his fascination with the gorilla's affinity to man and his own belief in evolution. Emerging from a shed ape skin is the upper half of a human male bearing a close resemblance to a youthful Akeley.[96] The piece aroused considerable controversy, appearing as it did in an era when religious fundamentalists were engaged in a national campaign against scientific knowledge about human origins that ran counter to their interpretation of the Bible. Finding its subject objectionable, the National Academy of Design declined to include the sculpture in its exhibit, although it accepted his bust of a gorilla, "The Old Man of Mikeno."[97] Akeley defended his work, explaining that he had not intended to suggest that man had descended from the gorilla but, rather, "that the gorilla, as the highest form of anthropoid that I know, and man had some common ancestors."[98] This was, of course, consistent with the most advanced teaching in his day on human evolution. "Chrysalis" was unveiled in Manhattan's West Side Unitarian Church in conjunction with a lecture on evolution.[99]

The 1920s in New York were anything but dull years for Akeley. By then he had achieved eminence as a preparator, and word of his African Hall project had spread widely enough to attract many students who wanted to work with him. These he carefully screened, accepting only the few whose love of nature and animals approximated his own and whose experience was minimal, for he believed he could more readily teach young aspirants who were not strongly tied to other preservation techniques.[100] From the beginning of his dream for the great museum re-creation of Africa, Akeley hoped that the undertaking would enable him to provide a training program that would produce a new generation of practitioners who could create a demand for high-quality work and thereby make a taxidermy career a dignified one.[101] While he taught his protégés the Akeley method, he continued to mount the animals he had collected, and the museum temporarily displayed them in standard glass cases until the permanent exhibit hall became a reality. Completed by 1925 were groups of elephants, rhinoceroses, okapi, and gorillas. Many skins awaited attention and much collection remained to be done if Akeley's grandiose conception was to be fulfilled.

All this work was expensive, of course, but there was also the cost of the contemplated building that loomed large before the frustrated planners. Akeley wanted to name the new display area "Roosevelt African Hall" in honor of his deceased friend and longtime supporter of the museum, and in all but one of his published references to the project he used that title. Acting on Akeley's estimate that the new structure alone would cost a million dollars, President Henry Osborn in 1922 appealed for a gift or endowment of the amount, emphasizing that the financing of the African Hall was the museum's highest priority.[102] From his perspective, Osborn felt that an appeal for such large sums would require very adroit treatment of prospective donors. Akeley, however, was not always ready to cooperate. Whereas many American museums were requesting big-game hunters to bring back some specimens for them, Akeley did his best to keep his institution from simply "ordering" animals in this fashion. When President Osborn was asked by an important museum benefactor if his son, about to embark for East Africa, could shoot some animals for the African Hall, Osborn agreed and requested Akeley to make the proper arrangements. An indignant Akeley explained that his uncompromising vision of the hall did not include that type of collecting. Only those intimately involved with the whole project, he insisted, could be trusted to select the specimens. Osborn admitted his mistake and agreed to make other museum space available for the socially prominent young hunter's trophies.[103]

Primary responsibility for directing the preparation of African Hall was given to James Clark, one of Akeley's closest associates, while the latter preferred to concentrate on field operations.[104] Ill-disposed though he was toward fund-raising, Akeley could not escape that essential task; after all, he was the architect of the whole plan and certainly the best-known figure for appealing to prospective backers. His proposal called for the numerous habitat groupings in African Hall to be underwritten by individual philanthropists who had to be sold on the project. When prominent hunters and conservationists deemed likely donors were identified, they were invited to Akeley's studio. There the man's conviction and sincerity often would win over his guests.[105] In this way money was brought in, but it was a slow process. Some museum officials thought Akeley was expecting too much from the institution as well as from everyone else. President Osborn, moreover, feared that Akeley would work himself to death before the project could be completed. Osborn tried to convince him to settle for a more modest design but to no avail.[106] For his part, Akeley was not above some subtle blackmail. Accusing museum leaders, somewhat unfairly, of resisting new ideas, such as his, he suggested that his interest in taxidermy had waned. His enthusiasm might be revived but only if he were allowed to proceed in his own way.[107]

It Akeley was discouraged by a lack of progress on his project, there were others at the museum who envied him and the support he enjoyed. Some of the scientists in other departments, particularly the anthropologists, resented the fact that the institution's funding was directed so lavishly toward expensive "publicity explorations," which were making the museum into a mounted zoo while important scientific studies done by their people went unpublished for lack of funds. Akeley the preparation man, they complained, outranked the heads of scientific departments.[108] But the object of their envy apparently was too bent on accomplishing his particular goals to pay attention to such institutional dissension.

Outside the museum, in what spare, nonworking hours were available, he had a social life that was often spent in the company of other naturalists and explorers. The prestigious Explorers' Club was a favorite haunt and a place where he was a frequent speaker.[109] And during this period personal problems reached a climax. Only two months after his return from the gorilla expedition, Akeley was sued for divorce. His wife of twenty-one years, who had been his ever-dependable associate on two of his African trips but from whom he had become estranged, charged him with cruelty, testifying that Akeley had once threatened her life. He in turn charged her with desertion. This messy case, which was discussed in the press, must have been an immense embarrassment.[110] Twenty months after the divorce, however, Akeley married Mary L. Jobe, an experienced traveler and outdoorswoman who had hiked through the Canadian Rockies. She would prove to be a valuable helpmate on his next and last African venture.

The early 1920s saw Akeley preaching conservation more fervently than ever. Big-game hunting in Africa was severely reducing the herds of the eastern territories, especially Kenya. Akeley and others feared that the region would soon be hunted out. It was his conviction that museums might one day provide the only existing examples of a once abundant African wildlife.[111] Perhaps his most eloquent appeal for more action on the problem was his 1926 article, "Have a Heart: A Statement and Plea for Fair Game Sport in Africa."[112] Here he recognized the destructive role of African hunters, especially those seeking ivory, but he insisted that "directly or indirectly, civilized [white] man is responsible for the rapid disappearance of wildlife in Africa."[113] The white settler, though justified in eliminating wild herds from his cultivated fields, nevertheless represented a major threat to game animals. There was plenty of land, Akeley suggested, that would not soon be needed by white farmers (he seems to have completely ignored the needs of black agriculturalists) and there the animals should be protected from all human predators.[114]

Whereas environmentalists of a later generation would note the inconsistency of those, like Akeley, who decried the threatened survival of rare species but nevertheless killed them in considerable numbers for museum exhibitions, he definitely could not see it that way. To Akeley the march of "civilization" was so inevitable, and its deadly effect on many animals so predictable, that scientific efforts to collect and mount them was a necessary service. The museums that did so, Akeley argued, played a "vital part in modern education" and thus justified his work. To those who believed that zoos and circuses served the same cause but more humanely by exposing live African animals to the Western public, he countered that animals in captivity were broken in spirit and no longer the creatures they were in the wild. The illusion of reality created by master taxidermists and other specialists who had studied the animals in their natural environment was a better portrayal of such creatures than the pitiful beasts chained in a circus or confined behind bars in a zoo.[115] Given the existing state of zoo exhibition in America, he was correct; Akeley could not foresee the impressive improvements in that field made since his day, but even if he had, he probably would not have considered it an adequate means of conveying a realistic impression of wild animals. Akeley deemed it particularly important for young people to observe what he and other progressive specialists could produce in museums so that succeeding generations would not continue to harbor distorted, if not totally erroneous, impressions of what Africa and its fauna were like.[116]

If protection of the animals was needed, then how could that be achieved? In view of the vested interests favoring continued unrestricted hunting, the prospect of winning support for a reserve or reserves was a daunting one. But Akeley moved. Refuge for the mountain gorilla, which he believed to be the most endangered species (he estimated that only 50–100 of them were left in the region he covered), was the first specific objective. As he and his party departed from the scene of his 1921 gorilla hunt on their way home, he conceived the idea of a sanctuary for that animal in the pristine wilderness embracing the three mountains, Mikeno, Karasimbi, and Visoke. It was his intent that it would include a biological research station and field laboratory.[117] Upon his return to New York he made arrangements to see the Belgian ambassador to the United States, Baron Emile de Cartier de Marchienne, to whom he related his recent African experiences and his conservation concerns. Subsequently a formal proposal was worked out through collaboration with John C. Merriam, Akeley's conservationist friend at the Carnegie Institution in Washington.[118]

The plan was presented to the Belgians in January 1923, and was supported by various American groups, including the New York Zoological Society and the U.S. Department of the Interior.[119] After Akeley and his colleagues pressed their case for the endangered gorilla so forcefully, the Belgian government responded favorably. Nobody was more pleased than Carl Akeley when, on March 2, 1925, King Albert I of Belgium, by royal decree, established the Parc National Albert in the Kivu District of the Belgian Congo. This, the first national park created in Africa, followed essentially the formula set out by Akeley. The latter subsequently recommended an enlargement of the preserve and, after his death, Mrs. Akeley collaborated with Belgian specialists in proposing a major extension. This came to fruition in 1929 when the King of the Belgians proclaimed that the original 24,000 hectares set aside in 1925 would now be expanded to 200,000 hectares of land in the Congo and in the neighboring Belgian territory (a League of Nations mandate) of Rwanda-Urundi. All wild animals here were protected, and regarding the gorilla in particular, its "destruction, capture or pursuit . . . as well as all forms of hunting this animal [were], absolutely forbidden."[120] Akeley certainly derived great satisfaction from his accomplishment.

He also found some time for writing. In 1920 his book, *In Brightest Africa*, was first released. Subsequently issued in several other editions, this widely read work was a collection of essays, most of which had been published in the AMNH's journal, *Natural History*, beginning in 1912. Apparently seeking the widest possible readership, Akeley and his publisher had chapters of the book reprinted in the popular periodical, *The World's Work* (1920–22). Modified versions of some chapters also appeared in *Boy's Life* (1924–25) and *Mentor* (1926). These writings provided some brief autobiographical details and an account of how he developed his taxidermy. More important, Akeley here conveyed his concern with saving Africa's animals and presented his vision of the great exhibit hall. Yet for most readers, the appeal of the book and articles lay in their exciting accounts of Akeley's adventures in the bush. Some of the latter, it must be admitted, were as thrilling as any contained in the rapidly growing literature on African travel up to that time. Such publications made Akeley more famous and undoubtedly served his purpose of gaining more support for African Hall.

In 1926 Akeley reached age sixty-two. While he no longer moved with the speed and agility of his youth, he nonetheless still though of himself and was considered by others as a vigorous man. Clearly, the years had taken their toll on him. Everyone who ever mentioned Akeley's work schedule noted how he continuously drove himself at a pace unbearable for most people. When engaged in a major project, which was most of the time, sleep meant little to him as he strove for perfection. Thus he was, as a later generation would have called him, a "workaholic." A close friend described him as looking older than his actual age, with craggy face, stooped shoulders, and scarred body.[121] The arduous African exertions had left him not only scarred but physically wasted. Neither age nor debility, however, could keep him from another trip to his beloved Africa. Perhaps he sensed that his time was quite limited and that it was necessary for him to take the lead in organizing another collecting venture. This was the period when American and European museums were engaged in a collection mania, as numerous expeditions went into eastern Africa on an unprecedented scale, endeavoring to provide their institutions with the material needed for ever more impressive displays.[122] Akeley's last field trip would be the most lavish African expedition heretofore organized by anyone.

The principal agent behind the new expedition was Daniel E. Pomeroy, a wealthy New York banker and member of the museum's board of trustees who chaired the African Hall Committee. Pomeroy was a friend of George Eastman, the Kodak Camera Co. magnate, and when he discovered in the autumn of 1925 that Eastman was interested in an African hunt, he saw an opportunity to serve the museum's purpose. He told Eastman of the long-proposed African Hall concept and arranged for Akeley to see him. After so often having his hopes dashed, the skeptical Akeley approached Eastman rather impatiently, wasting little time before bluntly asking him for one million dollars to get the African Hall underway. Declining to contribute that large a sum, the generous Eastman did offer to put up $100,000. It was agreed that Akeley, Pomeroy, Eastman, and the latter's friend Daniel B. Wenz, would share the costs of an expedition, with Pomeroy and Wenz also willing to finance an animal group each. Including Eastman's larger commitment, the funds available would allow the preparation of five such units.[123] This was the encouragement Akeley needed. It finally seemed as though his old vision might indeed come into being. This expedition, he wrote in his last published article, meant more to him than any earlier one because it was the "actual beginning of African Hall."[124]

It is interesting that Akeley now felt it necessary to explain to his superiors that in case any persons thought that the proposed expedition was just another rich men's hunt, he wanted it made clear that he would never be part of any such venture unless it was directed primarily toward the purposes of African Hall. And he urged the museum to cover the cost of housing in Africa for Eastman and Pomeroy.[125]

Planning and outfitting such a large venture must have been a formidable task. Akeley wanted to accomplish many things on this trip, probably realizing that it would be his last fieldwork. In addition to securing designated animals for the museum groups, he wanted to visit the great lion country of Tanganyika and then push on to Belgian territory once again where he would gather accessories and obtain the painted background for the gorilla group. For the latter, two carefully selected artists, William R. Leigh and A. A. Jansson, would join the Akeley mission. It was their job to sketch the general landscapes and particular vegetation for later paintings to set off the various animal displays in African Hall. While in Brussels on his way to East Africa, Akeley was asked to help carry out a survey of the recently established national park for a possible extension of its boundaries, something Akeley had encouraged.[126] It was an ambitious list of objectives and while trying to achieve them, Akeley had to remember that he was host to Eastman, an elderly millionaire who expected some attention even if his team was to be on its own much of the time.

The Eastman-Pomeroy-Akeley Expedition got underway when Akeley left the United States in early 1926, to be followed later by his partners. In Kenya, Akeley and his group, including his wife, Mary, worked inland for some weeks obtaining specimens and landscape paintings before heading back to the coastal port of Mombasa to meet the Eastman-Pomeroy party. He arranged comfortable quarters for his wealthy friends and saw that Eastman's safari was properly readied. This included such provisions as a special platform Akeley built on the front of the locomotive pulling Eastman's private train so that he could have the best possible vantage for observing wildlife while moving inland. But since Akeley was occupied with the work of collecting and preservation as well as supervision of his team of specialists, whereas the Eastman-Pomeroy group was only concerned with hunting, the two camps worked independently most of the time, often separated by considerable distances. The Eastman party which, counting African personnel, included thirty-seven people, used Nairobi as a main base from where it launched several quests for game, utilizing as many as six automobiles and trucks.[127]

Akeley and company, meanwhile, ventured into the northern part of Kenya to get giraffes, oryx, zebras, eland, and other species. In the region where he hunted in 1909 Akeley was disturbed by the vast tracts, once full of game, which were now practically empty. It confirmed his belief that his African Hall was the only hope for preserving something of the old, now rapidly vanishing, Africa.[128] This conclusion was of course emphasized in his report to the museum, an additional prompting to accelerate that project. During this phase of collecting Akeley was injured when his car struck a boulder, throwing his body against the steering wheel so forcefully that he tore cartilages from his breastbone.[129] This was just another of many painful reminders that Africa could exact a high price from those who insisted on confronting its untamed wilderness.

Attracted by reports of good lion country in the Serengeti Plains of Tanganyika, and desirous of linking up again with George Eastman's party, which was hunting in that territory, Akeley and associates traveled there in late July 1926. In particular, Akeley, hoping that Eastman by then had become sufficiently impressed with the importance of the museum team's work, wanted to solicit more financial support from him. He aimed to get another $500,000 but was unsuccessful.[130] They found the game herds more plentiful because large-scale hunting was less popular in Tanganyika. For three weeks lions were the main focus of their attention. In addition to hunting with Eastman and Pomeroy, Akeley worked with the professional nature photographer, Martin Johnson, who, along with his wife, Osa, was in the territory. Johnson was an old friend whose work had won Akeley's enthusiastic endorsement. Akeley, in fact, had been instrumental in getting the American Museum of Natural History to underwrite Johnson's African work.[131] Now the two men collaborated to record, with cameras Akeley had designed expressly for Johnson, some exciting scenes of the "king of beasts," including a Lumbwa lion-spearing episode similar to the Nandi performance that Akeley had such difficulty filming in 1910. As on that earlier occasion, Akeley recruited Africans to slay lions to obtain sensational motion pictures and, in addition now, to entertain his fellow hunters. Even though the lion was not an endangered species—indeed it was generally treated like vermin—this spectacle again was not consistent with his professed concern with wasteful killing.

In late August, while still in Tanganyika, Akeley contracted a severe fever. It was not a symptom of one of the expected tropical illnesses, however; this time the old Africa hand suffered a nervous breakdown.[132] Expending himself like a man obsessed with accomplishing everything on his last mission, Akeley simply pushed his body too far. He was so incapacitated that, lying in the back of a truck, he was forced to retreat 300 miles to Nairobi. The press reported in September that Akeley's breakdown was forcing him to leave the expedition and return to the United states.[133] But this was premature. Recovery required three weeks of rest in a nursing home, which prevented him from participating in the last big hunt of Eastman and Pomeroy. Eventually he felt well enough to continue his work. Shortly thereafter, in October, his two expedition partners and sponsors left for home.[134]

The next phase of Akeley's assignment was a trip to Uganda and on to the Belgian Congo, the purpose of which was to collect plant specimens for the gorilla exhibit in African Hall and, most important, to enable William Leigh to paint the scene of the Mount Mikeno vicinity that Akeley had determined would form the background for the gorilla group he had collected in 1921 and that was to have a prominent place in the African Hall. After a long journey of approximately 650 miles through British territory, the group reached the Belgian gorilla sanctuary in the Lake Kivu district in mid-November. From the old camp site of Rweru on Mt. Mikeno, the team of specialists was soon engaged in their respective tasks. Akeley, who planned to further his study of the gorilla in association with the Belgian scientist, J. M. Derscheid, who accompanied them, was pleased to introduce his wife to the misty but beautiful rain forest that had captivated his imagination ever since he first set eyes on it six years before. Not long after their arrival, however, he became feverish again. The artist William Leigh described his state as one of "deep melancholy."[135] Mary Akeley nursed him for several days, aware that his condition was steadily worsening but hopeful that the strength that always carried him through other illnesses would do so again. It was not to be. On November 17 he died. His widow, assenting to Akeley's stated desire, saw that he was buried close to the mountain camp in his beloved gorilla country.

On May 17, 1936, almost a full decade after his passing, Akeley African Hall was dedicated amid great fanfare before 2,000 AMNH members. This was preceded by a nationwide radio broadcast that described Akeley's dream, his career, and the long campaign that was necessary before the hall could materialize.[136] When the AMNH Board of Trustees met in 1927 and reviewed the record of how much money and effort had been invested in the project, acknowledging that Akeley had given his life for it, they agreed that completion must not be delayed much longer.[137] Ultimately, almost $1,000,000 was donated by twenty-three individuals to finance the habitat groups, and the City of New York, impressed by such private contributions, provided $1,250,000 for construction of the hall.[138] Despite some minor alterations, the great room that resulted remained true to Akeley's concept. And although only half of the habitat groups were installed at the time of its opening, the gallery level still awaiting sponsors for its displays, the magnificence of what had been achieved was readily apparent. Akeley's colleagues, many of them his former trainees, and the museum had carried on as he would have preferred. Back in 1925 President Osborn had advised Akeley that holding out for everything in the original plan, given its huge expense, might jeopardize realization of the whole scheme. Rather than "chasing the rainbows," Osborn suggested that work should begin on certain exhibits in order to interest the public and spur fund-raising. Akeley agreed to some temporary displays but demanded that the hall be built according to his ideas or not at all.[139] Osborn eventually understood and no longer attempted to inhibit Akeley's genius.[140]

Thanks to such loyalty to the designer and his plan, Akeley African Hall is the grandest display of animals ever presented by a museum of natural history. Nothing anywhere exceeds it in quality or in scale. Wildlife enthusiasts and armchair naturalists of a latter time can marvel at nature films produced with a photographic and video technology more advanced than anyone in Akeley's time could have envisioned. Such films can reveal heretofore hidden features of Africa's zoological wonders right in the viewer's home. Akeley could not have foreseen this as he argued for the necessity of accurate museum displays if the real Africa was to be preserved. But even those who appreciate the great contribution of modern film to animal study can still recognize the importance of African Hall and other exhibits like it.

Upon entering Akeley's memorial one first sees the huge central stand of eight elephants, some of which were shot and mounted by Akeley himself. Around this, in separate cases on two levels, are twenty-eight habitat groups. Each is hermetically sealed and artificially lit in such a way as to draw the viewer from the dimly lit central space into a scene of astoundingly realistic flora and fauna. The painstakingly constructed foliage surrounds preserved animals that represent the best of modern taxidermy. Sparing no detail or expense, James Clark and his associates constructed marvels of authenticity. The gorilla display, for example, contains seventy-five thousand artificial leaves and flowers. One berry bush in it took eight months to complete. Akeley-mounted gorillas appear strikingly against Leigh's superb painting in what has been called "the greatest diorama ever created".[141] African Hall set a new standard for museum exhibits that prevailed for many years.

Millions of museum patrons have passed through this monumental display since its opening, many of them children. The younger generation, Akeley hoped, would be so impressed with the wonders of his Africa that, when adults, they would work to prevent its animals from disappearing.[142] He wanted those who looked upon the exhibits to see not a fearsome land of wild terror but, rather, a "jungle peace" in "brightest Africa," the land he judged as the "garden spot of the world."[143] Some viewers undoubtedly have taken away an image of the continent in keeping with his vision. Yet, Africa indisputably was, as other underdeveloped tropical territories were, a land where the struggle for survival within the animal kingdom presented definite hazards for humans, especially uninitiated Westerners. Those aware of Akeley's own years in the bush, moreover, could not help but note the many perils he had faced during his African experiences. To a considerable extent, then, Americans influenced by Akeley would perceive Africa as a vast, primitive place not without its dangers, and primarily important for its animal life. This image would remain in the American consciousness for a long time.

A man totally devoted to the cause of conserving and preserving Africa's animals, Akeley gave little thought to the continent's human population. In his original design for African Hall (but not included in the finished room) various African peoples were to be represented in association with animals in bronze bas-reliefs above and outside the wildlife group compartments on the first floor, but these would not have been seen easily in the dimmer light outside the cases. In a way this conscious subordination of man to animals in the proposed exhibit room reflects Akeley's view of Africa. For him the animals indeed came first. In his book and articles about his African experiences, humans receive scant mention, and then only in relation to animal life. Akeley respected the courage and daring of the black lion hunters he photographed and acknowledged the bravery of his gun bearers on some occasions, but as "savages," he did not expect Africans to demonstrate honor or manliness.[144] On the other hand, Akeley developed a close relationship with a Kikuyu who became his most trusted factotum. This was "Bill," who joined the 1905 expedition as a thirteen-year-old tent boy and who was employed on two of Akeley's later safaris when he performed invaluable services. His real name was Wimbia Gikungu, but Akeley held that "a busy man cannot take the time to pronounce six syllables every time he calls a black boy."[145] While Bill was a special case, Akeley saw most Africans as simply anonymous carriers, cooks, gun bearers, and menials who could help him get to the beasts he needed for his exhibits. He left us no meaningful reflections about African society or culture. In most respects Akeley's attitudes were representative of Western commentators of that period who pictured Africa as a Garden of Eden whose native peoples were innocent children of nature. Africa was "the Land in Amber," preserving a way of life long forgotten in the developed countries, where the hunter could try to achieve mastery over himself and nature.[146]

Nor did Akeley record his views about Africa as a colonial territory. Again, everything was seen in connection with his collecting. British East Africa was judged a "sportsman's paradise" because it contained so much game and because its European administration was very helpful to hunters in providing clearances and licenses with a minimum of delay. Significantly, a railroad was available for transport through the country. The presence of a significant white settler population, furthermore, insured that Kenya could furnish all essential services and supplies as well as cars, mechanics, and spare parts that were, by the 1920s, in great demand by those who would reduce the travel time of their safaris. And by that time there were in Kenya more experienced African porters and camp men than any other territory could claim. The gorilla expedition of 1921 enabled him to see other parts of Africa but, true to form, he said nothing about the more than one-third of the continent he passed through for over six weeks except for some brief remarks about the animals sighted along the way. The reader of his account of this trip looks in vain, for example, for his thoughts about race relations in South Africa or the Rhodesias, or about mining and industrial development so important there. Like so many other Westerners who went to Africa in that period primarily for its wildlife, Akeley saw the continent strictly in nonpolitical terms.[147]

As a preparator, sculptor, author, leader of field expeditions, speaker, museum designer, and conservationist, Akeley certainly did much to generate interest in the so-called Dark Continent. His achievements and dedication to his field were a special inspiration to many young naturalists of his time. Those taxidermists he trained held prominent positions in the field for many years.[148] His emphasis on conservation was genuine. Later campaigners for the protection of Africa's wildlife would present their cause in the same terms he used, even if they were unaware of his pioneering efforts. In Akeley's time few people could believe that such huge, densely covered game lands could be significantly depleted. The case of the bison on the American prairie should have given them pause for concern, but Africa was, after all, far away, under European rule and it seemed destined for wholesale exploitation. Based on his sincere conviction that many species of African nammals were doomed to extinction, his African Hall was a noble conception, one meant for the best educational purposes, and it continues to serve such ends today. Akeley was one of the earliest voices raised in behalf of animal conservation in Africa and his success in convincing Belgian authorities to establish the first wildlife sanctuary there is perhaps his most significant legacy to the continent. It is indeed fitting that the most important modern scientific work on the gorilla has been conducted in the preserve he proposed.

Conclusion

In the near-century between T. J. Bowen's 1848 proposal to his church authorities for a mission to central Africa, and the posthumous opening of Carl Akeley's grand African Hall in 1936, the connections between Africa and the United States increased significantly. Following Bowen's lead, American missionaries ventured into numerous parts of the continent, apparently undeterred by the presence of tropical diseases which were fatal to many and left others, as in Bowen's case, with shattered health. In Nigeria his Baptist successors, both black and white, would create a durable network of mission posts. Ultimately some fifteen American Protestant denominations and several Catholic orders would be represented in the southern half of Nigeria. The non-Muslim territories there, first described to his countrymen by Bowen, in fact became one of the major areas for American mission work in Africa. These evangelists were encouraged to seek converts across much of tropical Africa by accumulating reports through the later nineteenth and early twentieth centuries about the backwardness of pagan societies there. While these Christian idealists did their religious work, they also provided some degree of education and, often, medical assistance to the local people. Of no little importance was the contribution toward literacy they made by compiling grammars and dictionaries of indigenous languages and by translating religious works into those languages. While European missionaries probably outnumbered their American counterparts in Africa during this period, the latter were both numerous and widespread.

There were fewer explorers from the United States. And Paul Du Chaillu was the first of them to gain any recognition. He and Henry Morton Stanley, another adoptive American (who later reclaimed British citizenship) whose exploits occurred in the period 1871 to 1889, certainly did as much as the explorers of any nations—with the exception of the Scotsman, David Livingstone—to awaken the outside world's interest in the generally unknown African interior. American explorers, including Bowen and Charles Chaillé-Long, contributed to the fast-growing body of literature on Africa in the second half of the nineteenth century.

Even though this writing did not, as seen in several studies here, always project an accurate, well-informed picture of Africa's human societies, it contributed toward a better understanding of the continent's geography and the variety of its flora and fauna. Consequently, Americans went out to Africa in larger numbers as travelers, hunters and scientists in the first decades of the twentieth century. Some of them, in turn, proceeded to add their own published accounts to the growing collection of Africana in the "developed" world.

Carl Akeley was one of these. His book and articles fascinated many readers in the 1920s. Akeley's early hunting expeditions in search of specimens for museum displays, which subsequently captivated the public, helped launch an era of such ventures as museums, zoos, and scientific societies tried to surpass one another in bringing Africa to America. This of course accelerated the trend in popular literature and motion pictures to exploit Africa as a source of vicarious thrills for the masses, especially in the period between the world wars. For every scientist or conservationist such as Akeley, however, there were many more hunter-adventurers who sought only to kill as much large game as possible. Americans of that sort did their part in decimating the natural heritage of Africa even while those converted to Akeley's views about the preservation of species were gaining new respect for African wildlife. Whatever the motives of those who focused on Africa's primitive wilderness, it was the animals rather than the people, which interested most Americans of that period.

Those Americans who, like Henry S. Sanford, promoted trade with Africa, did not see their hopes realized. Not only those looking for new commercial ventures, but also explorers such as Du Chaillu and Stanley expounded on the potential of trade between the United States and Africa, the latter whose territories contained a multitude of natural riches and whose societies represented important potential markets. But Africa before 1936—or, indeed, after that time—did not become a major focus of the American business community. Not only was the large domestic market their principal concern, but in the acquisition of many imported raw materials they had, in most cases, alternative sources of supply. In foreign trade Americans found a number of world areas more attractive than Africa, so they did not push very hard to become a bigger factor there. And, it must be borne in mind, Africa was largely under the control of European colonial powers after the partition of the continent in the 1880s. American competitors found various obstructions in their way when they challenged European firms in those colonies. Yet, admittedly, Sanford and other economic expansionists who insisted on the importance of trade with Africa exerted sufficient influence to affect U.S. foreign policy, as witnessed in the Congo affair with King Leopold II and in the associated Berlin Conference. Washington thereafter endeavored to facilitate growth in the African trade, providing assistance wherever possible but seeing only modest results as Europeans dominated the field.

As far as American economic interests were concerned, there was an African region that beckoned in a special way. This was South Africa, where striking mineral discoveries indeed captured the world's attention by the 1880s. John Hays Hammond was not the first from his country to seek wealth there, yet his story singled him out. Hammond's extraordinarily high salary, his successful and lucrative promotion of deep-level gold mining and, most of all, his newsworthy trial for participation in the Jameson Raid caper, made him the best-known American associated with South Africa. His colorful experience contributed to the American perception of that land as an El Dorado, thus drawing there increasing numbers of not just common fortune-seekers but also professional men, particularly engineers, a number of whom made significant contributions to the immense success of South Africa's mining industry. Not surprisingly, South Africa's gold shares became attractive to American investors. Moreover, Hammond led one of the industry's giants, Consolidated Gold Fields, Ltd., into the American investment field, and such involvement continued to grow through the decades before the Second World War. By the 1980s, South African investment in the American economy, especially the mining sector, was quite impressive.

In their separate fashions, then, all the subjects of the case studies herein added something to the conceptions that Americans formed about Africa in the period under consideration, as well as later. It was a dramatic time in the history of Africa's relations with the outside world, and these men determined that Americans would play a notable part in events that will continue to interest both their countrymen as well as Africans who want to understand their respective histories more fully.

Notes

Preface

1. Peter Duignan with Clarence Clendenen, *The United States and the African Slave Trade, 1619–1862* (Stanford, Calif.: Stanford University Press, 1963); Duignan with Clendenen, *Americans in Black Africa up to 1865* (Stanford, Galif.: Stanford University Press, 1964); Duignan with Clendenen and Robert Collins, *Americans in Black Africa, 1865–1900* (Stanford, Calif.: Stanford University Press, 1966); Duignan with L. H. Gann, *The United States and Africa: A History* (Cambridge: Cambridge University Press, 1984).
2. Peter Duignan, *Americans in Africa: A Preliminary Guide to American Missionary Archives and Library Manuscript Collections on Africa* (Stanford, Calif.: Stanford University Press, 1963); Duignan, *Guide to Research and Reference Works on SubSaharan Africa* (Stanford, Calif.: Stanford University Press, 1971); Duignan, *Handbook of American Resources for African Studies* (Stanford, Calif.: Stanford University Press, 1967).
3. Edward W. Chester, *Clash of Titans: Africa and U.S. Foreign Policy* (Maryknoll, N.Y.: Orbis Books, 1974); Edward H. McKinley, *The Lure of Africa: American Interests in Tropical Africa, 1919–1939* (Indianapolis: Bobbs-Merrill, 1974); Russel Warren Howe, *Along the Afric Shore: An Historic Review of Two Centuries of U.S. African Relations* (New York: Barnes & Noble, 1975); David Shavit, *The United States in Africa: A Historical Dictionary* (Westport, Conn.: Greenwood, 1989).

Chapter 1. Thomas Jefferson Bowen and Central Africa

1. H. A. Tupper, *The Foreign Missions of the Southern Baptist Convention* (Philadelphia, Pa. and Richmond, Va.: American Baptist Publication Society, 1880), pp. 362–72; Mary Emily Wright, *The Missionary Work of the Southern Baptist Convention* (Philadelphia, Pa.: American Baptist Publication Society, 1902), p. 144; Louis M. Duval, *Baptist Missions in Nigeria* (Richmond, Va.: Foreign Mission Board, Southern Baptist Convention, 1928), pp. 39–48; Peter Duignan and L. H. Gann, *The United States and Africa* (Cambridge: Cambridge University Press, 1984), pp. 92–98.
2. Thomas Jefferson Bowen, Diary, Bowen Papers (hereafter cited as BP), microfilm copy, Historical Commission of the Southern Baptist Convention, Nashville, Tenn.; Tupper, *Foreign Missions*, pp. 373–74; Duval, *Baptist Missions*, p. 48. This chronology refutes the claim in Wright, *Missionary Work*, p. 155; and Charles E. Maddry, *Day Dawn in Yoruba Land* (Nashville, Tenn.: Broadman Press, 1939), p. 38, that Bowen served in the Mexican War.
3. *Encyclopedia of Southern Baptists* (Nashville, Tenn.: Broadman Press, 1958), 1, pp. 457–60.
4. J. F. Ade Ajayi, *Christian Missions in Nigeria, 1841–1891* (Evanston, Ill.: Northwestern University Press, 1965), pp. 10–13.
5. Bowen's article in *Southern Baptist Missionary Journal* 3, No. 10 (Mar. 1849), 217.
6. Both of these multivolume sets were best-sellers in the 1840s and undoubtedly were found in many libraries. Richard C. Altick, *The English Common Reader: A Social History of the Mass Reading Public, 1800–1900* (Chicago: University of Chicago Press, 1957), pp. 282, 390. At the time of its publication, the section on African discovery in *Chamber's*

Miscellany 20 vols. (Edinburgh: W. and R. Chambers, 1845–47) was at least up-to-date, having been based on the most recent works. It is nevertheless an unfortunate fact that even the most "authoritative" encyclopedia of the day was far from an accurate source of data on the still little-explored Sudan.

7. Published in New York in 1844, this book followed the author's related study, *The Foulahs of Central Africa and the Slave Trade* (New York: privately printed, 1843).

8. Bowen's original mission proposal, entitled "Central Africa," *Southern Baptist Missionary Journal* 3, No. 6 (Nov. 1848), 126–27.

9. Ibid.

10. Ibid.

11. Ibid. 3, No. 10 (Mar. 1849), 219. In this instance Bowen borrowed his phraseology verbatim from *Chamber's Miscellany*, which, on the cited authority of William Hodgson, reported that the Fulani of "Central Africa" had introduced the Negro peoples of that region to the ideas of Mohammedanism, "which, however inferior and pernicious in themselves, were yet an advance upon the original Negro beliefs" (vol. 16, no. 142, p. 28.).

12. This view of African Muslims was shared by a number of British writers of the time. Philip D. Curtin, *The Image of Africa* (Madison: University of Wisconsin Press, 1966), p. 257.

13. E. A. Ayandele, *The Missionary Impact on Modern Nigeria, 1842–1914* (New York: Humanities Press, 1966), p. 120.

14. Bowen to James B. Taylor (chairman of the SBC Foreign Mission Board), 28 Dec. 1848, BP. Other Americans earlier had become interested in the commercial possibilities of the Niger area; see George E. Brooks and Frances K. Talbot, "The Providence Exploring and Trading Company's Expedition to the Niger River in 1832–33," *The American Neptune* 35, No. 2 (Apr. 1975), 242–58.

15. Bowen, "Central Africa," *Southern Baptist Missionary Journal* 4, No. 1 (June 1849), 14.

16. Laird was an English trader who organized an expedition to initiate trade up the Niger. Using two steamships, his party, which included the experienced Niger explorer, Richard Lander, and two British naval officers, ascended the river to its confluence with the Benue and a hundred miles farther up the latter stream. During their work between 1832 and 1834, 80 percent of the participants of this pioneering effort died, most from tropical diseases. Laird himself succumbed to wounds received in a skirmish with tribesmen on the lower reaches of the Niger. The trading results of the venture were negligible.

The mission of 1841 was more ambitious and had official government backing. Its objectives were to negotiate treaties with African chiefs banning the slave trade, to acquire scientific data on the riverine territories and, very importantly, to set up, at the confluence of the Niger and Benue, where Lokoja now stands, a model farm that would eventually develop into a settlement for freed slaves. Large and well-equipped, this expedition accomplished little and its death rate was so high that all experiments had to be abandoned. Its failure made a lasting impression and discouraged the British government from further involvement in the Niger region for many years. Later the regular use of quinine would enable more Europeans to survive the ravages of malaria.

17. Bowen, *Central Africa: Adventures and Missionary Labors in Several Countries in the Interior of Africa from 1849–1856* (Charleston, S.C.: Southern Baptist Publication Society, 1857), p. 25.

18. Ibid., p. 26.

19. Robin Law, *The Oyo Empire c. 1600—c. 1836: A West African Imperialism in the Era of the Atlantic Slave Trade* (Oxford: Oxford University Press, 1977), p. 259. In his revised account of Ilorin's political experience during this troubled period, Law proposes an earlier date for the Fulani assumption of control than other authorities; see pp. 255–60.

20. Bowen to Taylor, 1 Oct. 1850, BP; H. A. S. Johnson, *The Fulani Empire of Sokoto* (London: Oxford University Press, 1967), p. 143.

21. Bowen, *Central Africa*, pp. 27–29.

22. Bowen, Diary, BP. The inferiority of coastal peoples was a widely propagated view among whites in the first half of the nineteenth century. On the other hand, the superiority of interior groups such as the Fulani, was often attributed to white origins. Curtin likens this

theory to the later Hamite myth that has confused those writing Africa's history in modern times. Curtin, *Image of Africa*, pp. 233, 410–11.

23. The name "Nigeria" came into use in the late 1890s. As the British gained control of the region after Bowen's time there, they called the large northern area the Protectorate of Northern Nigeria; the territory south of the Niger and Benue Rivers was designated the Protectorate of Southern Nigeria. In 1914 these two were joined and henceforth the one British colony was known as Nigeria.

24. Bowen to Taylor, 1 July 1851, BP.

25. Samuel Johnson, *The History of the Yorubas* (London: Routledge and Kegan Paul, Ltd., 1921), p. 225; Sabori O. Biobaku, *The Egba and Their Neighbors, 1842–1872* (Oxford: Oxford University Press, 1957), pp. 14–17.

26. Jean Herskovits Kopytoff, *A Preface to Nigeria: The "Sierra Leonians" in Yoruba, 1830–1890* (Madison: University of Wisconsin Press, 1965), pp. 59–60.

27. Biobaku, *Egba and Their Neighbors*, chap. 3; Eva Krapf-Askari, *Yoruba Towns and Cities* (Oxford: Oxford University Press, 1969), p. 6.

28. Bowen to Taylor, 16 May 1851, BP; Kopytoff, *Preface to Nigeria*, p. 60.

29. Bowen to Taylor, 16 May 1851, BP.

30. E. A. Ayandele, *Nigerian Historical Studies* (London: Frank Cass, 1979), p. 61.

31. Ibid.; Johnson, *History of the Yorubas*, pp. 296–97.

32. Johnson, *History of the Yorubas*, p. 313.

33. Bowen, *Central Africa*, pp. 118–20; Johnson, *History of the Yorubas*, p. 314; J. F. Ade Ajayi and Robert Smith, *Yoruba Warfare in the Nineteenth Century* (Cambridge: Cambridge University Press, 1964), pp. 37–39.

34. Biabaku, *Egba and Their Neighbors*, p. 46.

35. Bowen, *Central Africa*, pp. 142–50; E. G. Parrinder, *The Story of Ketu, An Ancient African Kingdom* (Ibadan, Nigeria: Ibadan University Press, 1967), p. 47.

36. Bowen, Journal, 17 Jan. 1852. BP.

37. Bowen to Taylor, 28 Feb. 1842, BP.

38. Abeokuta, for example, saw a sizable Muslim population, who were refugees from northern cities caught in civil wars, streaming southward. Their settlement in Abeokuta was large enough to require two mosques and associated Koranic schools. Despite persecution by traditionalists who feared the growth of this militant religion, the Muslims maintained their position. T. G. O. Gbadamosi, *The Growth of Islam among the Yoruba, 1841–1908* (Atlantic Highlands, N. J.: Humanities Press, 1978), p. 25. This book provides an in-depth discussion of the spread of Muslims from northern cities southward as a result of protracted civil war.

39. Bowen, Journal, 18 Jan. 1852, BP. (Those Muslims who knew their own holy literature of course had heard of Jesus who is recognized in the Koran as an important prophet—but not the Son of God—who preceded Mohammad, the last and most significant of their prophets.)

40. Bowen, Diary, 1 Sept. 1855, BP.

41. Bowen to Taylor, n.d., BP.

42. Bowen, *Central Africa*, pp. 67, 199.

43. Bowen, Journal, 3 Apr. 1855, BP.

44. Ibid.

45. Bowen to Taylor, 1 Oct. 1855, BP.

46. S. A. Akintoye, *Revolution and Power Politics in Yorubaland, 1840–1843* (London: Longmans, 1971), p. 36; H. A. S. Johnson, *Fulani Empire of Sokoto*, pp. 142–44.

47. S. J. Hogben, *An Introduction to the History of the Islamic States of Northern Nigeria* (Ibadan, Nigeria: Oxford University Press, 1963), p. 161.

48. Bowen, *Central Africa*, p. 203.

49. *African Repository* 31 (Oct. 1855), 308.

50. Ayandele, *Missionary Impact*, pp. 120–25.

51. Sir Frederick D. Lugard, *The Dual Mandate in British Tropical Africa* (London and Edinburgh: Blackwood, 1923), pp. 593–96; Ayandele, *Missionary Impact*, pp. 129–37.

52. Bowen to R. R. Gurley, 6 Aug. 1857, *African Repository* 33 (Sept. 1857), 281.

53. Bowen's speech before the American Colonization Society, 19 Jan. 1858, Ibid. 34 (Feb. 1858), 43. Ayandele, in his extended introduction to the modern reprint of Bowen's *Central Africa* (London: Frank Cass, 1968) provides a good discussion of Bowen's emphasis

on the regeneration of Africa through the work of black Americans and other ex-slaves. See pp. xxxvi–xlii.

54. Bowen, *Central Africa*, p. 341.
55. *African Repository* 34 (Apr. 1857), 97; (May 1857), 129; (Aug. 1857), 225.
56. Bowen to Gurley, 23 Nov. 1858, *African Repository* 35 (Jan. 1859), 24; See also, Floyd J. Miller, *The Search for a Black Nationality: Black Emigration and Colonization, 1787–1863* (Urbana: University of Illinois Press, 1975), p. 184.
57. That decade brought the Fugitive Slave Act, the Kansas-Nebraska Bill, and the failure of John Brown's movement, all of which in various ways dashed blacks' hopes for changes in their status. See Hollis R. Lynch, "Pan Negro Nationalism in the New World before 1862," *Boston University Papers on Africa, 2* (Boston: Boston University Press, 1966), pp. 172–73.
58. Ibid., pp. 167–68, 171; Richard K. MacMaster, "Henry Highland Garnet and the African Civilization Society," *Journal of Presbyterian History* 48 (Summer 1970), 100–104; Howard H. Bell, "Negro Nationalism: A Factor in Emigration Projects, 1858–61," *Journal of Negro History* 47 (Jan. 1962), 46. See the society's constitution in *Apropos of Africa*, edited by Martin Kilson and Adelaide Hill (Garden City, N.Y.: Anchor Books, 1971), pp. 179–84.
59. Miller, *Search for a Black Nationality*, p. 183, Another important emigrationist who was strongly influenced by Bowen's *Central Africa* was Martin R. Delany, a rival of Garnet who also advocated settlement in Yorubaland. See Howard Bell's introduction to M. R. Delany and Robert Campbell, *Search for a Place: Black Separatism and Africa, 1860* (Ann Arbor: University of Michigan Press, 1969), pp. 14–17.
60. Bowen to A. M. Poindexter, 20 Oct. 1858; Bowen to Taylor, 23 Oct. 1858, BP.
61. Bowen to Taylor, 3 Dec. 1858, BP; Miller, *Search for a Black Nationality*, pp. 85, 197.
62. A. A. Constantine to Bowen, 1 Oct. 1859, BP.
63. Miller, *Search for a Black Nationality*, chap. 6.
64. Delany and Campbell, *Search for a Place, passim*.
65. Ibid., pp. 242, 248–9.
66. Bowen to Gurley, 6 Aug. 1857, *African Repository* 33 (Sept. 1857), 2. Bowen even suggested the name "nigritia" for the republic that he expected to result from black American emigration. Ibid., 281.
67. Bowen to the chairman of the House of Representatives' Committee on Commerce, 3 Feb. 1857; Bowen to Lippincott and Company, 21 Nov. 1868, BP; Richard K. MacMaster, "The United States Navy and African Exploration, 1851–1860," *Mid-America* 46 (1964), 200–202; Ajayi, *Christian Missions*, p. 48.
68. Moreover, Yoruba leaders repudiated their agreement to permit settlement, while Great Britain, whose interest in the Niger region had increased, was moving in certain ways to discourage a black American influx. See Bell, introduction to Delany and Campbell, *Search for a Place*, p. 20.
69. For a discussion of the condescending, colonialist view of the black emigrationists toward African societies, see Miller, *Search for a Black Nationality*, pp. 272–3.
70. Bowen, *Central Africa*, p. 342.
71. Livingstone even favored settling British convicts in eastern Africa. David and Charles Livingstone, *Narrative of an Expedition to the Zambezi and Its Tributaries*, 2 vols. (London: John Murray, 1865), 2, pp. 607–8.
72. *Grammar and Dictionary of the Yoruba Language with an Introduction and Description of the Country and People of Yoruba* (Washington, D. C.: Smithsonian Institution, 1858). For an evaluation of this work, see Ayandele, Introduction to Bowen's *Central Africa*, 1968 edition, pp. XLIV–XLVI.
73. Report of the Georgia State Hospital for the Mentally Ill, 24 Nov. 1875, BP.

Chapter 2. Jungle Adventure

1. Du Chaillu wrote eleven books, all but two of which, *Explorations and Adventures in Equatorial Africa* (New York: Harper, 1861); and *A Journey to Ashango-Land* (New

York: Harper, 1867), are considered "books for young readers." One expert discussing the midnineteenth century English book market claims that except for the work of David Livingstone, Du Chaillu's first book was the only best-seller in the field of travel, history, and biography in the period 1831-74. Richard Altick, *The English Common Reader* (Chicago: University of Chicago Press, 1957), p. 388. In England alone, *Explorations and Adventures in Equatorial Africa* sold 10,000 copies in two years. Richard West, *Congo* (New York: Holt, 1972), p. 23.

2. Kirk Foster, comp., *Supplement to Allibone's Critical Dictionary of English Literature and British and American Authors* (Philadelphia, Pa.: Lippincott, 1891), p. 517; *National Geographic Magazine* 14, 282; *New York Times*, 1 May 1903, p. 9; *Scientific American* 88, 355. And one contemporary writer who knew Du Chaillu stated that the latter was "born in America of French descent." Alfred H. Guernsey, "Paul Du Chaillu Once Again," *Harper's New Monthly Magazine* 38, 164.

3. *Appleton's Cyclopedia of American Biography*. Edited by James Grant Wilson and John Fiske, 6 vols. (New York: Appleton, 1888-91), vol. 2, pp. 240-41; *The Century Cyclopedia of Names*, 3 vols. (New York: Century Co., 1954), vol. 1, p. 345.

4. Edward Clodd, *Memories* (London: Chapman and Hall, 1916), p. 71. Clodd was a banking executive whose neighbor, Henry Bates, secretary of the Royal Geographical Society, often hosted many notable explorers. The first researcher to utilize Clodd's information about Du Chaillu was J. A. Rogers. See his book, *World's Great Men of Color*, 2 vols. (New York: Helga M. Rogers, 1946), vol. 1, p. 310. A French explorer who followed Du Chaillu to Gabon in the 1860s added to the confusion about the latter's antecedents when he referred to him as a "Senegalese Creole." Griffon Du Bellay, "Le Gabon," *Tour Du Monde* II (1865), 278. But Clodd's testimony is more convincing.

5. Rogers, *Men of Color*, vol. 1, p. 310.

6. Helen Everton Smith, "Reminiscences of Paul Belloni Du Chaillu," *Independent* 55 (1903), 1147.

7. Henry H. Bucher, Jr., "Canonization by Repetition: Paul Du Chaillu in Historiography," *Revue Française d'histoire d'outre-mer* 66 (1979), 17, n. 7.

8. Smith, "Reminiscences," p. 1147.

9. Ibid.

10. Michael Vaucaire, *Paul Du Chaillu: Gorilla Hunter* (New York: Harper, 1930), p. 18. It is interesting to note, however, that one writer estimates that Du Chaillu was born as late as 1837. Rogers, *Men of Color*, vol. 1, p. 310, and *Scientific American's* obituary (9 May 1903, p. 355) listed his birth year as 1838!

11. Paul changed the paternal name to the more aristocratic spelling, Du Chaillu. Bucher "Canonization," p. 16.

12. Ibid., p. 17.

13. Ibid.

14. Ibid.

15. Virginia Thompson and Richard Adloff, *The Emerging States of French Equatorial Africa* (Stanford, Calif.: Stanford University Press, 1960), pp. 4-5.

16. Griffon Du Bellay, "Le Gabon," 18-19; K. David Patterson, *The Northern Gabon Coast to 1875* (Oxford: Oxford University Press, 1975), pp. 90-92.

17. Bernard Schnapper, *La politique et le commerce français dans Le golfe De Guinée de 1838 à 1871* (Paris: Mouton, 1961), pp. 92, 97. See also, Guy Lasserre, *Libreville: la ville et sa region* (Paris: A. Colin, 1958), p. 60, which indicates that the French were envious of the British who were the sole beneficiaries of the practice of all ships, including French ones, landing intercepted slaves at Freetown, Sierra Leone.

18. Du Chaillu, *Explorations and Adventures*, p. 69.

19. Hampden C. DuBose, *Memoirs of Rev. John Leighton Wilson* (Richmond, Va: Presbyterian Committee of Publications, 1895), p. 147.

20. Smith, "Reminiscences of Paul Belloni Du Chaillu," p. 1146; Vaucaire, *Du Chaillu*, p. 8.

21. Smith, "Reminiscences of Paul Belloni Du Chaillu," p. 1146.

22. For this information, which supercedes that in previous biographical sketches of Du

Chaillu, we are indebted to Henry Bucher who sought diligently but unsuccessfully to find proof of Du Chaillu's American citizenship. See Bucher's "Canonization," pp. 18, 23.

23. Du Chaillu, *Explorations and Adventures*, p. XI; Vaucaire, *Du Chaillu*, pp. 9–10; Bucher, "Canonization," p. 18.

24. Du Chaillu, *Explorations and Adventures*, p. 26. The search for an inland healthy plateau region as a base for missionary service was suggested to Du Chaillu by the Reverend Wilson who himself had explored extensively beyond Mpongwe country. Du Bose, *Memoirs*, pp. 119–20. See also, Patterson, "Du Chaillu and exploration," 650.

25. Du Chaillu, *Exploration and Adventures*, pp. 25–26, 65.

26. J. Leighton Wilson, *Western Africa: Its History Condition and Prospects* (New York: Harper, 1856), p. 297.

27. Du Chaillu, *Explorations and Adventures*, pp. 36–39.

28. Ibid., p. 27; Vaucaire, *Du Chaillu*, p. 17; Patterson, "Du Chaillu and Exploration," p. 652.

29. Du Chaillu, *Explorations and Adventures*, p. 379. The sequence of Du Chaillu's travels presented here is not the one found in his book. Supposedly for the convenience of his readers, he chose not to record the journeys of his 1855–59 exploration in chronological order. One of the first to note the discrepancies this entailed was the unsigned reviewer (probably Winwood Reade) of *Explorations and Adventures* (first edition) in *The North British Review* 35 (1861), 223–50. See also, K. David Patterson, "Paul B. Du Chaillu and the Exploration of Gabon, 1855–1865," *International Journal of African Historical Studies* 7 (1974), 651, n. 19. Responding to censure over this problem, Du Chaillu corrected the chronology in a letter to *The Times* (7 June 1861) and in the preface of the second edition of *Explorations and Adventures*.

30. Ibid., p. 43.

31. Ibid., preface, p. X.

32. George Balandier, *The Sociology of Black Africa* (New York: Praeger, 1970), p. 88; K. David Patterson, *The Northern Gabon Coast to 1875* (Oxford: Oxford University Press, 1975), pp. 4–6, 125; David Birmingham, "The Forest and Savanna of Central Africa," in John Flint, ed., vol. 5, *The Cambridge History of Africa* (Cambridge: Cambridge University Press, 1976), p. 259; Christopher Chamberlain, "The Migration of the Fang in Central Gabon During the 19th Century," *International Journal of African Historical Studies* 11 (1978), 429–56.

33. George Wilson, *Western Africa*, pp. 302–5; Herbert Deschamps, *Quinze ans de Gabon: les débuts de l'éstablissement Français, 1839–1853* (Paris: Société Française d'Histoire d'Outre-Mer, 1965), p. 315. Benjamin Griswald, another American missionary, made contact with some Fang near the coast in 1844. James W. Fernandez, "Fang Representations under Acculturation," in Phillip Curtin, ed., *Africa and the West: Intellectual Responses to European Culture* (Madison: University of Wisconsin Press, 1972), p. 18. Robert B. N. Walker, an English trader with ten years' experience in Gabon, said he visited Fang villages on more than one occasion, spending days at a time with the people, and while he did not question that they were "notorious anthropophagi," he was highly skeptical of Du Chaillu's description of them. Walker, "M. Du Chaillu and His Book," a letter to the London *Daily Advertiser* abstracted in *The Athenaeum*, 21 Sept. 1861, p. 373; see also, Bucher, "Canonization," pp. 20–21.

34. Du Chaillu discussed the Fang extensively in pp. 92–130 of *Explorations and Adventures*. See also, his article, "The Great Equatorial Forest of Africa," *Fortnightly Review* 53 (June 1890), 785–88.

35. Du Chaillu, *Explorations and Adventures*, pp. 109–10.

36. Ibid., pp. 130–55.

37. K. David Patterson, "Early Knowledge of the Ogowe River and the American Exploration of 1854," *International Journal of African Historical Studies*, 5 (1972), 79; "Paul B. Du Chaillu and the Exploration of Gabon," 664; Bucher, "Canonization," p. 21.

38. Vaucaire, *Du Chaillu*, pp. 129–32. There has been some disagreement about Du Chaillu's writing ability, one commentator dismissing the "canard" that he could not write English coherently (West, *Congo*, p. 28). It is clear, however, that he needed considerable

help with composition. See his letter in Vaucaire's biography (pp. 133–34) which, although coherent, displays numerous errors in grammar and construction. This should not be surprising when one considers how brief Du Chaillu's acquaintance with English was at that point in his life. A British critic of Du Chaillu charged that the latter's first book was written for him by a New York journalist using the explorer's notes. Winwood Reade, *African Sketchbook*, 2 vols. (London: smith, Elder and Co., 1873), vol. 1 p. 146.

39. Vaucaire, *Du Chaillu*, pp. 129–30.
40. Ibid., pp. 131–32.
41. Du Chaillu, *Journey to Ashango-Land*, pp. VI–VII. Vaucaire, *Du Chaillu*, pp. 136–37; Wast, *Congo*, p. 23.
42. It was later said that this dispute, sometimes called the "Great Gorilla Controversy," was "one of the most bitter controversies ever engaged in by scientists." See Du Chaillu's obituary in the *New York Times*, 1 May 1903, p. 9. Another interesting discussion is in Wilfrid Blunt, *The Ark in the Park: The Zoo in the Nineteenth Century*. London: Hamish Hamilton, 1976, pp. 137–44.
43. *The Times* (London), 24 May 1861, p. 10; Bucher, "Canonization," pp. 19–20.
44. Robert B. N. Walker, "Mr. Du Chaillu and His Book," *Athenaeum* 1769 (21 Sept. 1861), 373–74; Bucher, "Canonization," pp. 20–21.
45. *The Times* (London), 7 June 1861, p. 10.
46. Ibid., p. 9.
47. Ibid.
48. *Globe* (London), 3 July 1861 as abstracted in *The Times* (London), 4 July 1861, p. 9, See also, West, *Congo*, p. 24.
49. Letter to *The Times* (London), 5 July 1861, p. 6.
50. Richard Burton to the editor of *The Times* (London), 8 July 1861, p. 10
51. Du Chaillu to the editor of *The Times* (London), 8 July 1861, p. 6.
52. Indeed, Burton was one who always seemed to be involved in such affairs. His dispute with his fellow explorer, John Speke, over which lakes were the actual sources of the Nile was not resolved until 1862 when Speke proved Burton's theory wrong.
53. Bucher, "Canonization," p. 20.
54. Du Chaillu, *Journey to Ashango-Land*, pp. VII–VIII, 414–15; Vaucaire, *Du Chaillu*, pp. 136–39; West, *Congo*, p. 24; Patterson, "Du Chaillu and Exploration," p. 654.
55. Thomas Savage and Jeffries Wyman, "Notice of the External Characters and Habits of the Troglodytes Gorilla, and a New Species of Orang from the Gabon River," *Boston Journal of Natural History* 5 (Dec. 1847), pp. 68–75. For a review of the early lore and then more scientific investigation of the gorilla prior to Du Chaillu's work, see Du Chaillu, *Explorations and Adventures*, pp. 388–94, 411–17; and Desmond and Ramona Morris, *Men and Apes* (London: Hutchinson, 1966), p. 74.
56. Wilson, *Western Africa*, pp. 366–67.
57. Ibid., p. 367.
58. Du Chaillu, *Exporations*, p. 345; Du Chaillu, "The Great Equatorial Rain Forest of Africa," *Fortnightly Review* 53 (June 1890), 780.
59. See, for example, his treatment of the gorilla in "The Great Equatorial Rain Forest," p. 780; and *King Mambo* (New York: Scribners, 1902), pp. 148–49.
60. Reade judged this subject so important that he discussed it at length in several writings (see, e.g., his *Savage Africa* [New York: Smith, Eldner and Co., 1864]; and *African Sketchbook*, vol. 1, pp. 146–47), but his best exposition is that in "The Gorilla as I Found Him," *Belgravia* 3 (1868), 230–39. Reade was not alone in doubting Du Chaillu's accounts of confrontations with gorillas. An American missionary in Gabon at the time denied that Du Chaillu had taken a gorilla out of Rio Muni country. Reade, "The Gorilla as I Found Him," p. 236.
61. Du Chaillu, letter to *The Times* (London), 1 Dec. 1862, p. 6.
62. Richard West, *Brazza of the Congo: European Exploration in French Equatorial Africa* (London: Jonathan Cape, 1972), p. 21; Geoffrey Bourne and Maury Cohen, *The Gentle Giants* (New York: Putnam, 1975), p. 31.
63. Reade, *Savage Africa*, p. 180.

64. George Schaller, *The Mountain Gorilla* (Chicago: University of Chicago Press, 1963), pp. 221–28.

65. In addition to detractors among Du Chaillu's contemporaries, Carl Akeley, who tracked and studied gorillas in the 1920s and who was very critical of Du Chaillu's characterization of the animal, discounted stories about its roar, stating that the sound was "nothing more than a throaty bark." Akeley, "Gorillas—Real and Mythical," *Natural History* 23 (Sept. 1923), 432.

66. Schaller, *Mountain Gorilla*, pp. 218, 225.

67. Richard Burton, *Two Trips to Gorillaland*, 2 vols. (London: Sampson, Low, Marston and Searle, 1876), vol. 1, preface, 44; West, *Congo*, p. 35.

68. George Schaller, *The Year of the Gorilla* (Chicago: University of Chicago Press, 1963), p. 5. Influenced by an earlier assessment not based on such extended or thorough fieldwork as that of Schaller, Henry Bucher reached a more negative conclusion on the worth of Du Chaillu's gorilla material. Bucher's authorities say "[Du Chaillu's] publications were so repudiated by the scientific world that even today they are considered first-rate examples of nature faking." Robert M. and Ada W. Yerkes, *The Great Apes: A Study of Anthropoid Life* (New Haven, Conn.: Yale University Press, 1929), p. 34, as quoted in Bucher, "Canonization," p. 22, n. 49. Yet, in another passage in the Yerkeses' study ignored by Bucher they admit that "the more we have used his [Du Chaillu's] publications, the more we have been impressed by the value of his observations . . . [and stripped of the fanciful embellishments, his work] would stand as by far the most important contribution to the natural history of the gorilla prior to the present century." *The Great Apes*, p. 127, as quoted in West, *Congo*, p. 28.

69. Du Chaillu, *Explorations and Adventures*, pp. 271–73, 314–17.

70. Dixon, *Natural History of the Gorilla*, p. 6.

71. Du Chaillu, *Explorations and Adventures*, pp. 104–5.

72. Burton, *Two Trips to Gorillaland*, vol. 1, p. 212; "A Day among the Fans," *Anthropological Review* 1 (1863), 47–48.

73. An old man admitted that certain clans were cannibals who ate only selected prisoners of war. Reade, *Savage Africa*, pp. 137–38, *Sketchbook*, vol. 1, p. 113.

74. Reade, *Savage Africa*, p. 38.

75. Alfred H. Guernsey, "Adventures in Gorilla Land," *Harper's New Monthly Magazine* 23 (June—Nov., 1861), 22.

76. Mary Kingsley, *Travels in West Africa* (London: Macmillan, 1897), pp. 330–32.

77. Henry H. Bucher, Jr., "The Mpongwe of the Gabon Estuary: A History to 1860," Ph.D. diss. (University of Wisconsin, 1977), p. 183; Patterson, "Du Chaillu and Exploration," p. 665.

78. The most extended development of this thesis is W. Arens, *The Man-Eating Myth: Anthropology and Anthropophagy* (New York : Oxford University Press, 1979), which attends to the African scene in pp. 83–96.

79. Joseph Ambouroué-Avaro, *Un peuple Gabonais, a l'aube de la colonisation: la Bas-Ogowe au XIXe siècle* (Paris: Karthala, 1981), p. 50.

80. Hubert Deschamps, *Tradition orales et archives au Gabon* (Paris: Berger-Levrault, 1962), pp. 84, 87, 102. See also, Alfred L. Bennett, "Ethnographical Notes on the Fang," *Anthropological Institute of Great Britain and Ireland Journal* 29 (1900), 83–85.

81. Abbé André Raponda Walker, *Notes d'histoire du Gabon* (Montpellier: Charité, 1960), p. 140; Ambouroué-Avaro, *Peuple Gabonais*, p. 50.

82. Du Chaillu, *Journey to Ashango-Land*, p. 19.

83. Ibid., p. 2.

84. Ibid., pp. 12–14.

85. Ibid., Preface, p. X.

86. Albert Bushnell to the secretary of the American Geographical and Statistical Society, 21 Nov. 1864, in *African Repository*, 41 (1865), 95.

87. Ibid.

88. Du Chaillu, *Journey to Ashango-Land*, pp. 124–38.

89. Ibid., pp. 315–23.

90. Ibid., p. 269. It is odd that Du Chaillu would have found reports of pygmies incredible. The little people had once been common inhabitants along the coast until eliminated by incoming Bantu groups. But even in the midnineteenth century there were creditable accounts of their existence not far from the littoral. Henry H. Bucher, "Mpongwe Origins: Historiographical Perspectives," *History in Africa* 2 (1975), 69.

91. Du Chaillu, *Journey to Ashango-Land*, pp. 315–23.

92. Du Chaillu, *Country of the Dwarfs* (New York: Harper, 1871), p. 259.

93. Du Chaillu, *Journey to Ashango-Land*, pp. 356–59.

94. Ibid., pp. 369–70.

95. In this endeavor Du Chaillu was assisted by H. W. Bates, a prominent naturalist who had produced a highly respected book on the Amazon River region. Vaucaire, *Du Chaillu*, p. 212.

96. *The Times*, (London), 9 Jan. 1866, p. 3.

97. Ibid.

98. 17 Jan. 1866, p. 7.

99. Ibid., 23 Jan. 1866, p. 5. See also, Vaucaire, *Du Chaillu*, pp. 210–11.

100. He first visited Sweden in 1871 and traveled through Scandinavia for about seven years; then in the 1880s he returned to Denmark and Norway. Vaucaire, *Du Chaillu*, p. 321.

101. Thomas Beer, *The Muave Decade* (New York: Knopf, 1926), p. 124; Vaucaire, *Du Chaillu*, pp. 288–92; Bucher, "Canonization," p. 26.

102. Alfred H. Guernsey, "Paul Du Chaillu Again," *Harper's New Monthly Magazine* 40 (1869–70), 201.

103. (New York, 1871).

104. Du Chaillu, *Stories of the Gorilla Country* (New York: Harper, 1867), p. 25.

105. Du Chaillu, *Journey to Ashango-Land*, p. 404.

106. Patterson, "Du Chaillu and Exploration," p. 660.

107. Du Chaillu, *Journey to Ashango-Land*, p. 436.

108. Du Chaillu, *Explorations and Adventures*, p.498.

109. Du Chaillu, *Journey to Ashango-Land*, preface, p. XIII.

110. The principal basis for his evaluation of Senegambian peoples was his brief visit to Senegal while sailing from France to Gabon, probably before 1850. While in Senegal, he joined a camel caravan from the coast northeastward into the fringe of the Sahara and then left it after two days to hunt ostriches in Wolof country. Du Chaillu, *My Apingi Kingdom, with Life in the Great Sahara* (New York: Harper, 1870), pp. 188–91; 207–12.

111. Du Chaillu, *Journey to Ashango-Land*, p. 285.

112. Dorothy Hammond and Alta Jablow, *The Myth of Africa* (New York: Library of Social Science, 1977), pp. 62–64.

113. Du Chaillu, *Journey to Ashango-Land*, p. 136.

114. Du Chaillu, *Explorations and Adventures*, pp. 356, 383–84; "Great Equatorial Forest," p. 784; Patterson, "Du Chaillu and Exploration," p. 660.

115. *The Times* (London), 11 Sept. 1861, p. 5.

116. Du Chaillu, *Journey to Ashango-Land*, p. 436; Patterson, "Du Chaillu and Exploration," pp. 661–62.

117. In one of his books Du Chaillu admitted that in the mid-1860s he suffered from extended ill-health resulting from his African venture. *King Mambo* (New York: Scribner, 1902), dedication, n.p.

118. Patterson, "Du Chaillu and Exploration," pp. 661–62.

119. Since some of his books were released in British and French editions, Du Chaillu undoubtedly contributed toward perceptions of Africa in those countries, but Britain and France had far more of their own nationals working in and writing about Africa than did the United States. In the latter Du Chaillu was the principal authority for many years. Henry Morton Stanley, his only major rival in this respect, published his first work on Africa only in 1874.

120. James R. Nesteby, "The Tenuous Vine of Tarzan of the Apes," *Journal of Popular Culture* 13 (Spring 1980), 483.

121. Richard A. Lupoff, *Edgar Rice Burroughs: Master of Adventure* (New Yerk: Ace Books, 1965), pp. 198–199.

122. Irwin Poges, *Edgar Rice Burroughs: The Man Who Created Tarzan* (Provo, Utah: Brigham Young University Press, 1975), p. 130.
123. Rudolph Altrocchi, *Sleuthing in the Stacks* (Cambridge: Harvard University Press, 1944), p. 95; Poges, *Burroughs*, p. 130.
124. Margaret Romer, "Edger Rice Burroughs, Creator of Tarzan," *Overland Monthly* March 1934, p. 6; Poges, *Burroughs*, p. 131.
125. Burroughs, *Tarzan of the Apes* (New York: Ballantine Books, 1984,) pp. 80–81; Du Chaillu, *Explorations and Adventures*, p. 83.
126. Du Chaillu, *Explorations and Adventures*, p. 93.
127. Burroughs, *Tarzan of the Apes*, p. 64.
128. Du Chaillu, *Explorations and Adventures*, p. 108; Burroughs, *Tarzan of the Apes*, p. 74.
129. Burroughs, *Tarzan of the Apes*, p. 74; Du Chaillu, *Explorations and Adventures*, p. 381.
130. The historian David Patterson provides a reasonable estimate of Du Chaillu's importance as an explorer in "Du Chaillu and Exploration," p. 663.
131. Du Chaillu, *Explorations and Adventures*, p. 102.
132. Ibid., p. 474.
133. Ibid., p. 291.
134. Ibid., p. 496.
135. Ibid., p. 381.
136. Ibid.
137. Ibid., p. 496.
138. Ibid., preface, p. VIII.
139. Ibid., p. 435.
140. Ibid., p. 239.
141. Hammond and Jablow, *Myth of Africa*, p. 28.
142. Reade, *Savage Africa*, p. 48; Patterson, "Du Chaillu and Exploration," p. 663.
143. Birmingham, "Forest and Savanna," pp. 259–60. The French were relatively uninterested in Gabon for either economic or political purposes until the 1880s, and came very close to turning it over to Great Britain. Henry Brunschwig, "French Exploration and Conquest in Tropical Africa from 1865," in L. H. Gann and Peter Duignan, eds., *Colonialism in Africa, 1870–1960, vol. I: The History and Politics of Colonialism, 1870–1914* (Cambridge: Cambridge University Press, 1969), p. 133.
144. Henry May to William H. Seward, 16 June 1863, Consular Despatches to the Department of State, Gabon, microcopy T-466.
145. Ibid.
146. Alfred H. Guernsey, "Adventures in Gorilla Land," *Harpers New Monthly Magazine* 18 (1861), p. 34.
147. A thoughtful and accurate discussion of Du Chaillu's impact on the American perception of Africa is found in Michael McCarthy, *Dark Continent: Africa as Seen by Americans* (Westport, Conn.: Greenwood Press, 1983), pp. 40–46; 129–32.

Chapter 3. In the Service of the Khedive

1. Ottoman Turkey's sovereignty over Egypt had been hollow for centuries as Mamluke (foreign white slave) dynasties ruled the country while ignoring Ottoman imperial claims to it. Napoleon Bonaparte led a French invasion of Egypt and destroyed Mamluke military power in 1798. The brief French occupation lasted only until 1801. Following the French withdrawal, surviving Mamlukes contested with Turkish forces, and within the latter several commanders vied with one another for control. When the smoke of this confusing conflict cleared after several years, Muhammad Ali, an Albanian officer in Ottoman service, was in charge. He was appointed governor (Wali) of Egypt in 1805 and also assumed the title of Pasha. His several successors (leadership remained in his family) inherited those

titles but Ismail, who ascended to power in 1863, managed to get the Ottoman sultan to confer a higher, more prestigious rank on him, one that at least suggested royal status if in fact it was less than that. Thus the title of Khedive was acquired by Ismail in 1866 and it became hereditary. Nevertheless, Ismail, like his predecessors, acknowledged the ultimate suzerainty of the Ottoman sultan by paying him an annual tribute. G. Douin, *Histoire du regne du Khedive Ismail*, 3 vols. (Rome: Egyptian Geographical Society, 1933–38), 1, chaps. 8, 13, 14.; P. J. Vatikiotis, *The Modern History of Egypt* (New York: Praeger, 1969), pp. 53–55; 79–80; Sidney N. Fisher, *The Middle East: A History* (New York: Knopf, 1969), pp. 263–64, 279–88.

2. Evidently the Khedive specifically stated his intention to use military force to win independence from Turkey. See Charles Chaillé-Long, *My Life on Four Continents*, 2 vols. (London: Hutchinson, 1972), vol. 1, p. 17; and Pierre Gordon Crabites, *Americans in the Egyptian Army* (London: George Routledge and Sons, 1938), pp. 42–45.

3. Crabites, *Americans in the Egyptian Army*, pp. 24–25; Duignan and Gann, *United States and Africa*, pp. 396–97, n. 16.

4. William Mc C. Dye, *Muslim Egypt and Christian Abyssinia* (New York: Atkin and Prout, 1880), pp. 495–500; Czeslaw Jesman, "American Officers of Khedive Ismail," *African Affairs* 59 (1958), 303.

5. Crabites, *Americans in the Egyptian Army*, p. 20.

6. William B. Hesseltine and Hazel C. Wolf, *The Blue and the Grey on the Nile* (Chicago: University of Chicago Press, 1961), pp. 9, 18–19., 40–41; Jesman, "American Officers," p.302.

7. Hesseltine and Wolf, *Blue and Grey*, pp. 4–9.

8. Chaillé-Long, Egyptian Service Contract, Chaillé-Long Papers, Manuscript Division, Library of Congress, Washington, D.C., container 1, folder 16 (hereafter cited as CP,1/6). This collection is not especially valuable to the researcher; it contains little that is not published in his books.

9. Chaillé-Long, *My Life*, vol. 1, p. 12; *National Cyclopaedia of American Biography* (New York: James T. White, 1909), 10, pp. 28–29; *Dictionary of American Biography* (New York: Scribners, 1957), vol. 3, pp. 591–92.

10. U.S., Congress, House, Committee on Military Affairs, Report no. 3160, *Charles Chaillé-Long: Adverse Report*, 59th Congress, 1st session, 1906, p. 3; Chaillé-Long, *My Life*, vol. 1, p. 8.

11. Chaillé-Long, *My Life*, vol. 1, p. 13.

12. Dabney H. Maury to F. T. Rivales, ?, 1869, CP, 1/2.

13. Chaillé-Long to George C. Taylor, 17 Nov. 1869, CP, 1/2.

14. Taylor to Chaillé-Long, 20 Dec. 1869, CP, 1/2.

15. Hesseltine and Wolf, *Blue and Grey*, p. 150.

16. Jesman, "American Officers," p. 303.

17. Ferdinand de Lesseps to Khedive Ismail, 10 May 1870, Egyptian Archives, Cairo, Judicial Reform File (1870–75), quoted in Crabites, *Americans in the Egyptian Army*, pp. 44–45.

18. Chaillé-Long, *My Life*, vol. 1, p. 32; Crabites, Ibid., pp. 42–45.

19. Crabites, Ibid., pp. 48–49.

20. Chaillé-Long, *My Life*, vol. 1, pp. 55–56.

21. Hesseltine and Wolf, *Blue and Grey*, p. 151.

22. Chaillé-Long, *My Life*, vol. 1, p. 61. The best description of Cairo life as experienced by the American officers is that in Hesseltine and Wolf, *Blue and Grey*, chap. 3.

23. U.S., Congress, House, Committee on Military Affairs, *adverse Report*, p. 3.

24. Hesseltine and Wolf, *Blue and Grey*, pp. 150–51.

25. Robert Collins, *The Southern Sudan, 1883–1898* (New Haven, Conn.: Yale University Press, 1962), p. 4.

26. P. M. Holt, *A Modern History of the Sudan* (London: Weidenfeld and Nicolson, 1961), pp. 61–63; Collins, Ibid.

27. Holt., Ibid., pp. 60–63; Richard Gray, *A History of the Southern Sudan, 1839–1889* (London: Oxford University Press, 1961), pp. 80–81.

28. Reginald Coupland, *The Exploitation of East Africa, 1856–1890* (Evanston, Ill.:

Northwestern University Press, 1967—reprint of 1938 edition), p. 272; Holt, *History of the Sudan*, p. 66.

29. John Marlowe, *Spoiling the Egyptians* (New York: St. Martins, 1975), p. 143.

30. R. Gray, *Southern Sudan*, pp. 80–81; Mekki Shibeika, "The Expansionist Movement of Khedive Ismail to the Lakes," in Yusuf Fadl Hassan, ed. *Sudan in Africa* (Khartoum: University of Khartoum Press, 1971), p. 142.

31. Charles Gordon to M. A. Gordon, 17 Nov. 1873; M.A. Gordon, ed., *Letters of General C.G. Gordon to his Sister, M.A. Gordon* (London: Macmillan, 1888), p. 69.

32. Ibid.

33. *Times* (London), 18 Aug. 1874, p. 8; see also, Pierre Crabites, *Gordon, The Sudan and Slavery* (London: George Routledge and Sons, 1933), pp. 28–30.

34. M. F. Shukry, ed., *"Equatoria under Egyptian Rule,"* Unpublished correspondence of Col. C. G. Gordon with Ismail, Khedive of Egypt and the Sudan, during the years 1876–76 (Cairo: Cairo University Press, 1953), introduction and p. 29.

35. Hesseltine and Wolf, *Blue and Grey*, pp. 152–53. Chaillé-Long himself admitted that even later, when he was in Uganda, he could not speak Arabic. See his book, *Central Africa: Naked Truths of Naked People* (London: Sampson, Low, Marston, Searle and Rivington, 1876), p. 94; and Edward A. Alpers, "Charles Chaillé-Long's Mission to Mutesa of Buganda," *Uganda Journal* 29 (1965), 4.

36. Chaillé-Long, *Central Africa*, p. 65.

37. George B. Hill, ed., *Colonel Gordon in Central Africa, 1874–79* (London: Thomas De La Rue and Co., 1885), p. 3. Chaillé-Long's actual rank was lieutenant-colonel.

38. The Egyptian scholar, M. F. Shukry, believes that Chaillé-Long distorted the facts of his meeting with Gordon to exaggerate his own importance. See his book, *Equatoria under Egyptian Rule*, p. 45.

39. Chaillé-Long, *My Life*, vol. 1, pp. 67–68. See also Chaillé-Long to the editor, 1 Mar. 1909, *Bulletin of the American Geographical Society of New York* 41, (Apr. 1909), 223.

40. Chaillé-Long, "General Gordon—More Soldier than Saint," manuscript, CP, 2/2. See also his book, *My Life*, vol. 1, pp. 67–68.

41. Shukry, *Equatoria under Egyptian Rule*, p. 44.

42. James R. Hooker, "Verney Lovett Cameron: A Sailor in Central Africa," in Robert I. Rotberg, ed., *Africa and Its Explorers: Motives, Methods and Impact* (Cambridge; Harvard University Press, 1970), p. 259.

43. Chaillé-Long, *Central Africa*, p. 38.

44. Khedive Ismail to Gordon, 30 Aug. 1874, in F. W. Moffit, "Some Despatches from Khedive Ismail to Major-General Charles Gordon," *Journal of the Royal African Society* 34 (Apr. 1935), 112.

45. Gordon to Khairy Pasha, 17 Aug. 1874, in Shukry, *Equatoria Under Egyptian Rule*, no. 19, p. 169. See also, Douin, *Khedive Ismail*, vol. 3, part 3, A, pp. 27, 89.

46. The circumstances of Chaillé-Long's appointment to Gordon's staff and his "orders" for the Uganda mission are thoroughly discussed in Alpers, "Chaillé-Long's Mission to Mutesa," pp. 3–4. See also, Douin, *Khedive Ismail*, vol. 3, 3, A, p. 89.

47. The mixture of nationalities was explained partly by Gordon's desire to give an international character to his work and thus make it more interesting to the "whole civilized world." Bernard M. Allen, *Gordon and the Sudan* (London: MacMillan, 1931), p. 15.

48. Further elaborating on his insistence that he went to Uganda under special orders from Ismail, Chaillé-Long stated in his last published account of the affair that Gordon wanted his American chief of staff to accompany him on the trip back to Khartoum but that he jumped off the steamer at the last minute and Gordon, unable to speak Arabic, could not get the boat's captain to turn back for him. See Chaillé-Long, *My Life*, vol. 1, pp. 87–88. Although Gordon was not, according to Chaillé-Long, opposed to his journey to Uganda, the commander nonetheless thought it an "utterly impracticable" venture, and while returning to Khartoum assumed the American had remained in Gondokoro. Chaillé-Long, *Central Africa*, p. 37. This is contradicted by Chaillé-Long's own journal that indicates that the night before he left for Khartoum "Gordon indicated to me his desire that I should visit M'tesa [sic], present him with gifts and reconnoiter the country." *Provinces of the Equator: Summary of the Letters and Reports of His Excellency the Governor General, part 1—Year*

1874 (Cairo, 1877), appendix 2, p. 37, quoted in Alpers, "Chaillé-Long's Mission to Mutesa," p. 5. Another member of Gordon's staff also reported that Gordon "sent" Chaillé-Long to Uganda. Romolo Gessi Pasha (ed. Felix Gessi), *Seven Years in the Soudan* (London: Sampson, Low and Marston, 1892), p. 79; see also, Shukry, *Equatoria under Egyptian Rule*, p. 45, and Crabites, *Gordon and the Sudan*, pp. 37–39.

49. Roland Oliver, "Discernible Developments in the Interior, c. 1500–1840," in Roland Oliver and Gervase Mathew, eds., *History of East Africa*, 2 vols. (Oxford: Oxford University Press, 1963), vol., 1, pp. 189–90; D. A. Low, "The Northern Interior, 1840–1884," Ibid., 331–36.

50. Low, "The Northern Interior," p. 334.

51. Zanzibar, an island off the East African coast, was the base of an important sultanate that controlled nearby islands and a significant stretch of the adjoining littoral. It was the center of a large slave-trading network and its merchants, many of them people of mixed African and Arab blood, called Swahilis, ranged far over the East African interior.

52. J. M. Gray, "Mutesa of Buganda," *Uganda Journal* 1 (1934), 32–39.

53. Gessi, *Seven Years in the Soudan*, p. 79.

54. Shukry, *Equatoria under Egyptian Rule*, p. 47.

55. Chaillé-Long, *Central Africa*. See also Hill, *Gordon in Central Africa*, pp. 16, 115.

56. Chaillé-Long, *Central Africa*, p. 36.

57. Shukry, *Equatoria under Egyptian Rule*, p. 47.

58. Douin, *Khedive Ismail*, vol. 3, pp. 28–29; R. Gray, *Southern Sudan*, p. 116.

59. Chaillé-Long, *My Life*, vol. 1, p. 90.

60. Chaillé-Long, *Central Africa*, pp. 81–91.

61. Ibid. pp. 106–8.

62. Chaillé-Long to R. Beardsley (U.S. consul in Cairo), 7 Nov. 1874, U.S. Consular Despatches, Cairo, vol. 9, no. 258, enclosure 1, microcopy T-41, roll 2.

63. For J. A. Grant's description of his mile-long canoe trip across Katonga Bay, an inlet on the western coast of Lake Victoria, see his *Walk Across Africa* (London: Blackwood and Sons, 1864), p. 207. Speke spent some eight days in the company of King Mutesa cruising along the shores of the lake in large canoes. Speke, *Journal of the Discovery of the Source of the Nile* (Edinburgh and London: W. Blackwood and Sons, 1863), pp. 314–19. The first to challenge Chaillé-Long's claim to have been first to sail the lake was Laurence Oliphant, "African Explorers," *North American Review* 124 (May—June 1877), 395–96. The historian E. Alpers, apparently unaware of these references, accepted Chaillé-Long's claim. "Chaillé-Long's Mission to Mutesa," p. 6.

64. Chaillé-Long, *Central Africa*, pp. 138–41.

65. Ibid., p. 306.

66. Chaillé-Long, *My Life*, vol. 1, 97; *Bulletin of the American Geographical Society of New York* 36 (Jan.—June 1904), 384–89.

67. Chaillé-Long to the editor, 20 Jan. 1904, *Bulletin of the American Geographical Society of New York* 36 (Jan.—June, 1904), 5; *My Life*, vol. 1, p. 164.

68. Hill, *Gordon in Central Africa*, p. 183; R. Gray, *Southern Sudan*, pp. 135, 184–85. One scholar allows that a treaty may have been signed by Mutesa but without his understanding of what it meant; thus it was merely "a scrap of paper." See J. M. Gray, "Mutesa of Buganda," 30–31. The last historian to investigate the matter of Chaillé-Long's alleged treaty concluded that perhaps some type of "letter" was signed but that Mutesa never intended to honor its provisions and in fact proceeded to ignore whatever agreement he may have made. Alpers, "Chaillé-Long's Mission to Mutesa," pp. 6–8. Also helpful is Shibeika, "Expansionist Movement," p. 152.

69. A. W. Graves, "The Physiography of Uganda: The Evolution of the Great Lakes and the Victoria, Nile Drainage System," *Journal of the Royal African Society*, 33 (1934), 66.

70. Chaillé-Long, *Central Africa*, p. 173.

71. Chaillé-Long to Beardsley, 7 Nov. 1874, U.S. Consular Despatches, Cairo.

72. In defense of Chaillé-Long it should be noted that his choice of troops in Khartoum was limited to some extent by orders from Cairo indicating which specific companies were to be transferred. Douin, *Khedive Ismail*, vol. 3, pt. 3, A, p. 126.

73. Hill, *Gordon in Central Africa*, p. 55.

74. Lord Godfrey Elton, *Gordon of Khartoum: The Life of General Charles George Gordon* (New York: Knopf, 1955), p. 154.
75. Ibid, p. 155.
76. Chaillé-Long, *Central Africa*, pp. 244–45.
77. Gordon had abandoned Gondokoro in Dec. 1874, declaring it too unhealthy for his headquarters, and moved north to Lado. Hill, *Gordon in Gordon in Central Africa*, pp. 43, 58, 60.
78. Chaillé-Long, *Central Africa*, p. 259.
79. Chaillé-Long, "The Black and Brown People of the Soudan," *Frank Leslie's Magazine*, Sept. 1884, p. 365.
80. R. Gray, *Southern Sudan*, pp. 46–69.
81. Chaillé-Long, *Central Africa*, pp. 273–74. Chaillé-Long claimed to have witnessed Azande cannibalism (Ibid, p. 287), but his tendency to sensationalize his depiction of African life has led Africanists to dismiss this. The respected German scholar-explorer George Schweinfurth, however, whose work is generally considered quite reliable, observed Azande anthropophagy on more than one occasion. See his book, *The Heart of Africa*, 2 vols. (London: Sanpson, Low, 1873), vol. 2, esp. pp. 17–19. The English anthropologist Evans-Pritchard, who devoted some of his extensive ethnographical research in the Sudan to the Azande, subjected practically all recorded references to their cannibalism to careful scrutiny. He convincingly judges Chaillé-Long's statements as merely conjecture, and though he gives little credit to Schweinfurth on the subject, he does not totally dismiss the latter's reports. Evans-Pritchard concludes his thorough but, in this writer's opinion, defensively partisan study by admitting that cannibalism probably did occur in Zandeland but not frequently. Moreover, he stresses that it was practiced mostly by other African groups who were conquered and gradually assimilated by the Azande. When outsiders such as Chaillé-Long and Schweinfurth, not understanding the complex ethnic mix that existed in some areas identified as Azande territory, detected cases of cannibalism among these peoples, they mistakenly associated the practice with "pure" Azande. E. E. Evans-Pritchard, "Zande Cannibalism," chap. 7 in his book, *The Position of Women in Primitive Societies and Other Essays in Social Anthropology* (London: Faber and Faber, 1965), pp. 133–64.
82. Hesseltine and Wolf, *Blue and Grey*, pp. 149–50.
83. The English trader, J. Petherick, an Italian hunter-adventurer, Carlo Piaggia, and the learned explorer Schweinfurth, had visited Azande lands between 1858 and 1870, the latter providing a good description of them in his book, *The Heart of Africa*, chaps. 13–17. See also, R. Gray, *Southern Sudan*, pp. 62–63. In 1859 an Italian priest, Franz Morlang, followed a route similar to that used later by Chaillé-Long that brought him within two days' travel of Makaraka. See the extract of his journal in Elias Toniolo and Richard Hill, eds., *The Opening of the Nile Basin: Writings by members of the Catholic Mission to Central Africa on Geography and Ethnography of the Sudan, 1842–81* (New York: Barnes and Noble Books, 1975), pp. 109–28. Evans-Pritchard, "Zande Cannibalism" (pp. 134–44), provides a useful survey of European visitors among the Azande. See also Douin, *Khedive Ismail*, vol. 3, part 1, p. 17, n. 1.
84. R. Gray, *Southern Sudan*, p. 53. Although he did not mention it in his own books, Chaillé-Long is credited by the historian P. Crabites with liberating slaves while among the Azande. *Americans in the Egyptian Army*, p. 158.
85. Chaillé-Long, *Central Africa*, p. 282.
86. Ibid., pp. 283–88.
87. Shukry, *Equatoria under Egyptian Rule*, p. 69.
88. Ibid., p. 70. The Turkish suzerain was encouraged to accommodate Ismail by financial inducements. The acquisition of Suakin, for instance, cost the Khedive an additional £15,000 ($75,000) annual tribute to Istanbul. *Times* (London), 9 July 1875, p. 5.
90. Ibid., p. 71.
91. Ibid., pp. 72–73.
92. E. R. Turton, "Kirk and the Egyptian Invasion of East Africa in 1875: A Reassessment," *Journal of African History* 11 (1970), 358.
93. Douin, *Khedive Ismail*, vol. 3, part 2, pp. 91–96; Coupland, *Exploitation of East Africa*, p. 276; Hesseltine and Wolf, *Blue and Grey*, p. 122.
94. Douin, *Khedive Ismail*, vol. 3, part 2, pp. 94–95.

95. Ibid.
96. Gordon to C. M. Watson, 28 Dec. 1874, cited in Stanley Lane Poole, *Watson Pasha* (London: J, Murray, 1919), p. 72; and Allen, *Gordon and the Sudan*, p. 37.
97. Gordon to Khairy Pasha, 21 Jan. 1875, in Shukry, *Equatoria Under Egyptian Rule*, no. 65, p. 211. See also, Allen, *Gordon and the Sudan*.
98. Chaillé-Long to Stone Pasha, 25 Jan. 1875, in Shukry, *Equatoria under Egyptian Rule*, no. 67, pp. 214–15. In fact, Gordon, probably hoping to rid himself of his American aide, did advise the Khedive to give Chaillé-Long responsibility for the land phase on the East African end of the operation. Nubar Pasha to Gordon, 17 Sept. 1875, in Moffit, "Some Despatches," p. 114; Douin, *Khedive Ismail*, vol. 3, part 3, p. 352.
99. Gordon to his sister, 21 Jan. 1875, in Hill, *Gordon in Central Africa*, p. 64; also quoted in Allen, *Gordon and the Sudan*, p. 37; and cited in Coupland, *Exploitation of East Africa*, p. 275.
100. Moffit, "Some Despatches," p. 115.
101. Ibid., p. 113.
102. Gordon to Khairy Pasha, 26 June 1875, in Shukry, *Equatoria Under Egyptian Rule*, no. 109, pp. 273–74.
103. Khedive Ismail to Gordon Pasha, 17 Sept. 1875, in E. A. Stanton, "Secret Letters from the Khedive Ismail in Connection with the Occupation of the East Coast of Africa," *Journal of the Royal African Society* 34 (1935), 276. This letter is also printed in Moffit, "Some Despatches," p. 114.
104. *The Times* (London), 2 July 1875, p. 9.
105. Ibid.; Coupland, *Exploitation of East Africa*, p. 277.
106. Beardsley to Hamilton Fish (U.S. secretary of state), 31 Aug. 1875, U.S. Consular Despatches, Cairo, 1875, vol. 10, no. 356, microcopy T-41, roll no. 2.
107. Khedive Ismail to McKillop, 7 Sept. 1875, quoted in P. Crabites, *Ismail, the Maligned Khedive* (London: George Routledge and Sons, 1933), pp. 114–16.
108. Khedive Ismail to Gordon Pasha, 17 Sept. 1875, in Stanton, "Secret Letters," p. 278.
109. Ibid.
110. Ibid.
111. Chaillé-Long, "General Gordon," manuscript, p. 23 CP. 2/2. In a newspaper interview Chaillé-Long said that Gordon, who wanted to be a "sultan" in Khartoum, offered him the "vice sultanate of Fatiko and Uganda." *Baltimore Sun*, 3 May 1902, p. 5. At the least this seems farfetched.
112. Chaillé-Long, *My Life*, vol. 2, p. 175. The historian E. R. Turton incorrectly states that McKillop and Chaillé-Long linked up in Suez and proceeded south together. "Egyptian Invasion of East Africa," p. 359.
113. Khedive Ismail to McKillop, 17 Sept. 1875, in Stanton, "Secret Letters," p. 271.
114. Ibid.; Shukry, *Equatoria under Egyptian Rule*, p. 85.
115. Chaillé-Long, *My Life*, vol. 1, p. 177. These actions were not in strict compliance with the Khedive's instructions and probably served to alert Zanzibar and the British to what was supposed to be a carefully guarded secret operation until it reached its destination. See Shukry, *Equatoria under Egyptian Rule*, p. 86.
116. Chaillé-Long, *My Life*, vol. 1, p. 178.
117. Ibid., 180.
118. Chaillé-Long initially assumed that he was the first Westerner to have explored the river. While aware that in 1865 a German, Baron von der Decken, traveled in the area, he mistakenly believed the latter was killed before he could proceed far beyond the river's mouth. Chaillé-Long, *Central Africa*, appendix, p. 327. Later he recognized that von der Decken had penetrated as far as Bardera (approximately 185 miles inland) but considered his own journey of 150 miles up the river as more significant because he lived to tell about it. Chaillé-Long, "Colonel Long on the Juba," *Bulletin of the American Geographical Society* 19 (1887), 197. See also, Chaillé-Long, *My Life*, vol. 1 p. 184.
119. Chaillé-Long, *My Life*, vol. 1, pp. 182–84.
120. Khedive Ismail to Mckillop, 29 Oct. 1875, in Stanton, "Secret Letters," pp. 280–81; see also, Shukry, *Equatoria under Egyptian Rule*, p. 87.

121. British determination to suppress the East African slave trade increasingly had become focused on Zanzibar. That island-state had responded to British pressure by taking various steps to reduce slaving and in return could expect London's help in its international relations. Even though British agents recognized that the sultan's authority along the coast north of Zanzibar was weak at best and often not recognizable, they agreed that the sultan was an essential factor in the antislavery struggle who, with British backing and encouragement, and sometimes intimidation, could make a big difference in this important campaign. See Coupland, *Exploitation of East Africa*, passim; J. M. Gray, "Zanzibar and the Coastal Belt, 1840–1884," Oliver and Mathew, *History of East Africa*, vol. 1, pp. 229–40.

122. Shukry, *Equatoria under Egyptian Rule*, p. 90.

123. Ibid.; Douin, *Khedive Ismail*, vol. 3, part 3, B, p. 687; Turton, "Egyptian Invasion of East Africa," p. 362.

124. M. Sabry, *L'empire 'Egyptien sous Ismail et l'interférence Anglo-Française, 1863–1879* (Paris: P. Geuthner, 1933), pp. 487–88.

125. Turton, "Egypian Invasion of East Africa," p. 359.

126. Alan Moorehead, *The White Nile* (New York: Dell Publishing Co., 1960), p. 188.

127. Shukry, *Equatoria under Egyptian Rule*, pp. 92–93; Douin, *Khedive Ismail*, vol. 3, part 3, B, p. 691.

128. Hill, *Gordon in Central Africa*, p. 151; Shukry, *Equatoria under Egyptian Rule*, p. 90.

129. In fact, Gordon was so despondent at this time that he was seriously considering resignation. Gordon to Khairy Pasha, 29 Sept. 1875, in Shukry, *Equatoria under Egyptian Rule*, no. 133, p. 125.

130. Chaillé-Long later charged that Gordon followed British orders not to meet the Egyptian expedition in East Africa. See his book, *L'Egypte et ses provinces perdues* (Paris: La Nouvelle Revue, 1892), p. 177; and *The Three Prophets* (New York: Appelton, 1886), p. 320; Shukry, *Equatoria under Egyptian Rule*, pp. 63–65. Hesseltine and Wolf, apparently accepting Chaillé-Long's opinion, state that Gordon simply "refused to exert himself." *Blue and Grey*, p. 90.

131. Shukry, *Equatoria under Egyptian Rule*, pp. 70–71, 90; Dye, *Moslem Egypt and Christian Abyssinia*, p. 82; R. Gray, *Southern Sudan*, pp. 180–83.

132. A respected explorer, naturalist, and colonial administrator who was a great admirer of Kirk, credited him with driving the Egyptians out of East Africa "with one frigate." Harry Johnston, *The Kilimanjaro Expedition* (London: K. Paul, Trench and Co., 1886), p. 22. But Turton ("Egyptian Invasion of East Africa," esp. pp. 360–63), demonstrates that Kirk's role was much less significant in this affair.

133. While Gordon was at work on the upper Nile and the McKillop expedition was underway, Ismail's forces also initiated an invasion of Ethiopia. This was a total disaster for Egypt, a defeat that proved far more costly and embarrassing to Ismail's regime than the East African venture. See Hesseltine and Wolf, *Blue and Grey*, chaps. 9, 10.

134. *New York Times*, 11 Nov. 1877, p. 5; Hesseltine and Wolf, *Blue and Grey*, pp. 299–30.

135. *New York Times*, 11 Nov. 1877, p. 5.

136. For a good discussion of the significance of the mixed courts and the difficulty Egypt had in obtaining European acceptance of them, see Marlow, *Spoiling the Egyptians*, chap. 10.

137. Chaillé-Long, *My Life*, vol. 1, pp. 239–45.

138. J. W. A. Nicholson, commander of U.S. naval squadron, to W. E. Chandler, secretary of the navy, 15 July 1882, copy, CP, 1/4; Chaillé-Long, *My Life*, vol. 1, pp. 246–47.

139. Earl of Cromer (Evelyn Baring) *Modern Egypt*, 2 vols. (New York, 1901), vol. 1, p. 289.

140. M. E. Chamberlain, "The Alexandria Massacre of 11 June, 1882 and British Occupation of Egypt," *Middle Eastern Studies* 13 (Jan. 1977), 17.

141. Chaillé-Long, *My Life*, vol. 1, pp. 250, 251, 267–68.

142. Those foreign nationals, such as Swedes and Swiss, whose countries were not represented among the naval forces in Alexandria, were hosted by others. Chaillé-Long

claimed to have rescued some 800 persons, but the American naval commander's report mentions only 130 refugees. Even this was too many for the naval vessels to accommodate, so some were transferred to an Italian merchant ship, which provided temporary quarters at a rate of $25 a day per person. Ibid., *New York Times*, 25 July 1882, pp. 1, 4.

143. Ibid., pp. 267–68.

144. Ibid., pp. 261–62. Baron de Kusel, *An Englishman's Recollections of Egypt, 1863–1887, with an Epilogue Dealing with the Present* (London: John Lane, 1914), p. 208; Chaillé-Long, interview with the *Baltimore Sun*, 3 May 1902, p. 5.

145. Chaillé-Long, *My Life*, vol. 1, pp. 259–62; Chamberlain, "Alexandria Massacre," p. 23.

146. Chamberlain, "Alexandria Massacre," p. 30.

147. Ibid., pp. 23–24, 33.

148. Chaillé-Long, interview with the *Baltimore Sun*, 3 May 1902, p. 5; and his speech before the American Geographical Society, 15 Feb. 1910, CP, 1/22; see also, *National Cyclopedia of American Biography*, x, 29.

149. J. W. A. Nicholson to secretary of the navy, 15 July 1902, CP 1/4.

150. Chaillé-Long, interview with the *Baltimore Sun*, 3 May 1902, p. 5.

151. *New York Times*, 5 Aug. 1883, p. 10.

152. Chaillé-Long, "England in Egypt and the Soudan," *North American Review* 168 (Jan.—June 1899), 579.

153. Gilbert Haven, "America in Africa, part I," Ibid. 125 (July 1877), 148–52.

154. Oliphant, "American Explorers," Ibid. (May–June 1877), 392.

155. Chaillé-Long, *My Life*, vol. 2, p. 543.

156. Ibid., 564; Chaillé-Long, interview with *Baltimore Sun*, 3 May 1902, p. 5; and his "Heroes to Order," *North American Review* 1634 (Jan.—June 1887), 507–13.

157. He finally referred to Stanley as "a fine specimen of a savage," *My Life*, vol. 1, p. 280.

158. Gordon to Chaillé-Long, 9 Dec. 1879, quoted in Chaillé-Long, *My Life*, vol. 2, pp. 533–34. Gordon also communicated his apology to Chaillé-Long through the *New York Times*, 23 Jan. 1880 and the *New York Herald*, 9 Dec. 1879 and 28 Jan. 1880. See also Chaillé-Long's letter in the American Geographical Society's *Bulletin* 41 (Apr. 1909), 224.

159. Chaillé-Long, *My Life*, vol. 2, p. 546.

160. Ibid.

161. Dorothy Middleton, "The Search for the Nile Sources," *Geographical Journal* 138 (June 1972). In a discussion that followed the public presentation of the paper upon which this article is based, the historian Kenneth Ingham had to inform the author that the gap in the knowledge left by Baker and Speke was filled in by Chaillé-Long. See Ibid., p. 222.

162. Chaillé-Long, *My Life*, vol. 1, p. 70.

163. Chaillé-Long, "England and Egypt in the Soudan," p. 572.

164. Chaillé-Long, interview with the *Baltimore Sun*, 3 May 1902, p. 5.

165. Ibid.

166. Allen, *Gordon and the Sudan*, p. 92; Elton, *Gordon of Khartoum*, pp. 135–36.

167. Chaillé-Long, *My Life*, vol. 1, pp. 81–83, 220; 2, p. 582; and his portrait of his one-time superior, "General Gordon as He Is," *New York Tribune*, 25 Jan. 1885, p. 5.

168. Chaillé-Long, *My Life*, vol. 1, p. 220.

169. Allen, *Gordon and the Sudan*, pp. 90–94; Crabites, *Gordon and the Sudan*, pp. 41–43; Elton, *Gordon of Khartoum*, pp. 160–63.

170. Chaillé-Long, *Central Africa*, p. 326.

171. Ibid., pp. 325–26.

172. Chaillé-Long, "Egypt, Africa and the Africans," pamphlet form of a speech before the American Geographical Society (New York, 1878), p. 36, CP, 4/1.

173. Chaillé-Long to his father, Littleton Long, 23 Apr. 1874, CP, 3/1.

174. Chaillé-Long, *Central Africa*, p. 121; Crabites, *Americans in the Egyptian Army*, pp. 163–64.

175. *American Register* (Paris), 7 Oct. 1876, p. 2. The author of this review remarked that "the brutal, selfish, cunning savage appears in the author's pages, as he really is and not what it is to be hoped."

176. Chaillé-Long to Beardsley, 7 Nov. 1874, enclosure no. 1 in Beardsley to the secretary of state, 28 Dec. 1874, U.S. Consular Despatches, Cairo, vol, 9, no. 258, microcopy T-41, roll 2.
177. Chaillé-Long, *Central Africa*, p. 18.
178. Ibid., p. 314.
179. Elton, *Gordon of Khartoum*, chap. 5.

Chapter 4. Henry Shelton Sanford

1. The Sanford Papers are housed in the General Sanford Memorial Library, Sanford, Florida (hereafter cited as SP). Microfilm copies of the collection are available at the Tennessee State Archives, Nashville (where the papers were cataloged). Africa-related portions of the papers on film are owned by the Ohio State University Library, Columbus, and the Hoover Institution, Stanford University, Stanford, California.
The American historian, Robert Stanley Thomson, in a series of three articles in the journal *Congo revue générale de la colonie Belge* (vols. 11 [1930], 295–336; and 12 [1931], 167–96, 335–52), published selected letters from the Sanford collection, which at that time was not easily accessible. In 1952 Leo T. Malloy published a laudatory booklet commissioned by the subject's granddaughter (*Henry Shelton Sanford, 1823–1891* [Derby, Conn.: Bacon Printing Co.,]) which was based on materials provided by Sanford's descendants. The Belgian scholar, François Bontink, later made available considerably more Sanford correspondence in his book, *Aux origines de l'état indépendant du Congo: documents tirés d' archives Américaines* (Louvain and Paris: Editions E. Nauwelaerts, 1966). As valuable as these contributions are, their primary purpose was to shed further light on the foundation of the Congo State, not to provide a full assessment of Sanford. The latter objective was the subject of the present writer's "Henry Shelton Sanford and the Congo," Ph.D. diss. (Ohio State University, 1967); and his article, "Henry Shelton Sanford and the Congo: A Reassessment," *African Historical Studies* 4 (1971), 19–39. Since then, Joseph Fry has published a well-researched biography, *Henry S. Sanford: Diplomacy and Business in Nineteenth Century America* (Reno: University of Nevada Press, 1982), which has been quite useful in the revision of the 1971 article, which is the basis for this chapter.
2. Carleton E. Sanford, *Thomas Sanford, The Emigrant to New England: Ancestry, Life and Descendants*, 2 vols. (Rutland, Vt., Tuttle Co., 1911), vol. 1, p. 628.
3. Fry, *Sanford*, p. 4.
4. Sanford's journals, SP 3/1–5; "Western Lands Accounts," 62/7–11.
5. Sanford's journals, SP, 3/7–9; Malloy, *Sanford*, pp. 11–14; Fry, *Sanford*, pp. 8–19.
6. Richard J. Amundson, "The American Life of Henry Shelton Sanford," Ph.D. diss. (Florida State University, 1963), p. 21.
7. "I do not consider him in his feelings a democrat, but a regular toady to aristocracy," wrote C. Remington to Pierce, 29 June 1835, U.S. Department of State, Appointment Papers: Applications and Recommendations for Office, Henry S. Sanford, Acc. 323, tray 164 (Washington, D.C. National Archives).
8. SP, boxes 34–44; Malloy, *Sanford*, pp. 17–18. Fry covers the Latin American work in *Sanford*, pp. 19–30.
9. Sanford to Secretary of State Lewis Cass, 30 Oct. 1857 (draft), SP, 116/7.
10. This phase of Sanford's career is discussed fully in Fry, *Sanford*, chap. 3, but see also, Francis J. Heppner, "Henry S. Sanford, U.S. Minister to Belgium, 1861–69" Master's thesis (Georgetown University, 1955), pp. 115–16 and *passim*. Sanford's direction of secret agents is treated in Harriet Chappell Owsley, "Henry Shelton Sanford and Federal Surveillance Abroad, 1861–65," *Mississippi Valley Historical Review* 48 (Sep. 1961), pp. 211–29.
11. President Grant nominated Sanford Minister to Spain in 1869 and selected a replacement for the Brussels post. When the Senate refused to confirm the Sanford appointment, the latter had to leave the Belgian ministry with no other diplomatic prospects.
12. Unsigned (probably Sanford), *Some Account of Belair, Also of the City of Sanford*,

Florida, with a Brief Sketch of Their Founder (Sanford, Fla.: no imprint, 1889), *passim*; Amundson, "American Life," chaps. 6–10.
  13. Sanford's accounts, SP, 8/12.
  14. Ibid.
  15. The most comprehensive account of Leopold and his African empire is A. Roeykens, *Léopold II et l'Afrique* (Brussels: Académie Royale des Sciences Coloniales, 1958). Two modern biographies that provide good coverage of the king's African projects are Neal Ascherson, *The King Incorporated* (New York: Doubleday, 1964); and Barbara Emerson, *Leopold II of the Belgians: King of Colonialism* (New York: St. Martin's, 1979). For Leopold's early investigation of possible fields for colonial enterprise, see L. LeFebre de Vivy, *Document's d'histoire precolonial Belge, 1861–1865* Brussels: Académie Royale des Sciences Coloniales, 1955); A. Roeykens, *Léopold II et la conférence géographie de Bruxelles, 1876* (Brussels: Académie Royale des Sciences Coloniales, 1958); and L. Greindl, *A la recherche d'un état indépendant: Léopold II et les Philippines* (Brussels: Académie Royale des Sciences d'Outre-Mer, 1962); Jean Stengers, "Léopold II entre l'extreme-Orient et l'Afrique (1875–1876), *La conférence de géographie de 1876* (Brussels: Académie Royal des Sciences d'Outre-Mer, 1976), pp. 303–74.
  16. By error, Sanford has been placed at the 1876 conference as the delegate of the American Geographical Society. See, exempli gratia, *Register of the Henry Shelton Sanford Papers* (Nashville: Tennessee State Historical Society and Archives, 1960), p. 5; and James P. White, "The Sanford Exploring Expedition," *Journal of African History* 8 (1967), 291. Sanford himself is quoted as having stated later, "I was a delegate from the United States to the first conference at Brussels in 1876" (*New York Times*, May 26 1885, p. 5), but this is at variance with official records, none of which indicate the presence of any American representatives. The American Geographical Society, moreover, did not list Sanford on its membership rolls until 1877. *Journal of the American Geographical Society* 8 (1876), 92; 9 (1877), 104. It is possible that Sanford was present at the meeting but only as an unofficial, unattached observer.
  17. Unable personally to attend, Latrobe shipped many American Colonization Society documents to Brussels in the belief that the conference would find the Liberian experience helpful in its deliberations and planning. John H. B. Latrobe to William Coppinger (secretary of the American Colonization Society), May 28 1876, Papers of the American Colonization Society (Library of Congress, Washington, D.C.), Letters Received (hereafter cited as ACS) vol. 224. See also, François Bontinck, "Le comité national américain de l'A.I.A.," *La Conférence de Géographie de 1876*, pp. 476–577.
  18. Robert Stanley Thomson, *Foundation de l'état indépendant du Congo* (Brussels: Office De Publicité, 1933) pp. 13–16; A. Roeykens, *Léopold II et la conférence géographique de Bruxelles*, 1876 (Brussels: Académie Royale des Sciences Coloniales, 1958), *passim*.
  19. Roeykens suggests that the monarch's collaboration with Sanford began in April or May 1877 (*Léopold et l'Afrique*, p. 258, n. 1). There is no data in the Sanford Papers which can date precisely Sanford's initial involvement.
  20. Bontinck, "Comité national Américain," pp. 478–88.
  21. Latrobe to Coppinger, 8 May 1877, ACS 227/106; Bontinck, "Comité national Américain," p. 487.
  22. *New York Times*, 3 June 1877, p. 3.
  23. Sanford to Latrobe, 30 July 1877, draft, SP, 29/16; Bontinck, *Origines*, p. 8. Latrobe to Sanford, 22 Sept. 1877, SP, 25/8; Bontinck, *Origines*, p. 17.
  24. Sanford to Latrobe, 30 July 1877, draft, SP, 29/10; Botnick, *Origines*, p. 8.
  25. The British, whom Leopold strongly desired to have in close collaboration with him in the association's work, decided to act independently of the international organization. Roeykens, *Léopold et l'Afrique*, pp. 348–51; Roger Anstey, *Britain and the Congo in the Nineteenth Century* (Oxford: Oxford University Press, 1962), pp. 60–64. Moreover, illness prevented Scheiffelin from attending the conference.
  26. Sanford to Latrobe, 30 July 1877, draft, SP, 29/10; Bontinck, *Origines*, p. 8.
  27. Bontinck, "Comité national Américain," p. 495.
  28. At that time Stanley was widely but incorrectly assumed to be an American. Born in Britain, he had come to the United States in 1858 and, in a rather bizarre chain of circumstances, served on both sides during the Civil War. Technically, therefore, he was

eligible for American citizenship but he did not become a naturalized citizen (and then quite secretly) until 1885. Finally in 1892, he regained his British citizenship. Richard Hall, *Stanley: An Adventurer Explored* (Boston: Houghton, 1975), pp. 125–31, 335–36, 345.

29. Cameron, heading an expedition for the Royal Geographical Society, crossed central Africa from the Indian Ocean to the Atlantic, emerging at Benguela, Angola in Nov. 1875. Visiting him in London shortly after his return, Leopold heard an encouraging report about the potential of the Congo basin. In fact, it seems that Cameron provided a major inspiration for Leopold's Brussels conference in 1876. See James R. Hooker, "Verney Lovett Cameron: A Sailor in Central Africa," in Robert I. Rotberg, ed., *Africa and Its Explorers: Motives, Methods and Impact* (Cambridge: Harvard University Press, 1973), p. 285.

30. Sanford to Bennett, undated draft, SP, 28/2; Bontick, *Origines*, pp. 22–23.

31. Sanford to Bennett, 7 Oct. 1877, draft, SP, box 28, folder 2; Henry Morton Stanley, *The Congo and the Founding of Its Free State*, 2 vols. (New York: Harper, 1885) vol. II, 21. See also Bontinck, *origines*, pp. 23–30; and Roeykens, *Débuts*, pp. 227–28.

32. Jean Stengers, "King Leopold and Anglo-French Rivalry, 1882–1884," in Prosser Gifford and William Roger Louis, eds., *France and Britain in Africa: Imperial Rivalry and Colonial Rule* (New Haven, Conn.: Yale University Press, 1971), p. 126.

33. By 1882 the name used for the paper organization was Association Internationale du Congo (AIC), but it too was only a facade, which Leopold carefully maintained to confuse everyone but his closest associates. Ascherson, *King Incorporated*, pp. 117–18.

34. The participants subscribed a total of 742,500 francs to the enterprise. Thomson, *Fondation*, p. 66. Sanford, whose financial position was unsound, did not become a member of the comité. Yet it is interesting to record that Stanley regretted the lack of American involvement and suggested that the royal funds be used to enter a subscription in Sanford's name. There is no evidence to indicate that this was done. Stanley to Sanford, 27 Feb. 1879, SP, 27/3. See also, A. Roeykens, *Les débuts de l'oevre Africaine de Léopold II, 1875–1879* (Brussels: Académie Royale des Sciences Coloniales, 1955), p. 353; Bontick, *Origines*, p. 50, n. 78; and Ascherson, *King Incorporated*, p. 108.

35. Sanford to Greindl, undated draft, SP, 29/2; Sanford to Greindl, 11 June 1878, draft, Ibid. 29/3; Bontinck, *Origines*, pp. 34–35.

36. The Dutch company did in fact fall into bankruptcy in May 1879. Despite the loss of capital this represented for the comité, Leopold was glad to be rid of the firm's principal director from the comité's leadership, for this powerful Dutchman was interfering with the king's plans. See H. L. Wesseling, "The Netherlands and the Partition of Africa," *Journal of African History* 22 (1981), 499.

37. Sanford to Leopold, 1 June 1879, draft, SP, 29/12; Bontick, *Origines*, pp. 83–84; extract in Robert Stanley Thomson, "Léopold II et le Congo révélés par les notes privées de Henry S. Sanford," *Congo revue générale de la colonie Belge*, 12 (1931), 180. Roeykens (*Débuts*, pp. 312–22) contends that Sanford was merely advocating a policy conceived by another of Leopold's advisors. Whatever the proposal's origin, Sanford worked hard to see it implemented.

38. Sanford's undated note, SP, 29/4; Sanford to Leopold, 1 June 1879, draft, SP, 29/12; Sanford to Jules Devaux (Leopold's secretary), undated draft, SP, 29/12; Bontinck, *Origines*, pp. 83–91; Thomson, *Fondation*, pp. 72–74.

39. Thomson, *Fondation*, pp. 73–74.

40. Greindl to Sanford, 18 Sept. 1878, SP, 24/18; Bontinck, *Origines*, pp. 39–41; Robert S. Thomson, "Léopold II et le Congo," 1, pp. 172–73.

41. Stanley to Sanford, 3 Sept. 1878; 28 Sept. 1878; 30 Sept. 1878; 19 Oct. 1878, SP, 27/2. The latter three letters are published in Bontinck, *Origines*, pp. 42, 43, 46.

42. Sanford to William M. Evarts, 25 Jan. 1879, draft, SP, 105/15.

43. Bontinck, *Origines*, pp. 63–73. The report subsequently submitted, however, was not positive.

44. Sanford to Blaine, 27 June 1881, U.S. Department of State, Miscellaneous Letters, part 2, June 1881 (Washington, D.C.: National Archives); Blaine to Sanford, 3 Sept. 1881, SP, 22/1.

45. Sanford to Greindl, 12 June 1878, draft, SP, 29/3; draft of Sanford speech, SP, 149/13; *New York Times*, 7 Mar. 1879, p. 8.

46. Sanford to Arthur, 1882, exact date unknown, draft, SP, 105/1. Several persons have

been suggested as authors of the scheme (Bontinck, *Origines*, p. 133, n. 4) but, considering his diplomatic experience, background in international law, and his earlier dealings with American officials, Sanford looms as the most likely one to have developed the idea and much of the strategy involved.

47. Jules Devaux to Sanford, 12 May 1883, SP, 25/19. There were several other considerations that made a recognized flag essential. See Meyer, "Henry Shelton Sanford and the Congo" (diss.), p. 71, n. 13.

48. Sanford to his wife, Gertrude Sanford, 27 Nov. 1883, SP, 83/7.

49. James D. Richardson, ed., *Messages and Papers of the Presidents*, 1789–1897, 20 vols. (Washington, D.C.: U.S. Government Printing Office, 1896), vol. 7, p. 175.

50. Frelinghuysen to Coppinger, 27 Dec. 1882, ACS, vol. 249; Latrobe to Coppinger, 24 Feb. 1882, Ibid., vol. 246; Sanford to Frelinghuysen, undated draft, SP, 29/9. Secretary Frelinghuysen's reservations were countered effectively by Sanford. Frelinghuysen to Sanford, 4 Aug. 1883, SP, 24/11; Sanford to Strauch, undated draft, SP, 29/16, Devaux to Sanford, 12 Dec. 1883, SP, 25/19; Bontinck, *Origines*, pp. 130–81.

51. *New York Herald*, 30 Dec. 1883, p. 5.

52. *New York Times*, 2 Jan. 1884, p. 2.

53. Ibid., 11 Jan. 1884, p. 3. The chamber's action carried weight in Washington where it was much discussed in the Senate. Morgan to Sanford, 1 Feb. 1884, SP, 26/5. See also, Fry, *Sanford*, p. 144.

54. Morgan's speech quoted in *African Repository* 43 (Jan, 1887), 18; Morgan, "The Future of the American Negro, "*The North American Review* 134 (1884), *passim*. Morgan actually favored the creation of a company "by act of Congress," which would provide official support for black emigration and the establishment of business and trade in Africa. Morgan to Henry S. Sanford, 19 July 1890, SP, 26/5. Sanford later suggested that the Congo could be "the ground to draw the gathering electricity from that black cloud spreading over the Southern states which . . . [is] growing with destructive elements." Sanford, "American Interests in Africa," *Forum* 9 (1890), 428.

55. Gibson to Sanford, 1890, SP, 24/12.

56. U.S., Congress, *Senate Report*, no. 393, 48th Cong. 1st session. For a discussion of Morgan's and Sanford's various maneuvers in winning Senate approval, see Bontinck, *Origines*, pp. 161–96; Meyer, "Sanford and the Congo" diss., 1967, pp. 89–99. Contributing in a minor way to our understanding of this episode is James L. Roark, "American Expansionism vs. European Imperialism: Henry S. Sanford and the Congo Episode, 1883–1885," *Mid-America* 60 (1978), 21–33. In this largely derivative article the author does not adequately credit previous work on the subject.

57. In a hostile article, newspaper unknown, Sanford was labeled "Blue Ribbon Sanford," the "gastronomic diplomat." See clipping in SP, 65/1.

58. During the Civil War, when all American diplomats in Europe strove to win support for the Union cause, Sanford explained to Secretary of State Seward: "This cannot be done simply by subsidizing certain organs of the press; it can be accomplished mainly over a table with good cheer and good liquor upon it and good company around it. I have the greatest faith in this best of weapons." Quoted in Heppner, "Henry S. Sanford," p. 22.

59. Latrobe to Sanford, 6 July 1888, SP, 25/9; John H. Latrobe, *Maryland in Liberia* (Baltimore: J. Murphy and Co., 1885), pp. 90–91.

60. S. E. Crowe, *The Berlin West African Conference, 1884–1885* (London: Longmans, Green and Co., 1942), p. 80.

61. It should be noted, however, that Leopold's plans were not precise on what each future step would be. The king, realizing that he could not draw on unlimited resources and uncertain how to move as he inaugurated his peculiar colonial venture, therefore could not have completely enlightened his associates. Jean Stengers, "King Leopold and Anglo-French Rivalry," pp. 124–25.

62. Devaux to Sanford, 6 Mar. 1884; 13 Mar. 1884, SP, 25/19; Bontinck, *Origines*, pp. 176–78.

63. U.S., Congress, Senate, *Executive Document*, no. 196, 48th Cong., 1st session, p. 348; E. Hertslet, *Map of Africa by Treaty*, 3 vols. (London: Frank Cass, 1967), vol. 1, 244–46.

64. Sanford's undated note, SP, 29/2. Morgan, always occupied with black emigration, hoped "to have a sensible Negro in the commission." Morgan to Sanford, 4 July 1884, Ibid., 25/5.
65. *New York Herald*, 30 Dec. 1883, p. 5; 3 Jan. 1884, p. 6.
66. Amos Lawrence to Sanford, 18 Nov. 1884, SP, 25/11. Lawrence, an old friend of Sanford, was a sales agent for several mills. Meyer, "Sanford and the Congo," diss., 1967, pp. 101–2.
67. Sanford to Morgan, 14 Apr. 1886, Morgan Papers (Library of Congress, Washington, D.C.), vol. 2; Bontinck, *Origines*, pp. 429–30.
68. Crowe, *Berlin Conference*, p. 81; Thomson, *Fondation*, p. 159.
69. Leopold to Sanford, 15 May 1884, in François Bontinck, "Onze lettres inédites de Léopold II à H.S. Sanford, de 1884 à 1887," *Bulletin des séances de l'académie royale des sciences d'outre-mer*, (1971–73), p. 464. In this article the author presents some correspondence that was not cataloged with the main collection of the Sanford papers in 1960. These letters were located only through Bontinck's diligent efforts to seek out all American materials bearing on the emergence of the Congo Independent State.
70. Ibid., p. 466.
71. For the negotiations in Paris, which produced this treaty, see François Bontinck, "L'entente entre la France et l'association internationale du Congo a la lumière des premièrs negotiations," *Etudes d'histoire Africaine* 2 (1971), 29–81.
72. See, especially, Stengers, "King Leopold and Anglo-French Rivalry," pp. 153–63.
73. Long the standard work on the conference, Crowe's *Berlin Conference* is still essential but should be used with Stig Forster, Wolfgang J. Mommsen, and Ronald Robinson, eds., *Bismarck, Europe and Africa: The Berlin Africa Conference 1884–1885 and the Onset of Partition* (London: Oxford University Press, 1988), which contains thirty studies of all aspects of the significant meeting, two of which deal with American participation. Also important are W. R. Louis, "The Berlin Congo Conference," in Prosser Gifford and William Roger Louis, eds., *France and Britain in Africa* (New Haven, Conn.: Yale University Press, 1971), pp. 167–220; William L. Langer, *European Alliances and Alignments, 1870–1890* (New York: Kropf, 1950), chap. 9; Ronald Robinson, John Gallagher with Alice Denny, *Africa and the Victorians* (New York: St. Martin's, 1961), pp. 160–77; and John D. Hargreaves, *Prelude to the Partition of West Africa* (London: Macmillan, 1963), pp. 328–37.
74. Kasson was a former congressman from Iowa and U.S. minister to Austria-Hungary (1871–77). A good study of Kasson, which includes a useful section on his work at the Berlin Conference, including his collaboration with Sanford, is Edward Younger, *John A. Kasson* (Iowa City: Iowa State Historical Society, 1955).
75. Kasson to Frelinghuysen, 23 Oct. 1884, telegram, no. 47. U.S. Department of State, Diplomatic Despatches from U.S. Ministers to Germany (Washington, D.C., National Archives), microcopy M–44, roll 52 (hereafter cited as DDG).
76. For Kasson's expansionist views in general, see his article, "The Monroe Doctrine in 1881," *North American Review* 133 (1891), 524–33; on Africa in particular, Kasson to Frelinghuysen, 15 Oct. 1884, no. 40; 3 Nov. 1884, no. 60, DDG, M–44/52.
77. Protocols of the West African Conference, Protocol 3, Annex 1, *U.S., Senate Executive Document No. 196*.
78. P. de Borchgrave (Leopold's secretary) to Sanford, 6 Dec. 1884, SP, 25/16; Bontinck, *origines*, p. 251; Thomson, "Léopold II et la Conférence," p. 337.
79. Sanford to Leopold, 10 Dec. 1884, draft, SP, 29/12; Bontinck, *Origines*, p. 254.
80. Baron A. Lambermont, a Belgian delegate to the Berlin Conference, handled the preliminaries and was to work with Baron E. Beyens, Belgian ambassador to France and former secretary of Leopold. Officially commencing formal talks for the king in Paris was Eudore Permex, member of the Belgian Parliament, who was assisted by another of Leopold's close collaborators, Emile Banning. Also on hand was Col. M. Strauch, secretary general of the AIC. See Banning, *Memoires politiques et diplomatiques* (Paris and Brussels: Renaissance de Livre, 1926), pp. 40–42. But in addition to this team Leopold could also count on the assistance of Arthur Stevens, a respected and influential Frenchman who had been the principal agent—albeit an unofficial one—in negotiating the so-called preemption treaty between the association and France in 1883. See Stengers, "King Leopold and

Anglo-French Rivalry," p. 154. In the 1884 discussions, however, Stevens found French officials far more difficult to deal with, especially since de Brazza was exerting his considerable influence to oppose Leopold's case. Ibid., pp. 154–55; and Bontinck, "Onze lettres inédites de Léopold II," p. 468. See also, Bontick, *Origines*, pp. 142–50, for the Paris negotiations.

81. De Montebello to Billot, 28 Dec. 1884, France, ministere des affaires étrangères, *Documents diplomatiques Français, 1871–1914*, 1st series, vol. 5 (Paris: Imprimerie National, 1933), no. 497.

82. Bontinck, *Origines*, p. 261. Even the British, it appears, viewed Sanford as a key man in the Paris deliberations and were willing to give him their assistance. Stanley to Sir William Mackinnon, 24 Dec. 1884, Mackinnon Papers (London: School of Oriental and African Studies), selected portions on microfilm owned by Cooperative Africana Microfilm Project (CAMP), Center for Research Libraries, Chicago, reel 3. See also Stanley to Sanford, 24 Dec. 1884, SP, 27/4; Bontinck, *Origines*, pp. 257–58.

83. Stanley to Sanford, 24 Dec. 1884, SP, 27/4; Bontinck, *Origines*, p. 258; Banning, *Memoires*, p. 41; Thomson, *Fondation*, pp. 245–46; Crow, *Berlin Conference*, pp. 185–95.

84. Sanford to Mackinnon, 25 Nov. 1884, Bontinck, "Onze lettres inédites de Léopold II," pp. 469–70. In Germany Leopold had another collaborator working in his behalf. The influential banker and friend of Bismarck, Gerson von Bleichroder, supported some of the Belgian king's African plans and helped Bismarck see advantages in German recognition of the association. See Marcel Luuel, "Gerson von Bleichroder, l'ami commun de Léopold II et de Bismarck," *Afrika-Tervuren* 8 (1963), 93–110; Fritz Stern, *Gold and Iron: Bismarck, Bleichroder and the Building of the German Empire* (New York: Knopf, 1977), pp. 402–9.

85. Sanford's undated note, SP, 29/2. Sanford had supported fully all association territorial claims in Dec. (Sanford to Mackinnon, 24 Dec. 1884, draft SP, 127/17; Bontinck, *Origines*, p. 259) but then realized compromise was essential in order to break the deadlock that was holding up the whole conference.

86. Banning, *Memoires*, pp. 41–61; Thomson, *Fondation*, pp. 267–79; Crow, *Berlin Conference*, pp. 165–75.

87. These territorial questions were difficult to settle because the Portuguese were reluctant to compromise on their claims, but eventually British pressure helped to make the Iberian state more flexible. The result was that while Portugal received recognition of its right to territory on both sides of the Congo mouth, Leopold kept a significant stretch of coastline north of the mouth (the right bank) and a corridor along the south shore to the highest navigable location, all of which would become important for the building of a railway that would bypass the rapids. Crow, *Berlin Conference*, pp. 174–75; Ascherson, *King Incorporated*, p. 134. Even in these negotiations Sanford did his part behind the scenes, encouraging his British contacts to do whatever they could to induce British authorities to force Portugal to make concessions. Sanford to MacKinnon, 2 Feb. 1885, MacKinnon Papers, reel 3.

88. Cros, *Berlin Conference*, pp. 149–50.

89. William Roger Louis, "The Berlin Congo Conference," in *France and Britain in Africa*, p. 217.

90. Stanley to Gertrude Sanford, 31 Oct. 1895, SP, 27/6; Bontinck, *Origines*, p. 377. For Sanford's own estimate of the high value of his Berlin work, see Sanford to Frelinghuysen, 14 Jan. 1885, draft, SP, 29/2; and Bontinck, *Origines*, pp. 287–89.

91. For a discussion of these policies, see David M. Pletcher, *The Awkward Years: American Foreign Relations under Garfield and Arthur* (Columbia: University of Missouri Press, 1962); Milton Plesur, *America's Outward Thrust: Approaches to Foreign Affairs, 1865–1890* (Dekalb: Northern Illinois University Press, 1971); and Justus D. Doenecke, *The Presidencies of James A. Garfield and Chester A. Arthur* (Lawrence: University of Kansas Press, 1981), chaps. 4, 8, 9, 10.

92. Bontinck, *Origines*, pp. 284–97; Meyer, "Sanford and the Congo," diss., 1967, pp. 154–58; Fry, *Sanford*, pp. 155–56.

93. Sanford to Amos Lawrence, 7 June 1886, draft, SP, 29/11.

94. The history of this venture has been traced in White, "Sanford Exploring Expedition" and Meyer, "Sanford and the Congo," diss., 1967, pp. 159–206. See also, Bontinck, *Origines*, pp. 346–61.

95. Sanford Exploring Expedition, "organization," SP, 32/7; Sanford to Jules Malou, undated draft, SP, 29/13.
96. Strauch to Sanford, 29 May 1886, Ibid., 29/16; Bontinck, *Origines*, pp. 351–52.
97. Sanford was still convinced in Oct. 1886 that the state was "doing all it can to promote my enterprise." Sanford to MacKinnon, 24 Oct. 1886, draft, SP, 127/6.
98. Emory Taunt to Sanford, 22 Aug. 1886, SP, 28/1; 17 Sept. 1886, 28/2; W. G. Parminter to Sanford, 14 Sept. 1886, SP, 26/7; A. B. Swinburne to Sanford, 14 Nov. 1886, SP, 27/14.
99. Stanley to MacKinnon, 28 Sept. 1886, MacKinnon Papers, reel 3.
100. H. M. Flagler to Sanford, 7 May 1888; H. S. Hewitt (for the mayor of New York) to Sanford, 14 June 1888, SP, 22/4.
101. Sanford's drafts, 14 Apr. 1888, SP, 22/4.
102. Interview in the *New York Herald*, 16 June 1888, p. 3.
103. Levita to Sanford, 28 Jan. 1889, SP, 125/10.
104. According to one estimate, between 1876 and 1885 the king threw more than 10 million francs into "the Congo abyss," and by 1890 had parted with 19 million for his Congo venture. Comte Louis de Lichtervelde, *Leopold of the Belgians* (New York: Century Co., 1929), p. 148.
105. For Leopold's attempts to negotiate loans in this period, see Alain Stenmans, *La reprise du Congo par la Belgique* (Brussels: Editions Technique et Scientifiques, 1949), pp. 71–75; and Emerson, *Leopold II of the Belgians*, pp. 142–50.
106. See Suzanne Miers, *Britain and the Ending of the Slave Trade* (New York: Africana Publishing Corp., 1975), pp. 201–6.
107. Salisbury was not only responding to British revulsion against the slave trade; he was becoming increasingly concerned with the importance of the Upper Nile region to Egypt (then under British control) and felt that growing Arab resistance to European advances in East Africa and the Upper Congo possibly represented an extension of the politico-religious movement begun by the Mahdi in the Sudan in 1884, which had closed that encroachment. Consequently, any effort that would check the Arabs south of the Sudan could only weaken the Mahdists and thus facilitate eventual reconquest of the Sudan. Roland Oliver, *Sir Harry Johnston and the Scramble for Africa* (London: Chatto and Windus, 1959), p. 139.
108. Suzanne Miers, "The Brussels Conference of 1889–90: The Place of the Slave Trade in the Policies of Great Britain and Germany," in Prosser Gifford and William Roger Louis, eds. *Britain and Germany in Africa* (New Haven, Conn. and London: Yale University Press, 1967), pp. 92–94. See also, S. J. S. Cookey, *Britain and the Congo Question, 1885–1913* (New York: Humanities Press, 1968), pp. 24–25.
109. Miers, *Britain and the Ending of the Slave Trade*, pp. 229–35.
110. Blaine to Sanford, 25 Apr. 1890, SP, 24/4; Bontinck, *Origines*, p. 369; Terrell to Blaine, 25 May 1890, no. 81, U.S. Department of State, Diplomatic Despatches from U.S. Ministers to Belgium (Washington, D.C., National Archives), microcopy M–193, roll T–27 (hereafter cited as DDB).
111. Terrell to Blaine, 20 Nov. 1889, no. 40, DDB, M–193/T–27.
112. Younger, *John A. Kasson*, p. 343; Meyer, "Sanford and the Congo," diss., 1967, pp. 154–56. For the case against both American participation in the Berlin Conference and Senate ratification of the Berlin Act by a leader in the successful opposition to the latter, see Perry Belmont, *An American Democrat: The Recollections of Perry Belmont* (New York: Columbia University Press, 1967), chap. 10.
113. Banning, *Memoires*, pp. 281–82.
114. Latrobe to Blaine, 7 Oct. 1889, copy, SP, 25/9.
115. Interview in the *New York Herald*, 14 Feb. 1889, p. 7.
116. Sanford to Blaine, 12 Dec. 1889, DDB, M–193/T–27. See also, Sanford, "American interests in Africa," pp. 421–22; 425–26.
117. Sanford wanted total prohibition of liquor sales in areas where it had not yet taken hold and the imposition of a substantial import duty where a market had already developed. Such a duty, of course, would disturb the free trade provisions of the 1884 treaty between the United States and Leopold's association, but Sanford convinced Blaine that they should yield the right to free trade on this specific point. Blaine to Sanford, 25 Apr. 1890. SP, 24/4; Bontinck, *Origines*, pp. 369–71; Meyer, "Sanford and the Congo," diss., 1967, pp. 222–23.

118. Terrell to Blaine, 24 May 1890, no. 94; Sanford to Blaine, 27 May 1890, DDB, M-193/T-27; Miers, *Britain and the Ending of the Slave Trade*, pp. 282-83.
119. Sanford to Blaine, 3 Apr. 1890, DDB, M-193/T-27; Miers, *Britain and the Ending of the Slave Trade*, pp. 178, 282-83.
120. Sanford to Blaine, 3 Apr. 1890; Terrell to Blaine, 2 May 1890, no. 80, DDB, M-193/T-27.
121. Sanford to Blaine, 3 Apr. 1890, DDB, M-193/T-27. For a discussion of the extent of gun imports, see R. W. Beachey, "The Arms Trade in East Africa in the Late 19th Century," *Journal of African History* 3 (1962), 451-61.
122. Sanford to Blaine, 3 Apr. 1890, DDB, M-193/T-27.
123. Hertslet, *Map of Africa by Treaty*, vol. 3, p. 60; Meyer, "Sanford and the Congo," diss., 1967), p. 228.
124. Terrell to Blaine, 10 May 1890, no, 88, DDB, M-193/T-38.
125. This treaty gave Leopold's association the equivalent of French recognition in return for a commitment to give France first option on the association's Congo claims, should termination of the latter operations prove necessary. Hertslet, *Map of Africa by Treaty*, vol. 1, 244-46.
126. Terrell to Baline, 10 May 1890, no. 88, DDB, M-193/T-28.
127. Sanford to Blaine, 3 Jan. 1890, DDB, M-193/T-27.
128. Sanford to E. M. Halford, 3 Jan. 1890, draft, SP, 29/3.
129. Sanford to Blaine, 27 May 1890, DDB, M-193/T-28.
130. Terrell to Blaine, 14 May 1890, no. 89, Ibid.
131. Sanford to Blaine, 27 May 1890, Ibid.
132. Sanford to Blaine, 14 May 1890, Ibid.
133. Terrell to Blaine, 22 May 1890, no. 93 (confidential), Ibid.
134. Interview in *New York Herald*, 14 Feb. 1889, p. 7.
135. Grenfell to Sanford, 23 June 1889; 23 Nov. 1889, SP, 24/19. It is interesting to note that Grenfell at this time was reluctant to speak out, explaining that "it is not the work of a missionary to criticize the policy of the state which furnishes protection and allows him to carry on his special work." To Sanford's disgust, Grenfell supported the state's claim that it must levy import duties if it were effectively to combat the slave trade (Grenfell to Sanford, 4 Apr. 1890, SP, 24/19).
136. Sanford to Blaine, 3 June 1890, DDB, M-193/T-27; Miers, *Britain and the Ending of the Slave Trade*, p. 286. n. 312.
137. Terrell to Blaine, 15 June 1890, no. 103, DDB, M-193/T-28. There was some sympathy with the United States' position. Several delegates admitted privately that the American stand was reasonable but that they had been instructed by their respective governments to support the Congo State's proposal on import duties. Terrell to Blaine, 15 May 1890, no. 90, DDB, M-193/T-28.
138. Terrell to Blaine, 5 July 1890, telegram, Ibid.
139. Sanford's undated draft, SP, 28/5.
140. Sanford to M. Leghait, n.d., abstracted in Banning, *Memoires*, pp. 280-90.
141. Walter La Feber, *The New Empire: An Interpretation of American Expansion, 1860-1898* (Ithaca, N.Y.: Cornell University Press, 1963), chap. 1.

Chapter 5. John Hays Hammond and the Jameson Raid

1. *The Jameson Raid* (Cape Town: Oxford University Press, 1951). The author was the first to use the revealing papers of Sir Graham Bower, imperial secretary to the British high commissioner for South Africa, who became an official scapegoat after the Raid.
2. *Conspirators in Conflict: A Study of the Johannesburg Reform Committee and Its Role in the Conspiracy Against the South African Republic* (Cape Town: Tafelberg-Uitgewers, 1967). Rhoodie was one of the first scholars to consult the papers of Charles Leonard, one of the principal conspirators in Johannesburg.

3. *The Autobiography of John Hays Hammond*, 2 vols. (New York: Farrar and Rinehart, 1935). Hammond omitted some features of his South African activities in this memoir written many years later.

4. Ibid., vol. 1, chap. 8.

5. Ibid., p. 177.

6. American mining experts who worked in South Africa receive attention in Clarence Clendenen, Robert Collins, and Peter Duignan, *Americans in Africa, 1865–1900* (Stanford, Calif.: Stanford University Press, 1966), chap. 7; Eric Rosenthal, *Stars and Stripes in Africa* (Cape Town: National Books, Ltd., 1968), chaps. 21, 25; Thomas J. Noer, *Britain, Boer and Yankee: The United States and South Africa, 1870–1914* (Kent, Ohio: Kent State University Press, 1978), pp. 30–34; Clark C. Spence, *Mining Engineers and the American West: The Lace Boot Brigade, 1849–1933* (New Haven, Conn.: Yale University Press, 1969), pp. 303–17.

7. John Hays Hammond, "South African Memories," *Scribners Magazine* 69 (Mar. 1921), 258; *Autobiography*, vol. 1, 201, 214, 218.

8. Hammond to Gen. Harry T. Hays, 8 Oct. 1895, Hammond Papers, Sterling Memorial Library, Yale University, box 2, folder 2 (hereafter cited as HP 2/2).

9. Ibid.

10. J. G. Lockhart and C. M. Woodhouse, *Rhodes* (London: Hodder and Stoughton, 1963), pp. 287–88; Ian Colvin, *The Life of Jameson*, 2 vols. (London: E. Arnold Co., 1922), vol. 1, 26–27; Van der Poel, *Jameson Raid*, pp. 2–3.

11. Hammond, *Autobiography*, vol. 1, 261–62.

12. Ibid., chap. 15.

13. Sir James Sivewright to Baron Carl Merck (private) 28 Sept. 1894, copy, Rhodes Papers, Rhodes House Library, Oxford, C.25.37(17).

14. Hammond had access to such information as Robert S. Swan, "Phallic Temples and Gold Reefs. Ancient Mining in Mashonaland," typescript of a mining survey, dated 9 May 1894, HP, 1/2. This report predicted that much gold was to be found in the ancient mines beyond the 85–100 feet depths worked in the early period.

15. C. J. Clark to Hammond, 27 Sept. 1894, HP, 1/3, 3.

16. Hammond, *Autobiography*, vol. 1, 277–80.

17. Ibid., 278; I. R. Phimester, "Rhodes, Rhodesia and the Rand," *Journal of Southern African Studies* 1 (October 1974), 78–83.

18. Various writers have drawn attention to the willingness, indeed eagerness, with which Rhodes and his associate Jameson adopted reckless, swashbuckling methods to gain their ends. The takeover of Lobengula's territories and the attempt to grab Manicaland and Gazaland from the Portuguese in 1890 do seem to point the way toward the Jameson Raid. See Lockhard and Woodhouse, *Rhodes*, pp. 292–93; Van der Poel, *Jameson Raid*, pp. 4–6; Julian R. E. Cobbin, "Lobengula, Jameson, and the Occupation of Manicaland, 1890," *Rhodesian History* 14 (1973), 39–56. John Flint, *Cecil Rhodes* (Boston: Little, Brown, 1974), p. 137.

19. The American engineer, Gardner Williams, who was Rhodes's managing director of DeBeers Mining Co. in Kimberley, had advised him that the Rand deposits were shallow and not worth serious attention. A. P. Cartwright, *Gold Paved the Way* (New York: St. Martins, 1967), p. 64.

20. Ibid., pp. 83–85; Robert V. Kubicek, *Economic Imperialism in Theory and Practice: The Case of South African Gold Mining Finance, 1886–1914* (Durham, N.C.: Duke University Press, 1979), pp. 99–100.

21. Frederick H. Hatch and J. A. Chalmers, *The Gold Mines of the Rand* (London: Macmillan, 1895), pp. 88–91; Cartwright, *Gold Paved the Way*, p. 61.

22. Hammond falsely claimed that he had originated the idea of deep mining and that Rhodes had then led the way in acquiring deep properties. Hammond, "South African Memories," p. 258; *Autobiography*, vol. 1, pp. 291–92; 296–97. Actually, others had promulgated the deep-level theory before Hammond even arrived in South Africa and Rhodes's competitors were the first to buy deep-level real estate. Hatch and Chambers, *Gold Mines of the Rand*, pp. 88–89; *South Africa*, vol. 30 (16 May 1896), 398; Cartwright, *Gold Paved the Way*, pp. 61–64. To his credit, however, Hammond disproved earlier

theories about temperatures below ground and correctly held that the heat factor in deep-mining would not be prohibitive. S. J. Truscott, *The Witwatersrand Goldfields: Banket and Mining Practice* (London: Macmillan, 1907), p.388.

23. He hired, for instance, the American geologist-engineer, George F. Becker, to study the Rand Fields and particularly the practicality of deep-mining. Becker to George H. Benson, 20 June 1896, George F. Becker Papers, Manuscript Division, Library of Congress, container 17, no. 2.

24. Consolidated Gold Fields of South Africa, Ltd., *The Gold Fields, 1887–1937*. London: Consolidated Gold Fields of South Africa, Ltd., 1937, p. 52; Kubicek, *Economic Imperialism*, p. 103.

25. But later Hammond emphatically denied that his report had launched the plan for the Raid. *Autobiography*, vol. 1, 290. See also, Robert I. Rotberg, *The Founder: Cecil Rhodes and the Pursuit of Power* (New York: Oxford University Press, 1988), pp. 524–25.

26. Vindex, *Cecil Rhodes, His Political Life and Speeches* (London: G. Bell, 1900), pp. 460–61.

27. Hammond, *Autobiography*, vol. 1, 217; Van der Poel, *Jameson Raid*, p. 29.

28. Charles Leonard, "Statement of Mr. Charles Leonard on the Position of the Uitlanders in the Transvaal with the History of the Franchise"—Supplement to *The African Critic*, 22 May 1897, pp. 1–2 [this was based on Leonard's testimony before the Parliamentary Commission of Inquiry (Great Britain, Parliament, *Parliamentary Papers* (House of Commons), Select Committee on South Africa, report no. 2 (London, 1894), hereinafter cited as *Blue Book 311* (1897)]; see also, J. S. Marais, *The Fall of Kruger's Republic* (Oxford: Oxford University Press, 1961), pp. 53–56.

29. Undated note by Sir Frederick Hamilton (editor of the Johannesburg *Star* at the time), Hamilton Papers, Rhodes House Library, Oxford, Afr.3.139.

30. Hammond estimated that explosives, including fuses and generators, amounted to nearly 10 percent of the total working costs of the mines. "The Transvaal Mines under the New Regime," *The Engineering Magazine* 23 (July 1902), 494. A more recent writer claims that explosives represented from 12 to 20 percent of mining costs. G. Blainey, "Lost Causes of the Jameson Raid," *Economic History Review* 18 (1965), 356.

31. Hammond, "Transvaal Mines," p. 494.

32. Lionel Phillips to Wernher, Beit and Co., 8 Nov. 1890 in *All that Glittered: Selected Correspondence of Lionel Phillips, 1890–1924*. Edited by Myrna Fraser and Alan Jeeves (Cape Town: Oxford University Press, 1977), no. 13, pp. 44–45; Hammond, *Autobiography*, vol. 1, pp. 304–5; Charles Leonard, *Statement*, pp. 20–21. For a discussion of the problems related to the recruitment of African labor and the retention of workers, see *Industrialization and Social Change in South Africa: African Class Formation, Culture, and Consciousness, 1870–1930*. Edited by Shula Marks and Richard Rathbone (New York: Longman, 1982), chaps. 2, 4, 5. The Transvaal Volksraad finally responded to several years of remonstrance by mine owners, when, in 1895, it passed a law that required Africans to carry special identification and provided penalties for job desertion. See Alan Jeeves, "The Control of Migratory Labor on the South African Gold Mines in the Era of Kruger and Milner," *Journal of Southern African Studies* 2 (Oct. 1975), 11.

33. George Becker to George H. Benson, 20 June 1896, Becker Papers, 17/2.

34. Blainey, "Lost Causes," p. 359. An excellent summary of the mining industry's problems with the state can be found in Peter Richardson and Jean Jacques Van-Helten, chap. 1, "The Gold Mining Industry in the Transvaal, 1886–1899," in Peter Warwick, ed., *The South African War 1899–1902* (London: Longman, 1980), esp. pp. 31–35.

35. Percy Fitzpatrick to H. Graumann, 11 Sept. 1888, in A. H. Duminy and W. R. Guest, eds. *Fitzpatrick: South African Politician, Selected Papers, 1888–1906* (Johannesburg: McGraw-Hill, 1976), p. 14.

36. Evidently there was a conspiracy to seize the military barracks and arsenal in Pretoria as well as public offices there and members of the government. Frederick W. Bell *The South African Conspiracy* (London: W. Heinemann, 1900), p. 26; Rhoodie, *Conspirators in Conflict*, pp. 24–25.

37. *Standard and Digger News* (Johannesburg), 22 Aug. 1892, p. 1.

NOTES 229

38. Sir Percy Fitzpatrick, *The Transvaal from Within* (London: W. Heinemann, 1899), p. 117.

39. J. P. R. Wallis, *Fitz: The Story of Sir Percy Fitzpatrick* (London: Macmillan, 1955), p. 38; C. Tsehloane Keto, *The Aftermath of the Jameson Raid and American Decision Making in Foreign Affairs, 1896.* Transactions of the American Philosophical Society, 70, pt. 8 (Philadelphia: American Philosophical Society, 1980), p. 11.

40. Statement by Sir Frederick Hamilton, Hamilton Papers, Afr.3.139; Vincent Harlow, "Sir Frederick Hamilton's Narrative of Events Relative to the Jameson Raid," *English Historical Review* 72 (1957), p. 288. Phillips also had been discussing the possibility of a Rand revolt with his employer, Alfred Beit, who was a close associate of Rhodes. Rotberg, *The Founder*, p. 524

41. Lionel Phillips to A. Beit, 16 June 1894, *All that Glittered*, no. 49, p. 79.

42. The Americans he helped to organize resolved that if forced into Kruger's military service, they would fire first at Boer officers. This, Hammond claimed, so intimidated the government that no Americans were drafted. J. H. Hammond, *The Truth about the Jameson Raid* (Boston: Marshall Jones Company, 1918), p. 22; Noer, *Britain, Boer and Yankee*, p. 45.

43. Harlow, "Sir Frederick Hamilton," pp. 289-90; R. V. Kubicek, "The Randlords in 1895: A Reassessment," *Journal of British Studies* 2 (1972), 88.

44. Harlow, "Sir Frederick Hamilton," pp. 289-90.

45. Van der Poel, *Jameson Raid*, pp. 9-10.

46. Loch's statement of 1 May 1896, Great Britain, *Parliamentary Debates* (Lords), 4th ser., 40, pp. 313-17; Van der Poel, *Jameson Raid*, pp. 16-17; Pakenham, *Jameson's Raid*, p. 146.

47. Sir Graham Bower, "Reminiscences of Sixteen Years Service in South Africa," unpublished manuscript copy, Rhodes House Library, Oxford, Mss. Afr.S. 63, p. 190; Rotberg, *Founder*, p. 525. Rhodes's often-quoted explanation of his intervention to prevent the Uitlanders from overthrowing Kruger themselves and establishing a new Transvaal administration that would draw all of South Africa around it without British involvement was, "I wasn't taking all this trouble [joining in the conspiracy] to turn out old Kruger and put J. B. Robinson [a powerful mine owner and Rhodes's enemy] and [certain others] in his place." S. Low, "Personal Recollections of Cecil Rhodes," *The Nineteenth Century and After* 4 (May 1902), 838-39.

48. Van der Poel, *Jameson Raid*, p. 22.

49. *Blue Book 311* (1897), q. 8959, p. 747; q. 9020, p. 477; Lionel Phillips, *Some Recollections* (London: Hutchinson, 1924), p. 141; G. Seymour Fort, *Alfred Beit, A Study of the Man and His Work* (London: I. Nicholson and Watson, 1932), p. 133.

50. Blainey, "Lost causes," pp. 364-65.

51. *Blue Book 311* (1897), p. vi; Fort, *Alfred Beit*, p. 133.

52. Phillips's employer, H. Eckstein and Co., managed the Transvaal operations of Wernher, Beit and Co.

53. Lionel Phillips to A. Beit, 16 June 1894, *All that Glittered*, No. 49, p. 79; Flint, *Rhodes*, p. 184.

54. Phillips, *Some Reminiscences*, p. 141; Flint, *Rhodes*, p. 184.

55. *Blue Book 311* (1897), q. 9060, p. 479.

56. Hammond, *Truth about the Jameson Raid*, p. 9; *Autobiography*, vol. 1, p. 320.

57. Hammond, *Autobiography*, vol. 1, p. 320.

58. It has been shown that Blainey ("Lost Causes of the Jameson Raid") was incorrect in emphasizing the significance of the financial crisis of 1895 as a cause of the capitalists' revolt, and that there was a qualitative difference between the deep-level holdings of the two largest firms, with CGFSA possessing the less desirable properties requiring both more capital and a longer period for development. Richard Mendelsohn, "Blainey and the Jameson Raid: The Debate Renewed," *Journal of Southern African Studies* 6 (Apr. 1980), 162-65.

59. Hammond, for example, had shares in a number of Rand operations, as well as in speculative ventures in Mashonaland. Hammond to E. F. Rhodes, 6 July 1895; Robert

Williams to Hammond, cable, 13 Feb. 1894, HP, 1/1 and 7. See also, Kubicek, *Economic Imperialism*, p. 104. For Phillips's position, see *Blue Book 311* (1897), qs. 7031–35, p. 371.

60. The South African historian J. S. Marais points out that Kruger was responding to what he considered to be an unreasonable position by Cape authorities. *The Fall of Kruger's Republic*, pp. 38–39.

61. *Standard and Digger News*, 21 Sept. 1895, p. 5. Kruger, succumbing to British and Cape pressure, reopened the drifts in early November, but the blockage on the railway was not quickly overcome and transport remained a problem. Anonymous Johannesburg resident, "The Story of an Amateur Revolution," *Fortnightly Review* 65 (Apr. 1896), 606.

62. Speech by Lionel Phillips to Chamber of Mines, The *Star* (Johannesburg), 11 Dec. 1895, p. 3. See also, Richardson and Van-Helten, "Gold Mining Industry in the Transvaal," pp. 31–35.

63. Phillips predicted "frightful losses to the industry," Phillips to A. Beit, 16 June 1894, *All that Glittered*, no. 49, p. 78; *Blue Book 311* (1897), qs. 7031–35, p. 371; qs. 9045–9058, pp. 478–79; *Star*, 14 Dec. 1895, p. 3.

64. Fitzpatrick, *Transvaal from Within*, 123; Van der Poel, *Jameson Raid*, p. 41.

65. Hammond to Frank Rhodes, Oct. 1895, Great Britain, Parliament, *Parliamentary Papers* (House of Commons), Report of the Select Committee of the Cape Assembly on the Jameson Raid, 29 May—17 June 1896 (C. 8380), Appendix A, no. 8, p. 109 (hereafter) cited as *Cape Blue Book* C. [8389] 1896); Robert White, diary, entry of Oct. 1895, Rhodes House Library, Oxford, Mss.Afr.S. 220–22.

66. *Blue Book 311* (1897), qs. 5972, 5974, p. 326.

67. Hammond to Gen. Harry T. Hays, 8 Oct. 1895, HP., 2/2.

68. *Blue Book 311* (1897), q. 7877, p. 410; Rhoodie, *Conspirators in Conflict*, pp. 30–31.

69. Rhoodie, Ibid., p. 31.

70. Ibid., pp. 35–37. One contemporary witness contended that many who joined the reform group did so unenthusiastically and only to ingratiate themselves with their employers. Hans Sauer, *Ex-Africa* (London: G. Bles, 1937), p. 276.

71. Hammond, *Truth about the Jameson Raid*, p. 29; Phillips, *Some Reminiscences*, pp. 142–43; H. O'Kelly Webber, *The Grip of Gold* (London: Hutchinson, 1936), p. 76; Rhoodie, *Conspirators in Conflict*, p. 39.

72. Rhoodie, Ibid., p. 37.

73. Hammond, *Truth about the Jameson Raid*, p. 29; Lionel Phillips, "From Inside Johannesburg," *Nineteenth Century*, vol. 42 (Aug. 1897), 210; Van der Poel, *Jameson Raid*, pp. 66–67.

74. Hammond, *Autobiography*, vol. 1, 322.

75. Ibid., p. 29; Edmund Garrett and E. J. Edwards, *The Story of an African Crisis* (Westminster: Constable and Co., 1897), pp. 73–74.

76. It might be assumed that Rhodes's brother was his principal operative on the Rand. Indeed, Frank Rhodes, said to be "brave, charming and universally liked," was in Johannesburg, but this unimaginative soldier was totally dominated by his younger brother who did not expect too much of him apart from military decisions. Even in the military sphere, however, Frank Rhodes was not dependable, preferring not to interrupt his regular social schedule in favor of seriously preparing for an uprising. His brother reportedly admitted he was a poor choice for leading a coup d'état. Fydell Edmund Garrett (close friend of C. Rhodes and editor of the *Cape Times*) to Agnes Garrett, 8 Jan. 1896, Gerald Shaw, ed., *The Garrett Papers* (Cape Town: Van Riebeeck Society, 1984), p. 49. See also, Harlow, "Sir Frederick Hamilton," pp. 302–3; Pakenham, *Jameson's Raid*, p. 66.

77. Hammond, *Autobiography*, vol. 1, pp. 326–27, 330; Cape Blue Book [C–8380, 1896], p. 85; Van der Poel, *Jameson Raid*, pp. 58–59; Noer, *Briton, Boer and Yankee*, p. 48.

78. Hammond, Ibid., 330. It is interesting to note that on this trip to Kimberley and Mafeking Hammond was accompanied by his wife, presumably to allay any suspicion of political intent.

79. Henry A. Wolff to S. W. Jameson, 14 Aug. 1896, copy, Howell Wright Collection,

Sterling Memorial Library, Yale University, box 19, folder 22; Hammond, *Autobiography*, vol. 1, 331; Van der Poel, *Jameson Raid*, p. 58.

80. *Blue Book 311* (1897), qs. 5972, 5974, p. 326; Hammond, *Autobiography*, vol. 1, pp. 320–21; Garrett and Edwards, *Story of an African Crisis*, p. 53; Van der Poel, *Jameson Raid*, p. 59; Pakenham, *Jameson's Raid*, pp. 80–81.

81. Hammond, *Autobiography*, vol. 1, 325; Keto, *Aftermath of Jameson Raid*, p. 12.

82. Colvin, *Jameson*, vol. 2, 89; Rhoodie, *Conspirators in Conflict*, pp. 45–46.

83. The neutrality of the Mercantile Association was attributed by some bigoted observers to the numerous "cowardly Jews" in its membership. Garrett and Edwards, *Story of an African Crisis*, p. 128.

84. Alf Brown to Howell Wright, 21 Feb. 1939, Wright Collection, 17/8.

85. Hammond, *Autobiography*, vol. 1, 319. See also, Alfred P. Hillier, *Raid and Reform* (London: Macmillan, 1898), p. 54.

86. Hillier, Ibid. The Johannesburg Reformers had not ignored the need to win over to their side those English miners and those unemployed on the Rand, who in some numbers sympathized with Kruger as he stood firm against his capitalist enemies. To provide relief for the jobless, in what was clearly a political move, a Present Help League and the related Kelley's Relief Stores were established in 1895 through the support of the Reform Committee. Charles van Onselen, *Studies in the Social and Economic History of the Witwatersrand, 1886–1914: vol. 2: New Nineveh* (New York: Longman, 1982), p. 126.

87. Bower, "Reminiscences," pp. 219–20.

88. *Star*, 24 Dec. 1895, p. 4.

89. *Standard and Digger News*, 27 Dec. p. 3; Garrett and Edwards, *Story of an African Crisis*, p. 125.

90. Douglas Blackburn and W. Warthman Caddell, *Secret Service in South Africa* (London: Cassell, 1911), pp. 274–77; Garrett and Edwards, *Story of an African Crisis*, p. 125; Bower, "Reminiscences," p. 221; Van der Poel, *Jameson Raid*, p. 64.

91. Van der Poel, Ibid., p. 67; Rhoodie, *Conspirators in Conflict*, p. 46.

92. *Cape Blue Book* [C–8380], 1896, p. 149; Rhoodie, Ibid., p. 49.

93. Harlow, "Sir Frederick Hamilton," p. 294.

94. *Cape Blue Book* [C–8380], 1896, pp. 5, 149.

95. Van der Poel, *Jameson Raid*, p. 73; Rhoodie, *Conspirators in Conflict*, pp. 46–47.

96. Rhoodie, Ibid., p. 46.

97. Thus, it is clearly not in accord with the facts to claim, as does Noer (*Briton, Boer and Yankee*, p. 46, 152 n. 6), that Hammond dominated the reform group or that he authored most of its protests. See Rhoodie, Ibid., p. 108.

98. Rhoodie, Ibid., p. 49.

99. *Blue Book 311* (1897), qs. 5050, pp. 283–84; qs. 6826–38, p. 362; Phillips, *Reminiscences*, p. 148.

100. Lionel Phillips, "From Inside Johannesburg," p. 207.

101. Richardson, *Messages and Papers of the Presidents*, vol. 9, pp. 655–58.

102. Phillips, "From Inside Johannesburg," p. 207; In fact, some determined British nationalists who were sympathetic with the reform movement informed Charles Leonard that they would support the revolt only if the Union Jack crowned the effort. John Scobie and H. R. Abercrombie, *The Rise and Fall of Krugerism: A Personal Record of Forty Years in South Africa* (London: W. Heinnemann, 1900), pp. 187–88. See also, *Star*, 19 Dec. p. 3; Garrett and Edwards, *Story of an African Crisis*, p. 82; John Hays Hammond, "The Jameson Raid and the World War," pt. 1, *Scribners Magazine* 79 (Apr. 1926), 229; Pakenham, *Jameson's Raid*, p. 218.

103. Lockhard and Woodhouse, *Rhodes*, p. 317.

104. Garrett and Edwards, *Story of an African Crisis*, p. 82.

105. Ibid., p. 83; Bower, "Reminiscences," p. 241.

106. Fitzpatrick, *Transvaal from Within*, p. 102; Van der Poel, Ibid., chap. 3.

107. *Blue Book 311* (1897), q. 7936, p. 415; Charles Leonard, *Papers on the Political Situation in South Africa, 1885–1895* (London: A. L. Humphreys, 1903), p. 380; Keto, *Aftermath of Jameson Raid*, p. 13.

108. Rhoodie, *Conspirators in Conflict*, p. 50.
109. *Star*, 24 Dec. 1895, p. 4. Many Boer families had in fact camped themselves in Church Square near the arsenal. Garrett and Edwards, *Story of an African Crisis*, pp. 145–46.
110. Hammond, *Autobiography*, vol. 1, p. 333. Hammond planned to have his men abduct Kruger and bring him to the Rand where, supposedly, he could be made to see reason. Hammond, "The Jameson Raid and the World War," pt. 1, p. 236.
111. Hillier, *Raid and Reform*, p. 55; Rhoodie, *Conspirators in Conflict*, p. 51.
112. Colvin, *Jameson*, vol. 1, p. 45.
113. *Cape Blue Book* [C–8380], 1896, p. 241; Fitzpatrick, *Transvaal from Within*, p. 122; Garrett and Edwards, *Story of an African Crisis*, p. 77; Harlow, "Sir Frederick Hamilton," p. 298.
114. *Cape Blue Book* [C–8380], 1896, p. 5; Van der Poel, *Jameson Raid*, p. 76.
115. Rhoodie, *Conspirators in Conflict*, p. 64.
116. Rhoodie, Ibid., charges Rhodes with intentionally deceiving the Johannesburg agents about his intentions and allowing Jameson to take the bit in his teeth; Van der Poel (*Jameson Raid*, pp. 85–86) suggests that Rhodes, while realizing that the plan had fallen through, simply did not act responsibly enough to see that Jameson was properly informed.
117. *Blue Book 311* (1897), p. 9; *Cape Blue Book* [C–8389], 1896, pp. 224–239; Pakenham, *Jameson's Raid*, p. 69.
118. *Blue Book 311* (1897), q. 5902, p. 324; Van der Poel, *Jameson Raid*, p. 78.
119. *Cape Blue Book* [C–8380], 1896, p. 150, 196; Hammond, *Autobiography*, vol. 1, p. 337; Van der Poel, Ibid., p. 28.
120. *Cape Blue Book* [C–8380], 1896, p. 198; Van der Poel, Ibid., p. 88.
121. *Star*, 30 Dec. p. 3.
122. Ibid., 28 Dec. p. 4.
123. Ibid.
124. Charles Thomas, *Johannesburg in Arms, 1895–96, Being the Observations of a Casual Observer* (London: Smith, Elder and Co., 1896), p. 20; Garrett and Edwards, *Story of an African Crisis*, p. 131.
125. *Star*, 30 Dec. 1895, p. 5.
126. Ibid., p. 3
127. Ibid., p. 4; Garrett and Edwards, *Story of an African Crisis*, p. 130.
128. *Star*, 30 Dec. 1895, p. 4; Hammond, *Autobiography*, vol. 1, pp. 337–38. Noer (*Briton, Boer and Yankee*, p. 48) has recently presented a distorted account of this episode. Unfortunately he depended on an unreliable work of Eric Resenthal, *Stars and Stripes in Africa* (Cape Town: National Books Ltd., 1968), and conveys the erroneous impression that Hammond was in command of the American community on the Rand. Although he wielded considerable influence, this was not the case. Moreover, Noer asserts that Hammond "sent" the engineers Jennings and Perkins, who worked for the Wernher, Beit firm, to meet with Kruger. In fact Hammond, who did not favor their mission to Pretoria, had nothing to do with their going.
129. *Standard and Digger News*, 1 Jan. 1896, p. 5.
130. Hammond to Poultney Bigelow, 28 Aug. 1896, copy, HP, box 7, letterbook no. 2, item 105; Hammond, *Autobiography*, vol. 1, p. 343.
131. *Standard and Digger News*, 1 Jan. 1896, p. 5; Hammond, *Autobiography*, vol. 1, p. 343; Garrett and Edwards, *Story of an African Crisis*, p. 162. Noer (*Briton, Boer and Yankee*, p. 49) suggests that Hammond was in charge of these meetings but his cited evidence does not support this. It is worth noting, moreover, that a group of about eighty Americans, calling themselves the "American Working Man's Committee," met at the Chamber of Mines office on the same evening (thirty-first) to express their opposition to the "so-called influential Americans who are paid by the Rhodes clique." They pledged their loyalty to Kruger. *Standard and Digger News*, 31 Dec. 1895, p. 3.
132. As in the case of the earlier secret committee, this new publicly acknowledged group was run by an inner executive, which was essentially the same handful of reform leaders as before. Rhoodie, *Conspirators in Conflict*, p. 71.
133. Thomas, *Johannesburg in Arms*, p. 32; *Star*, 31 Dec. 1895, p. 4; Hammond, "The

Jameson Raid and the World War," pt. 1, p. 230. In the latter article and in his *Autobiography* (vol. 1, 343–45) Hammond, recalling these events long afterward, incorrectly reverses the sequence of his activities during the hectic last day of 1895. See also, Rhoodie, *Conspirators in Conflict*, p. 73.

134. Hammond, *Autobiography*, vol. 1, p. 344.
135. *Star*, 31 Dec. 1895, p. 4; Rhoodie, *Conspirators in Conflict*, pp. 73–74.
136. Later these incriminating documents were dumped down a well of the Star building and all who knew of their existence were pledged to secrecy. Smith Le Roux to Maude Bower, 10 Feb. 1957, Sir Graham Bower Papers, Rhodes House Library, Oxford, S. 1279, no. 1. As Rhoodie demonstrates, however, Transvaal authorities did learn something about this episode. *Conspirators in Conflict*, pp. 74–75.
137. Thomas, *Johannesburg in Arms*, pp. 77–78.
138. Robinson to Chamberlain, 4 Feb. 1896, Great Britain, Parliament, *Parliamentary Papers* (House of Commons), 1896, 59 [C.7933], Correspondence concerning disturbances in South Africa, 1895–6, no. 219, p. 83.
139. *Star*, 31 Dec. 1895, p. 3; Thomas, *Johannesburg in Arms*, pp. 39–45.
140. Percy Fitzpatrick to Wife, 10 Jan. 1896, in *Fitzpatrick*, p. 32; Hillier, *Raid and Reform*, p. 61; Phillips, *Some Reminiscences*, p. 51; Thomas, Ibid., p. 36. Contrary to most accounts, not all guns were unpacked before the thirty-first. A small number had been brought out and distributed. See Anonymous, "Story of an Amateur Revolution," p. 607, whose author received a rifle before news of Jameson's march had reached the Rand.
141. Hillier, Ibid., pp. 61–62; Phillips, "From Inside Johannesburg," p. 212.
142. Hammond, *Autobiography*, vol. 1, p. 339.
143. Ibid., 339–349; Rhoodie, *Conspirators in Conflict*, p. 76.
144. *Star*, 2 Jan. 1896, p. 4; Percy Fitzpatrick to his wife, 5 Jan. 1896, in *Fitzpatrick*, p. 14.
145. Rhoodie, *Conspirators in Conflict*, p. 77.
146. *Star*, 31 Dec. 1895, p. 41; 1 Jan. 1896, p. 1; Mrs. John Hays Hammond, *A Woman's Part in a Revolution* (New York: Longmans, 1897), pp. 19–20; Hillier, *Raid and Reform*, p. 62.
147. Garrett and Edwards, *Story of an African Crisis*, p. 170.
148. Fitzpatrick, *Transvaal from Within*, p. 114. Blackburn and Caddell, *Secret Service*, pp. 281–84.
149. H. C. Fletcher to Howell Wright, 28 Dec. 1946, Wright Collection, 16/2.
150. *Star*, 3 Jan. 1896, p. 5; Garrett and Edwards, *Story of an African Crisis*, p. 172; Thomas, *Johannesburg in Arms*, p. 23; Frank Norris, "Street Scenes in Johannesburg During the Insurrection of January, 1896," *Harpers Weekly* 40 (7 Mar. 1896), 233; Anonymous, *From Manifesto to Trial: A Full History of the Jameson Raid and the Trial of the Members of the Reform Committee and of Dr. Jameson and His Staff* (Johannesburg: Argus, 1896), p. 48; Rhoodie, *Conspirators in Conflict*, p. 73.
151. Phillips, "From Inside Johannesburg," p. 215.
152. Ibid., pp. 214–15; Garrett and Edwards, *Story of an African Crisis*, p. 169; Hammond, *Autobiography*, vol. 1, pp. 345–46; Mrs. Hammond, *Woman's Part*, pp. 23–24.
153. Garrett and Edwards, *Story of an African Crisis*, pp. 175–76; Lockhart and Woodhouse, *Rhodes*, p. 239.
154. John C. Willoughby, "The Jameson Expedition: A Narrative of Facts," *Nineteenth Century* 42 (June 1897), 2; Poultney Bigelow, "White Man's Africa—Part 1: Jameson's Raid," *Harpers New Monthly Magazine* 93 (Nov. 1896), 817 (the author interviewed a doctor who accompanied Jameson); see also, Pakenham, *Jameson's Raid*, pp. 87–88.
155. H. A. Wolff to S. W. Jameson, 14 Aug. 1896, copy, HP, 3/6. An American journalist reported that on the thirty-first, when rumors were rife about the invaders' whereabouts, a member of the Reform Committee told the street crowd that Jameson was within three miles of the city and would be met by a mounted escort. Norris, "Street Scenes in Johannesburg," p. 233. See also, Garrett and Edwards, *Story of an African Crisis*, pp. 202–3; Phillips, *Some Reminiscences*, p. 160; Colvin, *Jameson*, vol. 2, p. 102.
156. R. A. Bettington, account of the Jameson Raid, p. 6, Wright Collection 17/6. This statement by a participant differs from the generally accepted version of the episode, which

has Frank Rhodes disregarding the pseudo-armistice and sending Bettington to Jameson. See, for example, Garrett and Edwards, *Story of an African Crisis*, pp. 202–3; Van der Poel, *Jameson Raid*, pp. 127–28.

157. Garrett and Edwards, *Story of an African Crisis*, pp. 209–10.

158. Percy Fitzpatrick to his wife, 5 Jan. 1896, *Fitzpatrick*, p. 28; Garrett and Edwards, *Story of an African Crisis*, pp. 209–10. Mrs. Hammond, *Woman's Part*, p. 31; Rhoodie, *Conspirators in Conflict*, p. 85.

159. Phillips, *Some Reminiscences*, p. 161.

160. L. S. Austin Fitzmaurice to Mrs. Alfred Brown, 2 Jan. 1896, Wright Collection, 17/11.

161. Commissariat Department of the Reform Committee, 4 Jan. 1896, Wright Collection, 17/13; Anonymous, "Story of an Amateur Revolution," p. 610; Rhoodie, *Conspirators in Conflict*, p. 75.

162. Anonymous, "Story of an Amateur Revolution," p. 610.

163. Maj. Charles J. White, autobiographical statement, filmed copy, Hugh Marshall Hole Papers, Sterling Memorial Library, Yale University.

164. Hammond, *Autobiography*, vol. 1, pp. 347–48. With many experienced men on hand, it is strange—indeed, almost incredible—that Hammond would have assumed such a hazardous command.

165. Thomas, *Johannesburg in Arms*, pp. 91, 95.

166. The leader of the Boer raiders later supplied a receipt for the cattle! Unpublished evidence of Mark R. Pascoe, copies of statements and documents relating to the Jameson Raid and Reform Committee, Johannesburg Public Library.

167. Hammond, *Autobiography*, vol. 1, pp. 351–352.

168. Ibid., 352, Mrs. Hammond, *Woman's Part*, pp. 34–35.

169. Natalie Hammond to Gen. Nathanial Harris, 29 Feb. 1896, HP, 2/6.

170. George Becker to Sara Becker, 12 May 1896, Becker Papers, 6/4.

171. J. C. Manion to Kruger, 10 Jan. 1896, Quoted in *Standard and Digger News*, 11 Jan. 1896, p. 8.

172. Various letters in HP, 3/1; The extensive campaign to assist Hammond through pressure on Washington was centered in California and New York where his family had very influential standing. See 30–38. Keto, *Aftermath of Jameson Raid*, pp. 22–27, Keto's work is a thorough study of the "Hammond affair" and its extensive impact on certain segments of American society as well as on the State Department.

173. Richard Olney to Sir Julian Pauncefote, 29 Apr. 1896, copy, HP, 3/2; Hammond, *Autobiography*, vol. 1, p. 361; Noer, *Briton, Boer and Yankee*, p. 50. It is worth noting that the American prisoners, when informed that Washington was arranging for British "protection" for them, opposed the move because they thought it might count against them with Kruger's government, which would be suspicious of any such British connection. See *Foreign Relations of the United States, 1896* (Washington, D.C.: U.S. Government Printing Office, 1897), pp. 562–69.

174. E. Solomon to C. W. Truslow, 31 Mar. 1896, HP, 3/2.

175. C. W. Truslow to Gen. Nathanial Harris, 9 Apr. 1896, HP, 3/2; Hammond, *Autobiography*, vol. 1, p. 376.

176. D. Chapin to President Grover Cleveland, 29 May 1896, *Foreign Relations of the United States, 1896*, p. 580.

177. William A. Cox, secretary of the U.S. Senate, to Paul Kruger, 28 Apr. 1896, copy, HP, 3/3.

178. Olney to T. C. Catchings, 4 June 1896, copy, HP, 3/3; Noer, *Briton, Boer and Yankee*, p. 52.

179. Mrs. John Hays Hammond, *Woman's Part*, p. 40; Hammond, *Truth About the Jameson Raid*, p. 43.

180. Cecil Rhodes provided the money for the fines.

181. Spence, *Mining Engineers in American West*, p. 304.

182. Marais, *Fall of Kruger's Republic*, pp. 132–35.

183. Cartwright, *Gold Paved the Way*, pp. 92, 112, 182; Paul Johnson, *Consolidated Gold Fields: A Centenary Portrait* (New York: St. Martins 1987), p. 38.

184. Hammond, *Truth about the Jameson Raid*, pp. 48–49; "The Jameson Raid and the World War," pt. 2, 386; *Autobiography*, vol. 2, p. 427. It is perhaps worth adding here that a recent writer has asserted that if the Jameson Raid had not been bungled at both Jameson's and the Johannesburg Reformers' ends, The Transvaal would have become British and the union of South African territories would have been achieved without the damaging prelude of the Anglo-Boer War. Consequently, he concludes less convincingly, the country would have progressed toward the establishment of a multiracial society with nothing like apartheid to stand in the way. Johnson, *Gold Fields*, p. 35. Obviously, neither Hammond nor anyone else implicated the affair had the last word on the Jameson Raid.

Chapter 6. Carl Akeley and the Preservation of African Mammals

1. Carl Akeley, *In Brightest Africa* (Garden City, N.Y.: Doubleday, Page and Co., 1920), p. 1. This is essentially an autobiography. Most chapters were previously published in several periodicals; in some cases the earlier versions contain information not included in the book; Mary L. Jobe Akeley, *The Wilderness Lives Again: Carl Akeley and the Great Adventure* (New York: Dodd, Mead, 1940), pp. 4–6. By his second wife, this is the only substantial biography of Akeley. Although more a hymn of praise than an objective assessment of the man, it is nevertheless an essential source of information. Another brief work, Seymour Gates Pond, *African Explorer: The Adventures of Carl Akeley* (New York: Dodd, Mead, 1957), was meant for young readers; not thoroughly researched, it is unreliable.

2. Roswell Ward, "Henry A. Ward," *Rochester Historical Society Publications* 24 (1948) (Rochester, N.Y.: Rochester Historical Society, 1948), p. 58; Mary Alice Evans and Howard Ensign Evans, *William Morton Wheeler, Biologist* (Cambridge: Harvard University Press, 1970), pp. 2–3.

3. In *Brightest Africa*, p. 5, Akeley mentions seven of his fellow workers at Wards who went on to significant careers.

4. Lewis Akeley (Carl's brother) to Mary Jobe Akeley, 6 Aug. 1937, Akeley Papers, American Museum of Natural History, New York, box 2, folder 9 (hereafter cited as APNY, 2/9.)

5. C. Akeley, *Brightest Africa*, pp. 3–7.

6. Frederic A. Lucas, "Akeley as a Taxidermist," *Natural History* 27 (1927), 148.

7. H. L. Ward to Mary Akeley, 5 Feb. 1940, APNY, 6/11; C. Akeley, *In Brightest Africa*, p. 8

8. Quoted in Geoffrey Hellman, *Bankers, Bones and Beetles: The First Century of the American Museum of Natural History* (Garden City: N.Y.: Natural History Press, 1968), p. 137.

9. *New York Times*, 17 Sept. 1885, p. 5; C. Akeley, *Brightest Africa*, p. 7; C. Akeley, "The Autobiography of a Taxidermist," *World's Work*, 41 (1920), 183; Lucas, "Akeley as Taxidermist," p. 146; John R. Russell, "Jumbo," *University of Rochester Library Bulletin* I (Nov., 1945), 13–16; James L. Haley, "The Colossies of His Kind: Jumbo," *American Heritage* 24 (Aug., 1973), 68; 82–83.

10. C. Akeley, *Brightest Africa*, p. 7; C. Akeley, "Autobiography of a Taxidermist," p. 183; Evans and Evans, *William Wheeler*, p. 7; Douglas Preston, *Dinosaurs in the Attic: A Excursion into the American Museum of Natural History* (New York: Natural History Press, 1986), p. 134.

11. P. T. Barnum to Henry A. Ward, 26 Sept. 1885, Henry A. Ward Papers, University of Rochester Library, folder 5; H. L. Ward to Mary Akeley, 5 Feb. 1940, APNY, 6/11; C. Akeley, "Autobiography of a Taxidermist," p. 183; *New York Times*, 17 Sept. 1885, p. 5; Russell, "Jumbo", pp. 15–20.

12. William Morton Wheeler, *Essays in Philosophical Biology* Cambridge: Harvard Univ. Press, p. 177.

13. Evans and Evans, *William Wheeler*, p. 50.
14. Nancy O. Lurie, *A Special Style* (Milwaukee: Milwaukee Public Museum, 1983), p. 15.
15. Evans and Evans, *William Wheeler*, pp. 52, 54.
16. Lewis Akeley to M. L. J. Akeley, Jan. 18, 1939, APNY, 2/9.
17. Evans and Evans, *William Wheeler*, pp. 5, 14, 23.
18. Wheeler, *Essays*, p. 179.
19. M. L. J. Akeley, *Wilderness*, p. 33.
20. Herbert Katz and Majorie Katz, *Museums U.S.A.: A History and Guide* (Garden City, N.Y.: Natural History Press, 1965), pp. 7, 13. See also, Frederic A. Lucas, "The Story of Museum Groups part 1," *The American Museum Journal* 14 (Jan. 1914), 3–13; and Robert G. Larson, "Museums of Natural History Revisited," *The Naturalist* 2 (1976), 8.
21. H. Severn Reger, "An Appreciation of William H. Werner," *The Oologist* 39 (Oct. 1922). 4–21; Frederic S. Webster, "The Birth of Habitat Bird Groups," *Annuals of the Carnegie Museum* 30 (Sept. 1945), 96–115.
22. Evans and Evans, *William Wheeler*, p. 51; Lurie, *Special Style*, p. 18.
23. Milwaukee Public Museum, *Ninth Annual Report* (Milwaukee, 1892), p. 10.
24. Lucas, "Akeley as Taxidermist," p. 151; M. L. J. Akeley, *Wilderness Lives Again*, p. 38.
25. Ibid, p. 36.
26. C. Akeley, *Brightest Africa*, p. 10; Wheeler, *Essays*, p. 179; Evans and Evans, *William Wheeler*, pp. 56, 72, 70, 78.
27. Katz and Katz, *Museums U.S.A.*, p. 130.
28. C. Akeley, *Brightest Africa*, p. 10.
29. The original plan called for the expedition to hunt in Mashonaland (part of what later became known as Southern Rhodesia) but an African rebellion against white rule there discouraged it. The next choice was the British East African Protectorate (later Kenya) where reports of rinderpest and tribal conflict forced yet another change of site. Somaliland, Elliot was told by recent travellers there, had ample game and, being closer to Europe, would be cheaper to reach. Elliot to F. J. V. Skiff, 21 Feb. 1896, Field Museum of Natural History Archives, Directors' Correspondence, 1893–1907; Field Columbian Museum, *Annual Report, 1896–97* (Chicago: Field Columbian Museum), 1897, p. 184.
30. Field Columbian Museum, *Annual Report, 1896–97*, p. 186.
31. C. Akeley, "The Wild Ass of Somaliland: A Story of Hunting in Desert Africa," *Natural History* 14 (Mar. 1914), 114; C. Akeley, *Brightest Africa*, pp. 116–17; M. L. J. Akeley, *Wilderness Lives Again*, pp. 41–48.
32. C. Akeley, *Brightest Africa*, pp. 97–101.
33. Ibid., pp. 75–76.
34. Field Museum of Natural History, *Annual Report for 1906* (Chicago: Field Museum, 1907), p. 27.
35. Ibid., p. 132; Delia Akeley, *Jungle Portraits* (New York: Macmillan, 1930), pp. 79–81; M. L. J. Akeley, *Wilderness Lives Again*, p. 79.
36. Patricia M. Williams, "The Museum 'Trademark'," Field Museum of Natural History, *Bulletin* 39 (Jan. 1968), 2.
37. Jonas Platt, "Making Wild Animals Live Forever," *Technical World Magazine* 20 (Sept. 1913), 92; Frederic A. Lucas, "Evolution in Museum Technique," *Scientific American* (June 1922): p. 399.
38. C. Akeley, *Brightest Africa*, pp. 11–13. See also, James Clark, *In the steps of the Great Museum Collector, Carl Ethan Akeley* (New York: M. Evans, 1968), pp. 27–28.
39. Platt, "Wild Animals," p. 93.
40. C. Akeley, "Carl Akeley and His Work," *Mentor* 12 (June 1924), 27.
41. C. Akeley, *Brightest Africa*, pp. 173–74; M. L. J. Akeley, *Wilderness Lives Again*, p. 222.
42. C. L. Dewey, who worked with Akeley at the time and who later became president of the Cement Gun Co., pointed out that, contrary to popular belief, Akeley never used the spraying apparatus to build up plaster manikins for his large animal mountings. "My Friend Ake," *Nature Magazine* 10 (Dec. 1927), 391.
43. Ibid.; C. Akeley, *Brightest Africa*, pp. 164–65; Ralph C. Davison, "The Cement

Gun: Plaster Work Done with a Hose," *Scientific American* 107 (Jan. 1912), 44-45 (which provides illustrations of the uses to which the commercial machine was put).

44. James L. Clark, *Good Hunting: Fifty Years of Collecting and Preparing Habitat Groups for the American Museum* (Norman: University of Oklahoma Press, 1966), p. 8.

45. Wheeler, *Essays*, p. 81.

46. C. Akeley, "Carl Akeley's Own Story," *Mentor* 14 (Jan. 1926), 27. See, also, Delia Akeley to D. C. Davies, 25 May 1927, Field Museum Archives, Directors' correspondence, 1893-1907.

47. C. Akeley, contract with Field Museum of Natural History, 6 Mar. 1908, Akeley Papers, University of Rochester Library, Rochester, New York, box 1, folder 10 (hereafter cited as APR, 1/10).

48. Andrews, *Beyond Adventure*, p. 110.

49. H. C. Bumpus to Carl Akeley, 18 Apr. 1908, APR, 6/5.

50. C. Akeley, "Elephant Hunting in Equatorial Africa with Rifle and Camera," *National Geographic Magazine* 23 (Aug. 1912), 794. Carl Akeley to Herman Bumpus, 20 July 1910, quoted in *American Museum Journal* 10 (Oct. 1910), 186-87. When he was engaged in his own search for a prime specimen, Akeley admitted to being "elephant mad." Akeley to Henry Fairfield Osborn, 30 Oct. 1910, American Museum of Natural History Archives, A-1/796.

51. C. Akeley, "Elephant Hunting," pp. 779-810.

52. Delia J. Akeley, *Jungle Portraits*, p. 234.

53. C. Akeley, *Brightest Africa*, pp. 146-47.

54. Arthur H. Fisher, "Lion Spearing in the African Jungle, *Travel* 26 (Aug. 1916), 9. Akeley never said much about his illnesses or injuries suffered during his safaris, and only the most crippling infirmities could slow him down. Characteristically, he referred to his serious disability in Uganda in 1909 as only "a considerable strain." C. Akeley, *Brightest Africa*, p. 69. Fisher, "Lion Spearing," p. 10. The lion spearing episode occurred in the latter part of the expedition, by which time funds were fully expended. In order to stay longer, Akeley wired his banker and tried unsuccessfully to mortgage some rural property he owned in Clarendon, N.Y. M. L. J. Akeley, *Wilderness Lives Again*, p. 363.

55. M. L. J. Akeley, *Wilderness Lives Again*, p. 12.

56. Lucas, "Akeley as Taxidermist," p. 148.

57. C. Akeley, *Brightest Africa*, p. 158.

58. C. Akeley to Sir James Hayes-Sadler (governor of British East Africa), 22 Mar. 1909, APR, 6/5; C. Akeley to Ernest D. Lewis (Editor of the *Roosevelt Quarterly*), 13 Jan. 1925, APR, 5/16. Roosevelt's respect for Akeley's courage, knowledge of animals and hunting prowess is apparent in the numerous references to Akeley in Theodore Roosevelt and Edmund Heller, *Life-Histories of African Game Animals*, 2 vols (New York: Scribner, 1914).

59. C. Akeley, *Brightest Africa*, pp. 160-62; Theodore Roosevelt, *African Game Trails* (New York: Scribner, 1927), pp. 346-50; Kermit Roosevelt, "Akeley the Explorer," *Natural History* 27 (Mar.—Apr. 1927), 118-19.

60. C. Akeley to Ernest Lewis, 13 Jan. 1925, APR, 5/16.

61. Akeley, *Brightest Africa*, p. 162.

62. First published in 1910, it has been reissued several times since. Akeley wrote the introduction for the 1927 memorial edition.

63. C. Akeley to Gifford Pinchot, 5 Apr. 1919; Akeley to Henry Cabot Lodge, 10 Apr. 1919, APR, 4/11; Edith Kermit Roosevelt to Roosevelt Memorial Association, 11 Apr. 1921 (signed by five other family members), APNY, 1/6. Pictures of Akeley's final model can be seen in Dewey, "My Friend Ake," p. 390.

64. C. Akeley, *Brightest Africa*, pp. 45-52; Delia Akeley, "Saving Carl Akeley After His Bout with an Elephant," *Literary Digest* 96 (Mar. 3, 1928), 58-60; Delia Akeley, *Jungle Portraits*, pp. 238-51. C. Akeley's notes on the incident, APNY, 1/6.

65. D. Akeley, *Jungle Portraits*, pp. 85-95.

66. C. Akeley, notes on 1909-10 expedition. APNY, 3/7. Even before his injury Akeley had been advised that gorilla hunting would require more extensive preparation than he had been able to do. Richard J. Cunningham to Akeley, 14 Mar. 1910, APR, 6/7.

67. Henry L. Ward to Akeley, 18 Jan. 1911, APR 6/8.

68. Hellman, *Bankers, Bones and Beetles*, p. 1.
69. Plan for African Hall, APR, 1/3; C. Akeley, *Brightest Africa*, p. 252.
70. Plan for African Hall.
71. Fisher, "Lion Spearing," p. 13.
72. C. Akeley, *Brightest Africa*, pp. 166–68; Andrews, *Beyond Adventure*, pp. 123–24; F. Trubee Davison, "Akeley the Inventor," *Natural History* 27 (1927), 124–29.
73. Davison, "Akeley the Inventor," p. 128. This article includes pictures of several models of the Akeley camera. See also, Akeley, *Brightest Africa*, p. 172.
74. Andrews, *Beyond Adventure*, p. 125.
75. Clark, *Good Hunting*, p. 50; James L. Clark, *In the Steps of the Great Museum Collector, Carl Ethan Akeley* (New York: M. Evans, 1968), p. 63.
76. American Museum of Natural History, *Annual Report 1922* (New York, 1923), p. 31.
77. Ibid.
78. M. L. J. Akeley, *Wilderness Lives Again*, p. 159.
79. Ibid.
80. Henry F. Osborn to C. Akeley, 1 Apr. 1912, APR, 6/8.
81. C. Akeley, notes on a meeting with Henry F. Osborn, 28 May, 1912, Ibid.
82. Mary Hastings Bradley, "In Africa with Akeley," *Natural History* 27 (Mar.—Apr. 1927), 163. Mrs. Bradley also published a longer account of her experience on this trip but gives Akeley relatively little attention in it. See her book, *On the Gorilla Trail* (New York: Appleton, 1923).
83. C. Akeley to Herbert and Mary Bradley, 11 July 1921, APR, 7/3.
84. C. Akeley, *Brightest Africa*, pp. 190–98. His collection of gorilla data is in APNY, 6/1–6.
85. C. Akeley, *Brightest Africa*, pp. 198–226. Bradley, "In Africa with Akeley," p. 168. Bradley, *On the Gorilla Trail*, p. 112; Andrews, *Beyond Adventure*, pp. 128–31. The motion pictures were made possible by Akeley's special modifications of his camera, which enabled him to operate in reduced light with a telephoto lens.
86. Bradley, "In Africa with Akeley," pp. 165, 168.
87. C. Akeley, *Brightest Africa*, chaps. 8, 9; C. Akeley, "Gorillas: Real and Mythical," *Natural History* 23 (Sept.—Oct. 1923), 428–47.
88. *New York Times*, 15 Mar. 1922, p. 18.
89. C. Akeley, "Gorillas," p. 438.
90. Russell H. Tuttle, *Apes of the World: Their Social Behavior, Communication, Mentality and Ecology* (Park Ridge, N.J.: Noyes Publications, 1986), pp. 237–38; George Schaller, *The Mountain Gorilla* (Chicago: University of Chicago Press, 1963), pp. 215–17.
91. C. Akeley, *Brightest Africa*, pp. 230–31.
92. Bradley, "In Africa with Akeley," p. 169.
93. C. Akeley to Robert Yerkes, 8 June 1922, APR, 7/4; C. Akeley, *Brightest Africa*, pp. 248–50; C. Akeley, "Gorillas," p. 447.
94. Pictures of these sculptures can be seen in "The Sculpture of Carl Akeley," *Field Museum of Natural History Bulletin* 51 (Jan. 1980), 6–8; C. Akeley, "African Hall: A Monument to Primitive Africa," *Mentor* 13 (Jan. 1926), 10–15; and Clyde Fisher, "Carl Akeley and His Work," *Scientific Monthly* 24 (Feb. 1927), 97–118.
95. Bronze copies were acquired by the Field Museum in Chicago in 1926.
96. It, too, is pictured in "The Sculpture of Carl Akeley," p. 9.
97. *New York American*, 17 Mar. 1924, p. 5.
98. Ibid. Another account attributed this rejection to the sculpture's "lack of merit." See *South Bend Tribune*, 25 Apr. 1924, p. 4.
99. *New York World*, 17 Mar. 1924, p. 7; *South Bend Tribune*, 25 Apr. 1924, p. 4; see also, *New York Times*, 6 Dec. 1926, p. 7.
100. C. Akeley to Mrs. Paul Dutton, 24 Jan. 1921, APR, 7/2.
101. C. Akeley, "African Hall: A Monument of Primitive Africa," *Mentor* 13 (Jan. 1926), 11.
102. C. Akeley, *Brightest Africa*, p. 266.
103. C. Akeley to Osborn, 7 Oct. 1925, APNY, 1/4.

104. Clark, *Good Hunting*, p. 51, 64.
105. M. L. J. Akeley, *Wilderness Lives Again*, p. 220; Daniel E. Pomeroy, "Akeley's Dream Comes True," American Museum of Natural History, *Complete Book of African Hall* (New York: American Museum of Natural History, 1936), p. 8.
106. Andrews, *Beyond Adventure*, p. 137; Hellman, *Bankers, Bones and Beetles*, p. 140.
107. C. Akeley to Osborn, 12 Jan. 1920, APR, 6/14.
108. Hellman, *Bankers, Bones and Beetles*, p. 163.
109. Herbert L. Stoddard, *Memoirs of a Naturalist* (Norman: University of Oklahoma Press, 1969), pp. 190–91.
110. *Chicago Daily News*, 22 Mar. 1923, p. 1; *Chicago Daily Tribune*, 22 Mar. 1923, p. 3; *New York Times*, 23 Mar. 1923, p. 40. In the divorce settlement Akeley agreed to turn over all his property to Delia. *New York Herald Tribune*, 30 July 1927, p. 10.
111. C. Akeley, "African Hall," pp. 20–21.
112. *Mentor* 13 (Jan. 1926), 47–50.
113. Ibid., p. 48.
114. Ibid., pp. 48–49.
115. C. Akeley, "African Hall," pp. 10–11; Preston, *Dinosaurs in the Attic*, p. 82.
116. C. Akeley to Thornton W. Burgess, 27 June, 1921, APR, 7/2.
117. C. Akeley to Robert Yerkes, 8 June, 1922, APR, 7/4; C. Akeley, *Brightest Africa*, pp. 248–50; C. Akeley, "Gorillas," p. 447; Baron de Cartier De Marchienne, "Akeley the Conservationist," *Natural History* 27 (Mar.—Apr. 1927), 115–17.
118. C. Akeley, "Have a Heart: A Statement and Plea for Fair Game Sport in Africa," *Mentor* 13 (1926), 50; Akeley, "Africa's Great National Park," *Natural History* 29 (Nov. 1929), 639–40; M. L. J. Akeley, *Akeley's Africa*, p. 241.
119. M. L. J. Akeley, "Africa's Great National Park," pp. 641.
120. Ibid., p. 649.
121. Andrews, *Beyond Adventure*, pp. 93–94.
122. Edward McKinley, *The Lure of Africa: American Interests in Tropical Africa, 1919–1939* (Indianapolis: Bobbs-Merrill, 1974), pp. 126–27. It is odd that a study of hunting in Kenya during this period makes no mention of these numerous museum collecting missions. E. I. Steinhart, "Hunters, Poachers and Gamekeepers: Towards a Social History of Hunting in Colonial Kenya," *Journal of African History* 30 (1989), 247–264.
123. Pomeroy, "Akeley's Dream Comes True," pp. 8–9.
124. C. Akeley, "Carl Akeley's Own Story," p. 31.
125. C. Akeley to Trubee Davison, 7 Aug. 1925, copy, APNY, 1/14
126. M. L. J. Akeley, "Africa's Great National Park," pp. 643–44.
127. George Eastman, "A Safari in Africa," *Natural History* 27 (Mar.—Apr. 1927), 534.
128. Pomeroy, "Akeley's Dream Comes True," p. 10.
129. Eastman, "Safari in Africa," p. 537.
130. When asked later if he obtained the additional money from Eastman, Akeley replied, "The old tightwad didn't give me a cent." William Leigh, *Frontiers of Enchantment* (New York: Simon, 1940), pp. 111, 131.
131. M. L. J. Akeley, *Akeley's Africa*, p. 129. The museum sent Johnson on a five-year mission. A corporation was established, with a fund of $150,000, to finance the various phases of his work. He was directed to make his permanent base in Nairobi and from there travel to various game areas for filming a "priceless record" to be part of the institution's collection. American Museum of Natural History, *The American Museum and Education: Fifty-Sixth Annual Report* (New York, 1925), p. 16; Martin Johnson, "Camera Safaris," *Complete Book of African Hall*, p. 48.
132. *New York Times*, 1 Dec. 1926, p. 1.
133. Ibid., 20 Sept. 1926, p. 3.
134. M. L. J. Akeley, *Akeley's Africa*, pp. 146–52.
135. Leigh, *Frontiers of Enchantment*, p. 252.
136. *New York Times*, 17 May, 1936, p. 3.
137. Pomeroy, "Akeley's Dream Comes True," p. 10.
138. Fred Smyth (AMNH bursar) to M. L. J. Akeley, 5 Mar. 1940, APNY, 2/7.
139. C. Akeley's notes on meeting with Osborn, 9 May, 1925, Ibid., 1/4.

140. C. Akeley to Osborn, 7 Oct. 1925; Osborn to C. Akeley, 14 Oct. 1925, Ibid.
141. Preston, *Dinosaurs in the Attic*, p. 84.
142. C. Akeley to Thornton W. Burgess, 27 June, 1921, APR, 7/2.
143. C. Akeley, *Brightest Africa*, p. 254.
144. Ibid.
145. Carl and M. L. J. Akeley, *Adventures in the African Jungle* (New York: Dodd, Mead, 1930), p. 27.
146. Hammond and Jablow, *Myth of Africa*, chap. 8. See also, Donna Haraway, *Primate Visions: Gender Race and Nature in the World of Modern Science* (New York: Routledge, 1989), pp. 48–54, which provides a radical feminist's perspective on these matters.
147. McKinley, *Lure of Africa*, p. 119.
148. See, among the many tributes to his work, David M. Walsten, "The Legacy of Carl Akeley," *Field Museum of Natural History Bulletin* 57 (Jan. 1986), 5–25.

Bibliography

Unpublished Sources

American Museum of Natural History Archives, New York, N.Y.
   Directors' Correspondence
   Carl Akeley Papers
Center for Research Libraries, Chicago, Ill.
   William Mackinnon Papers (microfilm copy)
Field Museum of Natural History Archives, Chicago, Ill.
   Directors' Correspondence, 1893–1903
   Carl Akeley File
Historical Commission of the Southern Baptist Convention, Nashville, Tenn.
   Thomas Jafferson Bowen Papers
Johannesburg Public Library, Johannesburg, South Africa.
   Copies of documents relating to the Jameson Raid
Library of Congress, Washington, D.C.
   American Colonization Society Papers
   George F. Becker Papers
   Charles Chaillé-Long Papers
   John Tyler Morgan Papers
National Archives, Washington, D.C.
   U.S. Department of State, Appointment Papers: Applications and recommendations for Office
   U.S. Department of State, Diplomatic Despatches from Ministers to Belgium and Germany (microfilm copies)
   U.S. Department of State, Consular Despatches from Cairo, Cape Town, Boma, and Gaboon (microfilm copies)
   U.S. Department of State, Miscellaneous letters
The Ohio State University Library, Columbus.
   Henry Shelton Sanford Papers (microfilm copy)
Rhodes House Library, Oxford, United Kingdom.
   British South Africa Company Papers
   Sir Graham Bower Papers
   Sir Federick Hamilton Papers
   Cecil Rhodes Papers
   Robert White Diary
University of Rochester Library, Rochester, N.Y.
   Carl Akeley Papers
   Henry Augustus Ward Papers
Sterling Memorial Library, Yale University, New Haven, Conn.
   John Hays Hammond Papers
   Hugh Marshall Hole Papers
   Howell Wright Collection

Published Documents and Correspondence

Bontinck, François. *Aux origines de l'état indépendent du Congo: documents tirés d'archives Américaines*. Louvain and Paris: Editions E. Nauwelaerts, 1966.

Duminy, A. H., and Guest, W. R., eds. *Fitzpatrick: South African Politician, Selected Papers, 1888–1906*. Johannesburg: McGraw-Hill Book Co., 1976.

France. Ministère des Affaires Etrangere. *Documents diplomatique français, 1871–1914*. 1st series, v. Paris: Imprimerie National, 1933.

Frazer, Myrna, and Jeeves, Alan, eds. *All that Glittered: Selected Correspondence of Lionel Phillips*. Cape Town: Oxford University Press, 1977.

Gavin, R. J., and Betley, J. A., eds. *The Scramble for Africa: Documents on the Berlin West African Conference and Related Subjects, 1884–1885*. Ibadan, Nigeria: Ibadan University Press, 1973.

Gordon, M. A. *Letters of General C. G. Gordon to his Sister, M. A. Gordon*. London: Macmillan and Co., 1888.

Great Britain. *Parliamentary Debates* (House of Lords). 4th series, London: H. M. Printing Office, 1872–1914.

———. *Parliamentary Papers*. c. 4205. "Correspondence Respecting the West African Conference" (May—Nov. 1884). London, 1885.

———. c. 4241. "Further Correspondence Respecting the West African Conference" (Nov.—Dec. 1884). Africa no. 3, 1885.

———. c. 4284. "Correspondence with Her Majesty's Ambassador at Berlin Respecting the West African Conference" (Dec. 1884 – Feb. 1885). Africa no. 2, 1885.

———. c. 7933, c. 8063 "Correspondence Concerning Disturbances in the South African Republic, 1895–96."

———. "Report from the Select Committee on British South Africa, 11–14 August 1896."

———. "Reports from the Select Committee on South Africa (Jameson Raid)."

———. c. 8380. "Report of the Select Committee of the Cape Assembly on the Jameson Raid, 29 May–17 July 1896."

Hertslet, E. *Map of Africa by Treaty*. 3 vols. London: Frank Cass, 1967.

Hill, George B., ed. *Colonel Gordon in Central Africa, 1874–1879, from Original Letters and Documents*. London: Thomas De La Rue and Co., 1885.

LeFebve de Vivy, L. *Documents d'histoire précolonial Belge, 1861–1865*. Brussels: Académie Royale des Sciences Coloniales, 1955.

Richardson, James D., ed. *Messages and Papers of the Presidents, 1789–1897*. 20 vols. Washington, D.C.: U.S. Government Printing Office, 1896.

Shaw, Gerald, ed. *The Garrett Papers*. Cape Town: Van Riebeeck Society, 1984.

Shukry, M. F., ed. *Equatoria under Egyptian Rule: Unpublished Correspondence of Col. C. G. Gordon with Ismail, Khedive of Egypt and the Sudan, during the Years 1874–1876*. Cairo: Cairo University Press, 1953.

Stanley, Henry Morton. *Unpublished Letters*. Edited by Albert Maurice. London: W. and R. Chambers, Ltd., 1957.

Stanton, E. A. "Secret Letters from the Khedive Ismail in Connection with the Occupation of the East Coast of Africa." *Journal of the Royal African Society*. 34 (1935), 272–83.

U.S. Congress. House. *Executive Document 156*. 48th Cong., 2nd sess., 30 Jan. 1885.

———. *Executive Document 1*. 49th Cong., 1st sess., 8 Dec. 1885.

———. *House Report 2665*. 48th Cong., 2nd sess., 28 Feb. 1885.

———. Senate. *Executive Document 196*. 49th Cong., 1st sess., 30 June 1886.

———. *Executive Document 77*. 49th Cong., 2nd. sess., 5 Feb. 1887.

———. *Senate Report 393*. 48th Cong., 1st sess., 13 Mar. 1884.
——— Department of State. *Papers Relating to the Foreign Relations of the United States*. Washington, D.C.: U.S. Government Printing Office, 1865–1900.

Primary Published Sources

African Repository (Journal of the American Colonization Society).
Akeley, Carl E. "African Hall: A Monument to Primitive Africa." *Mentor*. 13 (Jan. 1926), 10–22.
———. "Autobiography of a Taxidermist." *World's Work*. 41 (Dec. 1920), 177–95.
———. *In Brightest Africa*. Garden City, N.Y.: Doubleday, Page and Co., 1920.
———. "Bill: My Kikuyu Gun-Bearer, and Some of Our Adventures Together in East Africa." *World's Work*. 41 (Apr. 1921), 594–607.
———. "Carl Akeley's Own Story." *Mentor*. 13 (Jan. 1926), 23–32.
———. "Elephant Hunting in Equatorial Africa." *Natural History*. 12 (Feb. 1912), 43–62.
———. "Elephant Hunting in Equatorial Africa with Rifle and Camera." *National Geographic*. 23 (Aug. 1912), 779–810.
———. "Elephant Hunting on Mt. Kenya; A Woman Wins the Record Pair of Elephant Tusks for a Sportsman's License in British East Africa." *Natural History*. 15 (Nov. 1915), 322–38.
———. "Elephants: Experience of a Representative of the American Museum of Natural History." *World's Work*. 41 (Nov. 1920), 73–92.
———. "An Episode of a Museum Expedition." *Natural History*. 14 (Dec. 1914), 304–8.
———. "Flamingos of Lake Hannington, Africa." *Natural History*. 12 (Dec. 1912), 304–8.
———. "Gorillas—Real and Mythical." *Natural History*. 23 (Sept.—Oct. 1923), 428–47.
———. "Hand to Hand with a Leopard and Some Experiences with Rhinos." *World's Work*. 41 (Feb. 1921), 393–402.
———. "Have a Heart: A Statement and Plea for Fair Game Sport in Africa." *Mentor*. 13 (Jan. 1926), 47–50.
———. "Hunting the African Buffalo; One of the Most Dangerous of Big-game Animals in British East Africa," *Natural History*. 15 (Apr. 1915), 151–61.
———. "Hunting Gorillas in Central Africa." *World's Work*. 44 (June 1922), 169–83.
———. "Hunting Gorillas on Mt. Mikeno." *World's Work*. 44 (July 1922), 307–18.
———. "Hunting Gorillas in Central Africa, III." *World's Work*. 44 (Aug. 1922), 393–99.
———. "Is the Gorilla Almost a Man?" *World's Work*. 44 (Sept. 1922), 525–33.
———. "Lion Spearing." *Mentor*. 13 (Apr. 1925), 47–50.
———. "Martin Johnson and His Expedition to Lake Paradise." *Natural History*. 24 (May—June 1924), 284–88.
———. "Martin Johnson's African Photographs: A Series of Wild Animal Photographs, and a Big-game Hunter's Opinion of Them." *World's Work*. 46 (June 1923), 184–92.
———. "My Acquaintance with Lions." *World's Work*. 41 (Jan. 1921), 277–88.
———. "Roosevelt in Africa." Forward to Roosevelt, Theodore, *African Game Trails*. New York: Scribners' Sons, 1924, memorial edition, pp. IX–XX.
———. "Theodore Roosevelt and Africa." *Natural History*. 19 (Jan. 1919), 12–14.
———. "The Wild Ass of Somaliland: A Story of Hunting in Desert Africa." *Natural History*. 14 (Mar. 1914), 112–17.
———, and Akeley, Mary L. Jobe. *Adventures in the African Jungle*. New York: Dodd, Mead & Co., 1930.

———. *Lions, Gorillas and Their Neighbors*. New York: Dodd, Mead & Co., 1932.

Akeley, Delia. *"J. T., Jr.": The Biography of an African Monkey*. New York: Macmillan and Co., 1929.

———. *Jungle Portraits*. New York: Macmillan and Co., 1930.

———. "My First Elephant." *All True: The Record of Actual Adventures that Have Happened to Ten Women of Today*. New York: Brewer, Warren and Putnam, 1931.

———. "Jungle Rescue." *Colliers*. 81 (11 Feb. 1928), 10, 36, 38–39.

———. "Notes on African Monkeys." *Natural History*. 18 (Dec. 1918), 670–83.

———. "Saving Carl Akeley after His Bout with an Elephant." *Literary Digest*. 96 (3 Mar. 1928), 58–60.

Akeley, Mary L. Jobe. "The Africa Nobody Knows: A Bright Continent Where the Last Frontier Is Vanishing." *World's Work*. 56 (June 1928), 180–88.

———. "Africa's Great National Park: Carl Akeley's Gorilla Sanctuary and Biological Survey Station Becomes a Reality." *Natural History*. 29 (Nov.—Dec. 1929), 638–50.

———. "Belgian Congo Sanctuaries." *Scientific Monthly*. 33 (1931), 289–300.

———. *Carl Akeley's Africa: The Account of the Akeley-Eastman-Pomeroy African Hall Expedition*. New York: Dodd, Mead and Co., 1929.

———. "Carl Akeley's Last Journey: A Visit to the Gorilla Sanctuary in the Belgian Congo." *World's Work*. 56 (July 1928), 250–59.

———. "In Giraffrica: Hunting a Noble Beast." *World's Work*. 55 (Mar. 1928), 536–45.

———. "In the Land of His Dreams: Last Chapter of Carl Akeley's 1926 Expedition." *Natural History*. 27 (Nov. 1927), 525–32.

———. "Lions! Seeing Them Face to Face." *World's Work*. 55 (Apr. 1928), 652–62.

———. "National Parks in Africa: The Extension of Wild-Life Conservation." *Science*. 71 (11 Dec. 1931), 584–88.

———. *The Wilderness Lives Again: Carl Akeley and the Great Adventure*. New York: Dodd, Mead and Co., 1940.

American Museum of Natural History. Annual Reports.

———. *The Complete Book of African Hall*. New York: American Museum of Natural History, 1936.

———. "War Service of Carl Akeley." *Natural History*. 18 (Nov. 1918), 618–19.

Andrews, Roy Chapman. *Beyond Adventure: The Lives of Three Explorers*. New York: Duell, Sloan and Pearce Co., 1924.

———. "My Museum Complex." *World's Work*. 58 (Oct. 1929), 55–59.

Anonymous, *From Manifesto to Trial: A Full History of the Jameson Raid and the Trial of the Members of the Reform Committee and of Dr. Jameson and His Staff*. Johannesburg: Argus, 1896.

Anonymous Johannesburg Resident. "The Story of an Amateur Revolution." *Fortnightly Review*. 65 (Apr. 1896), 605–12.

Banning, Emile, *Memoires politique et diplomatiques*. Paris and Brussells: Renaissance du Livre, 1926.

Barrett, Samuel Alfred. "Mr. Akeley, Our First Taxidermist." *Yearbook of the Public Museum of the City of Milwaukee*. 6 (1 Sept. 1927), 193–95.

Bell, Frederick W. *The South African Conspiracy*. London: W. Heinemann, 1900.

Belmont, Perry. *An American Democrat: The Recollections of Perry Belmont*. New York: Columbia University Press, 1967.

Blackburn, Douglas, and Caddell, Worthman. *Secret Service in South Africa*. London: Cassell, 1911.

Bowen, Thomas Jefferson. *Central Africa: Adventures and Missionary Labors in Several Countries in the Interior of Africa from 1849–1856*. Charleston, S.C.: Southern Baptist Publication Society, 1857.

———. "Central Africa." *Southern Baptist Missionary Journal*. 3 (Nov. 1848), 126–27.

———. *Grammar and Dictionary of the Yoruba Language with an Introduction and Description of the Country and People of Yoruba*. Washington; D.C.: Smithsonian Institution, 1858.

Bradley, Mary Hastings. *Alice in Jungleland*. New York: D. Appleton and Co., 1922.

———. "In Africa with Akeley." *Natural History*. 27 (Mar.—Apr. 1927), 161–72.

———. *On the Gorilla Trail*. New York: D. Appleton and Co., 1923.

Burton, Richard F. *Abeokuta and the Cameroons Mountains*. 2 vols. London: Tinsley Bros., 1863.

———. "A Day amongst the Fans." *Anthropological Review*. 1 (1863), 43–54.

———. *Two Trips to Gorillaland and the Cataracts of the Congo*. 2 vols. London: Sampson, Low, Marston and Searle, 1876.

"Carl Akeley and His Work: Naturalist, Big-game Hunter, Taxidermist, Sculptor and Inventor." *Mentor*. 12 (June 1924), 20–28.

Cartier de Marchienne, Emile de Baron. "Akeley, the Conservationist." *Natural History*. 27 (Mar.—Apr. 1927), 115–17.

Chaillé-Long, Charles. "The Black and Brown People of the Soudan." *Frank Leslie's Magazine*. (Sept. 1884), 357–66.

———. *Central Africa: Naked Truths of Naked People*. London: Sampson, Low, Marston, Searle and Rivington, 1876. [reprint Farnborough, England: Gregg International Publishers, Ltd. 1976].

———. "Colonel Chaillé-Long on the Juba." *Bulletin of the American Geographical Society of New York*. 19 (1887), 194–98.

———. "Egypt Under the Viceroys." *The Era*. 2 (Mar. 1903), 245–61.

———. *L'Egypt et ses provinces perdues*. Paris: La Nouvelle Revue, 1892.

———. "England in Egypt and the Soudan." *North American Review*. 168 (Jan.—June 1899), 570–80.

———. General Gordon as He Is." *New York Tribune*. 25 Jan. 1885, p. 7.

———. "General Gordon: The Hero and the Man." *Belford Magazine*. (Sept. 1890), p. 31.

———. "Heroes to Order." *North American Review*. 144 (Jan.—June 1887), 507–13.

———. Interview with the *Baltimore Sun*. 3 May 1902, p. 5.

———. Letter to the editor. *Bulletin of the American Geographical Society of New York*. 41 (Apr. 1909), 222–24.

———. *My Life on Four Continents*. 2 vols. London: Hutchinson and Co., 1912.

———. "The Nile Sources and the African Problem." *Harpers*. 34 (5 July 1890), 530–531.

———. "The Part of the Nile which Colonel Chaillé-Long Discovered." *Bulletin of the American Geographical Society of New York*. 61 (1909), 222–24.

———. *The Three Prophets: Gordon, the Mahdi and Arabi*. New York: D. Appleton and Co., 1886.

———. "The Uganda Protectorate and the Nile Quest." *Bulletin of the American Geographical Society of New York*. 36 (1904), 36–54.

———. "Uganda and the White Nile." *Journal of the American Geographical Society of New York*. 8 (1876), 285–304.

———. "Voyage au Lac Victoria-Nyanza et au pays Niam-Niam." *Bulletin de la Société de Géographie*. (Oct. 1875), pp. 1–15.

Chambers, Robert, and Chambers, William, "African Discovery." In *Chambers' Miscellany of Useful and Entertaining Tracts*. Edinburgh: W. and R. Chambers, 1845, 16, no. 142, pp. 1–32.

Clark, James L. *Good Hunting: Fifty Years of Collecting and Preparing Habitat Groups for the American Museum*. Norman: University of Oklahoma Press, 1966.

———. *In the Steps of the Great Museum Collector, Carl Eathan Akeley*. New York: M. Evans, 1968.

Clodd, Edward. *Memories*. London: Chapman and Hall, 1916.

Davison, Ralph C. "The Cement Gun: Plaster Work Done With a Hose." *Scientific American*. 106 (13 Jan. 1912), 44–45.

de Kusel, Baron. *An Englishman's Recollections of Egypt, 1863–1887 with an Epilogue Dealing with the Present*. London: John Lane, 1914.

Dewey, C. L. "My Friend 'Ake'." *Nature Magazine*. 10 (Dec. 1927), 387–391.

Du Bose, Hampden C. *Memoires of Reverend John Leighton Wilson*. Richmond, Va.: Presbyterian Committee of Publications, 1895.

Du Chaillu, Paul Benoni. *Adventures in the Great Forest of Equatorial Africa and the Country of the Dwarfs*. New York: Harper and Bros., 1890.

———. *In African Forest and Jungle*. New York: Charles Scribners' Sons, 1903.

———. *The Country of the Dwarfs*. New York: Charles Scribners' Sons, 1902.

———. "Descriptions of New Species of Animals Discovered in Western Equatorial Africa. Skull of a Manatee." *Proceedings of the Boston Society of Natural History*. 7 (1859–61), 296–304; 358–67.

———. "Equatorial Africa, with an Account of the Race of Pygmies." *Journal of the American Geographical Society of New York*. 2 (1870), 99–112.

———. *Explorations and Adventures in Equatorial Africa*. New York: Harper and Bros., 1861.

———. "The Great Equatorial Forests of Africa." *Fortnightly Review*. 53 (June 1890), 777–90.

———. *A Journey to Ashango-Land*. New York: Harper and Bros., 1867.

———. *King Mambo*. New York: Charles Scribners' Sons, 1902.

———. *Lost in the Jungle*. New York: Harper and Bros., 1869.

———. *My Apingi Kingdom*. New York: Harper and Bros., 1870.

———. "Résumé des voyages effectués de 1856 à 1859 dans l'Afrique equatoriale occidentale." *Bulletin de Société géographique* 3 (1862), 133–47.

———. *Stories of the Gorilla Country*. New York: Harper and Bros., 1868.

———. *Wild Life under the Equator*. New York: Harper and Bros., 1869.

———. *The World of the Great Forest*. New York: Charles Scribners' Sons, 1900.

"Du Chaillu's *Explorations and Adventures*." *North British Review*. 35 (1861), 219–52.

"M. Du Chaillu and His Detractors." *Littell's Living Age*. 70 (1862), 473–75.

Dye, William McC. *Muslim Egypt and Christian Abyssinia*. New York: Atkin and Prout, 1880.

Eastman, George. *Chronicles of an African Trip*. Rochester: privately printed, 1927.

———. "A Safari in Africa." *Natural History*. 27 (Nov. 1927), 533–38.

Field Museum of Natural History. Annual Reports.

Fitzpatrick, Percy. *The Transvaal From Within*. London: William Heinemann, 1899.

Garrett, Edmund, and Edwards, E. T. *The Story of an African Crisis*. Westminster: Constable and Co., 1897.

Gessi, Romolo. (ed. Gessi, Felix). *Seven Years in the Soudan*, London: Sampson, Low and Marston, 1892.

Grant, James Augustus. *A Walk Across Africa*. London: Blackwood and Sons, 1864.

Gray, John, Owen, Richard, and Walker, Richard. "Correspondence on the Gorilla." *Athenaeum*. no. 1769 (21 Sept. 1861), 372–74.

Griffon du Bellay, M. T. "Le Gabon." *Le tour du monde*. 12 (1865), 273–304.

Guernsey, Alfred H. "Adventures in Gorilla Land." *Harper's New Monthly Magazine*. 23 (1861), 16–34.

———. "Du Chaillu, Gorillas and Cannibals." *Harper's New Monthly Magazine*. 36 (1867–68), 582–94.

———. "Paul Du Chaillu Again." *Harper's New Monthly Magazine*. 38 (1868–69), 164–74.
———. "Paul Du Chaillu Once More." *Harper's New Monthly Magazine* 40 (1869–70), 201–13.
Hammond, John Hays. *The Autobiography of John Hays Hammond*. 2 vols. New York: Farrar and Rinehart, 1935.
———. "Gold Mining in the Transvaal, South Africa." *Cassier's Magazine*. 22 (July 1902), 187–211.
———. "The Gold Mines of the Witwatersrand, South Africa." *Engineering Magazine*. 14 (Feb. 1898), 733–51.
———. "The Jameson Raid and the World War." *Scribner's Magazine*. 79 (Mar.—Apr. 1926), part 1—pp. 227–39; part 2—pp. 376–86.
———. "South Africa and its Future." *North American Review*. 164 (Jan.—June 1897), 233–48.
———. "South African Memories." *Scribner's Magazine*. 69 (Mar. 1921), 257–78.
———. "The Transvaal Mines under the New Regime. *Engineering Magazine*. 23 (July 1902), 489–96.
———. *The Truth about the Jameson Raid*. Boston: Marshall Jones Company, 1918.
Hammond, Natalie Harris. *A Woman's Part in a Revolution*. New York and London: Longmans, Green and Co., 1897.
Hillier, Alfred P. *Raid and Reform*. London: Macmillan and Co., 1898.
Hodgson, W. B. *The Foulahs of Central Africa and the Slave Trade*. New York, privately printed, 1843.
———. *Notes on Northern Africa*. New York: Wiley and Putnam, 1844.
Hutchinson, G. T. *Frank Rhodes, A Memoir*. London: W. Clowes and Sons, Ltd., 1908.
Johnston, Sir Harry H. *The Kilimanjaro Expedition*. London: K. Paul, Trench and Co., 1896.
Johnson, Martin. "Camera Safaris." *Natural History*. 37 (Jan. 1936), 47–54.
Kasson, John. "The Congo Conference and the President's Message." *North American Review*. 142 (Jan.—June 1886), 231–52.
Latrobe, John H. *Maryland in Liberia*. Baltimore: J. Murphy and Co., 1885.
Leigh, William. *Frontiers of Enchantment*. New York: Simon and Schuster, 1940.
———. "Painting the Background for the African Hall Groups." *Natural History*. 27 (Mar.—Apr. 1927), 142–52.
Leonard, Charles. *Papers on the Political Situation in South Africa, 1885–1895*. London: A. L. Humphreys, 1903.
———. "The Situation in the Transvaal." *New Outlook*. 53 (4 Apr. 18896), 621–23.
Loring, W. W. *A Confederate Soldier in Egypt*. New York: Dodd, Mead and Co., 1884.
Low, Seth. "Personal Recollections of Cecil Rhodes." *The Nineteenth Century and After*. 4 (May 1902), 828–48.
Lucas, Frederic A. "Akeley as a Taxidermist." *Natural History*. 27 (Mar.—Apr. 1927), 142–52.
McCutcheon, John Tinney, *In Africa; Hunting Adventures in the Big Game Country*. Indianapolis: Bobbs-Merrill, 1910.
Milwaukee Public Museum. Annual Reports.
Morgan, John Tyler. "The Future of the American Negro." *North American Review*. 139 (July—Jan. 1884), 194–212.
New York Herald. 1883, 1884, 1888, 1889.
New York Herald Tribune. 1927.
New York Times. 1877, 1879, 1884, 1885, 1922, 1923, 1926, 1936.

New York World. 1924.

Norris, Frank. "Street Scenes in Johannesburg during the Insurrection of January, 1896." *Harper's Weekly Magazine.* 40 (7 Mar. 1896), 233.

Phillips, Lionel. "From Inside Johannesburg." *Nineteenth Century.* 42 (Aug. 1897), 206–16.

———. *Some Reminiscences.* London: Hutchinson and Co., 1924.

Mrs. Lionel Phillips. *Some South African Recollections.* London: Longmans, Green and Co., 1899.

Pomeroy, Daniel Eleazer. "Akeley's Dream Comes True: The Akeley Memorial African Hall—A Monument to the World's Greatest Wonderland of Wild-life." *Natural History.* 37 (Jan. 1936), 5–10.

Reade, Winwood, *African Sketchbook.* 2 vols. London: Smith, Elder and Co., 1873.

———. "The Facts about M. Du Chaillu." *Galaxy.* 3 (1872), 853–62.

———. "The Gorilla as I Found Him." *Belgravia.* 3 (1863), 230–39.

———. "The Habits of the Gorilla." *American Naturalist.* I (1867), 177–80.

———. *Savage Africa.* New York: Smith, Elder and Co., 1864.

Review of Paul Du Chaillu's Explorations and Adventures in Equatorial Africa. *North British Review.* 35 (1861), 219–52.

Review of Winwood Reade's "Notes on the Derbyan Eland, the African Elephant and the Gorilla." *Proceedings of the Zoological Society.* 1863, p. 169.

Roosevelt, Kirmit. "Akeley the Explorer." *Natural History.* 27 (Mar.—Apr. 1927), 118–19.

Roosevelt, Theodore. *African Game Trails: An Account of the African Wanderings of an American Hunter Naturalist.* 2 vols. New York: Scribners' Sons, 1910.

———, and Heller, Edmund. *Life Histories of African Game Animals.* 2 vols. New York: C. Scribners' Sons, 1914.

Sanford, Henry Shelton. "American Interests in Africa." *Forum.* 9 (June 1890), 409–29.

———. "Report on the Conference of the International African Association, 1877." *Journal of the American Geographical Society.* 9 (1877), 103–8.

Sauer, Hans. *Ex Africa.* London: G. Bles, 1937.

Savage, Thomas, and Wyman, Jeffries. "Notes of the External Characters and Habits of the Troglodytes Gorilla, and a New Species of Orang from the Gabon River." *Boston Journal of Natural History.* 5 (Dec. 1847), 68–75.

Scobie, John and Abercrombie, H. R. *The Rise and Fall of Krugerism: A Personal Record of Forty Years in South Africa.* London: William Heinemann, 1900.

Smith, Helen Everton. "Reminiscences of Paul Du Chaillu." *Independent.* 55 (1903), 1146–48.

Speke, John Hanning. *Journal of the Discovery of the Source of the Nile.* Edinburgh and London: W. Blackwood and Sons, 1863.

The Standard and Diggers' News (Johannesburg), 1895, 1896.

The Star (Johannesburg), 1895, 1896.

Stanley, Henry Morton. *The Congo and the Founding of Its Free State.* 2 vols. New York: Harper and Bros., 1885.

Thomas, Charles. *Johannesburg in Arms, 1895–1896, Being the Observations of a Casual Observer.* London: Smith, Elder and Co., 1896.

The Times (London). 1861, 1862, 1874, 1875, 1883.

Toniolo, Elias, and Hill, Richard., eds. *The Opening of the Nile Basin: Writings by the Members of the Catholic Mission to Central Africa on Geography and Ethnography of the Sudan, 1842–1881.* New York: Barnes and Noble Books, 1975.

Tucker, Charlotte Maria. *Abeokuta; or Sunrise Within the Tropics.* New York: R. Carter and Bros., 1853.

Willoughby, John C. "The Jameson Expedition: A Narrative of Facts." *Nineteenth Century.* 42 (June 1897), 9–21.

Wilson, John Leighton. *Western Africa: Its History, Condition and Prospects.* New York: Harper and Bros., 1856.
Wheeler, William Morton. "Carl Akeley's Early Work and Environment." *Natural History.* 27 (Mar.—Apr. 1927), 133–41.
———. *Essays in Philosophical Biology.* Cambridge: Harvard University Press, 1939.

Secondary Works

Ajayi, J. F. Ade. *Christian Missions in Nigeria, 1841–1891.* Evanston: Northwestern University Press, 1965.
———, and Smith, Robert. *Yoruba Warfare in the Nineteenth Century.* Cambridge: Cambridge University Press, 1964.
Akintoye, S. A. *Revolution and Power Politics in Yorubaland, 1840–1843.* London: Longmans, 1971.
Allen, Bernard M. *Gordon and the Sudan.* London: Macmillan and Co., 1931.
Alpers, Edward A. "Charles Chaille-Long's Mission to Mutesa of Buganda." *Uganda Journal.* 29 (1965), 1–11.
Altick, Richard. *The English Common Reader: A Social History of the Mass Reading Public, 1800–1900.* Chicago: University of Chicago Press, 1957.
Altrocchi, Rudolph. *Sleuthing in the Stacks.* Cambridge: Harvard University Press, 1944.
Ambouroué-Avaro, J. *Un peuple gabonais a l'aube de la colonisation: Le Bás-Ogowe au xix^{e}siecle.* Paris: Karthala, 1981.
Amundson, Richard J. "The American Life of Henry Shelton Sanford." Ph.D. dissertation. Florida State University, 1963.
Anstey, Roger. *Britain and the Congo in the Nineteenth Century.* Oxford: Oxford University Press, 1962.
Ascherson, Neal. *The King Incorporated.* New York: Doubleday and Co., 1964.
Ayandele, E. A. *The Missionary Impact on Modern Nigeria, 1842–1914.* New York: Humanities Press, 1966.
———. Introduction to Thomas J. Bowen's *Central Africa*, second edition, London: Frank Cass, 1968, pp. VII–L.
———. *Nigerian Historical Studies.* London: Frank Cass, 1979.
Balandier, George. *The Sociology of Black Africa.* New York: Praeger Publishers, 1970.
Balch, Edwin S. "American Explorers of Africa." The *American Geographical Review.* 5 (Apr. 1918), 271–87.
Beachy, R. W. "The Arms Trade in East Africa in the Late 19th Century." *Journal of African History.* 3 (1962), 451–61.
Beer, Thomas. *The Muave Decade.* New York: Alfred Knopf, 1926.
Bell, Howard. Introduction to Delany, M. R., and Campbell, Robert. *Search for a Place: Black Separatism and Africa, 1860.* Ann Arbor: University of Michigan Press, 1969, pp. 1–22.
Bennett, Alfred L. "Ethnological Notes on the Fang." *Anthropological Institute of Great Britain and Ireland Journal.* 29 (1900), 66–98.
Biobaku, Sabori O. *The Egba and their Neighbors, 1842–1872.* Oxford: Oxford University Press, 1957.
Biographie Colonial Belge. 5 vols. Brussels: Librarie Falk Fils, 1948–59.
Birmingham, David. "The Forest and Savanna of Central Africa." In *Cambridge History of Africa.* vol. 5. Edited by John Flint. Cambridge: Cambridge University Press, 1976.
Blainey, G. "Lost Causes of the Jameson Raid." *Economic History Review.* 18 (1965), 350–66.

Bontinck, François. "Le comité national Américain de l'A.I.A." *La Conférence de géographie de 1876*. Brussels: Académie royale des Sciences d'Outre-Mer, 1976, pp. 476–577.

———. "L'entente entre la France et l'association international du Congo à la lumière des premièrs negotiations." *Etudes d'histoire Africaine*. 2 (1971), 29–81.

———. "Onze lettres inédites de Léopold II à H.S. Sanford, de 1884 à 1887." *Bulletin de l'Académie Royale des Sciences d'Outre-Mer, 1971–1973*, 462–82.

Brooks, George E., and Talbot, Frances K. "The Providence Exploring and Trading Company's Expedition to the Niger River in 1832–33." *The American Neptune*. 35 (Apr. 1975), 242–58.

Brunschwig, Henry. "French Exploration and Conquest in Tropical Africa from 1865–1898." In *The History and Politics of Colonialism, 1870–1914*. Vol. I of *Colonialism in Africa, 1870–1960*, Edited by Duignan and L. H. Gann. 4 vols. Cambridge: Cambridge University Press, 1969.

Bucher, Henry H. "Canonization by Repetition: Paul Du Chaillu in Historiography." *Revue Française d'histoire d'outre-mer*. 66 (1979), 15–32.

———. "John Leighton Wilson and the Mpongwe of Gabon: The Spirit of 1776 in Mid 19th Century Western Africa." *Journal of Presbyterian History*. 54 (1976), 291–315.

———. "The Mpongwe of the Gabon Estuary: A History to 1860." Ph.D. dissertation, University of Wisconsin, Madison, 1977.

———. "Mpongwe Origins: Historiographical Perspectives." *History in Africa*. 2 (1975), 59–89.

———. "The Village of Glass and Western Intrusion: An Mpongwe Response to the American and French Presence in the Gabon Estuary, 1842–1845." *International Journal of African Historical Studies*. 6 (1973), 363–400.

Butler, Albert E. "Transplanting Africa." *Natural History*. 33 (1933), 533–44.

Butterfield, Roger. *The Prodigious Life of George Eastman*. Chicago, Time Inc., 1954.

Cartwright, A. P. *Gold Paved the Way*. New York: St. Martins Press, 1967.

———. *The Corner House: The History of Johannesburg*. Cape Town and Johannesburg: Purnell and Sons, Ltd., 1936.

Chamberlain, Christopher. "The Migration of the Fang into Central Gabon During the 19th Century." *International Journal of African Historical Studies*. 2 (1978), 429–56.

Chamberlain, M. E. "The Alexandria Massacre of 11 June, 1882 and British Occupation of Egypt." *Middle Eastern Studies*. 13 (Jan. 1977), 14–39.

Chester, Edward W. *Clash of Titans: Africa and United States Foreign Policy*. Marynoll, N.Y.: Orbis Books, 1974.

Clendenen, Clarence, Collins, Robert, and Duignan, Peter. *Americans in Africa, 1865–1900*. Stanford, Calif.: Stanford University Press, 1966.

Clendenen, Clarence, and Duignan, Peter. *Americans in Black Africa up to 1865*. Stanford, Calif.: Standford University Press, 1964.

Cobbin, Julian R. E. "Lobengula, Jameson and the Occupation of Manicaland, 1890." *Rhodesian History*. 14 (1973), 39–56.

Collins, Robert. *The Southern Sudan, 1883–1898*. New Haven, Conn.: Yale University Press, 1962.

Colvin, Ian. *The Life of Jameson*. 2 vols. London: E. Arnold and Co., 1922.

Consolidated Gold Fields of South Africa Limited. "*The Gold Fields*," *1887–1937*. London: Consolidated Gold Fields of South Africa, Ltd., 1937.

Coupland, Reginald. *The Exploitation of East Africa, 1856–1890*. Evanston, Ill.: Northwestern University Press, 1967.

Cookey, S. J. S. *Britain and the Congo Question, 1885–1913*. New York: Humanities Press, 1968.

Crabites, Pierre Gordon. *Americans in the Egyptian Army*. London: George Routledge and Sons, 1938.

———. *Gordon, The Sudan and Slavery*. London: George Routledge and Sons, 1933.
———. *Ismail, The Maligned Khedive*. London: George Routledge and Son, 1933.
Cromer, Earl of. *Modern Egypt*. 2 vols. New York: Macmillan Co., 1901.
Crowe, S. E. *The Berlin West African Conference, 1884–1885*. London: Longmans, Green and Co., 1942.
Cutright, Paul Russell. *Theodore Roosevelt the Naturalist*. New York: Harper, 1956.
Curtin, Phillip. *The Image of Africa*. Madison: University of Wisconsin Press, 1964.
Davison, F. Trubee. "Akeley the Inventor." *Natural History*. 27 (Mar.—Apr. 1927), 124–49.
Deschamps, Herbert. *Quinz ans de Gabon: Les début de l'éstablissement Français, 1839–1853*. Paris: Societé Française d'Histoire d'Outre-Mer, 1965.
———. *Traditions orales et archives au Gabon: contribution a l'ethnohistoire*. Paris: Berger-Levrault, 1962.
Dickerson, Mary Cynthia. "The New African Hall Planned by Carl E. Akeley. *Natural History*. 14 (May 1914), 175–87.
Dixon, A. E. *The Natural History of the Gorilla*. New York: Columbia University Press, 1981.
Doeneke, Justus D. *The Presidencies of James A. Garfield and Chester A. Arthur*. Lawrence: University of Kansas Press, 1981.
Douin, G. *Histoire du regne du Khedive Ismail*. 3 vols. Rome: Egyptian Geographical Society, 1933.
Duignan, Peter, and Gann, L. H., eds. *The United States and Africa: A History*. Cambridge: Cambridge University Press, 1984.
Dunbar, A. R. "European Travellers in Bunyoro-Kitara, 1862–1877." *Uganda Journal*. 23 (1959), 107–17.
Duval, Louis M. *Baptist Missions in Nigeria*. Richmond, Va.: Foreign Mission Board of the Southern Baptist Convention, 1928.
Elton, Lord Godfrey. *Gordon of Khartoum: The Life of General Charles George Gordon*. New York: Alfred Knopf, 1955.
Emerson, Barbara. *Leopold II of the Belgians: King of Colonialism*. New York: St. Martins' Press, 1979.
Encyclopedia of the Southern Baptists. vol. 1. Nashville, Tenn.: Southern Baptist Convention, 1958.
Evans, Mary Alice, and Evans, Howard Ensign. *William Morton Wheeler, Biologist*. Cambridge: Harvard University Press, 1970.
Evans-Pritchard, E. E. *The Position of Women in Primitive Societies and Other Essays in Social Anthropology*. London: Faber and Faber, 1965.
Fernandez, James. "Fang Representations under Acculturation." In *Africa and the West*. Edited by Phillip Curtin. Madison: University of Wisconsin Press, 1972, pp. 3–48.
Fisher, Arthur H. "Lion Spearing in the African Jungle." *Travel*. 27 (Aug. 1916), 8–13.
Fisher, Clyde. "Carl Akeley and His Work." *The Scientific Monthly*. 24 (Feb. 1927), 97–118.
Fisher, G. Sydney. *The Middle East: A History*. New York: Alfred Knopf, 1969.
Flint, John. *Cecil Rhodes*. Boston: Little, Brown and Co., 1974.
Forster, Stig; Mommsen, Wolfgang J.; and Robinson, Ronald, eds., *Bismarck, Europe, and Africa: The Berlin Africa Conference 1884–1885 and the Onset of Partition*. London: Oxford University Press, 1988.
Fort, G. Seymour. *Alfred Beit, A Study of the Man and His Work*. London: I. Nicholson and Watson, 1932.
Fraser, James Earle. "Akeley the Sculptor." *Natural History*. 27 (Mar.—Apr. 1927), 120–23.

Fry, Joseph, *Henry S. Sanford: Diplomacy and Business in Nineteenth Century America*. Reno: University of Nevada Press, 1982.
Gardinier, David. *Historical Dictionary of Gabon*. Metuchen, N. J.: Scarecrow Press, 1987.
Gaulme, Francois. *Le Gabon et son ombre*. Paris: Karthala, 1988.
Gbadamosi, T. G. O. *The Growth of Islam Among the Yoruba, 1841–1908*. Atlantic Highlands, N.J.: Humanities Press, 1978.
Gifford, Prosser. "King Leopold and Anglo-French Rivalry, 1882–1884. In *Britain and France in Africa*. Edited by Prosser Gifford and William Roger Louis. New Haven, Conn.: Yale University Press, 1971, pp. 121–66.
———, and Louis, William Roger, eds. *Britain and Germany in Africa*. New Haven, Conn.: Yale University Press, 1967.
Gray, John Milner. "Mutesa of Buganda." *Uganda Journal*. 1 (1934), 22–49.
———. "Zanzibar and the Coastal Belt, 1840–1884." In *History of East Africa*. vol. I. Edited by Roland Oliver and Gervase Mathew. Oxford: Oxford University Press, 1963, pp. 212–51.
Gray, Richard. *A History of the Southern Sudan, 1839–1899*. London: Oxford University Press, 1961.
Graves, A. W. "The Physiography of Uganda: The Evolution of the Great Lakes and Victoria Nile Drainage System." *Journal of the Royal African Society*. 33 (1934), 103–14.
Greene, Dorothy S. "Carl Akeley Again Penetrates the African Jungle." *Natural History*. 21 (July—Aug. 1921), 428–30.
Greindl, L. *A la recherche d'un état indépendant: Léopold II et les Philippenes*. Brussels: Académie Royale des Sciences d'Outre-Mer, 1962.
Hall, Richard. *Stanley: An Adventurer Explored*. Boston: Houghton Mifflin, 1975.
Hammond, Dorothy, and Jablow, Alta. *The Myth of Africa*. New York: Library of Social Science, 1977.
Hammond, Harold E. "American Interest in the Exploration of the Dark Continent." *Historian*. 18 (Spring 1956), 202–29.
Harraway, Donna. *Primate Visions: Gender, Race, and Nature in the World of Modern Science*. New York and London: Routledge, 1989.
Harlow, Vincent. "Sir Frederick Hamilton's Narrative of Events Relative to the Jameson Raid." *English Historical Review*. 72 (1957), 279–305.
Hatch, Frederick H., and Chambers, J. A. *The Gold Mines of the Rand*. London: Macmillan and Co., 1895.
Hellman, Geoffrey. *Bankers, Bones and Beetles: The First Century of the American Museum of Natural History*. Garden City, N.Y.: Natural History Press, 1968.
Heppner, Francis J. "Henry S. Sanford, U.S. Minister to Belgium, 1861–1869." M. A. thesis, Georgetown University, 1955.
Hesseltine, William B., and Wolfe, Hazel C. *The Blue and Grey on the Nile*. Chicago: University of Chicago Press, 1961.
Hogben, S. J. *An Introduction to the History of the Islamic States of Northern Nigeria*. Ibadan, Nigeria: Oxford University Press, 1967.
Hole, Hugh Marshall. *The Jameson Raid*. London: Phillip Allen, 1930.
Holt, P. M. *A Modern History of the Sudan*. London: Weidenfeld and Nicolson, 1961.
Hooker, James R. "Verney Lovett Cameron: A Sailor in Central Africa." In *Africa and its Explorers: Motives, Methods and Impact*. Edited by Robert Rotberg. Cambridge: Harvard University Press, 1970, pp. 255–94.
Howard, Lawrence C. *American Involvement in Africa South of the Sahara, 1801–1860*. New York: Garland Publishing Co., 1988.
Howe, Russell Warren. *Along the Afric Shore: An Historic Review of Two Centuries of U.S.-African Relations*. New York: Barnes and Noble Books, 1975.
Huffstodt, Jim. "The Akeley Legacy." *Outdoor Highlights*. 14 (6 Jan. 1985), 10–14.

Icenogle, David. "The Expeditions of Chaillé-Long." *Aramco World Magazine.* 29 (Nov.–Dec. 1978), 2–7.
Jeeves, Alan Henry. *Migrant Labour in South Africa's Mining Economy: The Struggle for the Gold Mines' Labour Supply, 1820–1920.* Kingston, Canada: McGill-Queen's University Press, 1985.
Jesman, Czeslaw. "American Officers of Khedive Ismail." *African Affairs.* 57 (Oct. 1958), 302–7.
Johnson, H. A. S. *The Fulani Empire of Sokoto.* London: Oxford University Press, 1967.
Johnson, Samuel. *The History of the Yorubas.* London: Routledge and Kegan Paul, Ltd., 1969.
Katz, Herbert, and Katz, Marjorie. *Museums U.S.A.: A History and Guide.* Garden City, N.Y.: Natural History Press, 1965.
Kennedy, John Michael. "Philanthropy and Science in New York City: The American Museum of Natural History, 1868–1968," Ph.D. dissertation, Yale University, 1968.
Keto, C. Tsehloane. *The Aftermath of the Jameson Raid and American Decision Making in Foreign Affairs, 1896.* Transactions of the American Philosophical Society, 70 pt. 8. Philadelphia: American Philosophical Society, 1980.
Kingsley, Mary. *Travels in West Africa.* London: Macmillan and Co., 1897.
Kirk, John Foster. *Supplement to Allibone's Critical Dictionary of English Literature and British and American Authors.* Philadelphia: J. B. Lippincott, 1891.
Kopytoff, Jean Herskovits. *A Preface to Modern Nigeria: The "Sierra Leonians" in Yoruba, 1836–1890.* Madison: University of Wisconsin Press, 1965.
Krapf-Askari, Eva. *Yoruba Towns and Cities.* Oxford: Oxford University Press, 1969.
Kubicek, Robert V. *Economic Imperialism in Theory and Practice: The Case of South African Gold Mining Finance, 1886–1914.* Durham, N.C.: Duke University Press, 1979.
———. "The Randlords in 1895: A Reassessment." *Journal of British Studies.* 2 (1972), 84–103.
LaFeber, Walter. *The New Empire: An Interpretation of American Expansion, 1860–1898.* Ithaca, N.Y.: Cornell University Press, 1963.
Lane-Poole, Stanley. *Watson Pasha.* London: J. Murray, 1919.
Langer, William L. *European Alliances and Alignments, 1870–1890.* New York: Alfred Knopf, 1950.
Langlands, Bryan W. "Early Travellers in Uganda: 1860–1914." *Uganda Journal* 26 (1962), 55–71.
Lasserre, Guy. *Libreville: la ville et sa region.* Paris: A. Colin, 1958.
Law, Robin. *The Oyo Empire, c. 1600-c. 1836: A West African Imperialism in the Era of the Atlantic Slave Trade.* Oxford: Oxford University Press, 1977.
Lichtervelde, Louis, Comte de. *Leopold of the Belgians.* Translated by Thomas H. Reed and H. Russell Reed. New York: Century Co., 1929.
Lockhart, J. C., and Woodhouse, C. M. *Rhodes.* London: Hodder and Stoughton, 1963.
Louis, William Roger. "The Berlin Congo Conference." In *France and Britain in Africa.* Edited by Prosser Gifford and William Roger Louis. New Haven, Conn.: Yale University Press, 1971, pp. 167–220.
Low, D. A. "The Northern Interior, 1840–1884." In *History of East Africa.* Edited by Roland Oliver and Gervase Mathew. 2 vols. Oxford: Oxford University Press, 1963, vol. 2, 297–351.
Lucas, Frederic A. "Akeley as a Taxidermist." *Natural History* 27 (1927), 142–52.
———. "The Story of Museum Groups," parts 1 and 2. *The American Museum Journal* 14 (Jan.–Feb. 1914), 2–16; 51–66.
Lugard, Sir Frederick D. *The Dual Mandate in British Tropical Africa.* London and Edinburgh: Blackwood, 1923.
Lupoff, Richard A. *Edgar Rice Burroughs: Master of Adventure.* New York: Ace Books, 1965.

Lurie, Nancy O. *A Special Style*. Milwaukee: Milwaukee Public Museum, 1983.
Luuel, Marcel. "Gerson von Bleichroder, l'ami commun de Léopold II et de Bismarck," *Afrika-Tervuren*. 8 (1963), 93–110.
Lynch, Hollis R. "Pan Negro Nationalism in the New World Before 1862." *Boston University Papers on Africa. vol. 2*. Boston: Boston University Press, 1966.
MacMaster, Richard K. "Henry Highland Garnet and the African Civilization Society." *Journal of Presbyterian History*. 48 (Summer 1970), 95–112.
Malloy, Leo. *Henry Shelton Sanford, 1823–1891*. Derby, Conn. Bacon Printing Co., 1952.
Marais, J. S. *The Fall of Kruger's Republic*. Oxford: Oxford University Press, 1961.
Marks, Shula, and Rathbone, Richard. *Industrialization and Social Change in South Africa: African Class Formation, Culture and Consciousness, 1870–1930*. New York: Longmans, 1982.
McCarthy, Michael. *Dark Continent: Africa as Seen by Americans*. Westport, Conn.: Greenwood Press, 1983.
McKinley, Edward. *The Lure of Africa: American Interests in Tropical Africa, 1919–1939*. Indianapolis: Bobbs-Merrill, 1974.
Mendelsohn, Richard. "Blainey and the Jameson Raid: The Debate Renewed." *Journal of Southern African Studies*. 6 (Apr. 1960), 27–46.
Meyer, Lysle E. "Henry Shelton Sanford and the Congo." Ph.D. dissertation. Ohio State University, 1967.
Middleton, Dorothy. "The Search for the Nile Sources." *Geographical Journal*. 138 (June 1972), 40–58.
Miers, Suzanne. *Britain and the Ending of the Slave Trade*. New York: Africana Publishing Corp., 1975.
———. "The Brussels Conference in 1889–90: The Place of the Slave Trade in the Policies of Great Britain and Germany." In *Britain and Germany in Africa*. Edited by William Roger Louis and Prosser Gifford. New Haven, Conn.: Yale University Press, 1967, pp. 83–118.
Miller, Floyd J. *The Search for a Black Nationality: Black Emigration and Colonization, 1787–1863*. Urbana: University of Illinois Press, 1975.
Moorehead, Alan. *The White Nile*. New York: Dell Publishing Co., 1980.
Morris, Desmond and Ramona. *Men and Apes*. London: Hutchinson, 1966.
Murphy, Robert Cushman. "Carl Ethan Akeley." *Curator*. 7 (1964), 307–20.
Nesteby, James R. "The Tenuous Vine of Tarzan of the Apes." *Journal of Popular Culture*. 13 (Winter 1979), 483–87.
Noer, Thomas J. *Britain, Boer and Yankee: The United States and South Africa, 1870–1914*. Kent, Ohio: Kent State University Press, 1978.
Olds, Elizabeth Fagg. *Women of the Four Winds: The Adventures of Four of America's First Women Explorers*. Boston: Houghton Mifflin, 1985.
Oliphant, Lawrence. "African Explorers." *North American Review*. 124 (May—June 1877), 233–48.
Oliver, Roland. "Discernible Developments in the Interior, c. 1500–1840." In *History of East Africa*. Edited by Roland Oliver and Gervase Mathew. 2 vols. Oxford: Oxford University Press, 1963. vol. 1, pp. 169–211.
———. *Sir Harry Johnson and the Scramble for Africa*. London: Chatto and Windus, 1959.
Owlsley, Harriet Chappell. "Henry Shelton Sanford and Federal Surveillance Abroad, 1861–1865." *Mississippi Valley Historical Review*. 48 (Sept. 1961), 211–29.
Pakenham, Elizabeth. *Jameson's Raid*. London: Weidenfeld and Nicholson, 1960.
Parrinder, E. G. *The Story of Ketu, An Ancient Yoruba Kingdom*. Ibadan, Nigeria: Ibadan University Press, 1967.
Patterson, David. "Early Knowledge of the Ogowe and the American Exploration of 1854." *International Journal of African Historical Studies*. 5 (1972), 75–90.

———. *The Northern Gabon Coast to 1875.* Oxford: Oxford University Press, 1975.

———. "Paul Du Chaillu and the Exploration of Gabon, 1855–1865." *International Journal of African Historical Studies.* 7 (1974), 647–67.

Phimester, I. R. "Rhodes, Rhodesia and the Rand." *Journal of Southern African Studies.* 1 (Oct. 1974), 74–90.

Pitollet, Camille. "La découverte de l'explorateur Du Chaillu." *Tropiques: revue des troupes coloniales* 339 (Feb. 1952), 51–58.

Platt, Jonas. "Making Wild Animals Live Forever." *Technical World Magazine.* 20 (Sept. 1913), 90–94.

Plesur, Milton. *America's Outward Thrust: Approaches to Foreign Affairs, 1865–1890.* Dekalb: Northern Illinois University Press, 1971.

Pletcher, David M. *The Awkward Years: American Foreign Relations under Garfield and Arthur.* Columbia: University of Missouri Press, 1962.

Podmore, Charles R. "Carl Akeley, Taxidermist and Sculptor. *African Wild Life.* 14 (Dec. 1960), 323–27.

Poges, Irwin. *Edgar Rice Burroughs: The Man Who Created Tarzan.* Provo, Utah: Brigham Young University, 1975.

Preston, Douglas. *Dinosaurs in the Attic: An Excursion into the American Museum of Natural History.* New York: Natural History Press, 1986.

Raponda-Walker, André. *Notes d'histoire du Gabon.* Montpelier: Impr. Charité, 1960.

———. *Rites et croyances des peuples du Gabon.* Paris: Présence Africain, 1962.

———, and Reynard, Robert. "Anglais, Espannols et Nord-Américains au Gabon au xix^c siècle." *Bulletin de l'Institute d'études centrafricaines.* 12 (1956), 253–79.

Reger, H. Servern. "An Appreciation of William H. Werner." *The Oologist* 34 (Oct. 1922): 4–21.

Register of the Henry Shelton Sanford Papers. Nashville, Tenn. State Historical Society and Archives, 1960.

Rhoodie, Denys. *Conspirators in Conflict. A Study of the Johannesburg Reform Committee and its Role in the Conspiracy against the South African Republic.* Cape Town: Tafelberg-Uitgewers, 1967.

Rideing, William H. "Two Explorers and a Literary Parson." *McClure's Magazine.* 34 (Nov. 1909—Apr. 1910), 214–20.

Rittenhouse, Mignon. *Seven Women Explorers.* New York: Lippincott, 1964.

Roark, James L. "American Expansionism vs. European Imperialism: Henry S. Sanford and the Congo Episode, 1883–1885." *Mid-America.* 60 (1978), 21–33.

Robinson, Ronald, and Gallagher, John, with Denny, Alice. *Africa and the Victorians.* New York: St. Martins' Press, 1961.

Roeykens, Auguste. *Léopold et l'Afrique.* Brussels: Académie Royale des Sciences Coloniales, 1958.

———. *Léopold II et la conférence géographie de Bruxelles.* Brussels: Académie Royale des Sciences Coloniales, 1956.

———. *Les débuts de l'oeuvre africaine de Léopold II, 1875–1879.* Brussels: Académie Royale des Sciences Coloniales, 1955.

Rogers, J. A. *World's Great Men of Color.* 2 vols. New York: Helga M. Rogers, 1946.

Romer, Margaret. "Edgar Rice Burroughs, Creator of Tarzan." *Overland Monthly.* (Mar. 1934), pp. 67, 70.

Rosenthal, Eric. *Gold! Gold! Gold!: The Johannesburg Gold Rush.* New York: Macmillan Co., 1970.

———. *Stars and Stripes in Africa.* Cape Town: National Books Ltd., 1968.

Rotberg, Robert I. *The Founder: Cecil Rhodes and the Pursuit of Power.* New York: Oxford University Press, 1988.

Russell, John R. "Jumbo." *University of Rochester Library Bulletin* I (Nov. 1945), 12–20.

Sabry, M. *L'empire Egyptian sous Ismail et L'interférence Ango-Française, 1863–1879.* Paris: P. Geuthner, 1973.

Sanford, Carleton E. *Thomas Sanford, The Emigrant to New England: Ancestry, Life and Descendants.* 2 vols. Rutland, Ver.: Tuttle Company, 1911.

Saunders, John Richard. *The World of Natural History—as revealed in the American Museum of Natural History.* New York: Sheridan House, 1952.

Schaller, George. *The Mountain Gorilla.* Chicago: University of Chicago Press, 1963.

——. *The Year of the Gorilla.* Chicago: University of Chicago Press, 1964.

Schnapper, Bernard. *La politique et la commerce Français dans le golfe de guinée de 1838 à 1871.* Paris: Mouton, 1961.

Schweinfurth, George. *The Heart of Africa.* 2 vols. London: Sampson Low, 1873.

Serpell, David. "American Consular Activities in Egypt." *Journal of Modern History.* 10 (1938), 344–54.

Shavit, David. *The United States in Africa: A Historical Dictionary.* Westport, Conn.: Greenwood Press, 1989.

Shibeika, Mekki. "The Expansionist Movement of Khedive Ismail to the Lakes." In *Sudan in Africa.* Edited by Yusuf Fadl Hassan. Khartoum, Sudan: University of Khartoum Press, 1971.

Southern Baptist Missionary Journal. 3 (1849).

Spence, Clark C. *Mining Engineers and the American West: The Lace Boot Brigade, 1849–1933.* New Haven, Conn.: Yale University Press, 1969.

Stengers, Jean. "King Leopold and Anglo-French Rivalry, 1882–1884." In *France and Britain in Africa: Imperial Rivalry and Colonial Rule.* Edited by Prosser Gifford and William Roger Louis. New Haven, Conn.: Yale University Press, 1971.

Stenmans, Alain. *La reprise du Congo par la Belgique.* Brussels: Editions Techniques et Scientifiques, 1949.

Stern, Fritz. *Gold and Iron: Bismarck, Bleichroder and the Building of the German Empire.* New York: Alfred Knopf, Inc. 1977.

Taylor, Orville. "Thomas J. Bowen: A Man for All Seasons." *Viewpoints.* 8 (1982), 51–61.

Thomson, Robert Stanley. *Fondation de l' état indépendant du Congo.* Brussels: Office De Publicité, 1933.

——. "Léopold II et la Conférence de Berlin: Documents inédits provenant de la correspondence particulière de l'Hon. Henry S. Sanford." *Congo Revue Générale de la Colonie Belge.* 12 (Oct. 1931), 325–52.

——. "Léopold II et le Congo révélés par les notes privées de Henry S. Sanford." *Congo revue générale de la colonie Belge.* 12 (Feb. 1931), 168–96.

——. "Leopold II et Henry S. Sanford: Papiers inédites concernant le Rôle Joué par un diplomate Américain dans le création de l'E.I. du Congo." *Congo Revue Générale de la Colonie Belge.* 11 (Oct. 1930), 295–331.

Truscott, S. J. *The Witwatersrand Goldfields: Banket and Mining Practice.* London: Macmillan and Co., 1907.

Turton, E. R. "Kirk and the Egyptian Invasion of East Africa in 1875: A Reassessment." *Journal of African History.* 11 (1970), 355–70.

Tuttle, Russell H. *Apes of the World: Their Social Behavior, Communication, Mentality and Ecology.* Park Ridge, N.J.: Noyes Publications, 1986.

Van der Poel, Jean. *The Jameson Raid.* Cape Town: Oxford University Press, 1951.

Van-Helten, Jean Jacques. "The Gold Mining Industry in the Transvaal, 1886–1899." In *The South African War.* Edited by Peter Warwick. London: Longman, 1980.

van Onselen, Charles. *Studies in the Social and Economic History of the Witwatersrand, 1886–1914.* volume 2—*New Nineveh.* New York: Longman Inc., 1982.

Vatikiotis, P. J. *The Modern History of Egypt.* New York: Praeger, 1969.

Vaucaire, Michel. *Paul Du Chaillu: Gorilla Hunter*. New York: Harper and Bros., 1930.
Vindex (F. Verschoyle). *Cecil Rhodes, His Political Life and Speeches*. London: G. Bell, 1900.
Wallis, J. P. R. *Fitz: the Story of Sir Percy Fitzpatrick*. London: Macmillan and Co., 1955.
Walston, David M. "The Legacy of Carl Akeley." *Field Museum of Natural History Bulletin*. 57 (Jan. 1986), 5–25.
Ward, Russell. *Henry A. Ward*. Rochester Historical Society Publications, No. 24. Rochester, N.Y.: Rochester Historical Society, 1948.
Warwick, Peter, ed. *The South African War, 1899–1902*. London: Longmans, 1980.
Wauters, A. J. "Le Général Sanford: La reconnaissance de l'association du Congo." *Le Mouvement Géographique*. 7 May 1911, pp. 61–73.
Webber, H. O'Kelly. *The Grip of Gold*. London: Hutchinson, 1936.
Webster, Frederic S. "The Birth of Habitat Bird Groups." *Annals of the Carnegie Museum*. 30 (1945), 97–118.
Welbourn, Frederick B. "Speke and Grant at the Court of Mutesa." *Uganda Journal*. 25 (1961), 220–23.
Wesseling, H. L. "The Netherlands and the Partition of Africa." *Journal of African History*. 22 (1981), 495–509.
West, Richard. *Congo*. New York: Holt, Rinehart and Winston, 1972.
White, James P. "The Sanford Exploring Expedition." *Journal of African History*. 8 (1967), 291–302.
White, Norman E. "He Makes 'Stuffed Animals' Look Like Living Ones." *American Magazine*. 98 (Oct. 1924), 62–65.
Wilhelm, Donald. "A Wonderful Preserver of Wild Animals." *American Magazine*. 79 (June 1915), 56–57.
Williams, Patricia M. "The Museum Trade Mark." *Bulletin of the Field Museum of Natural History*. 39 (Jan. 1968), 2–5.
Wright, Lenoir Chambers. *United States Policy Towards Egypt, 1830–1914*. Jericho, N.Y.: Exposition Press, 1969.
Wright, Mary Emily. *The Missionary Work of the Southern Baptist Convention*. Philadelphia: American Baptist Publication Society, 1902.
Younger, Edward. *John A. Kasson*. Iowa City: Iowa State Historical Society, 1955.

Index

Abedare Mountains, 170
Abeokuta, 21, 22, 23, 24, 204 n.38
Abomey, 24
Aden, 90
African Civilization Society, 30, 31
African Game Trails (T. Roosevelt), 177
African Hall. *See* Akeley African Hall
African Repository, 29
Afrikaansche Handelsvereeniging, 109
Aggasiz, Louis, 162
Akeley, Carl, 160, 164, 187; association with T. Roosevelt, 176–77; cement gun, 172–73; conservation ideas, 160, 176, 188, 189, 197; designs and manufactures motion picture camera, 180, 183; designs T. Roosevelt memorial, 178; divorce, 188; elephant data, 174–75; elephant hunting, 170, 174, 178, 179; expedition to Africa, 1896, 168–70; expedition of 1905–6, 170; expedition of 1909–11, 174, 176–79; expedition of 1921, 181–85; expedition of 1926, 192–94; at Field Museum, 168–74; First World War Service, 173, 180–81; friendship with W. Wheeler, 163, 165, 166, 167, 168; gorilla data, 184; gorilla hunting, 182–84; influence on Americans' image of Africa, 196–97; life in New York City, 186, 187, 188; lion hunting, 176, 193; marriages, 170, 188; near-fatal encounter with elephant, 178–79; survives leopard's mauling, 169; taxidermy, 162–68, 170, 171, 172, 173, 174, 179, 180, 186, 195, 196; view of Africans, 196–97; work at Wards Natural Science Establishment, 162–65; work habits, 164, 166, 171, 183, 187, 190, 191; writing, 188, 190, 196; youth, 162. *See also* Akeley Camera; "Akeley method" of taxidermy
Akeley, Delia Denning, 170, 174, 178, 188
Akeley, Mary L. Jobe, 188, 192, 194
Akeley African Hall: Akeley's high standard for, 186, 195; collection of materials for, 194; dedication of, 195; delays in implementing Akeley's design, 179, 181; description of, 195; George Eastman's crucial support for, 191; emphasized in Akeley's writing, 190; genesis of plan for, 179; models for, 185; fund-raising for, 186–87; significance of, 196, 197
Akeley Camera, 180, 183, 193
"Akeley method" of taxidermy, 171, 172, 237 n.50
Albert, King of the Belgians, 160, 190
Albert Nyanza, Lake, 70, 74, 78, 79, 97
Alexandria: British bombardment of, 93; Chaillé-Long's early duties in; 1882 riots in, 92, 93
Amazons, 24
American Baptist Convention, 17
American Board of Foreign Missions, 17, 36
American Civil War, 31, 32, 63, 66, 67, 105
American Colonization Society, 29, 30
American Committee of the International Commission of Brussels, 107
American Geographical Society, 97, 111
American image of Africa, 8; Akeley and, 196–97, 199–201; Chaillé-Long and, 98–100; Du Chaillu and, 33, 53–62; missionaries and, 15
American Museum of Natural History, 164, 167, 174, 179, 191, 193, 194, 195
Americans in Johannesburg (1895–96), 146, 148, 149, 229 n.42
Anglo-Boer War, 128, 157, 158, 159
Anglo Portuguese Treaty (1884), 116
Apingi people. *See* Puno people
Arabi, Colonel Ahmed, 92, 94
Arthur, Chester A., 118
Arts Commission of Washington, 178
Ashango people. *See* Massangou people
Ashira people. *See* Shira people
Association international du Congo. *See* Association international pour l'exploration et civilization d'Afrique central
Association international pour l'exploration et civilization d'Afrique central, 106, 108, 109, 110, 111, 112, 113, 114, 119

Azande people, 81, 82, 83. *See also* Cannibalism: among Azande

Ba Beker (Bugandan emissary), 75
Bab-el-Mandab, 84
Badagry, Slave Coast, 20, 21
Bahr al-Ghazal, Sudan, 70
Baker, Samuel, 70, 75, 84, 99, 100
Baker Relief Expedition, 84–85
Baraka, Gabon, 38
Barghash, Sultan of Zanzibar, 86, 87, 90
Barnato, Barney, 130
Barnum, P. T., 164, 165
Barth, Heinrich, 43
Bechuanaland, 141, 154, 182
Becker, George, 155
Beit, Alfred, 139, 145
Belgian Congo, 179, 182, 195
Bennett, James Gordon, 108
Benue River, 203 n.16
Berbera, Somaliland, 84
Berlin Act (1885), 118, 119, 120, 121
Berlin Conference (1884–85), 114; Sanford's work at, 116, 117, 118, 119, 121, 122
Bettington, R. A., 152, 153
"Bill." *See* Gikungu, Wimbia
Bismarck, Otto von, 116, 118, 224 n.84
Black American colonization in Africa, 29–32, 105, 111–12, 125
Blaine, James G., 110, 121, 123
Blair, Montgomery, 67
Blaque Bey, 66
Boers, 35, 130, 132, 135, 143, 147, 150, 152, 153
Bouet-Willaumez, Edouard, 36
Bowen, Thomas Jefferson: in Abeokuta, 23; assessment of his work, 31–32; barred from Sokoto Caliphate, 27; book, *Central Africa*, 29; conceives "Central Africa" mission, 18–20; death, 32; difficult travel in Yorubaland, 24–25; early life, 17; establishes mission stations, 25, 26, 28; fluctuating estimate of Yoruba people, 25, 27; helps Abeokutans repel Dahomeans, 23; in Illorin, 26–28; impressed by Fulani people, 26–27; in Ketu, 24–25; in Liberia, 21; military experience in Southern U.S., 17; promotion of U.S. trade with Yorubaland, 19, 29, 32; racial views of, 19, 21, 25, 27, 32, 203 n.22; support for black American colonization in Yorubaland, 28, 29, 30, 31, 32; view of Islam, 19, 26; work with Yoruba language, 23, 32
Boy's Life, 190

Bradley, Alice, 182
Bradley, Herbert, 181, 182, 183
Bradley, Mary, 181, 182, 183
Brazza, Pierre Savorgnan de, 114, 116, 118
Brightest Africa (Akeley), 190
Britain, 68, 83, 92, 93, 95, 97, 98; acquieses in Egypt's Red Sea expansion, 84, 86; antislavery efforts, 120; diplomacy during opening of the Congo, 116; imperialism in South Africa, 158–59; military intervention in Egypt, 93; pressures Egypt out of East Africa, 89, 90, 91; support of Zanzibar, 90
Brite, James, 178
British East African Protectorate, 170, 174. *See also* Kenya
British Museum, 43, 168
British Somaliland, 169
British South Africa Company, 131, 133, 142, 143
Brockport Normal School, 162
Bruce, David, 162
Brussels Act (1890), 125
Brussels Anti-Slavery Conference (1889–90), 121–25
Brussels Conference of the International Commission of the Association international pour l'exploration et civilization d'Afrique central (1877), 107
Brussels Geographical Conference (1876), 106
Bucher, Henry H., Jr., 35, 37, 206–7 n.22, 209 n.68
Buganda, 74, 75, 76, 77, 78, 79
Bumpus, Herman, 174
Bunyoro-Kitara, 74, 76
Burroughs, Edgar Rice, 57, 58, 59, 62; du Chaillu's influence on, 58, 59; inspiration for Tarzan character, 57
Burton, Richard, 44, 48, 49, 96
Buxton, Thomas F., 18

Caillé, René, 18
Cairo, 64, 71, 72, 75, 79, 84, 85, 86, 87, 89, 92; Chaillé-Long in, 68, 83, 91
Cameroons, 41
Cameron, Verney Lovett, 72, 108
Camma people. *See* Nkomi people
Cannibalism: among Azande, 82, 215 n.81; among Fang, 41, 44, 47, 48, 49, 58
Cape Colony, 131, 132, 133
Cape Town, 139, 145, 146, 147, 148, 155, 182
Cape Guardafui, 86
Cape Lopez, 40, 61
Cape St. Catherine, 38
Cape St. Johns, 37

INDEX

Carmel School for Girls (New York), 35, 37
Carnegie Institution, 189
Carry, Lott, 17
Central Africa: Adventures and Missionary Labors... (Bowen), 28, 29
Central Africa: Naked Truths of Naked People (Chaillé-Long), 72, 77, 78, 100
Chaillé-Long, Charles, 84, 85, 90, 99, 100, 101; acting U.S. consul in Alexandria during 1882 riots, 92–94; adds "Chaillé" to his name, 67; alleges Azande cannibalism, 82, 215 n.81; appointed Gordon's chief of staff, 71; battles Nyangbara, 81, 83; Civil War (U.S.) experience, 67; controversy over naming of Lake Kioga, 96–97; death, 95; discovers Lake Kioga (Hussein), 79; disgusted by Mutesa of Buganda, 77; distributes women to his men, 81–82; distrust of Britain, 97–98; early minor duties in Egypt, 68; employed in New York, 67, 91; estranged from Gordon, 80–81; expedition to Azandeland, 81–82; falsifies accomplishment in Buganda, 78, 214 n.68; family background, 67; fights with Kaba Rega's men, 79–80; life after Egypt, 94–95; literary attack on Gordon, 98, 217 n.130; marriage, 95; mission to East Africa, 87–91; mission to Uganda, 71–80, 213 n.48; positive estimate of Baganda; rewarded by Khedive Ismail, 83; sails on Lake Victoria, 77–78; studies law, 91; view of Africans, 99, 100; works in Egypt's mixed courts, 91–92
Chaillé-Long, Marie Hammond, 95
Chamber of Mines (Johannesburg), 137
Chamberlain, Joseph, 154
Chambers' Miscellany, 18
Chicago Public Library, 57
Chicago Tribune, 174
Chicago, University of, 167, 173
Chimpanzees, 47
"Chrysalis" (Akeley sculpture), 185–86
Church Missionary Society, 28
City of Washington (Gabon), 42
Civil War. *See* American Civil War
Clapperton, Hugh, 18
Clarendon, New York, 162, 167
Clark, James, 174, 187, 195
Clark, William, 26
Clark University, 167
Cleveland, Grover, 95, 119, 145, 156
Clodd, Edward, 33, 206 n.4
Columbia University Law School, 91
Columbian Exposition. *See* World's Columbian Exposition
Comité d'études du Haut Congo, 109, 110

Committee on Monumental Memorials, 178
Congo Independent State, 118–26; Sanford's company thwarted by, 119, 120, 122–25
Congo River, 38, 57, 104, 108, 109, 116, 117, 118
Consolidated Gold Fields of South Africa, 131, 137–38, 140, 141, 149; Hammond's Association with, 135, 139, 157, 158
Corée ou chösen, la terre du calme, La (Chaillé-Long), 95
Corisco Island, 17, 40
Country of the Dwarfs (Du Chaillu), 53
Crawford, J., 52
Critchley, J. W., 165
Crowther, Samuel, 21
Cunningham, Richard, 170

Dahomey, 23, 24
Daly, Charles P., 106, 107
Darfur, 70
De Beers Consolidated Mines, 130, 142
de Bono, Andrea, 82
de Cartier de Marchienne, Baron Emile, 189
Delaney, Martin R., 204 n.52
Delegoa Bay, 132
Denham, Dixon, 18
Dennard, J. S., 25, 26
Derscheid, J. M., 194
Dodson, Edward, 169
Dom Pedro III, Emperor of Brazil, 68
Du Chaillu, Charles Alexis, 33, 35, 38
Du Chaillu, Paul Belloni: American citizenship in doubt, 37; claims confirmed by later explorers or researchers, 44, 45, 46, 47; confusion about place and date of birth, 33, 35, 206 n.2; criticism of his African work, 43, 44, 45, 46, 47, 48, 52; discovers pygmies, 51; exaggerates Fang cannibalism, 47–49, 207 n.33; exaggerates gorilla's ferocity, 46; first expedition to Gabon (1855–59), 38–42; gorilla controversy, 45–47; hopes for African development, 59–61; impact on Americans' image of Africa, 53–57; 61–62, 210 n.110; importance as explorer, 59; influence on E. R. Burroughs's conception of Tarzan character, 57–59; interest in Scandinavia, 33, 52; as lecturer, 52–53; mistakenly claims new ape species, 47; as naturalist, 40, 43, 59; popularity of his books, 53, 205–6 n.1; racial views, 51, 54, 55, 56; second expedition to Gabon (1863–65), 49–52; stereotypical view of African

culture, 54, 55, 56; teacher in girls' school, 35; writing, 33, 38, 42, 43, 52, 53, 54, 55, 56, 57, 58, 59, 60, 61, 62, 207–8 n.38

East Rand Proprietary Mine, 145
Eastman, George, 191, 192, 193, 194
Eastman-Pomeroy-Akeley Expedition (1926), 192–94
Edward, Prince of Wales, 85
Edward VII, King of England, 97
Egba people, 20, 23, 204 n.38. *See also* Yoruba people
Egypt: British intervention and occupation, 92–94; expansion in East Africa, 85–91; expansion in the Levant, 63; expansion on Red Sea coast, 84; expansion on Upper Nile, 69, 70, 71, 72, 74, 75, 76, 77, 78, 79; relationship with Ottoman Turkish Empire, 63, 85, 211 n.1; in Sudan, 64, 68, 69, 70, 81–83. *See also* Ismail, Khedive of Egypt
Ekstein and Company, 137
Elephants, 160, 165, 171, 174, 178, 179
Elliot, Daniel G., 168, 169, 173
Encyclopaedia Britannica, 18
English, George Bethune, 64
Equatoria Province, Sudan, 70, 84, 85, 100
Ethiopia, 91
Ethnological Society (British), 44
Explorations and Adventures in Equatorial Africa (Du Chaillu), 43, 45, 58
Explorers' Club, 188

Fajulu, Sudan, 81
Fang people, 40, 41, 48, 49, 58. *See also* Cannibalism
Farrar, George, 145, 149, 155
Fathers of the Holy Spirit, 36
Fernan Vaz (Omboué) Gabon, 42, 50
Field, Marshall, 168, 172, 173
Field Columbian Museum. *See* Field Museum of Natural History
Field Museum of Natural History, 168, 170, 171, 173, 176
Fitzpatrick, Percy, 142, 149, 155
"Flag crisis," 145–47, 231 n.102
Florida, 17, 105
Fodio, Usuman dan, 20
Foreign Relations Committee (U.S. Senate), 111
Fort d'Aumale, Gabon, 36
Foweira, Sudan, 80
Fowler, Sir William, 168
France, 66, 68, 83, 95; competition with Leopold II over Congo, 111, 114, 117, 118; in Gabon, 35, 36, 37, 59, 114; treaty with Leopold II, 114, 115
Frankfurt, 104
Frelinghuysen, Frederick T., 111, 112, 114
Frere, Sir Bartle, 85, 107
Fulani people, 18, 19, 20, 55

Gabon, 114; development of French sphere of interest in, 35–37; Du Chaillu and, 38–46, 48–52, 55, 57
Gabon River, 36, 37, 38, 43
Garfield, James A., 118
Garnet, Henry Highland, 30
Geographical Society of Vienna, 81
George Washington Corps, 149
German-English Academy (Milwaukee), 165–66
Germany, 104, 116. *See also* Berlin Conference
Gezo, King of Dahomey, 23, 24
Gibson, R. L., 112
Gikungu, Wimbia ("Bill"), 196, 197
Gold Fields American Development Company, 158
Gold mining: north of the Limpopo River, 132–33; in South Africa, 130–31, 135, 136, 137, 138, 139, 140, 156–57
Goldie, George, 97
Goncalves, Lopo, 35
Gondokoro, Sudan, 71, 74, 76
Goodale, Harvey, 20, 21
Gordon, Charles George, 74, 75, 96; accepts governorship of the Sudan, 70; Chaillé-Long's literary attacks on, 98, 100; and Egypt's East Africa venture, 84, 85, 86, 87, 88, 90; relationship with Chaillé-Long, 71, 72, 80, 81, 85
Gorillas: Akeley and, 160, 161, 179, 182, 183, 184, 185, 189, 194, 195, 198; Du Chaillu and, 38, 41, 44, 45
Grant, J. A., 69, 77, 78, 96
Greindl, Baron Jules, 108
Grenfell, George, 124
Grey, John Edward, 43

Habitat groups, 166–67, 180, 195
Hall, Priscilla, 182
Hamilton, Frederick, 144, 146, 147
Hammond, John Hays, 135, 140, 141, 146, 148, 149, 150, 151, 154, 155, 157, 158, 159; and Americans on the Rand, 137–38, 143, 145–46, 149, 232 n.128, 131; arrested and tried, 154–56, assesses mineral potential north of the Limpopo River, 132, 133, 135; early life and education, 128; early mining and industrial experience, 128–30;

INDEX

encourages deep-mining, 135; enters Rhodes's plot against Kruger's government, 139; his many tasks for Reform Committee, 142, 143, 144, 150; joins Rhodes's mining firm, 131; justifies Jameson Raid, 158–59; lured to South Africa, 130; position on "flag question," 145, 146, 149; prepares to assault Boer camp, 153; readies strike force against Pretoria arsenal, 143, 232 n.110; scouts Jameson's invasion route, 142; sentenced to death, 156; unable to prod other reformers to action, 144–45; works for GFSA from London, 157; writing, 158
Hammond, Natalie Harris, 155, 157, 230 n.78
Harper and Brothers Company, 42
Harrison, Benjamin, 123
Hausaland, 20
Heidelberg, University of, 104
Heller, Edmund, 170
Hill, Robert, 20, 21
Hodgson, W. B., 18, 19
Hornaday, William T., 167, 171
Hornaday process, 171
Hussein, Lake. *See* Kioga, Lake

Ibrahim, Lake. *See* Kioga, Lake
Igboho, Yorubaland, 20
Ijayi, Yorubaland, 26
Illorin, Yorubaland, 20, 26, 27
Imperial British East Africa Company, 170
Ishogo people. *See* Shogo
Islam, 19, 26, 100, 204 nn.38, 39
Ismail, Khedive of Egypt, 72, 74, 82, 85, 86, 88, 89, 100; East African Expansionism, 83–91; economic crisis, 91; efforts to suppress slave trade, 69, 87, 90; employment of foreigners, 64, 65, 66, 67, 70, 71; European education and influence, 69; deposed, 92; discharges American officers, 91; hires American officers, 64, 66, 67, 68; imperialistic designs, 64, 69, 71, 83–84, 86; policy toward Ottoman Turkey, 64, 68, 84. *See also* Egypt

Jameson, Leander Starr, 128, 135, 140, 141, 153; accompanies Hammond and Rhodes to Matebeleland, 132, 133; assembles force at Pitsani, 144; fails to stir Johannesburg to revolt, 144–45; marches to defeat, 147–48, 149, 152; obtains letter of invitation from Reform Committee, 142; on trial, 154
Jameson Raid, 128, 151, 153, 154, 156, 157, 159; delays, 145–48; failure of, 152; initial plan, 138–42

Jansson, A. A., 192
Johannesburg, 130, 135, 139, 140, 141, 142, 143, 146, 147; during abortive rising associated with Jameson Raid, 148–54
Johnson, Martin, 193, 239 n.31
Johnson, Osa, 193
Jones, John Paul, 63
Journey to Ashango-Land (Du Chaillu), 52, 56
Juba River, 86, 88, 90

Kaba Rega, King of Bunyoro-Kitara, 76
Karasimbi, Mount, 183, 184, 189
Kasson, John A., 116, 177
Kellerman, W. F. G., 75
Kenya, 170, 174, 176, 177, 178, 179, 182, 187, 188, 192, 197. *See also under* Akeley, Carl
Kenya, Mount, 170, 178
Ketu, Kingdom of, 24, 25
Khartoum, 64, 71, 74, 80, 85, 98
Kilimanjaro, Mount, 84
Kimberley, Cape Colony, 130, 133, 142
Kingsley, Mary, 48, 49
Kioga, Lake (Lake Hussein, Lake Ibrahim), 79, 80, 96–97, 98, 100
Kipling, Rudyard, 57
Kirk, John, 90, 91, 97
Kismayu, Somaliland, 88, 89
Kissenyi, Belgian Congo, 182
Kivu, Lake, 182, 190, 194
Kneeland, S., 42–43
Kodak Camera Company, 191
Koran, the 26, 204 nn. 38, 39
Kruger, Paul, 158; alienates Uitlanders, 135, 136, 137, 138, 140, 144, 157; challenges Rhodes's ambitions, 132; offers concessions to Uitlanders, 151; pardons Reform Committee members, 156; receives Uitlander delegations, 148, 151–52
Krugersdorp, Transvaal, 152, 153

Lacy, John H., 25, 26
Lado, Sudan, 81, 83
Laird, Macgregor, 20, 203 n.16
Lamu, East Africa, 89
Lancer, Bishop and Company, 61
Lander, John, 18
Lander, Richard, 18
Latrobe, John H. B., 106, 107
Lavigerie, Cardinal Charles M. A., 120
Lawlin, Richard, 61
Lawly, A. L., 147
Leigh, William R., 192, 194
Leonard, Charles, 139, 141, 145, 146, 147, 149, 155

Leopold II, King of the Belgians, 103, 104, 119, 124, 125, 126; alienates Sanford, 119, 120; calls geographical conference (1876), 106; conciliates France on Niari-Kwilu region, 118; decides to acquire African territory, 106; dominates AIA, 109; exploits Brussels Antislavery Conference (1890), 121, 123; hires Stanley, 108, 109; heavy investment in Congo venture, 120; interests at Berlin Conference (1884–85), 117, 118, 224 n.84; preemption treaty with France, 114; Sanford's services to, 105, 106, 107, 108, 109, 111–13, 114, 116, 117, 118
Liberia, 17, 29, 31, 32, 107, 112
Libreville, Gabon, 36
Limpopo River, 132
Lincoln, Abraham, 104–5
Liquor and arms trade in Africa, 102
Livingstone, David, 32
Lobengula, Chief of the Ndebele (Matabele), 132
Loch, Sir Henry, 138
Lodge, Henry Cabot, 178
London, 49, 50, 157, 158; center of dispute over Du Chaillu's findings, 43–44, 52
Low, Abiel A., 111
Low, Seth, 111
Lugard, Frederick, 28

Mafeking, Cape Colony, 142
Mahdi, 98
Makaraka people, 81
Malone, T. A., 44
Mandingo (Mandinka) people, 21
Marno, M., 81
Mashonaland, 132
Massangou people, 51–52
Massawa, Ethiopia, 84
Matabeleland, 132, 135
Maury, Major General Dabney H., 67
McCutcheon, John T., 174
McKillop, H. F., 87, 88, 89, 90
Mein, Thomas, 146
Mentor, 190
Mercantile Association (Johannesburg), 148, 231 n.83
Merriam, John C., 189
Metropolitan Museum of Art, 185
Mexico, 128, 129
Mikeno, Mount, 183, 184, 189, 194
Miller, Martha, 182
Milwaukee, 165, 166, 167
Milwaukee Public Museum, 166, 167, 179
Missionaries, 15; in the Congo, 120, 124; in Gabon, 17, 36, 37, 38; in Liberia, 17; in northern Nigeria, 28; in Sudan, 69, 82; in Yorubaland, 21, 23–28
Mixed Courts of Egypt, 91–92
Mombasa, Kenya, 84, 85, 170, 192
Morgan, John Tyler, 111, 112, 113, 222 n.54
Mott, Henry, 66
Mott, Thaddeus, 66, 67
Mouaou Kombo, Gabon, 51
Mpongwe people, 38, 40, 48
Mruli, Sudan, 78, 80
Muhammad Ali (Viceroy of Egypt), 63–64
Muhammad Said (Viceroy of Egypt), 69
Muslims, 19, 26, 27, 28
Muni River, 40
Murchison, Sir Roderick, 50
Mutesa, King of Buganda, 72, 74, 75, 76, 97, 100; and Chaillé-Long, 77–78
My Life on Four Continents (Chaillé-Long), 100

Nairobi, 170, 176, 192, 194
Nandi people, 176, 185, 193
Natal, 131
National Academy of Design, 186
National Geographic Magazine, 174
Natural History, 190
Natural History Society of Boston, 43
Ndebele (Matabele) people, 132, 152
Netherlands, The, 122, 125
New York, 67, 91, 164, 166, 173, 174, 179, 195
New York Chamber of Commerce, 111
New York Herald, 108, 111, 114
New York State Colonization Society, 30
New York Star, 95
New York Times, 94, 111
New York Zoological Park, 171
New York Zoological Society, 189
Niam-Niam. *See* Azande people
Niari-Kwilu region, 117, 118
Niger River, 20
Nigeria, 28, 204 n.22. *See also* Sokoto Caliphate
Nile River, 64, 66, 69, 70, 77, 78, 79, 81, 82, 90, 97, 174, 177
Nkomi people, 42, 50, 51, 61
Notes on Northern Africa (Hodgson), 19
Nubar Pasha, 70, 91
Nubians, 99
Nupe, Kingdom of, 27
Nyangbara people, 81, 83

Obongo people. *See* Pygmies
Ogbomosho, Yorubaland, 26
Ogboni Society, 23

INDEX

Ogooué River, 41, 42, 59, 114
"Old Man of Mikeno" (Akeley sculpture), 186
Olney, Richard, 155
Orange Free State, 131
Orungu people, 40
Osborn, Henry Fairfield, 180, 181, 186, 187, 195
Ottoman Turkish Empire, 63, 64, 66, 68, 211 n.1
Oyo Empire, 23

Parc National Albert, 160, 190
Paris: Chaillé-Long in, 83, 94; Sanford in, 104, 117, 118
Paris Geographical Society, 83
Park, Mungo, 18
Pennsylvania Academy of Fine Arts, 185
Penny Cyclopedia, 18
Phillips, Lionel, 137, 139, 140, 141, 143, 145, 151, 152, 153, 155
Pinchot, Gifford, 178
Pitsani, Bechuanaland, 141, 147
Place du Consuls (Alexandria), 93
Political Reform Association (Johannesburg), 137
Pomeroy, Daniel E., 191, 192, 194
Port Durnford, East Africa, 89
Portugal: interest in Congo region, 116, 117; in Gabon, 35
Pretoria, 143, 146, 148, 149, 151, 152
Puno people, 55, 60
Purdy, Erastus, 84
Pygmies, 51, 52, 53, 81, 83

Rand, the, 130, 132, 135, 136, 137, 138, 139, 140, 147, 154, 157
"Randlords" (mine owners and capitalists of Johannesburg), 137, 140, 149
Reade, Winwood, 49, 52; corroborates Du Chaillu's findings on Fang cannibalism, 48; disturbed by Du Chaillu's book, 45; visits Gabon to discredit Du Chaillu, 45–46
Rea Sea, 83, 84, 87
Reform Committee, 152, 155, 156; agrees on rising, 142; capitulates to Kruger, 154; confusion and irresolution among leaders, 145; creates police force, 143; delays uprising, 144–45, 146–47; disagreement over flag issue, 146, 147, 149; gives Jameson letter of invitation, 142; Hammond's importance in, 142–43; leaders arrested, 154; military preparations, 143, 150, 153; negotiates with Kruger, 151; as provisional government on the Rand, 149, 150, 151, 153; tries to prevent Jameson's march, 147
"Requiem" (Akeley sculpture), 185
Réunion (island), 33
Richmond-African Missionary Society, 17
Rhodes, Cecil, 134, 146, 152; architect of plot against Kruger's government, 139; fails to stop Jameson's march, 147; imperialistic designs, 131, 132; and Hammond, 131, 132, 133, 135, 137, 139, 141, 142, 145, 252 n.180; links to officials in London, 138, 140; and Reform Committee, 141, 144, 149, 150, 151
Rhodes, Frank, 141, 144, 146, 152, 155, 230 n.76
Rhodesia, 131. *See also* Mashonaland and Matabeleland
Rhoodie, Denys, 128
Rider Haggard, H., 57
Robinson, Sir Hercules, 138, 150, 152, 154
Rochester, New York, 162, 163
Rockefeller, John D., 119
Roman-Dutch law, 156
Roosevelt, Kermit, 177
Roosevelt, Theodore, 176, 177
"Roosevelt African Hall," 186
Roosevelt (Theodore) memorial project, 178
Royal Geographical Society, 43, 50, 52, 69, 97
Royal School of Mines (Freiberg, Germany), 128
Rubaga, Buganda, 76
Rwanda-Urundi, 190
Rweru (Akeley's camp), 190

St. Petersburg, 33
St. Thomas, Ontario, 164
Salisbury, Lord, 120
Sandilands, Gordon, 153
Sanford, Henry S.: business enterprises and investments, 105, 119, 120; closeness to Leopold II, 108; death, 125; disillusioned by Leopold II, 123–25; early fascination with Europe, 103–4; early life, 103; first diplomatic posts, 103–4; helps recruit H. M. Stanley, 108; interest in Black American colonization in the Congo, 112, 125, 126; member of International Commission of AIA, 107; naïveté regarding Leopold II's true intentions, 108, 109, 113; promotes U.S. trade with Congo, 110, 113, 114, 117, 119, 123, 124, 125, 126; his trading company in the Congo, 119, 120; U.S. delegate to Berlin

Conference (1890), 121–25, 225 n.117; U.S. minister to Belgium, 104–5
Sanford, Nehemiah Curtis, 102
Sanford Exploring Expedition, 119, 120
Sanford, Florida, 105
Sanford Papers, 102, 219 n.1
Sangatanga, Gabon, 40
"Saro." *See* Sierra Leonians
Sandinavia, 33, 52
Schieffelin, Henry M., 107
Schoeff, General A. P., 67
Schweinfurth, George, 52, 107
Seke people, 40, 41
Senegal, 36
Senegambia, 55
Serengeti Plains, 193
Seward, William H., 164
Shaw-Kennedy, Vernon, 170
Sheffield Scientific School. *See* Yale University
Shekiani people. *See* Seke people
Sherman, General William T., 66, 68
Shippard, Sir Sidney, 154
Shira people, 50
Shogo people, 55
Shona people, 132
Sierra del Crystal Mountains, 40
Sierra Leone, 23, 36
Sierra Leonians, 23, 32
Slave Coast, 20
Slave trade: Atlantic, 35, 36, 40; in East and Central Africa, 89, 120, 121; in Gabon, 40; in Indian Ocean, 85, 89, 217 n.121; in Sudan, 69
Slavery in Africa, 36, 40
Smithsonian Institution, 177
Société du Haut-Congo pour le commerce et l'industrie, 120
Sokoto Caliphate, 20
Somaliland. *See* British Somaliland
South African Republic (Transvaal), 128, 130, 135, 136, 137, 141, 149, 154, 155, 156, 157, 158
Southern Baptist Convention, 17
Southern Baptist Convention Foreign Mission Board, 18, 15, 16
Speke, John Hanning, 69, 77, 78, 96, 101
Sportsman's Show, New York, 1895, 176
Standard and Digger News (Johannesburg), 144, 151
Standard Bank of South Africa, 143
Stanley, Henry Morton, 52, 53, 96, 118; association with Sanford, 108–10, 119, 126
Stanley Field Hall, 171
Star (Johannesburg), 144, 150, 151
Stephenson, Fred, 174

Stevenson, Adlai, 156
Stone, General Charles Pomeroy, 66, 68, 83, 84, 91, 92
Sudan, 64, 68, 69, 70, 71, 74, 75, 83, 95
Sunday Star (Washington), 95
Swahili people, 74. *See also* Zanzibaris

Tana River, 86
Tanganyika, 182, 192, 193
Tanganyika, Lake, 118, 182
Tarzan (fictional character), 57–59
Tarzan of the Apes (Burroughs), 57, 58, 59
Taxidermy, 197; Akeley's new techniques, 171, 172, 181, 186; crude early methods, 163, 164, 165, 166, 171. *See also* Habitat groups
Taylor, Zachary, 104
Teague, Colin, 17
Terrell, Edwin H., 121, 124, 125
Tewfik, Khedive of Egypt, 92
Three Prophets (Chaillé-Long), 100
Times (London), 43, 52, 86, 111, 146
Townshend, Henry, 21
Transvaal. *See* South African Republic
Transvaal National Union, 137
Trimble, A., 151
Turkey. *See* Ottoman Turkish Empire

Uasin Gishu Plateau, Kenya, 176, 177
Uganda, 71, 72; Akeley in, 170, 174, 176, 177, 179, 194; Chaillé-Long in, 76, 80. *See also* Buganda; Bunyoro-Kitara
Uganda Railway, 170
Uitlanders: anticipating Jameson's march, 145–53; grievances against Kruger's government, 135, 136, 140, 141, 143, 144, 145, 150, 151, 153, 156, 157, 158, 228 nn.30 and 32, 231 n.86
Ukerewa, Lake. *See* Victoria, Lake
Union Jack, 149, 231 n.102
Union of South Africa, 182
United States: agrees to revisions of Berlin Act, 125; fails to ratify Berlin Act, 119, 121; recognizes Leopold II's association, 112; signs Brussels Act, 125; small interest in Gabon, 61
United States Department of the Interior, 189
United States Department of State, 155
United States Geological Survey, 128
United States House of Representatives, 31
United States National Museum, 167
United States Senate, 31, 112, 125
Urondogani, Buganda, 78
Usuman dan Fodio, 20
USS *Ticonderoga*, 110

Van der Poel, Jean, 128

Vaucaire, Michel, 35
Venezuela boundary dispute, 145
Victoria (Nyanza), Lake, 69, 72, 74, 79, 84, 87, 88, 97, 170; Chaillé-Long and, 77–78
Visoke, Mount, 189
Vierklur (South African Republic's flag), 146, 149
Virginia Beach, Virginia, 95
Virunga Range, 183

Walker, R. N., 43
Walker, William, 38
Ward, Henry Augustus, 162; employs Akeley, 163–65; and Field Museum, 168; and Milwaukee Public Museum, 166
Ward's Natural Science Establishment, 162, 163, 164, 165
Washington, D.C., 104, 181
Washington Academy (Maryland), 67
Washington College (Trinity College), Connecticut, 102
Webster, Harrison, 163
Weed, Thurlow, 104

Wenz, Daniel B. 191
Wernher, Beit and Company, 139, 140
West Side Unitarian Church (New York City), 186
Wheeler, William Morton, 163, 165, 166, 167, 168, 173
White, Robert, 141
Williams, Gardner, 142
Wilson, John Leighton, 37, 38, 45
Witwatersrand. *See* Rand
Wolff, Henry A., 143
Wolof people, 55
World's Columbian Exposition, 167, 168
World's Work, 190
"Wounded Comrade" (Akeley sculpture), 185

Yale University, 128, 163, 164
Younghusband, Francis, 146
Yoruba people, 23, 24, 25, 31. *See also* Egba people

Zaire, 160
Zanzibar, 86, 87, 88, 89, 90, 214 n.51
Zanzibaris, 74, 75